Father's Day 2009

Dear

Sa

to meet my Uncle Richard, who was a remarkable man, but collected here is his life's work; some of it is difficult reading thanks to Richard's obsession with words and what you could do with them, but if you do manage to get around to reading some of it, perhaps you will come to know him a little. He would have liked you immensely and I think that you would have liked him too.

Love, Jonathan

Published in 2008 by Park Corner Press, 76 Stansfield Drive,
Grappenhall, Warrington WA4 3EA

A CIP record for this book is available from the British Library

ISBN 978-0-9560305-0-4

In the name of the author,
the publisher and editor of this book dedicate it
to his nephews.

AN UNKNOWN PLANET?
Writings by Richard Ogden

Richard A. Ogden

Edited by Mark O'Sullivan

Illustrations by Jonathan Standing

Published by Park Corner Press,
Warrington

Contents

Foreword

The author

I first met Richard Ogden in a bar at King's College, Cambridge, in 1970. We were both 19, born within a month of each other; unlike me, he looked like a Norse god, all massy blond hair and giant frame. But no Norse god ever had Richard's personality. He was unfailingly kind, gentle and generous. He took a fundamental delight in words, was well-read, and curious, and humorous, and brilliant. He drew much of his sustenance from literature and music, loving the greatest of the classics, but also difficult modern works such as those of Becket or Joyce, Schoenberg or Ligeti. And he always took great pleasure in the genuinely creative, the ingenious, the new perspective. He loved discussions of (say) a range of science-fiction authors, or of the novels of H G Wells or P G Wodehouse, but was also fascinated with the genuine advances of literature, including American fiction as represented by, say, Thomas Pynchon or Donald Barthelme.

We left Cambridge in the mid-70s. For most of us the radical 1960s spirit was fading. Some of us went into commerce and the liberal professions, others into the public sector – into structures which would contain and direct our lives for many years. Richard chose a harder path. Along with the fundamental values of his background, he retained his love of the northern fells; but he only briefly returned to the North. He spent a time in Bristol, and later went west again, first teaching in Cornwall and then to Plymouth. In that concrete city he, with the serendipity which he often enjoyed, rented an ancient house full of character in the Barbican, and found a job at the Theatre Royal. But even that was too constricting. He returned further west to Penzance, coming into a little money which enabled him to buy a friendly cottage at Park Corner.

He had an all-consuming devotion to books and music. He was attracted at Cambridge to Wagner, whose works sought to combine the two, and I remember staying up with him for a marathon 19-hour session listening to *Der Ring des Nibelungen* on records from beginning to end – *Götterdämmerung* ended about 7 am, and we were exhausted, but he felt the next step was to put the first record on all over again... His taste later developed away from Wagner. Indeed, it was always open to change: for many years he disdained Mozart, but in his last letter to me, in January 2005, he said that he was now finding many delights in Mozart's chamber music – and added that he had been impressed recently by the Streets' *A Grand Don't Come for Free*, introduced to him by his young friend Charlotte Potter and her boyfriend Rob. His collection of books and CDs was large and impressive, and he also got constant pleasure from the works which passed through his hands in his time with Pat and Claire at Penzance Rare Books.

Richard was not a recluse. He was known about Penzance, as an *habitué* in a number of the pubs, for his involvement in theatre and other activities, as a regular at the arthouse cinema showings. He was often seen, alone or in company, wandering the countryside round about, maybe on the way to Lamorna or Men Scryfa. He remained close to his family in Manchester and latterly Falmouth, and to friends not only in Cornwall but elsewhere in Britain and in France and Spain. And he got on easily with children too, though he had none of his own – moreover, I recall Richard in 2004 at Tamsin Bretsky's wedding, sitting in the garden surrounded by young people, and he was often in the Dock Inn with Rob and Charlotte. Yet Richard was a very private man. Though affable, he was quiet. He did not cultivate a wide circle of acquaintance. But to those of us, young and old, who were privileged to be his friends, he gave love and loyalty in great abundance.

The word that I associate with Richard is humanity, in its fullest sense – as someone who both fully inhabited what it means to be human, and was also deeply immersed in the world of letters. Many of us are made inhumane by a complex society which has the power to reduce us to thin roles as consumer or bureaucrat, or else by the insistent demands of meretricious mass media. Richard rejected both. With a Cambridge degree and his huge natural talent, he could have made money, or acquired power and influence. But he was not interested in these things. So long as he had books and music, contact with friends, simple food and the occasional pint in a pub, he had the basis of contentment. And in conversation he showed an enviable depth of reading and thinking, an aliveness to the whole range of human experience, a subtle and playful humour, a delightful sense of the use of words, a capacity to create and build and enrich.

Being the man he was, he would have been an outstanding novelist. This was his ambition. He wrote an excellent first novel while at Cambridge (which is included in this collection, and inspires its title), though with characteristic humility he was dissatisfied with it and refused to seek publication. Thereafter for many years he was gripped by problems of writer's block, something which caused him much frustration. Only in later years did this inhibition begin to lift, with the help of Margaret Snow and others, and he wrote poetry of charm and value. We must regret that in the end the great novel was not written.

The book

In April 2005 Richard died suddenly and unexpectedly from an embolism following a routine operation at the tragically young age of 53. His sister Jane and I, along with other friends, spoke about how his life had been devoted to writing, and how sad it was that he had never been published. We knew the reason: he set himself standards so high that he never felt that anything was really quite finished or ready. But we decided that despite this we should put together for publication some of his writings, illustrated by his nephew, Jonathan Standing.

The papers Richard left behind were not in order. He wrote usually in manuscript, in pencil, in exercise books or reporters' notebooks, with rubbings out and crossings out, and stories again and again redrafted from the very beginning with professionalism and perfectionism; once or twice, works had been typed out on a typewriter, maybe with a carbon copy or two. Much of what he wrote was unfinished, for reasons which one can in part understand from a diary fragment he wrote about his writer's block.

I have done my best with what survives to show in this book a representative sample of his work: a novel, a play, short stories, poetry – science fiction, Gothic tales, modernist and more conventional pieces. I have claimed an editor's licence, on behalf of the reader, to make a few changes and additions which it seemed to me that Richard might have made had he lived. Still, it is not sure that all the stories are finished. But I believe that the contents of this volume demonstrate clearly his powerful and astonishingly versatile talent, and form a collection which people will read with pleasure. If, to some others beyond Richard's mourning friends, it conveys the spirit which lies behind it, then it will have done its job.

Mark O'Sullivan
Drummore, Wigtownshire
Summer 2008

The Life of St Gwinear*

ACT 1: Cornwall, Ireland and Brittany

Prologue

By St Gwinear's tomb in a Cornish wood:
A heavily wooded graveyard at twilight. Large tomb midstage. Bert enters, followed by a reluctant Greta from left.

GRETA: Oh, Bert, we've come miles! We're miles away from the village! Oh, let's go back, please! We can come again tomorrow.

BERT: We're here, Greta. This is the place. Listen, there's the blackbird; his name is Okmar and he has four wives and twenty-seven chicks.

GRETA: Oh, but it's late! It's nearly dark! My Dad'll be furious when I get home! He'll be sitting there by the fire – an – an when I get in he'll grab me an he'll say – 'Right my girl!' or – or 'Well, you little toad' or 'You – you –

---

* When Richard first came to Cornwall he taught for a time at Penzance Girls' Grammar School. His interest in drama would crystallise before long, when he was to to move to becoming Assistant Stage Manager at the Theatre Royal in Plymouth, and perhaps it was no wonder that he saw the opportunity for the Grammar School girls to put on a play under his direction. What may have given more surprise was the play. Richard wrote it himself, basing it on the ancient Cornish Life of St Gwinear. St Gwinear is commemorated in the name of a village and parish to the east of Penzance near Hayle, and his Life is one of only two to have survived destruction in the Reformation. I suppose that Richard came across a translation of it in the Morrab Library, a singular institution in Morrab Gardens near his Penzance home.

According to the legend, St Gwinear was an Irish prince and pupil of St Patrick who because of his faith was exiled to Brittany by his father King Clito. After his father died, he was asked to succeed. Rejecting the crown, he and his sister Piala and others set sail as a party of 777 missionaries to evangelise Cornwall. The local tyrant, Teudar (a figure known from other Cornish tales, and said to be buried at Hayle) killed many in Gwinear's party, and later martyred Gwinear himself.

Richard was fascinated by the history and mythology of the Dark Ages, and his treatment is sensitive and assured. He draws the rather disparate elements of the Gwinear story together with a framing device which cunningly unites the figure of St Patrick, so relevant to the legend, with a romantic story involving a boy, a girl and her parents which must have gone down very well with his schoolgirl actors. Taking full advantage of the need of school performers for a large number of parts, he creates a kaleidoscope of varied characters (though limiting to 7 the number of Gwinear's party of evangelists, having no doubt concluded that the 777 of the original tale was conventional Celtic reduplication, quite apart from being unmanageable on even the largest of school stages). He did not maintain a master copy of his manuscript, but kept a number of the production scripts used by his actors, many of which he seems to have amended in response to events as rehearsals and performances went along. Hence the editor has had to use more judgement here than elsewhere in arriving at a final text. Regrettably the text of the two songs has been lost; their melody was no doubt by C T Cooper, who is credited in the programme with composing the music. One or two of the scripts showed lighting directions; these have been omitted. *Editor's note* you paddle-steamer!' an he'll FLAY me! He'll stick pins in me an hot coals an lock me in the shed all night with the cockadrills...

BERT: (*Who has been listening to the bird*) What a beautiful song! I nearly know it now, only he can glide so much better, and his tone is so much prettier. Come and sit with me, and listen properly.

GRETA: Oh. Oh, Bert, it's a GRAVE. We can't sit here Bert. There's someone buried! Someone DEAD. It might be my great-grandad.

(*Bert grabs her hand and pulls her towards the tomb*).

He'll come an lurch over our shoulders with 'is eyes blazing an stretch out his hoary arms and drag us down into the murky depths of the earth to feed on slugs an worms an snakes an 'orrible white writhing willow-roots FOR EVER, GLOATING...

BERT: (*Pushing her over to the tomb*). Sit down. No-one will see us here, you needn't worry.

(*They sit on the tomb but Greta is obviously unhappy. She snivels and whimpers*).

GRETA: It's not nice, Bert ... souls in torment ... they come out in the moonlight.

(*In sudden desperation Greta jumps off the tomb. Bert is still holding her hand. When their arms are fully extended they realise that their hands are stuck together. For a moment they stare at their locked hands in stupefaction*).

GRETA: Oh, Bert, whatever has happened?

BERT: Let go, you little fool.

GRETA: (*Sobbing with fright*). I can't! Oh, I want to go home, I'm frightened.

BERT: (*Slipping down from tomb*). Twist your arm around. No, not like that. Like this.

(*They go through a series of intricate manoeuvres, twisting and turning in an effort to extricate themselves*).

GRETA: It's no good. Oh Bert, it's a judgment. I said it was wrong. My dad...

(*She sinks sobbing to the ground at the foot of the tomb, pulling Bert down with her*).

(*Blackbird sings off*).

BERT: Oh, pack it in, Okmar.

GRETA: Bert, what are we going to do?

(*Long pause. Enter from right St Patrick. He walks wearily towards L, stops in front of tomb – no surprise. He slowly climbs the steps, sits on top step at left front of tomb, leans staff against knee, takes off hat and fans himself with it*).

PATRICK: Well, Winnie, here I am. Back again.

GRETA: 'Oos that Bert?

BERT: I don't know – Can't ... see ...

GRETA: It must be 'im – from the grave. Oh Bert, we're in for it now.

BERT: Keep quiet, can't you.

PATRICK: Oh, but I didn't expect to find you in this sorry state, Winnie, sure I didn't. And it's a grim story they've been telling me round about here, how you had yourself chopped by the bloody tyrant Teudar, and how he murdered all our good friends. Still, boy, it's the only way to go out, as I told you long ago, a pretty spot to lie in with the birds too; and you did wonderful work here, before you went. It's a beautiful church they've built for you. Have you seen it? Strong grey stone, rising straight towards our Father. I'd only like to know, Winnie, have you finished? Are you still here, or have you gone for good? You'd show yourself to old Patrick, if you were here?

(*Greta begins to whimper again*).

BERT: (*Whispering*). Oh, shut up, woman ... you bird-brain, he'll hear you.

PATRICK: Is that you, Winnie? Or is it only the little birds? Oh, I remember that Teudar alright. A bitter man, blind to all good but that of bloodshed and perniciousness. And even you could do nothing for him, Winnie. Well, I shall certainly visit him while I am here. To be crucified upside down is the worst I can expect; and it is so hard to see him sink into that pool of liquid fire, scratched and torn by the devil's talons.

(*Squeals from Greta. Patrick stops and peers around*).

PATRICK: That's no birds, brother Patrick – it's a female human girl with a soul (*Pause*) if she hasn't lost it. (*Pause, peering*) Where are you, my little bird? (*Pause. Sees B & G who are tensely silent*). Well, God be with you, what's this? (*Rising from his seat with extreme difficulty*) Sure and I didn't see you there. Is it some trouble you're in? (*Pauses over them and looks down*). Well bigod if it isn't two little ones making spring joy. Hi, (*Tapping G with his staff*) did I not hear you call out?

BERT: What are you, sir, a god? Or a spirit? Forgive us that we don't kneel to you, sir; we would surely do you proper reverence, but we are inextricably entangled.

PATRICK: Why, indeed I'm only an ordinary boy like yourself. It is good to see respect in the young, but ...

BERT: (*Perhaps a little ashamed – aggressive and suspicious*). What's your name then?

PATRICK: I'm Patrick.

BERT: Patrick what?

PATRICK: (*Slightly puzzled*). Well, Patrick – Saint. Saint Patrick.

BERT: There's no-one called Saint lives around here.

GRETA: Oh, sir, can you do miracles? Can you get us out of this?

PATRICK: (*As if beginning a long speech*). If it is good that I wish to do, I can indeed achieve wonderful things, by God's grace. When His will and mine are the same – and often now I can see through to the Right, for I have lived with Him a long time -

BERT: You are a god, then?

PATRICK: Oh, no, no. There were times when people thought me so, quite wrongly. When I sent the worms packing from my country – ha! that was wonderful to see them boiling out of the heather, swarming into the sea ...

GRETA: O-o-h ... don't say they've ...

BERT: You aren't dead, are you?

PATRICK: Well, I'll tell you now. It's a strange thing, but I can't remember. I've been imprisoned and tortured a good number of times – burying up to the neck, I've had that – and sinking in the sea with a bag of stones – but it quite escapes me whether I – whether my hurt – was ever, so to speak, mortal. To tell you the absolute honest truth, I get my story mixed up with the others. (*Pause. Nod towards tomb*). Even young Winnie's. (*Pause laughing*). But here I am talking, and I'm using up your night for you. I must be getting on. Ought to see a bit more life in you, eh? (*Prodding them with his staff*). You can do wonderful things yourselves, eh? (*Prods them again, is unable to pull staff away. Tussles with it*). Well, here's some bewitching.

(*Greta and Bert both speak at once, beseeching*).

GRETA: Oh, don't go, sir, don't go ...

BERT: It's what we told you, we're stuck like this ...

GRETA: Please help us if you can ...

BERT: We'll burn a sacrifice – I can get a cow ...

(*The staff comes away suddenly, Patrick sits down hard. He has pulled the young people into a new and uncomfortable position. They fidget, trying to get used to this new discomfort, while Patrick talks as if to himself*).

PATRICK: That was pride. And disrespect. Pride and disrespect did that. Oh, Lord; (*Reaches for his hat, holds it in his lap*). Oh, Lord, when will I know you better? (*He ponders mournfully*).

(Ow *and* Ooh! *quietly from G & B*).

GRETA: Please sir ...

PATRICK: Yes, now, these poor children – (*He tries to get up, fails*). It's that you're unable to disentangle yourselves – you are in a complex and mysterious way interlocked, and as it were, cemented together, is that it?

GRETA: Yes, sir, that's the truth of the matter – we've been tugging and pulling fit to burst, an' now my dad'll be out looking for us with 'is lash and 'is tweezers, like as not, and it's 'orrible to think of what 'e'll do if he finds us like this.

PATRICK: And what were you doing, can you tell me, to land in this fearful predicament?

BERT: We were ...

GRETA: We fell.

PATRICK: You fell, eh? Fell, is it? Well, maybe I'm able to do something. It's a most extraordinary happy chance that you've fallen so close to my young friend Gwinear's monument. If he and I cannot intercede for you, no-one can, I'll tell you that. But it'll be a matter of getting you over onto the slab, so his spirit can enter into you the more easily ...

GRETA: O-o-h, sir, is that really what we've got to do?

(*After much hauling and pushing, with interjections of 'Ow!' and 'That hurts' from the young people, Patrick discovers that he is unable to move them*).

PATRICK: (*Panting*). I'll fetch my rascal of a squire ... to help ... (*Right*) Angus! (*Shouts*) Angus! ... (*Normal voice*) he's never there ... always up to something miles away from where he should be ... (*Shouts*) Angus! ... it's a hard task to lay upon a poor saint. (*He waits, no-one appears*).

BERT: If you lifted us on edge sir, made a kind of wheel ...

PATRICK: Y'know I think there might be some sense in that. We can but try it, anyhow. (*Strenuous efforts to carry out the suggestion*).

BERT: Perhaps if you used your staff, sir, as a lever ...

(*Patrick thinks, then, muttering vehemently to himself, he attempts to prise them into position. After several abortive attempts they move slightly. Tremendous strain and they begin to move*).

PATRICK: (*Muttering*) Move, ya' blethering, footling, rotten, excommunicated heap of rammidgings ...

(*Patrick falls flat on his face. G & B now in a wheel-like position, totter and roll slightly back and forth*).

PATRICK: (*Mutters in a testy manner, then rises to his knees, retrieves hat, holds it against his chest*). Dear Lord, only You are perfect. (*Pause*).

BERT: I think you could move us quite easily now, sir.

PATRICK: Yes, yes, let's see now. (*Rises*) Ha ha! Yes, easy as pie! (*He makes a great game of pushing them the rest of the way, laughing gleefully*). Like being a boy again! (*They bump against the bottom step and stop*).

PATRICK: Ah, but now here's the difficult part, I'll bet. (*He attempts to pull them up the steps*).

PATRICK: Angus! (*No response*). Well, that's as far as I can get you my dears. But never mind, let's try it where you are – you're on the monument that's the important thing. (*Begins to move down the steps*).

BERT: (*Strangled voice*). This isn't terribly comfortable.

PATRICK: That's alright, we'll have you out of that in no time. (*Raises arms in air*). Lord ... Lord, see these two children prostrated before you, their union is not pleasing to them; by your divine mercy rend them asunder, so that they may be two again. This is Patrick speaking to you, Lord. (*Pause*) Any good?

BERT: (*Struggling*) No, perhaps you weren't loud enough.

PATRICK: I think it will have to be the full service. Are you sure you can think of no reason why this misfortune should have befallen you?

BERT: Well ...

GRETA: Oh, sir, you can't be thinking of taking us to the church like this. Do try again, PLEASE.

PATRICK: Once more, then. (*Raises arms*) Lord, through the agency of my young friend Gwinear here entombed, relieve these young people of their embarrassing juxtaposition, or if You be for any reason unwilling to do what we ask, then through Your servant Gwinear as heretofore, show us some sign or portent that we may know. This is Patrick. (*long pause*)

(*Enter Angus, carrying a dead blackbird*).

ANGUS: I got a dead bird, Pat.

(*Patrick grabs him by the scruff of the neck*).

PATRICK: Angus, Angus, it's a horrible deed to hurt and destroy the Lord's creatures ...

ANGUS: But it was squaking like ...

PATRICK: And I've told you before you mustn't call me Pat, and now there are strangers here.

ANGUS: But ... (*He looks down at B & G*) What's wrong with them?

PATRICK: Now Angus, there's something I want you to do for me.

ANGUS: Why are they upside down?

PATRICK: I want you to go into the village ...

ANGUS: What happens if you kick them ... (*He aims an experimental kick but P drags him back by the ear*).

PATRICK: Angus, listen to me, will you? Go into the village, fetch some people with branches so they can carry these two to St Gwinear's church.

ANGUS: Alright.

(*Patrick takes away his crossbow*).

PATRICK: I'll look after this devil's engine while you're gone. And hurry now. (*Angus leaves reluctantly, looking over his shoulder at B & G*).

ANGUS: Did the Good Lord make them like that?

PATRICK: Go on now.

ANGUS: Alright (*Exit slowly*).

BERT: I always said it was bunkum, all that praying. Sacrifices, we need.

PATRICK: Oh, don't go saying things like that, boy. Winnie will fix this for you once we get you into his church, but don't go making him angry. Everything is for the best, you can be sure of that. If the Good Lord wants you to remain joined for the moment, he is bound to have a very good reason for it. Our lives are governed even to the smallest detail by a sensible and consistent plan.

BERT: It all seems pretty disorganised to me. I should think there are five or six gods all quarrelling about us at this moment.

GRETA: Is this really St Gwinear's tomb, sir?

PATRICK: Yes, indeed, his inscription is on it. Why, did you know Gwinear?

GRETA: No ... well, I saw him of course, and since he died I've been into his church any number of times, but my dad doesn't know, and when he finds out that I was carried in like this, and by all the neighbours ... (*dissolves into tears*)

PATRICK: He was a great servant of the Lord, and a very good friend of mine. I'll tell you about him, if you like. It will pass the time while we wait. I first met him many years ago, when he was still a boy. I was in Ireland – oh, a glorious country, believe me. What a life that was! Roaming all day over the moors, wandering by the side of lovely streams, sleeping at night on the mountainside, watching the sun rise and set. The animals would come and talk to me in those days, rabbits and geese and little stag-beetles, and if I met a fellow traveller, then I passed the Word on to him, and told him about our Saviour. Now it happened that the news of my journeying went on before me, and one day a man came to me who said that in a certain town only two or three miles away, the kings of seven kingdoms thereabouts chanced to be at that moment engaged in a week of feasting, and if I passed that way, they would welcome a visit from me.

I rejoiced to hear that these people were thirsting so for knowledge of our Lord, and that very evening I was striding down the hillside to where the little town lay …

Scene I

A feast in the castle of Clito, King of Kulcharnie in Ireland and Gwinear's father

Song

GWINEAR: What's that you're playing now, Ulric?

ULRIC: (*Wheezing, toneless voice*) Oh, that's not a song boy, which is to say it is not a song which I have previously put together inside my head, telling to all people of the wonderful events of my life, such as many a song I carry about with me. It is more a song of the harp herself, to which I listen to know whether she is happy among those things she remembers, and is ready to sing of them tonight, or whether she is old and dead and good for no more than answering to my fingers. It is no use to make the harp do your will if you are not acquainted with her mood. *(He has not raised his head from the strings, and now only half raises it, shouting*). Give us some peace, you women! (*They happen to be in a huddle and take no notice*).

GWINEAR: (*Leaning very far forward in order to touch the harp, finally squats in front of the fire at Ulric's feet*). The harp has a spirit of her own then?

ULRIC: Everything has a spirit, boy. If you are to be a singer as you say, you must remember not to let the spirit be obscured by the thing. It is the spirit which will be in your songs. You must learn to know all the gods and not to make them jealous by paying attention to only one of them. It is hard; there are as many gods as there are stones and men. Even Lucius will tell you that.

GWINEAR: Lucius? (*U. looks up and nods towards the sleeping L. G. looks over his shoulder*). Oh, the Roman … (*Puzzled*) but he says that only those things we can touch are real, there's nothing else. He thinks that when we die we just rot and that's the end of it. He's very depressing to talk to.

ULRIC: Ach! You needn't think that anyone truly believes such stuff at bottom, young Gwinear, however much noise they might make about it. Fill Lucius with wine and you'll learn the names of more gods than your daddy's sacked villages.

GWINEAR: Does wine always make people more religious?

ULRIC: Oh, it is very important, very important. That and music … (*At a particularly violent gust of laughter from the women, U. loses patience and shouts more loudly, in great exasperation*). You hedonistic bunch of cacophonies, I've told you once! We're having a serious philosophical discussion here, and how you can expect a man to listen to his harp with this rumpus going on …

ERILA: *(She turns away from the other two at first as if only for a moment, but then gradually becomes interested in her own speech and moves towards Ulric, Gwendal following, Urdusk involved with the dice-players).* Is it you there Ulric, making that CLANG, CLANG, BONK! like a dragon in an ironworks? We cannot hear ourselves speak for your infernal twanging! No wonder you cannot sing in tune if that's the best you can do with the harp. Every night you torment us with your wailing as if you were tormented, possessed by devils.

GWENDAL: And now look, he's teaching poor Gwinear to do the same.

ERILA: *(As if to Gwendal, but also for Gwinear, Urdusk and dice-players, who are all listening).* Oh, heaven help us, not two of them! I shan't sleep at night for the devils in my head!

DODRAN: *(Perhaps obscured by general hubbub).* Devils in your bed more like! *(He is soundly cuffed by Urdusk. This leads to a mock fight which ends in Urdusk's sitting on Dodran's knee).*

GWENDAL: I tell you, Ulric, you'd better sing more sweetly if you want to keep your entrails. His Majesty King Clito looked most dyspeptic at the end of that song last night.

ERILA: Oh, that one last night! *(She thumps Gwendal, hilariously stumbling over potatoes towards centre, between R. and L. tables where child is sitting, in order to mimic Ulric).* It killed the whole feast. King Olf beat his wife senseless after that one! *(she inadvertently tramples on child 5 and absently thrusts him aside with her foot. He sprawls face-down on a group of potatoes and makes feeble attempts to rise, holding a potato in each hand, feet and knees slipping on other potatoes. Erila stands in an exaggeratedly bent posture, clutching an imaginary harp and waving her hand over the strings, throws her head back and half wails, half-screeches an improvised song, the excruciating tune of which is suggested by the notes Ulric, ignoring her, is still emitting. Everyone else except Lucius and the children watches her).*

Oh, I am a drunken, smelly old man
Who has lived too long ...

(Loud applause and thumping of the table from dice-players. Gwinear watches impassive).

GWENDAL: *(Clutching Erila's arm and continuing her song)*

And I'm going to sing yes another
Inc-e-redibly tedious old song ...

(More applause and laughter from Urdusk and the dice-players. Erila and Urd. are laughing too, leaning against each other).

... About kelpies and suchlike things
That don't exist ...

ERILA: *(Thumping Gwendal, her singing impeded by laughter, becoming a shout)* ...

...Unless I fall over from being ... from b ...

(They both make attempts to complete the line, but incapacitated by laughter, at last collapse against each other, with thunderous applause from dice-players).

GWENDAL: *(emerging from the embrace, stumbling towards Ulric)*. Here, give us the harp, Ulric, we'll see if we can get this to some proper music. *(She grabs the harp; we hear the thump of her hand against the body of the harp, and the discordant vibrations of the strings in the ensuing struggle. Ulric resists, shrinking into his chair and making whines and whimpers of protest).*

GWINEAR: Leave him, Gwendal.

GWENDAL: Come on, ya great huddle of mothballs ...

GWINEAR: *(Rising from his knees; much louder)* I said leave him!

(Silence but for giggles of Urdusk, snores of Lucius and sounds of the potato game. Gwendal slowly releases harp and steps back, Ulric unwinds grunting, checking harp for damage.

Meanwhile, children I – 4, intrigued by child 5's plight, have slightly amended the game, first by rolling the potatoes as close to him as possible then rolling them so that they stop by him and heap up round him; now they are positively flinging them at his head. Encouraged by the blows he has struggled back more or less to his original position, but now a potato strikes home particularly hard and he bursts into desperate, deafening, baby-like weeping. The game stops, children I – 4 try to dissociate themselves from him. Everyone else ignores him. Erila leans back against a table, fidgeting with her fingers).

GWENDAL: To be sure we was only fooling, Gwinear.

GWINEAR: *(glares at her, then turns to Ulric)*. Ulric can you give us a song now before dinner? *(Ulric still obviously in a huff, qualified assent, half-rising when Gwinear says ...)* Their Majesties may not be able to eat in any case.

(Ulric shuffles to spot where E and G performed, gathering furs about him. He glares venomously at them, who link arms and commiserate with one another, moving to chairs behind table on right, where they sit. U. prepares to sing but child 5 is still bawling; U. kicks out violently and child 5 shoots across the floor, hitting the inner front leg of right table with his head, then lies still. Gwinear rushes over to administer first aid. Ulric adopts a position which is very similar to Erila's earlier imitation of it, plays a few introductory bars, and begins to sing).

Song

At the very first notes Lucius, who has so far been sleeping profoundly, starts up in his chair and anxiously looks about him; when the song itself begins he moans piteously and tries to bury himself in his arm chair. He goes through a series of contortions trying to block out the sound, groaning at intervals, clapping cushions against his ears and piling them over his head. Gwinear's first move having reached child 5 is to prop him against the table leg, loosen his clothing and fan him with the hem of his own shirt. There should be blood if possible. Next he grabs child 2, who looks guilty, and sends him through rear door on an errand. Then he clears space on the table and lifts child 5 onto it. Erila and Gwendal prod wound and idly discuss chances of survival. Child 2 returns with enormous roll of bandage. Hands it to Gwinear who gives it to the women indicating they should bandage child's head. Erila holds roll and lets out bandage while Gwendal wraps it round head, not very competently. Gwinear sits on table behind and to right of Ulric. Fetching a flute from out of his tunic, he accompanies song with it.

CLITO: *(Approaching pair made by Gwinear and Ulric, drunkenly clapping arm round Gwinear's shoulders; jogged by Gwinear's dancing, speech slurred with drink).* Gwinrrbr ... Gwb ... Gwi ... Winnie ... m'boy ... 'smusic; I thought ... I thought, there's no fucher int. Ol 'Ulric, no good – sti 'thi' mud. Drone, drone, oooheoo *(Wails a distorted version of the ballad)* ... Iw's WRONG! This's good, m'boy. This'll sell! 'Sbound't' sell!

ULRIC: *(Dropping to his knees as if in obeisance but in fact exhausted, fingers still working frantically at the harp).* I can't go on much longer, Your Majesty ... I'm not used to this ...

CLITO: *(Jogged off Gwinear's shoulders, half-falls and saves himself by grasping Ulric's shoulders),* 'Salright, Ulrick! You're doing great! *(staggers off, resuming drunken version of ballad – OUT OF THIS rises first appearance of the two tunes sung together)*

OLF: Leave her alone! I got here first!

CLITO: Don't you speak like that with me, Sir Olf. I dance with who I like.

GWENDAL: Your Majesties, can I settle this? *(C. hits her)*

OLF: But you can have Dodran there.

CLITO: Thass a man. Are you suggesting I should dance with a man?

OLF: You were dancing with Gwellum a minute ago. *(A tug-of-war has developed, O. on her left arm, C. on her right. She faces front).*

CLITO: *(Now going to O. and grabbing the place where his lapels would be).* Are you making an incineration?

OLF: No, no, only dear Ethel is not often out of the way, and I enjoy a bit of female companionship.

CLITO: Well it's my party, alright? *(Thrusts him out of the way but he returns infuriated; there is a fight which ends in a lucky blow from O. knocking C. out. C. falls on the already prostrate Fergus and O. claims Gwendal).*

FERGUS: *(Very drunk) (Taking over Urdusk tries to raise him but, having failed, goes and gets Anselm, who since tripping over Lucius and Child 5 (Lucius shouting "Help") during F. & S's duet, has been trying unsuccessfully to untangle him).*

UGRAMOND: Y'great hog, Tusc! Look at this, he's eating the lot! *(S., V. and A. all dash round to their chairs and fall too).*

End of Song

ULRIC: *(Petting Gwinear and leading him back towards fireplace. Meanwhile there is light applause from dice-players).* That was quite well done, Gwinear, quite good.

ARNO: Excellent!

GWELLUM: Bravo!

ULRIC: *(Ignoring them)* Only, do you not feel that there was perhaps more brain than heart in your music? All your notes were in the exact right place, and flowed beautifully together, and yet there was a coldness about them, as if you did not believe the things they were saying.

GWINEAR: (*Looking at him with earnest attention*)
To tell the truth, the music went so fast that I had no time to do more than put the notes in their right places.

SPANGAR: (*Mouth full*) Come and have something to eat, you two. (*Ulric and Gwinear confer silently, move towards table*). Must take it out of you, all that twiddling.

ULRIC: (*Going first, between tables 2 & 3 stopping to observe and perhaps prod Lucius, Child 5, Fergus, Clito*). There are certainly some casualties of our performance.

SPANGAR: Don't worry about them they're happy enough. It was Olf did for those two. (*Inaudible comment from Olf*) – he'll be in trouble if they remember. Come and sit by me, Gwinear, tell me more about this fluting of yours. Seems to me you're too damn good at it for a king's son. (*Gwinear obeys, Ulric sits next to Tusc at table 3. Loud knocking at door to left*). What is it?

ARNO: I think it was all nonsense what Ulric said. Too intellectual, indeed! Your playing was wonderful, exciting. Just look at the effects of it.

GWINEAR: It's kind of you, Arno; but he knows what he's talking about. Perhaps music isn't my vocation after all. But I felt so sure!

ANSELM: Don't you think we ought to wake Clito, at least?

UGRAMOND: Come in, will you!

ANSELM: We are eating his food, after all.

SPANGAR: Perhaps you're right. Gwellum, put some water on His Majesty. Then come and eat. And Dodran, for the gods' sakes go and see who that is.

ATTENDANT: It's the saint, sor. The saint from Cornwall, sor, he's come, sor, the saint from Cornwall's come, sor. St Patrick, sor. Shall we bring him in, sor?

DODRAN: He says it's St Patrick come from Cornwall; he's come, Patrick the saint. From Cornwall. Shall they bring him in?

SPANGAR: Yes, yes, it'll be a distraction.

DODRAN: You're to bring him in.

CLITO: A horse! A horse! Get that horse! Kick him off it! Keep away from me, you dogs! One step more and you're sliced beetroot! Help, Gwinear, help me! There's blood in my eyes! Just wait till I can see, you hell-froth! Just wait till Gwinear comes! No-one can fight me and Gwinear! You'll all be burned alive for the great god Ogbad: Ogbad'll swallow your foul souls and slaver on your ashes! Let go, Slug, Tapeworm, Salamander!

LUCIUS: It's me, your majesty! Friend! Friend! I'm Lucius! I'm on your side!

CLITO: (*Quieting*) Who? What? Who do you say you are?

LUCIUS: Lucius, Your Majesty. I live in your castle.

CLITO: Never heard of you! (*Struggles with sword again*).

LUCIUS: Yes! Yes! Lucius the Roman! I was dropped on your shores by pirates. I've given you good service.

CLITO: Lucius! Thank the gods I've found you! We've got our work cut out here, boy. There are thousands of 'em, horrible little crawling maggots on our land. We've got to squash them, Lucius!

LUCIUS: I think you're wanted, Your Majesty. There's a visitor.

CLITO: Ha! What's this? A prisoner!

LUCIUS: Should I keep this, do you think?

CLITO: Get off, worm!

OLF: (*Whispers*) Has he said anything about me?

ANSELM: (*Also whispering*) No, not yet. I don't think he remembers. I'd keep out of the way if I were you.

(*Exit Urdusk for more potatoes*)

PATRICK: (*Seeming to wake up*) Is it his majesty King Clito of Kulcharnie I'm looking at?

CLITO: Hold your tongue!

(*to Attendant and Guards; trying to stride about purposefully, testing strength and sharpness of sword*) Alright, unstring him. You've done the rack and the crushing with stones? Let's start cutting bits off.

ATTENDANT: It's the saint, sor. The saint from Cornwall sor. He said he was coming, sor. The saint from Cornwall – you knew he was coming, sor. You asked him to come, sor. You was pleased to think, sor, that if he was to come with his speechifying and his workings of miraculous happenings, sor, he'd be a pleasing diversion and a maker of exciting merriment at your feast, sor. St Patrick, sor; there's not a serpent been seen in Ireland since he come, sor ...

CLITO: (*High voice*) I'm not listening to this claptrap! He's from Cornwall – alright, nail him to a table and we'll have a game. (*Still testing the sword, Child 3 still imitating him*).

SPANGAR: (*Standing*) With due respect, Clito, and this being a fine meal, all the same I think we should hear what he says first.

CLITO: (*Looking round*) Clito? Who do you mean, Clito? ... Ah!

SPANGAR: This might be a pet of the Cornish king, if Cornwall's invented kings yet. We don't want to infuriate any Cornish king, the gods alone know what'd happen.

CLITO: (*Genuine puzzlement*) Aren't we fighting the Cornish already? (*aggressive*) Isn't Kulcharnie good enough for any louts from oversea? (*Waving sword in air, imitated by Child 3*).

SPANGAR: We're not fighting them as far as I know, and from what I've heard Cornwall's good enough for a united Ireland, which as you know we haven't got. And remember, this man is a sort of guest.

CLITO: (*Considering, fingers on chin*) Well, I don't remember inviting any saint. What are you then? (*P begins to speak but is interrupted with a prod*). A spy, I've no doubt! And what are you supposed to do? Recitations and conjuring tricks? Let's hear it then. (*Pause with a prod*). Come on, say your piece. (*Pause. Patrick moves feebly as if trying to rise. Clanking of chain*).

PATRICK: I'm ... I'm sure, Your Majesty, my delivery would be much improved if I was standing up.

CLITO: What do you take me for? Get on with it!

PATRICK: But you were having some revelry before I came in; it'd be a shame for me to interrupt, I'm afraid my performance is dry stuff, whereas I enjoy nothing better than a good song and dance.

CLITO: (*Becoming furious*) Make your bloody speech, you Cornish bucket-of-guts!

PATRICK: (*Very hesitant*) You wouldn't have such a thing as a glass of wine, would you ...?

CLITO: (*Standing over Patrick, sword in air*) Are you going to give us a poem, or do I chop you where you lie?

PATRICK: (*During speech Clito retires and stands with point of sword on ground, leaning against pommel in quite an elegant posture, though swaying visibly, with expression of deep concentration*). Very well, I shall do what I can ... with your help, Lord ... although the circumstances are not what I should have wished. I come to tell you a thing which is wonderful; it is a miracle such as no man has ever performed or even dreamed; its rehearsal is a cure for all the troubles you have now, for all those you have had in other years, for all those whose pain you are yet to feel. If you should love a girl who repays you with sneers and cold words, if her presence for you is an unanswerable question, so that you become with her something that is not yourself, my speech will be the answer to the question. If it is simply that your head throbs and spins and you are unable to follow the thoughts that fly; if you try to speak, write, carve, build, and find that your meaning loses itself in the whirlpool, and you are staring blindly after all at the wall or at some silly thing, my speech will restore your meaning to you, and make sense of the thing you are looking at. If you have fought your way to the centre of the battle through a mass of men who lie reeking, whose hot blood smothers you from head to foot, and then you find your lust turning to some sickness you cannot name, my speech will tell you what that sickness is, and show you how to swallow it. (*Slight movement, clinking of chain*). There <u>is</u> a king in Cornwall, called Teudar. He is the most unhappy man I ever saw. I have tried to bring him this speech, but every time he has been too frightened to look at it closely, and ever since he has refused to understand it. Now it has so invaded him that he imagines it governs the world, and that everyone is as troubled by it as he. He has a god called Gog who started life as a very unimportant demon, and whom Teudar has now promoted to the top of the tree. (*Patrick's own laughter*). You are sensible men; you will hardly believe the absurd things this imagined spirit insists on. Poor Teudar believes that the only method of keeping Gog at bay is to kneel in front of his statue every day at dawn, having himself whipped 60 times with fresh birch-twigs by his servants. (*Much louder laughter and murmuring from audience*). If only he knew, the world is much more simple than that. There is no need to sort out the politics of the gods, or to decide which of them wants what ... (*longish pause, slightly heavier delivery*) ... there is only one God; (*sharp intake of breath from audience; Ulric starts to his feet, Clito comes to attention, all much more alert*). He asks nothing of us, and He has no name; (*with each statement now there is a new reaction of anxiety in the audience. Clito moves towards Patrick threateningly but Gwinear comes over to him and holds his arm, watching Patrick, both of them stare at Patrick fascinated*). He has one son, born of a woman, who is half-god, half-man. (*Rising babble obscures P's speech; Ulric is heard to say "This is not right"; Lucius, free of his bonds, shows interest and is moving towards Patrick*). The son's name is Jesus, and he lives in each one of you. The part of Jesus which is in you is what you hear saying, when you are with your troublesome girl, to treat her kindly in spite of ...

CLITO: I'm not listening to anymore of this! Lucius, you're a sensible man, what do you think of this? Here, lift him up, let Lucius take a look. What do you think? Burning, cutting, crushing, drowning?

LUCIUS: I've heard something of this before; the man Jesus was in fact a lunatic my people freed from his misery a few centuries ago. I've never actually seen one of his followers before, however. To be quite frank I thought the thing had died out long ago. It's quite picturesque though, don't you think? Hey, I say, is it true you've come from Cornwall?

PATRICK: I'd hardly started ... that was only by way ... by way of a prologue ...

LUCIUS: From Cornwall, are you?

PATRICK: Eh? ... yes, that's where I've come from.

LUCIUS: I don't know it myself. Not far from Wales, though, they tell me?

PATRICK: Er, no, it's not far.

LUCIUS: Well, I know Wales very well – I was stationed there, you know. Lovely country!

PATRICK: Yes, grand.

LUCIUS: I say, you wouldn't know of any ships going that way? The thing is, I've managed to get myself rather stranded here, and if there should be any of my people still left in Wales ...

CLITO: Alright, that's enough! Pick him up, put him on the table, here, clear the table, bring it forward. I'm not dealing with a dangerous madman like that until he's in little pieces.

PATRICK: Look, is it really vital to keep me chained up like this?

GWINEAR: Wait a moment.

PATRICK: Ah, thank you, young man.

GWINEAR: Come and sit down. Can you walk?

PATRICK: This is really very kind. You wouldn't have a glass of wine, would you?

GWINEAR: Get some wine, Erila.

PATRICK: Ah! It is good to see respect in the young.

CLITO: What do you think you're doing, you idiot? Gwinear! Are you deaf? Leave that man alone! He's not right in the head! He'll send you mad with his talk! Ach, the boy's never had any sense. This man is the enemy, we're going to cut him up. Now stop your damn fool playing about.

GWINEAR: What on earth is the matter? Patrick's our guest.

CLITO: He is against our country – he has blasphemed – he is a danger to everything we hold dear.

GWINEAR: I think that's all an exaggeration, he seems perfectly alright to me. I don't see why we shouldn't treat him like a human being.

CLITO: What ... what ... do you know ... I tell you ... look ... I tell you, boy, either you get upstairs to bed, now, without another word, or you get out of my castle for good – out of my country too – and you take your smelly friend with you! Go to his blasted pagan Cornwall if you like!

GWINEAR: Very well. Come on Patrick.

SPANGAR: Are you sure this is wise, Clito?

CLITO: If you expect me to keep him here when he's declared himself against all religion, all morality ...

SPANGAR: It is unfortunate that he feels that way, but perhaps his beliefs are not the only point ...

CLITO: Don't tell me what's the point and what isn't, Spangar, or you'll be out too.

ARNO: You are making a mistake, Your Majesty. If Gwinear leaves he will not be alone.

CLITO: You can all go, if you like. You're nothing to me. At least there'll be one man left who knows the difference between right and wrong.

ARNO: I'm coming with you, Gwinear. Dodran'll come too and Gwellum.

LUCIUS: I say, you don't have any idea which direction you're heading in, do you? I mean, if you're going East ...

KATHRYN: What's this Erila's been telling me? Drunken brawling and lewd talk ... Ah! Piala!

ETHEL: Where is he? Where is he? He's in here somewhere, the swine.

OLGA: Oh not again! Fergus, Fergus, when will you learn some sense?

KATHRYN: Gwinear! How could you let this happen? Your own sister!

GWINEAR: Oh, is that Piala?

KATHRYN: Clito, are you responsible for all this?

CLITO: Er, no ... Kathryn ... don't er ... worry ...

KATHRYN: Where are they going?

ETHEL: Where's Dodran?

KATHRYN: Clito, what's been happening?

End of Scene I

Interlude

Begins in a place near Clito's castle,
and then advances in time and place to the wood in which the prologue was set

PATRICK: (*To audience*) Oh, yes? And I suppose I know what you're about thinking. I suppose it would happen that you know my story better than I do myself, and think, "surely Patrick would never have had any dealings with such s..."

ANGUS: I can't find it, Pat.

PATRICK: What is it, boy? What is it you can't find?

ANGUS: The village, Pat. I can't find it.

PATRICK: But ... you simple little child ... did I not tell you to follow the path that brought us out here this morning?

ANGUS: Yes, and I remembered that, so I went looking for the path, and I recognised it because of some holes I'd dug, but when I started following it it just brought me back here. I got a branch, though – a big one.

PATRICK: But this is no use, Angus, how can we possibly carry those people on this?

ANGUS: I thought we could sort of thread them with it, like a needle ...

PATRICK: Oh no, no, no, I've had experience of that sort of thing – we don't want to kill them. No, we must have smaller branches, and fasten them together.

ANGUS: We could break this one up.

PATRICK: No, no, you really have not the most basic practical sense. We'll find them on the ground.

ANGUS: Shall I go and put this back in the earth, then?

PATRICK: Angus, just come with me, will you.

GRETA'S FATHER: Well, well, who might you be? And what are you doing with this tree?

ANGUS: I was just going to put it back, sir, but he wouldn't let me.

PATRICK: You must excuse the boy, his intentions are good. Of course we should replant the tree, but we have a most complicated and urgent matter to settle. We will, of course, come again in the morning and put everything to rights.

G.F: Oh, you'll come again in the morning, is that the idea? You think this tree will lie happy here and wait for you to come again in the morning? As if it didn't know your sort better than to expect you two days running in the same spot! I tell you, we've had enough of you in this wood. You come here with your camp-fires and your caravans, leaving gates open, trampling through cornfields ... do you realise that these trees are my livelihood? And as if it wasn't enough for you to destroy everything in sight, you go performing your magic and your miracles all over the place, bewitching the land and the people till they can't go anywhere without seeing white spots in front of their eyes and dying of horrible wasting diseases. No-one can go walking in the woods at night – you take our daughters and perform unspeakable rites with them on your blood-drenched altars ... there isn't ... well, you, my lad, will go now and put that tree back where you found it or else your Mummy and Daddy will never like to see you again.

ANGUS: Yes, sir.

PATRICK: Er, do you have a daughter, sir?

G.F: What do you know about my Greta? What have you done with her, you abominable necromancer? Where's that pig of a Bert? If the pair of you have been ... if you've had ... tell me where she is, you wretch, or I'll reach down your throat and pull out your insides bit by bit!

PATRICK: Indeed there's no need to go to such extremes sir; please don't alarm yourself unduly. There's nothing seriously amiss with the girl; so far as I know, she's still er ... intact, and likely to remain so. To put it another way, she's even more intact than before.

G.F: What do you mean? What's happened?

PATRICK: It's just that there's been a slight accident, sir.

G.F: Ha! Serves her right, the little hussy! And how have you got mixed up with this?

PATRICK: It simply happens that such ... cases are a, a speciality of mine, and the young lady requested my help.

G.F: And is there a dirty-looking young scoundrel with yellow hair hanging around her?

PATRICK: He is constantly by her side – a touching devotion.

G.F: Oh, yes?

PATRICK: Sad to say, the boy was involved in the accident also ... nothing but a fall, you understand.

G.F: Hmph! It's not the only accident he'll have tonight, either.

PATRICK: Well, I should advise perhaps leaving the treatment to me for the moment, but if you'd like to come and see the invalids?

G.F: Yes, very well, let's go and see them. Er, ... thank you.

Exeunt

End of Interlude

Scene II

A hunt in the country surrounding the palace of Prince Étienne of Britanny

GWINEAR: Is this really the man, after all? He seems very young still but he will die very soon, yes. He breaks if you touch him. He's not frightened, though, is he? He's laughing! I think he's ready to do what you ask. He's ready for you. Ah! Who sent you?

HYA: I don't know. I don't know where I've come from.

GWINEAR: You've got blood on your clothes, like me.

HYA: Yes, it's the same blood. You killed me and broke me in pieces. It was strange, like coming out of sleep.

GWINEAR: It was just the same with me. I woke up when I was looking at you in the pool... at least I think it was you.

HYA: You look like me.

GWINEAR: Am I one of your broken off pieces do you think?

HYA: No, no, that's the only one. Oh, don't. I don't like it; I hated being inside it; I couldn't sort out the moments from one another; I couldn't feel the days passing; all I could feel were needs and fears making me run, and I couldn't understand them – I even saw only crude and simple things, as if it was through a veil of blood.

GWINEAR: How long were you like this? How did you come to be inside it?

HYA: I've said, I don't know how long. Someone evil put me inside it, out of hatred. Would you get rid of it please?

GWINEAR: Sit down and let me wash your face, so I can see you better. What's your name?

HYA: Hya.

GWINEAR: We're just the same, "Hya and I". But no-one hates me – except perhaps my father, and he's simply blind. How could it be that someone hated you? Can you remember anything about it? Tell me. What were you doing when you were changed?

HYA: (*Thinks*) I was only a little girl ... I live with my father, and I had to cook and clean for him ... but I didn't like the work, so he beat me and I ran away ... I slept three nights in the hills ... I don't think it was this country ... on the third night I was woken up by some people who were having a dance and a feast in the hills at night ... they wanted me to eat and dance with them ... their food was horrible, but I ate some because I was so hungry ... and I was frightened of them, but I loved them because I was lonely ... it was very exciting to dance with them, and exhausting ... but they wouldn't let me stop ... just when I was about to faint and fall, their master came ... he held me up and laughed in my face ... then they all laughed, and he shouted and threw me down the hill ... that's all.

GWINEAR: And this is the man who hated you? What was he like? Describe him to me.

HYA: He was a giant ... he was black, as if it was always night-time around him ... he had horns, and fire came from his mouth ...

GWINEAR: (*Nodding*) I know him.

HYA: You know him? But how ... how did you meet him? This may have been centuries ago, in another country.

GWINEAR: Well, I haven't actually met him, yet, but I know of him – and it's not a description you could easily mistake for someone else's. He's the Emperor Satan – he's immortal, and very powerful – he rules most of the world, although surprisingly few people have heard of him.

HYA: Who are you, then, that you're likely to meet him?

GWINEAR: I'm just the same as you, we know that. I am a servant of his great Rival – and so are you. You have met him – so shall I – and he will be the first man to show me real hatred. The Master we both serve was here just now, and he told me nearly everything that will happen; He's left... No, He never leaves, but He has stepped back to let us see things as clearly as we can for ourselves. And, look, the clearest thing is that you have defeated Satan, and that somehow, I shall defeat him too.

HYA: Where is the Master?... I don't see him.

GWINEAR: Oh, you won't see Him, He is invisible, but He is always ...

HYA: Oh, show me somewhere to hide, quickly! Where are they? Over there? I must run, I must run ...

GWINEAR: It's alright, it's alright Hya ... haven't I said the Master is here? You need never fear for yourself again. Never give danger or pain or death the slightest thought, even when the knife is in the act of falling. He is always there with His wings spread around you. Let your thoughts always fly to Him, and stop there.

Besides, they're not hunting you any more. You have nothing to do with their games and their killing. <u>You</u> are hunting <u>them</u> now, them and all men. You must learn the best way to know them, and then trap them, control them, bind them to the life God wants them to lead.

HYA: Are you very close to our Master?

GWINEAR: I've only just now discovered quite <u>how</u> close. I saw him in the pool before I saw you – or rather I saw myself, and I saw him in my own face. He gives off light all the time, and his face is always moving in thousands of different ways, so that you can never see Him whole. The face spoke to me – or rather it told me about myself, and what I was to do.

HYA: And what is that?

GWINEAR: Well, first I must disconnect myself from all the world's affairs, I suppose. I must give up possessions and pastimes and all that sort of thing – then I must live in complete peace for a time, and listen to what else the Master has to tell me. He will tell me where to go in order to do His work.

HYA: Where do you live now? With the Master?

GWINEAR: I've been living with the Prince, in his castle, but that must stop now.

HYA: Which Prince is he?

GWINEAR: Oh, the Prince of this country. He's a good man, but very rich. I must avoid him – him and all my friends – for a short time. I must find a place in the woods or among rocks somewhere.

HYA: Oh, can I come with you?

GWINEAR: No, of course not. I must live in peace, I said. You would interfere with God's presence in my mind.

HYA: But I'm like you ...

GWINEAR: Yes, you, too, must look for solitude, now, while you still have no friends or ties. You must be sure that God has chosen you. When we both ... The Prince is coming. He must get no opportunity to change my mind. Goodbye.

HYA: Wait! What's your name?

GWINEAR: Gwinear.

HYA: Goodbye.

VINCENT: Gilbert, is this not where he said to stop?

GILBERT: I cannot see, Vincent, as you well know. If there is any question of stopping I am for it with all my heart.

MAURICE: I know the place, I think. He said where the rocks make a point with the bushes, didn't he?

VINCENT: That's what he said, but ... I don't remember any spring here, do you?

MAURICE: A spring? No. That's certainly a spring though, isn't it?

GILBERT: Look, are we stopping here or not?

VINCENT: One hears of springs that come suddenly out of the ground. There are rivers underground which sometimes burst their banks.

GILBERT: I'll throw this thing off in a minute!

MAURICE: Look, the pool has no outlet.

GILBERT: Are you going to help me?

MAURICE: It is just spreading over the grass all the time! What are you doing, Gilbert? You know what will happen if that gets broken!

VINCENT: Have some sense, Gilbert!

GILBERT: That's all very well, but I don't intend to sit quietly holding that thing up while you two discuss geology. He can take the front on the way back, that's all I can say.

VINCENT: Alright, alright, there's no need to get heated.

MAURICE: This is where he said to stop, anyway.

GILBERT: And you know very well that the one who takes the front gets to sit in it. You can take the front on the way back, that's all I can say.

VINCENT: Quiet, Gilbert, here he comes!

PRINCE: Well, where is he then?

ARNO: I can only suppose that he went on following the deer.

PRINCE: On foot? I know he's fit, but there are limits even to <u>his</u> speed.

DODRAN: He'd already hit the deer with an arrow, Sire. She was wounded and staggering.

PRINCE: And none of you followed him? <u>Not one?</u>

ARNO: He was far away, sire, and none of us could hope to catch him.

DODRAN: Besides, we knew you would want to know what was happening ...

ARNO: And he could always find his way back, he knows this country by now.

GWELLUM: Look, something's happened here. There's blood.

ARNO: Blood? He's been here. He's been fighting, or something. Look for him, will you? He may be lying here somewhere. What's the matter with you three? Look for him! What's the point of just standing there?

PRINCE: He wasn't alone. There are two sets of footprints.

GWELLUM: Here! He killed the deer. Look, here's the skin. It's still wet.

PRINCE: Then where's the carcass? Has anyone found the carcass?

VINCENT: He must have carried it away.

PRINCE: By himself? One man carry a great bleeding thing like that? And why did he not take the skin as well? Why take the carcass and not the skin? The skin is <u>more</u> use than the carcass!

GWELLUM: But he was not alone, Sire. You said yourself that there are two sets of footprints. One took the front feet and one took the back.

PRINCE: But who was it? And why didn't they wait here? Where have they gone? I know who it was. It was one of you, wasn't it? I know how you've been talking to each other, thinking I didn't know what you were saying.

Well, I know everything here, do you understand? You think I've been giving him too much, and not enough to you, don't you? You think he's going to be a Minister, and you're just going to be cast aside. One of you has been here and killed him, and hidden his body.
Then you skinned the deer because you thought I'd see the blood, and you came back and told me you'd seen him running off because you thought I wouldn't bother. Well, listen to me, will you? You're going to find him, and bring him to the palace in the next three days. I'm going back now and if you're seen again in the Palace without Gwinear, you die in the dungeons. And if you're not back with him in three days, all my army and all my subjects will be looking for you. Every man in the country will be your enemy. There'll be no escape for you. Vincent!

VINCENT: My Lord?

PRINCE: You'll stay with them, and help them search.

VINCENT: Stay ... but ...

PRINCE: If they try to cross the border, kill them one by one.

VINCENT: But ... your Majesty ...

PRINCE: Well, what is it?

VINCENT: If ... they've murdered ... what if ... what if they kill me?

PRINCE: You ... Take me back. You stay where you are! Well, what are you waiting for? Remember – three days!

DODRAN: I suppose we should start looking, then.

GWELLUM: Not a good day's sport.

ARNO: What do you think has happened to him?

GWELLUM: He's off hunting more deer, I've no doubt. It's funny, this morning I thought, 'This is going to be a great day !' Then there was that race over the plain, and when I saw him stare after the deer I shouted "Run, Gwinear! After her! Go get her!" I loved him! I loved all of us and the Prince! I thought, 'This is where I belong. This is Gwellum, for life!'

DODRAN: What about this other person?

ARNO: Was it Patrick, I wonder? He'd been talking about Patrick.

DODRAN: You don't think it's at all unlikely. He wasn't happy. Oh, he drank with us and he liked the prince well enough, but he was never entirely comfortable at parties. I wonder why he upsets so many people. Especially kings.

GWELLUM: Well, look, if he's gone with Patrick, they can't have got far. Let's get after them.

DODRAN: Yes, we only have to find him and we're safe. When we explain he'll come back, won't he?

ARNO: I don't know.

DODRAN: I hope he's alright.

ARNO: Yes.

GWELLUM: It's this way, I think.

DODRAN: Wait a minute. What about him?

ARNO: I suppose he'd better come with us.

DODRAN: That's what the Prince said, wasn't it? Should I tell him, do you think?

ARNO: Yes, go on.

DODRAN: Er ... Vincent! Are you coming, then?

VINCENT: You people just keep walking, alright? You know what you've got to do. You just start looking, alright? I'm right behind you, so don't try anything.

DODRAN: Vincent, what's the matter with you? Don't you remember last night at cards, winning all that money off me?

VINCENT: Just keep back. I don't trust any of you people. You might lose money to us happily at night, when you're drunk, but in the morning you're quite capable of saying we've stolen it, and getting us hanged. Gwinear's the only rich man with any respect for the truth. Now you're going to look for him, and if you don't find him I'm going to do exactly what the Prince said.

DODRAN: But, Vincent, you know we're Gwinear's friends. You heard us talking just now – we're worried about him.

VINCENT: Acting, that's all that was. You knew I was here listening – you wanted to lead me, into a.... make me think I was alright.

GWELLUM: You realise, don't you, Vincent, that there are three of us and only one of you?

VINCENT: You just ...

ARNO: Don't hurt him.

DODRAN: What about the horns?

GWELLUM: Yes, he would brain us with one of those.

VINCENT: Go on, kill me, I've done my duty.

GWELLUM: Get up, you idiot! Stop making a fool of yourself.

VINCENT: Be careful! I'm a desperate man!

ARNO: Come, Vincent, we'll look for Gwinear together.

VINCENT: Do what you like with me. I don't care what happens to me now.

ARNO: Now, there's no need to feel like that. We're all in the same situation, you know. If we don't manage to find Gwinear, we're all going to be in trouble.

End of Scene II

Interlude

The scene does not change,
but the time and place become involved with those of the prologue

LUCIUS: Good evening.

MARCEL: Good evening, sir. It seems you have those bushes well under control.

LUCIUS: Yes, it isn't terribly difficult after an hour or so of practice. It's just a question of judging the distance correctly, I've found ... and of course the density of the bush.

MARCEL: It being part of your object to avoid destroying the bush completely, I imagine.

LUCIUS: Exactly. If possible they should be saved and used again.

MARCEL: Tell me, does someone follow you collecting the leaves in a sack?

LUCIUS: Oh no, no. The leaves are essentially a useless by-product. All that is required of me is to thoroughly frighten any small animals and birds who might be sheltering in the bush, so that they make a dash into the open for safety, and can then be pursued by the hunters.

MARCEL: Ah! I understand. Have you been in the Prince's employment for long?

LUCIUS: I do not see myself precisely as an employee of his, but I have in the past performed a variety of odd jobs about the palace to which my abilities seem suited. This is the first time I have been set to this particular task and frankly I don't think I will readily undertake it again. To be truthful, the futility of the exercise has already begun to depress me. I tried to explain how much more efficient it would be to group the hunters <u>around</u> the bush so that they could leap on the animals as soon as they emerged, but there is something about the French – begging your pardon – which makes them blind to good Roman logic.

MARCEL: It seems in a way unkind to disillusion you still further with your work, but I must tell you: the hunt has been abandoned, and the Prince has gone home.

LUCIUS: Ah! Then there's little point in my continuing.

MARCEL: Very little.

LUCIUS: How did you come to know this? Were you also involved in the hunt?

MARCEL: No, I happened to meet just now a group of the hunters who were looking for someone lost. I am simply returning home from my work as usual. I always use this path.

LUCIUS: What is your work?

MARCEL: I have a small ship-building firm. Sloops, ketches, fishing-smacks, dhows, junks, triremes; or anything smaller, a canoe, a coracle, water-wings ... we do a certain amount of business in bath-tubs too, chamber-pots, or any vessel for the kitchen – we make the finest sieves in France.

LUCIUS: Really? Do you by any chance supply the Prince's serving-bowls?

MARCEL: Those stoneware models with the leaf design? Yes, they're one of our lines.

LUCIUS: This is most interesting. Do you know, I think I may be able to put some business in your way. Not the sieves and the bowls, but the ships ... I've been thinking of taking a short trip myself, to Wales – you know Wales?

MARCEL: Yes, it's not far. You could do that in a smallish sailing-boat, with, say, six oars ... It needn't be terribly expensive, apart from the labour. The labour is always the major item. Would you be in a position to provide your own oarsmen? I have one or two ...

LUCIUS: But, by Jove, what's this extraordinary machine? Have you made this too?

MARCEL: Oh, the bicycle? Yes, merely a labour-saving device I thought up to reduce costs. The idea is that by turning these pedals with the feet, one causes the wheel to revolve at great speed.

LUCIUS: And what is the purpose of that?

MARCEL: Oh, the applications are many. There are a number of attachments, which can be put in the place of this rubber tyre; a cutting-edge, sand-covered paper for smoothing wood ... one man can do the work of three.

LUCIUS: Why is there this second wheel?

MARCEL: H'm ... that and the tyres and handles were added in order to facilitate transportation of the machine. I take it home every night, you see, and keep it by my bed. There are still some problems to be ironed out, unfortunately. At the moment, unless the revolving wheel is held clear of the ground the whole machine has a tendency to move along in the direction of the wheel, taking its operator with it.

LUCIUS: Surely that could be very easily overcome. A simple metal stand with a hinge, attached to the frame here ...

MARCEL: Yes, yes, those are the very lines on which I've been working! You must come home with me and look over the plans. Have a glass of wine or something – and I think there's rabbit tonight. I have some other projects on the go which may be of interest to you. Now – you're contemplating a sea-voyage: well, I have devised a method of applying the bicycle principle to propulsion through water...

LUCIUS: What's that?

MARCEL: It's the spirits. This is one of their favourite spots.

LUCIUS: Spirits?

MARCEL: I've often met them here on my way home. It's nothing to worry about, just be prepared for the abnormal. And I think it would be as well if we concealed ourselves. Here...

LUCIUS: Are these things real, then, in France?

MARCEL: It's not strictly speaking a question of France, but that we happen here to come close to a different world entirely, and certain things are in the habit of crossing over. That spring, for example, was never there before.

GRETA: But, dad, I've been going out with Bert since I was six, and he's <u>promised</u> he'll marry me.

BERT: What?!

GRETA'S FATHER: No-one's going to marry you when I've done with you. You'll be fit for nothing but scrubbing floors, you'll have to drag yourself along the ground. There won't be a bone in your body; the men'll all spit on you when you crawl past; that'll be an end to your pouting and your flaunting, your rolling in the grass, your perfume, your vile bewitching of honest men, your ...

BERT: Ouch! That was me!

PATRICK: Sir, I must most positively ask you to moderate your wrath more effectively. Here we are, having travelled little more than fifty yards in the last half-hour, and all because of these constant stoppings and belabourings. It does the conveyance no good at all, and at the present rate these two will be old and past caring before we reach the church. Besides, the poor souls have troubles enough, without needing to be bruised all over their bodies.

BERT: He's right you know.

G.F: You keep out of this, lout!

PATRICK: Let us stop and rest, in any case. I can only pray that my staff is still intact here; so much is difficult for me without it.

LUCIUS: What church do they mean?

MARCEL: I don't know – there's no church in these parts.

G.F: You're right to reprove me, sir, but I'm a rough and violent man by nature, and I have only to think of this lascivious, deceitful, dirty-minded …

GRETA: Oh, dad!

PATRICK: Well, we'll, say no more about it. Let's concentrate on more important questions. I find myself beginning to have doubts, for instance, as to the direction we should be taking through this wood.

BERT: What if you, Patrick, took the back of the stretcher, and he took the front, as knowing the way better?

GRETA: Oh, yes!

G.F: I told you we'd had enough from you! If you think I'm going to take my eyes off you …

PATRICK: Well, you know it's not an entirely ridiculous suggestion. Tell me, can you see the path we should be taking?

G.F: Of course … it's … er … what… well, I'll be …

PATRICK: Is that a person we could ask, behind that bush? Hello, there! I say!

GRETA: Oh, who is it?

LUCIUS: He means us. Are you going to speak to him?

MARCEL: Well …

PATRICK: Don't be alarmed. We're just ordinary travellers.

MARCEL: There isn't usually any harm. Will you stand too?

LUCIUS: You first.

PATRICK: We've lost our way. How do you do?

MARCEL: I'm alright, so far.

PATRICK: Would you be good enough to tell us where we are?

MARCEL: You are in La Foret des Champignons.

G.F: What's he talking about? Why's he dressed like that?

PATRICK: I think it may be magic we have to deal with here.

GRETA: Oh, who is it?

PATRICK: And in what country is this forest?

MARCEL: It is in Britanny.

G.F: Of course it's in Britain, what d'you expect?

LUCIUS: …the realm of the Prince of Britanny, who was here not long ago.

PATRICK: And quite different from Britain, whether in my day or this fellow's.

LUCIUS: But we are on our way to the coast.

G.F:	And we need to get on elsewhere too.
PATRICK:	Yes, the magic feels to be strengthening, and we don't want to get too lost. My staff has not lost its usefulness: we need to go on in this direction.
MARCEL:	Who were they? And where are we? What do you have there?
LUCIUS:	It's a compass-clock. It tells you where you are and when it is, in relation to all the other possible places and times.
MARCEL:	Now that is something I have wondered about for a long time.
LUCIUS:	It doesn't seem very happy. We go along here.

Exeunt

End of Interlude
Scene III

On the coast of Britanny

MARCEL:	Well, boys, how's it going? You have the boilers full, and all the parts moving freely?
NAVVY 1:	Yes, sir. We had a loose blade on the starboard paddle, but that's all fixed.
NAVVY 2:	I've put oil in all the places on the plan and the fire is lit.
NAVVY 3:	And there's enough coal to go to Greenland and back.
MARCEL:	Good, good: and the funnel?
NAVVY 4:	It's clear now, sir.
MARCEL:	Well, that must be about all. Why not stop for dinner now, then afterwards we'll find a place for the chronometer there. We have perhaps an hour before they go.
ARNO:	How does it work?
LUCIUS:	It's this dial on the top. You turn it round.
ARNO:	And what do you mean by "when it is"?
LUCIUS:	Well, you know, it's...
VINCENT:	Don't ask me.
LUCIUS:	... it's the, er – whether it's night or day.
MARCEL:	Ah, you're looking at the chronometer. Yes, a very subtle device.
GWELLUM:	Marcel, have you got more paper? I've nearly covered all the last lot.
MARCEL:	Well, I hope you're using it wisely, Gwellum. Is your writing any smaller?
GWELLUM:	I'm afraid I've spoiled a couple of sheets with crossing-out.
MARCEL:	H'm – you can wash them once or twice, you know, without any ill effect. Still, of course you should have some more. And come up here, anyway, I want you to see this. Now, I'll explain the working of the chronometer. Here, these are for you. You seemed to be having difficulty in understanding the machine's function. Well, as soon as you've grasped that the rest of it – the operation and so on – will appear very simple. And there's no need to be worried about it, because you

will almost certainly not have to depend on the machine at all. For Cornwall you'll be going directly north, which means that the sun must rise on your right and set on your left, always being forty or fifty degrees behind you.

GWELLUM: Wait a moment – how can it be behind us and to the left of us?

MARCEL: Well... it is a complete hemisphere above you we're discussing – the sun does move in at least three dimensions.

ARNO: Yes, Gwellum, that's perfectly clear.

MARCEL: So, you have a method of keeping to your course by observing the sun. You also, naturally, can tell by the same means roughly what time of day it is – whether time to get up, time to go to bed, and so on. Similarly with the moon at night. Here Gwellum has a table of certain key positions. Alright Gwellum? Now, you will observe that on the dial here are two indicators which are connected so as to describe a constant angle; there's one for time and one for position. Each corresponds to one of these series of letters on the dial – Gwellum, look – N, for North.

GWELLUM: N, for North.

MARCEL: S for South

GWELLUM: S, yes.

MARCEL: E, for East, and

GWELLUM: E, and ...

MARCEL: W for West. And here's midday, here's mid-morning, and so on. Now if you want to establish the direction you're taking, you make an estimate as to the time of day, then move the time-indicator thus until its shadow – its shadow, mind – falls on the name of the time you have chosen; then you revolve the direction scale until the shadow of the direction-indicator falls on the name of North. And there you are. If, similarly, you wish to know the time, you make an estimate of your direction, and follow the same process in reverse. Is that all clear now?

LUCIUS: I think I understand, but – if the original estimate is made simply by observation, is the final reading not similarly a mere approximation?

MARCEL: Ah, no, no. You see, having guessed at the time and then found your direction, you can proceed to make a more accurate estimate of the time based on this first result, and then repeat the process using your new estimate. And so on, as many times as you like, achieving greater accuracy each time.

MARCEL: Of course, one should adjust slightly the angle between the indicators every morning, but this is perhaps a little too complicated for beginners. You can always write to me from Cornwall if you need further advice.

GWELLUM: What's this one?

MARCEL: Ah, that one's very important. It's your map of the channel. It does say so at the top, look. This is Brittany, with an X for where we are, and this is Cornwall, and here is the line along which you'll travel.

GWELLUM: Yes, but ... I mean, these are just lines. I mean, what do you mean "This is Brittany, this is Cornwall"?

MARCEL: Oh, I see. I see, they're pictures of the places. Pictures, as if seen from above, with the names written on them. Here, for example, is the end of the land of Cornwall, where it goes into the sea, and so I have written "Land's End" to help you identify it. You will have to be very careful in going round that point, because of all the rocks which I have marked here as little spots. And here, a little further round, is the place where you should be landing. Can you see the name of it?

GWELLUM: Yes, it is, two lines straight down with one across, that's "Huh", then "Eh" – Heh – then "LL"? Yes? Heh-ll. HELL?!

MARCEL: Hell, yes. Oh, not that Hell, Gwellum, don't worry. The name is merely a coincidence. Hell is a small port in the north of Cornwall. I don't know a great deal about it, but it is an important place. The king lives there – King Teudar – and many travellers pass through it, especially in the summer months.

LUCIUS: Another point, Marcel. Of course I realise that this may not be at all important – and indeed it by no means challenges the validity of your machine – but, apart from its use in the process of direction-finding, why would we ever need to know the time of day?

MARCEL: Oh, good gracious me, it's sometimes of the highest importance – indeed, vital – to time one's actions correctly when at sea. This matter of the embarkation for example – you're to leave as the tide is turning – well, it's now just after midday which means it should be almost high tide, and indeed it is high tide. Yes – mm – I'm afraid it's later than I thought. In fact you should have started about half an hour ago.

GWINEAR: It's almost time to go.

MARCEL: Yes – I'm afraid – we've just discovered – Gwinear – it's rather more than time to go. I don't think – no – I shouldn't advise setting out now. The currents, you know. It's especially important to consider the currents when setting out and arriving, and I've worked out that particular aspect of your journey for you very precisely, so that you don't need to bother about it provided you keep an eye on the time. Now, I'm very sorry, but you'll have to wait for the next tide – and meanwhile I'll make the necessary alterations in Gwellum's itinerary. Now, the next tide is...

GWINEAR: Thank you, Marcel. There's no need for that, we have time to do everything that's necessary. Are you coming with us?

MARCEL: Well, no. I have my wife and child here, you see – the same goes for my men, most of them.

GWINEAR: Yes, of course.

MARCEL: And I thought, if I planned everything out for you, and gave you the chronometer – your friends all know what they've got to do, now –

GWINEAR: Yes, Marcel, I hope we shall be able to show our gratitude to you sufficiently in time. And there is time for all of us. Shall we go? Who is doing what? Who has the steering?

MARCEL: Vincent has said he will take the wheel ...

VINCENT: Yes, the wheel, I'm doing that. It's on the poop. You have to stop it turning.

MARCEL: He'll be directed by Gwellum, of course, who is in overall charge of the navigation.

GWINEAR: Good. And the fire, who is in control of that?

MARCEL: Ah, that's Dodran. Where is Dodran?

GWELLUM: He was down on the beach ...

DODRAN: Here I am. The fire is going well, we can get up steam at any time.

GWELLUM: Ah, there you are – good, you've started ... what? Dodran, what is that you've got in your hand?

DODRAN: What?.... oh, this ... I don't know. Ha ha. I ... picked it up without thinking.

GWELLUM: Dodran, you ... you ... you've been eating <u>food</u>, haven't you? While we've been working there, improving our minds until they hurt, you've been sitting making merry and <u>wallowing</u> in dissipation. You really <u>are</u> a rotten, lousy hypocrite. All that ...

ARNO: Gwellum, calm down. We don't have time for this sort of thing.

GWELLUM: Oh, I see! I see! We've got time for long talks about me and what a pig I am, but when it comes to Dodran – dear old Dodran – stuffing himself with sausages and making a swine of himself, we just leave him to it! All that stuff about "I'm quite willing to do all the work" and "Writing isn't hard Gwellum, I can do it for you" – Pah! Get out of the way, you make me sick! <u>Stuff</u> the time! He's not getting away with lazing about <u>and</u> eating food.

GWELLUM: Let go! .... Wretched frogs! ... It's nothing to do with you.... <u>Will</u> you get off me! ... Alright! Give me that!

GWINEAR: Gwellum!

GWELLUM: *(Noise of response, without looking up)*

GWINEAR: Are you ready Gwellum?

GWELLUM: Yes, I'm just eating my sausage. You don't mind if I eat my sausage, of course? What little sausage Dodran's left I mean. I trust it's alright for anyone who isn't Dodran to eat a sausage?

GWINEAR: Of course it's alright. You eat as much as you like. Now, shall we be starting? Dodran – the steam, you know what to do.

DODRAN: Yes.

GWINEAR: Marcel, would you direct the other? I'm afraid I can't help very much.

MARCEL: Yes, of course. Come on, you four, let's get this chronometer aboard. Lucius! The maps, please.

TRUMPETER: Étienne Trois, Prince de la Forêt des Champignons, Régent de la Bretagne, Gardien de la Vraie Religion, Général de tous les ...

PRINCE: Gwinear!

One of my cowherds told me you were here – I came straight away. But what are you doing? Why are you dressed like that? You've been away for weeks! What was the matter? Was something wrong at the palace? You must come back with us now. All your friends can come too. Did they find you?

GWINEAR: Yes, they found me. They're going away with me now, to Cornwall.

PRINCE: What do you mean, going away? You must come back.

GWINEAR: No. Thank you for everything you gave us, especially your friendship; but we must go immediately. I told you once that something like this might happen, and tried to explain, but then I didn't fully understand it myself. Perhaps it wasn't clear.

PRINCE: I thought you were just talking wildly.

GWINEAR: Yes – and you would think the same if I tried again. Marcel, carry on, would you?

PRINCE: Look, Gwinear, there's something else – someone else to see you. You'll go back with them if not with me. Fetch them now. They came to the palace to find you. They've come from Ireland. This isn't for you, this voyaging, this sackcloth.

TRUMPETER: Katrine, Ancienne Reine de Kulcharnie (*pron. as if in French*) en Irlande, Veuve du regretté Clito, Roi...

PRINCE: Here he is – we've found him. He says they're going to Cornwall – but he'll listen to you, don't worry. It's your mother and sister, Gwinear, from Ireland. Go on now, tell him your message.

GWINEAR: Mother.

KATHRYN: Gwinear; are you well?

GWINEAR: Yes; indeed I have never been better. But why are you crying? Is all not well with my father?

KATHRYN: Oh, Gwinear, he's dead. He died three months ago, and now the castle is empty and barren, everyone has left. We live all alone in the hall, and thieves and beggars come right into the castle. Even the wolves steal out of the larder. We haven't the strength to do anything.

GWINEAR: How did he die?

KATHRYN: After you had gone he was always drunk, and raged about the castle, even more than before. Then one night he was drinking in the watch-tower, and he thought he saw you and came rushing out and ... and he fell all the way down the stairs! At the bottom he was all ... in a pool of ... I could hardly recognise him!

DODRAN: Has my father not come to help you?

KATHRYN: No! Dodran ... Olf stays all the time in his kingdom and they say he's gathering an army to ... to come and kill us all, and take Kulcharnie.
That's why ... Gwinear, we want you back; you must come and be king, then we'll be safe again, and happy ... and Olf will be our friend as he used to be.

GWINEAR: Have you seen Patrick again, since we left?

KATHRYN: Yes, he came once, and helped us as much as he could, but he wouldn't stay. He talked with Piala a long time, and made her cheerful. Poor Piala – she has been lame since the night you went, when Ulric kicked her and Lucius fell on her. Patrick says she will be a queen one day.

GWINEAR: Piala?

PIALA: My Lord?

GWINEAR: No, I'm not your king, and never will be.

PIALA: You serve my King, and I will follow you until I know how to serve Him on my own account.

GWINEAR: Ah. Patrick has brought you a long way, then.

PIALA: Helped by my love for you, and the trust I have in you.

GWINEAR: But is this so? Are you sure? Remember how Dodran used to say he would marry you and make you queen of his country when Olf was dead. You used to dream about him at night.

DODRAN: Hey, Gwinear!

GWINEAR: Why not take him now, and make him king of Kulcharnie?

DODRAN: Gwinear, what are you talking about?

PIALA: Don't say any more. I have no country now.

ARNO: Then come with us.

KATHRYN: But, Gwinear, you're leaving me alone! And Kulcharnie!

GWINEAR: Mother ... you're not alone. I know you won't come with us, but we are not deserting you, and what is more important, our Lord will never desert you. I know you'll understand this in time, and you will also see that neither Kulcharnie nor any other earthly kingdom has any importance. Goodbye now.

MARCEL: Everything is ready. Goodbye.

GWINEAR: Goodbye, Marcel.

PRINCE: Gwinear, you don't know what you're doing! You haven't thought! You're a fool, Gwinear, you're a fool!

GWINEAR: Yes, I'm a fool.

TRUMPETER: Messieurs et Mesdames, vous verrez maintenant l'embarquement pour la Cournailles des sept ...

PRINCE: Oh, shut up!

MAURICE: Vincent! It is you! What? ... eh? What's the matter? ... oh, he's not going to hurt you now, he knows it's not your fault. We wondered what had happened to you, we all thought you were lost. This boy's got your job now: he's too big for his boots, but he's much better on the trumpets than you ever were. Mind you, he'll get your job back with no trouble – his nibs can't abide the boy.

TRUMPETER: Qu'est-ce qu'il y a, Maurice? Qui est cet ...

MAURICE: Oh, buzz off, you little pipsqueak.

TRUMPETER: C'est moi qui sonne des trompettes, tu le sais ...

MAURICE: I said go away! I'll be glad when you come back, Vincent, I can tell you. Do you know, that little wretch refuses to carry the weapons when we're hunting? I've got to carry all the weapons, and my end of the throne! It's too much.

VINCENT: Maurice, look, don't make a fuss, please.

MAURICE: Mind you, it's not all bad, I've got the back end now – it's much easier. I was demoted because I complained so much. Gilbert wasn't happy about that. Hey, Gilbert! Gilbert! It's Vincent here!

GILBERT: Oh, yes?

VINCENT: Maurice, don't!

ARNO: Vincent, are you ready? Come on!

MAURICE: Gilbert, I say, it's Vincent! Come and say hello! Where are you? What are you doing round there?

GWELLUM: Vincent!

TRUMPETER: Maurice, qu'est-ce qu'il a dit?

MARCEL: Alright? Come ashore now, boys, and cast off!

MARCEL: Goodbye, my friends! Good luck!

NAVVY: Look, they've left something.

MARCEL: It's their food. Here, don't forget your provisions!

HYA: Gwinear! Gwinear!

HYA: Gwinear! Where is he? Oh … is he … has he … he's going …

MARCEL: My dear – he's gone – with his friends – we can't stop them, now – what is it?

HYA: Oh, I must go with them, I should be with them!

MARCEL: There, the sea is nothing, you can follow them. We'll build you a ship.

HYA: I must go.

End of Scene III

ACT 2: Cornwall

Scene I

The tower of Teudar, King of Cornwall

TEUDAR: Worm! Worm! Can you see now, Worm?

WORM: The light is breaking. You should sleep.

TEUDAR: I've slept too long. Can you see?

WORM: The light is in my eyes like splinters. There is only a dazzle. A star. I can see nothing.

TEUDAR: You're lying, Worm.

WORM: You don't know I'm lying. You cannot know.

TEUDAR: Tell me what you see!

WORM: There is no-one. There is the mist. The rock is hidden. A crow eating mutton: eating <u>my</u> worms.

TEUDAR: What is the crow?

WORM: Only a crow. Hooded. A selfish creature.

TEUDAR: What else?

WORM: They are alive in the cottage: there is smoke. Gog makes no sign: he is under the earth. The sea is quiet, like clay. There is a ship, still.

TEUDAR: A ship. What is the ship?

WORM: There is fire in it, and strength; it cuts into Gog's side. There is no-one. They are hidden.

TEUDAR: Who are they?

WORM: You have seen them for yourself. You see them now.

TEUDAR: The seven? Who come against Gog?

WORM: He is troubled: he stirs. He cannot sleep, but his thoughts clash one against the other. Anger grows in him like bread. His dreams, like yours, glow and drip.

TEUDAR: Agh! There are seven: five walk erect, one must peer ahead of him, one is lame.

WORM: They will appear again.

TEUDAR: What more can you see? What do they bring? Do they carry a bird?

WORM: No, they have no bird. He who carries the bird is yet to come. They have sticks, a cross like Gog's. They have no weapons. They scorn the power of metal and fire, though such brought them across the sea. A spirit goes with them; they have given up to it all power, all pride, all their rights as men. And yet it is a pallid, sickly thing without blood. It hovers round them like dust in sunlight. They think its light hides them, but Gog sees them. They think no pain can scatter it from their minds, but Gog will show them the pain that turns all faith to ash. Gog is strong under the earth. Light is nothing to him.

TEUDAR: <u>All</u> is nothing to Gog, Worm. We live until he crushes us. There are no greater fools than these who defy him with hope and the things of the air, thinking only that the air is above the earth.

WORM: Gog will blot them out as if they had never been.

TEUDAR: Come, Worm, we must watch them die. He will want us to see and fear him. Let us go up.

WORM: Yes, he will want us to see. But we shall not see them from the tower. They will die in the wood, where they cannot be seen from the air. And we must not only see the death, but, as ever, be Gog's slaves, his tools. Here is the slayer of Gog's enemies.

TEUDAR: Yes, I shall serve Gog. But, Worm, he hates me. He hates me in everything he has made.

WORM: Yes, Lord, you are hated by all things. Your servants, eaten by hatred of you, roam your country killing and spoiling in your name. Your voice is in every man's nightmares, your face is a story to frighten children. The dogs and the sheep run at the smell of you; the wolves disdain to eat the rubbish from your kitchen. You know that I, your most faithful and truthful friend, will at the end choke your life out with a knotted scarf: I might be plotting the deed at this moment. Every movement you make shows how you revolt from yourself: You are filled with disgust by everything you see, everything you think. And at the centre of this world that pulses with hatred of Teudar sits Gog, who made you out of the fiercest, purest hate that burned in him when he was young. To him you are a loathsome, poisoned scab on his world, reminding him always of his own suffering. You will live only so long as you cause pain.

TEUDAR: And at these seven new deaths, Worm, will he be satisfied? Or do our little splashes of blood only anger him?

WORM: He does not give thanks or encouragement. He gives nothing. We can only do what we think he asks, and never try to rise higher than a pestilence or the scum on a drain. Kneel before him now: let us show that we know our own foulness.

TEUDAR: Is he there?

WORM: A part of him. He is coiled at the foot of our walls. His breath comes up to us.

TEUDAR: What is he thinking?

WORM: He cannot think. He waits. He feels the seven who crawl on his skin. He pants with thirst for them. In a moment he will shake off sleep and show his claws. He waits to know that you are there. He waits for the smell of your blood.

TEUDAR: I am ready for him. Worm. The light. There is no need for light. Let him take my blood in darkness.

WORM: Now he has found us.

Scene 2

A ruined cottage

LUCIUS: Why is it suddenly dark? Where have we got to?

GWELLUM: Obviously it's a cottage, Lucius. The darkness is caused by the walls and the roof, full of holes though they are.

LUCIUS: Well, isn't that odd! I thought it was just a heap of stones and we were walking round it. Why didn't we knock on the door?

GWELLUM: There is no door; and I should not think there is anyone to open it for us, in any case.

DODRAN: Be still: listen for anyone who moves.

PIALA: There <u>is</u> someone …

GWINEAR: Where are you? Come, show yourself to us.

LUCIUS: It seems to me that …

PIALA: What is it there? Someone is suffering.

ARNO: I can vouch for that. Something has me by the leg here and won't let go. I don't know – whether it's a snake or –

PIALA: No, no, snakes are long and thin, and they have scales like fish, and no legs.

VINCENT: Some of the really big ones have legs.

PIALA: This is a woman. Don't be scared of us, my dear – we are people too. Ow!

GWINEAR: Let go of my friend's leg, please. Now what did you mean by biting him? Do you like to be called a snake?

OLD WOMAN: Ach, you little brat, don't talk to me – you must be half daft – what's the good of talking to me like that? You come tramping through my house, a whole squadron of you – is it <u>your</u> leg hurts when I bite him? Come closer, I'll bite <u>you</u>!

GWINEAR: You must forgive us for coming into your house unasked, we did not know you were here, and it is cold and wet outside.

O.W:	Cold and wet! He's dafter than I thought! Come in here because it's wet! Get out, vermin! I don't want your greasy talk, I'll be sick listening to it.
GWINEAR:	Nonetheless my friends would like to sit in here until ...
GWELLUM:	Gwinear!
GWINEAR:	Let go of her. Stop it, madwoman! In the name of God, stop it! ... to sit in here for a time, I was saying, and perhaps share any food which you have. Or would you like us to find food for <u>you</u>? Shall we try to make a fire?
VINCENT:	Has she stopped?
GWELLUM:	Is she still alive?
LUCIUS:	Try to be sensible, Gwellum.
PIALA:	Shall I help you to stand?
O.W:	What did he say about Gog?
PIALA:	I'm sorry – what did you say?
O.W:	I said what did he say about Gog?
PIALA:	He mentioned God. God, not Gog.
O.W:	God, Gog, Gog, God, what does it matter, there's no difference! Just get out of my house, slither back into your pit, I'm drowning in your slime! I can't stand, I've got no legs, I'm a snake, I've got to creep through your filth, I'm a snake like Gog, keep out of my way or I'll crush you like a bladder!
DODRAN:	Here's some bread, Gwinear, and cider.
O.W:	Leave it! Thief! Rat! Leave my food! You're no better than ...
GWINEAR:	Bring it to me, Dodran.
DODRAN:	It's rather foul, all of it. The bread is like pondweed.
GWINEAR:	That hardly matters. None of us has the delicate appetite he used to have. Thank you.
O.W:	Thieving pigs! Bloodsuckers!
GWINEAR:	Thank you, it was a good meal.
GWELLUM:	By God, it <u>is</u> good!
GWINEAR:	No, you've had enough.
O.W:	Ach, eat it! I couldn't stomach it myself – I hope you vomit your lungs out.
GWELLUM:	It's extraordinary! How did you <u>know</u> I'd had enough? I'd forgotten what it was like to feel full. Poof! I think I'd better sit down.
O.W:	What are you doing? Where are you getting them? You're making them out of your slime! They stink of you!
GWELLUM:	The little shrew! Did she hide all this when she heard us coming?
ARNO:	No, Gwellum. It is a gift from God.
LUCIUS:	I'm completely unable to understand this. There is as much cider in the jug as there was at first – and it has become clear, as if the scum had been scraped off it.
VINCENT:	He's right! It's clear, like water.

GWELLUM: Let me see. It's the most wonderful thing I've ever seen! You hardly have to lift it. You could just have a tube connected to your mouth – you could sit there for ever!

O.W: Ezeky! Hag! Come out! Ezeky! There's food here! Come out, you old flea bags!

Oh, what a sight. What noble figures of men. It fills me with joy to see you again, such tasty fat lumps of snake-fidder. You still hear, then, when it's something you like to listen to? And you think you're hungry, I've no doubt? Well, there it is. Don't ask me <u>what</u> it is. It might be stones – Gog – Venom – it's air for all I know – you're both too old and stupid to know the difference anyhow. Look out for those seven dung-beetles that brought the stuff, they've got a vicious bite. This is how they trap their prey; there's nothing they like better than a dry, crisp old crone.

GWELLUM: Have some cider.

GWINEAR: Arno, Piala, Dodran, come here, you're making them nervous.

O.W: You can get out now, you've done enough. I don't want you growing here like mushrooms.

HAG: <u>Are</u> there any mushrooms?

GWINEAR: Is there nothing else we can do for you?

O.W: Yes, I told you – get out!

PIALA: We'll go in a minute, madam, but won't you talk with us a little before we leave? Can you tell us who you are and why you live like this? And we'd welcome any facts you can give us about the country we're in, because we know nothing of where we're going.

O.W: Who we are? And why we live? What kind of questions are those? You're the magicians, not us. We're people ten million to ten million and two and I suppose it's none of your business anyway. As to the country you're in, you can't have been in it long.

PIALA: We have been here a week, and have done little but grow confused. We have met very few people; but we knew God would lead us to you before long.

O.W: Liar! Gog knows nothing about us! No-one knows about us! We've stayed in here since we were born, so we've stayed alive. If you knew anything you'd not be roaming about, <u>you'd</u> find yourselves a hole too. But there's not room here. Clear out! I'm not saying any more!

GWINEAR: Do you not know of any other people who live nearby?

EZEKY: There's that daft woman we saw …

O.W: Huh! A lot of good it'd do you to go looking for <u>her</u>! As if she hadn't proved she was mad by living on the lakeside, she walks about pretending to be a doctor, and tries to make other people live <u>with</u> her! She's dangerous.

GWINEAR: Where is the lake?

O.W: Follow the river.

GWINEAR: Well, ...

O.W: That is, if you've always had a longing to see the inside of a serpent. There are probably worse ways to go. All deaths are slimy in Cornwall.

GWINEAR: ... thank you very much for your hospitality. We will leave you now, and get on our way.

VINCENT: What does she mean, about insides of serpents?

O.W: You've heard of Teudar, I expect?

GWINEAR: Yes, we know the name.

O.W: The lake is one of his nasty hobbies. When Gog made Teudar, wanting to make the vilest thing the world had ever seen, he bungled his first two or three tries – they turned out as giant serpents, so Gog dropped them in the lake and tried again. The first thing Teudar did when he rose out of Gog's spittle was to go and find these abortions, and he's looked after them ever since. There are twenty or thirty of them now, all monstrous and vicious. No-one except that madwoman gets past them. If you're not eaten you die of their breath, or sink in their slime. Of course, whether they'll stomach you I don't know. Most likely they'll throw you up again all over the shore.

PIALA: Thank you. You have been a great help to us.

GWINEAR: Please remember us. Goodbye.

VINCENT: We're not going to that lake, are we?

PIALA: Of course we must go to the lake, Vincent.

GWELLUM: We'll throw some of this bread for them, then they'll take no notice of us.

VINCENT: Oh, I should have listened to Maurice! He didn't want me to come on this trip!

LUCIUS: Come, Vincent, all will be well. You must have faith, it is the answer to everything. No-one was more surprised than I to find this was so.

VINCENT: I'm trying to have faith!

DODRAN: Arno! There's a door! Surely when we arrived that was just a bare hole?

ARNO: You're right, Dodran. God does more for us than we deserve, it seems. There are many things about our mission which I cannot understand – but it is not necessary to understand. Come on, let's go.

O.W: Bah! Good riddance to them! They won't try to get round me again in a hurry. You two were a great help, as usual. You'd be in a pitiful state if you didn't have me to look after you.

HAG: Do you know the secret of this jug?

O.W: Don't ask questions! What good will it do you to know how it works? Perhaps it's the biggest jug in the world, I don't know. As soon as you know what it is it'll be empty. It'll be empty anyway some day soon, so make the most of it.

EZEKY Look – all the holes have gone. Our roof is thatched all over.

O.W: Yes, it's gloomier than ever.

HAG: They weren't as bad as you say, those people.

O.W: Just shut up and eat your bread before it melts. The only people we see are tramps, and all tramps are bad. No-one travels if he has a natural home – all these restless types have got evil deeds on their minds. They come changing things – what's the good of change? If you're not hungry you've got indigestion. Change just confuses you – they change things to put you off your guard. It didn't work with me, though.

HAG: He said we should remember them.

EZEKY: Remember them's all we can do – they'll never come back here.

Scene 3 Part 1

Teudar's lake of serpents

TEUDAR: Where are they now, Worm?

WORM: They follow the river. It is the river that passes under the tower, slow, and black. Cakes of scum gather at the edges. They watch the long weed coiling, they glimpse the creatures that live under stones. Some times the current is streaked with scarlet; sometimes it bears the products of your dungeons, food for Gog's children. They try to sing, but already the song twists in their mouths, and their hearts are like lumps of clay in their bodies.

TEUDAR: And are we to meet them by the lake?

WORM: No, the lake will not be the end for them, but they must suffer there. Already Gog's children smell their approach, and come slowly twisting up from their caves on the lake-floor.

WORM: Every creature among them is blind. Some are headless, some have great white eyes that bulge and sway. They blunder into one another, coiling together like the weed. They suck and champ, blow and billow. The water is thick, like old milk.

TEUDAR: Are they hungry now? Will they be disappointed?

WORM: They have no such thoughts or feelings. There is no light inside them. They are like seething mud-pools, or the black whirl-winds that suck everything into themselves; they are animate things – objects that live without reason, having only malice. As for what they will do, let us wait.

Scene 3 Part 2

VINCENT: Lucius! Gwellum! Look! He can't want us to go through there. He's not human if he makes us go through there.

GWELLUM: There you are, Lucius! A perfect example! Are they real or aren't they?

LUCIUS: You must not fall into the error of assuming a thing is real simply because you see it, Gwellum. You should try looking through my spectacles sometime – then you would perhaps realise how foolish it is to put so much trust in sight. Why, on the occasion of my first meeting with Marcel... Good Heavens!

VINCENT: Oh, if only Marcel were here! He was a sensible, practical man – he'd have made a special boat, or something –

LUCIUS: Yes, this argument that sight is the one infallible arbiter of the real, apart from contradicting what you were saying before, is a most unchristian argument ...

DODRAN: Yes, it's their breath makes the smell. I suppose it's poison, and that's how they kill?

ARNO: Everything about them is poisonous – the sight of them, the sounds they make, their claws and teeth and skin. Without God's help we should have fallen already; we'd be on the way to death, imagine ourselves in Hell.

PIALA: This is Hell.

GWELLUM: Shall I look at the map?

ARNO: Gwinear, can you go on? Should we stop here?

GWINEAR: No, we must get round here as quickly as we can. I will go in front – let me have the cross – with Piala – and you and Dodran wait until last. There is the path; it's narrow, but there is no need to be at all afraid. These things are only empty monstrosities. Whether they exist or not I don't know but I'm sure the only existence possible to them is a half-hearted, powerless existence, likely to become nothing at any moment. Come on, Vincent – just hold on to Lucius, he will explain away these monsters for you.

Go back! Leave us! You pitiful, idiot creatures – what do you think you are, that we should be afraid of you? How can you think that we should give you our lives? We are God's creatures; His beauty, His power, His love, are all ours; listen to us, and you will hear God! Now, who should be afraid? You are afraid, and full of shame! You are no more than stinking lumps of earth, half-fashioned. You have no place in the world; the world belongs to us, through the grace of God. If you kill us all, you will be no less vile. You may suck the bones of our friend until you retch, and tremble with horror at what you have done, but he has life forever, and nothing can ever make you live. Sink back now into your slime, and tell your foul master what I have said. Never attempt to rise again. Go!

Go on now, they will not trouble us any more.

Scene 4 Part I

Beneath the tower of Teudar

VINCENT: Poor Lucius! He was only just saying how I wasn't to worry, because they couldn't do anything, and then one of them grabbed me with its ... and he ... and (sobs)

GWELLUM: Come on, Vincent, come and sit down. I know it doesn't mean much to you yet, but Lucius is fine now. He's got nothing to do with all that filth on the lake-bottom. He's having a marvellous time. Do you realise – he's just discovered Everything There Is To Know! Imagine how Lucius is enjoying that!

VINCENT: I thought he was peculiar at first – stuck-up, you know – but he wasn't. It wasn't important, all that –

PIALA: We've been told about you. Those three old people, in the cottage up the river – you live here –

HYA: Yes, I've stayed here since I came – twenty days – I don't know. I watch the creatures in the lake. I've waited for one of them to show a sign, but it hasn't happened. Now they've gone back to nothing again. Sometimes I go looking for people, but it is even harder to deal with them.

PIALA: Can you tell us – we also, you see, have not been here long –

HYA: I know who you are. I've been waiting for you. I saw you set out in your ship, and I could hardly bear to see the water widening between us; it seemed a long time that I was empty and cold without you, only God came to help me and then He stayed with me all the time, so I hardly needed anyone else. When I saw you coming round the lake it was as if I had been with you from the beginning, in Clito's castle ...

GWELLUM: You saw us come? You sat there and watched? You ... well, you might have helped!

HYA: Yes – your friend was killed – but – I knew, you see. I knew he was to die here. I know a lot, now. There was nothing I could do to help. I should have come to meet you, but as it was I could only wait and feel you coming closer –

GWINEAR: Hya.

HYA: Gwinear.

GWINEAR: You know where you are, now?

HYA: Yes, there is no possibility of my going to the wrong place now. At first it was <u>your</u> face I followed, or rather carried with me, as I had seen it in the pool. I knew <u>everything</u> about it. But of course it <u>wasn't</u> your face in the pool, not exactly. It wasn't you I was looking for, but God. Now I always know where to find Him. I see you both; and Gwinear has his own beauty, not only God's.

GWINEAR: <u>I</u> am happy, too. Will you come down?

HYA: Yes.

ARNO: Who is this, Gwinear? Is she the girl you told us about?

DODRAN: I thought you were a story he'd made up. But you're even better than the story.

HYA: I never doubted that you were real.

GWELLUM: Look, this is all very nice, and it's good to hear that <u>some</u> things are real, at least, but I'd still like to know why she didn't come and lend a hand when we were in trouble – especially if she reckons we're her friends. I mean, there's a time and place for sitting in a trance and looking at faces, but all this stuff about "no possibility of getting to the wrong place" – I mean, how far can you go with that sort of thing? One more person pulling might have made all the difference.

PIALA: Gwellum, you know what you're saying isn't right. I heard you telling Vincent...

GWELLUM: Yes, I know, I'm sorry. It's just that I'm changing too fast. I'm afraid of going mad. All this is too close to madness. How do you know it's God's face, or if it's not some great delusion? It's so big, and the colours – and it moves like something mad – it's like when you lie down in bed after one of Clito's parties. They said in the cottage she was mad – "That madwoman" they called her – and I just think we ought to be more careful, that's all. I mean, how much do we know about her? Do we know where she's come from? She's supposed to come from the same place as us, is that it? Well, how did she get here so fast? H'm? Did Marcel just put together another sea-bicycle, a faster one, just like that? Or what?

HYA: No, it was God brought me, it had nothing to do with any man. He carried me, on an oak-leaf.

GWELLUM: Well, there's nothing more to be said, is there? God carried her on an oak-leaf! Did you hear that, Vincent? An oak-leaf!

VINCENT: Eh? What?

GWELLUM: She sailed from Brittany on an oak-leaf. Had to keep baling out, of course, because of the kinks in the edge. A dandelion would have been better, or a pine-needle. Well, that's all I wanted to know, you carry on. I'll just sit down for a while. I just wonder what Lucius would have thought about coming from Brittany to Cornwall on a leaf.

DODRAN: I think he'd have been a little more polite than you, at least!

GWELLUM: Alright, I'll shut up. Perhaps you knew Lucius better than I did. I'll just close my eyes and rest for a while.

HYA: I threw it in the water and it seemed to grow, then I stepped onto it.

PIALA: Yes, yes. You're coming with us now?

HYA: Yes, I am coming with you, aren't I?

GWELLUM: Very useful girl to have around! Marvellous what she can do with leaves!

DODRAN: Oh, do shut up, Gwellum!

GWELLUM: Sorry!

DODRAN: She does happen to know a good deal more than you about this place, even if it were not perfectly obvious that she belongs with us.

GWELLUM: I won't say any more.

ARNO: Can you tell us anything about the people here, where we should go to find them? You've got no notion, Gwinear?

HYA: There are some people, but they don't come out much. They're afraid of the king. There's a village – or an encampment, rather, in that direction, up through the wood.

ARNO: Have you been there?

HYA: Well, only once so far, I'm afraid. I thought I should find a job, or perhaps make some friends among the beggars, you know – just to make a start. I realise it wasn't a very good idea. I soon found that they were all beggars, and had no use for friends. One or two of them showed some interest in me at first, but as soon as I told them I had nothing they left me alone. I walked round the place peering into their huts and calling them to come out, but for a whole day I didn't see anyone at all. I sat in the space in the middle of their camp but no-one ever came through it. I found odd bits of food half-buried in the mud – some old leaves, splinters of wood, you know –

ARNO: Very good!

HYA: – and towards night I started chewing some of these things, but then one by one they came out and tried to shoo me away. They didn't come together, it wasn't a mob, but one would come out and throw things at me, then another rushed at me and tried to hit me – it went on for hours. By the time it was dark I was confused – I'd been trying to talk to them when they came out, but they were too quick. I couldn't do any more, so I started back through the wood. It wasn't that God had left me, He hadn't. He did <u>something</u> there through me, I know. It's just that the Cornish are especially difficult I think. The king has them in a spell, and they can't get out of it. They won't take anything new.

DODRAN: We must go there at once! We'll be invincible! They're obviously desperate for the very thing we can give them. This coming out in ones and twos, throwing things – that's no resistance. We'll have them rejoicing in no time. The place will be a continuous festival! Come on, you two.

HYA: It <u>is</u> the seven of us together that will be remembered.

GWELLUM: What? We're going now? Alright. We're off, Vincent. There's more to do before we sleep, it seems.

ARNO: Look, wait a moment. Wouldn't it make more sense to sleep first, and go to the village in the morning? There's no point in going and waking everyone up, then falling asleep ourselves. We need a rest, and perhaps we should talk about what we're going to do. Besides, Gwellum will be in a better mood in the morning.

GWELLUM: Yes, we'll go and sleep. It's alright as far as I'm concerned.

DODRAN: Gwinear, what do you think? Do we go straight away, or do we sleep now?

GWINEAR: I know I, for one, must have some rest. There are too many things coming all at once just now. There is nothing to be done while we are still thinking about Lucius, all in our different ways – and quarrelling over him.

GWELLUM: It's not Lucius… it's just…

PIALA: Hya, where can we go to sleep? We can't stay by this lake. I'm sure that's what's making everyone grumpy, the mist and everything. We'd all get a chill, sleeping here.

HYA: Well, we can go into the wood – there's a shelter there and it's warmer. I know some places where <u>one</u> can lie down.

PIALA: Into the wood, then – come on, we'll find somewhere.

ARNO: Are you alright, Gwinear?

Scene 4 Part 2

DODRAN:	Gwinear, what's the matter?
GWINEAR:	I don't know. I'd like to rest here a moment.
ARNO:	Are you tired? Shall we sleep here and not go on?
GWINEAR:	Yes, I'm tired, that's it.
ARNO:	Here, sit down.
PIALA:	We'll stop here. It doesn't matter about the lake, we can bear it for one night.
GWINEAR:	No, you go ahead and – find a place to sleep – somewhere better than this – a bit of grass, you know, to lie on. I'll follow in a minute.
ARNO:	I'll stay with you.
GWINEAR:	Yes, if you like. And Hya, will you stay too?
GWELLUM:	It was talking to those monsters did it – it must have been a big effort, making that speech.
GWINEAR:	Yes. You go and sleep now – there are plenty of trees to lie under.
PIALA:	Come on, Gwellum, let's start looking.
VINCENT:	There's a path goes through here, look.
DODRAN:	You'll be alright?
GWINEAR:	Yes, yes. You go on, they'll need you.
GWELLUM:	Well, goodnight; I'll see you in the morning.
GWINEAR:	Yes, Gwellum. Everything will look better in the morning.

Scene 4 Part 3

WORM:	Is everything done?
TEUDAR:	I don't know. You – who just left me – is it fastened at the neck?
WORM:	Yes, I can see. There is not a chink of light. Come now. Time also is lacking.
TEUDAR:	You are lying to me, Worm. When we leave here, light and time will flood me. I shall be lost.
WORM:	You cannot know such things.
TEUDAR:	Yes, I know! And this – this is a dog that knows only what you tell it. You! Bring a torch; put it close so that I can feel the heat of it.
WORM:	No! In one minute Gog will move away from us. You have only to choose, King, between your floods of light and the blackness Gog will leave behind him.
TEUDAR:	Stand around me then – all of you – two in front, one behind.
WORM:	No – this one will stay. Four must do it. I shall take his place behind you. Now we must go, or the four will become seven again.
TEUDAR:	Yes, Worm, I know nothing. Lead us – go before us.

Scene 5 Part 1

Outside the village near the tower of Teudar

GWINEAR: You know that there's little time for us here?

HYA: Yes, I know.

GWINEAR: And you still mean to come with us?

HYA: Yes, of course.

GWINEAR: Then that's all. I'm ready to go on again now – Arno? – shall we follow the others?

ARNO: Wait. There's no time, you say. This village, then, that Hya knows. Are we to make no impression on it?

GWINEAR: Well, perhaps we can do nothing in person; but already there is more happening there than ever before. God has spoken there. The first thing they know, when they wake, is that something has happened to change them all; that is an impression.

ARNO: Yes, I understand that – but I don't see our part in it; it seems as if we've been wandering from place to place, a great unwieldy throng of us, with only the very smallest notion of where we were going, and why there in particular. When we left Ireland we just let the wind take us, and in a way the wind has been taking us ever since.

GWINEAR: God's wind.

ARNO: Yes, God's wind, but – ever since we got here, we haven't done anything.

HYA: You're too proud Arno. It's enough to be what you are – you don't have to tell the story of it as well. Remember Patrick – he wouldn't let such thoughts bother him – he would have a glass of wine now, and trust in God.

ARNO: You know Patrick?

HYA: Oh, yes. Did you not realise? I met him in Brittany, while you were still there. He is the only man who knows exactly how much we have done. He is very experienced in these matters. He knows all the stories that will be told about us, and all the monuments that will be built for us…

ARNO: What's that?

GWINEAR: It's beginning already.

HYA: That's Dodran's voice.

ARNO: Is this what we came for?

GWINEAR: Yes. We must go at once.

Scene 5 Part 2

PIALA: There's a space here – perhaps – but there's a big bump in the middle, and – yes, nettles.

DODRAN: Well, it doesn't matter, we can all huddle round Vincent. We can lie on top of him, he won't mind.

PIALA: But – do you think Gwinear will want that? He has to think about what we are to do tomorrow; he doesn't want to be getting mixed up with people's feet all through the night. And he said a piece of grass – find a piece of grass to lie on.

DODRAN: Oh, he was only talking generally. He doesn't want to be treated like someone special, I'm sure. We're all his friends, after all. Why, I've known him to wake up many a time without the smallest notion of how he came to be sleeping where he was.

PIALA: I think you take him too much for granted, all of you. Don't you see that almost the whole weight of our mission is on him? You don't consider how talking with God has changed him; you see in him only the boy you used to know in Ireland, but there is almost nothing of that boy left. See how he asked Hya to stay with him, and no-one else. Will he not want to go on talking quietly with her when they come?

DODRAN: He can talk if he wants. Gwellum and I sleep quietly, we don't fidget. It's only Vincent snores.

PIALA: We ought to wake him up and put him somewhere else. If he lay across, like that there'd be all this space ...

DODRAN: Oh, really, do we have to disturb him? The poor man has had a dreadful day – he loved old Lucius. Why should we make him face it all again so soon? Besides, he'll wake up before long without our help. You know how he dreams – he lives in a world peopled with monsters. Everything we do is food for his nightmares. Think how those creatures from the lake are swarming now in his head, and all our faces surrounding him full of anger and pain. He never sleeps long.

PIALA: Well, perhaps we could just lift him gently, and turn him round without waking him. Come on, you take his head.

DODRAN: Oh, very well.

VINCENT: What? Leave me alone. I've got nothing. You stay as you are, don't bother with me.
No, no. I'm not one of them. I carry the spears. You take no notice...

DODRAN: Gwellum, will you come and help us with this man? He's far away.

GWELLUM: H'm? You know, Lucius was right about putting too much trust in the eyes. These artificial spy-holes of his are much better. They make a tremendous difference to this picture of our journey, too. It was all just funny-shaped lines before, but now I can see Brittany all clear and bright here, then <u>this</u> country, all black and murky – and then the sea – it was the sea I had most trouble with before. Come and look at this. Here's the place where we had to go round because of the rocks. You can see it all there, look – the wind, and the spray, and the land looming up through it all.

DODRAN: I don't – quite – see what you mean, Gwellum. I mean, this is all writing, isn't it? And it's not supposed to deal with all those things that change, like the sea.

GWELLUM: No – it all changes, look – the land as well. Here, try it through these.

DODRAN: Well, I see <u>more</u> now...

GWELLUM: That's Wales. There's something between Wales and Cornwall. I don't know what. You can see better with the little windows.

DODRAN: Yes – m'm – a river, perhaps – or a – a small sea.

GWELLUM: Wales is where Lucius wanted to go – where all his intellectual friends live. We must go across when we've finished here, and tell them what's happened to him.

VINCENT: Wha'? Are we there now?

DODRAN: Where, Vincent?

VINCENT: Heaven. Are we there? We were going there together. They'd cut us off from the earth.

PIALA: Have you been getting into fights again?

DODRAN: No, we're not there. We've a long way to go yet.

VINCENT: Oh, now I've got to start again! It was the wrong ladder. They'll come again here. Don't wake me till we've got there.

GWELLUM: Looks as though we're in for a troubled night.

PIALA: It's a restful-looking spot. Gwinear will lie happy there. The grass is thick, and soft.

DODRAN: It must be rich earth there, to grow such grass.

PIALA: You don't suppose it's damp, do you?

DODRAN: The leaves dropped by the trees have fed it, and the corpses of animals dying in the shade.

GWELLUM: Vincent will have killed a few more, lying there.

PIALA: Just so long as it's not damp. It's still warm.

DODRAN: I'll sit and keep it until Gwinear comes.

PIALA: You won't fall asleep there, will you?

DODRAN: No no, I'm not tired.

PIALA: You'll tell him we saved the place specially?

DODRAN: Yes, he'll lie here, don't fret.

PIALA: Then I'll go to sleep myself. Goodnight.

DODRAN: Goodnight.

PIALA: You'll say goodnight to the others for me?

DODRAN: Mm-mm.

PIALA: Goodnight, Gwellum.

DODRAN: Here, Gwellum. I shan't be looking at anything for a while.
What? Who <u>are</u> you? Get up! Gwellum! Vincent! They're here! They want to ...

PIALA: Gwinear! Gwinear! Someone go to him!

VINCENT: They're murdering me! I knew ...

Scene 5 Part 3

WORM: That is good for now. These four are dead.

TEUDAR: And where are they, Worm? Who has them now?

WORM: I cannot tell you; but there is nothing good beyond corruption.

TEUDAR: I hear a scuffing and panting still. What is that?

WORM: Nothing. The souls have gone and make no sound. But you have no time to listen – do not let the fear drain from your mind. Think of your creatures stinking in the pool, of Gog's breath on you if you fail; your sword ...

TEUDAR: Yes. He is in me. Worm ... help ... Worm. The three. Worm! Stay! Are they here?

WORM: They are here.

Scene 5 Part 4

ARNO: Ah ... you ... !

GWINEAR: Arno! Stop!
It seems we must lie in this place, Arno – Hya. There should be no questioning or struggle. God has said that our work on earth will stop now – so let us give our lives to Him as He gave Himself for us. Be happy. There is no need for us to fear these men who take only our bodies – the one we should fear is he who might have killed our souls.

TEUDAR: Hope as you wish, boy, but do not try to fly to your God. You are bound to my earth, and even now you begin to rot.

GWINEAR: And you know who might have killed our souls, you poor, wretched king. It is his work you do. But he will leave you desolate. There is no hope in him. Already he is withdrawing from this land; when he has gone you will shrink and die, and oblivion will take you forever.

Interlude

While the scene is shifting from the previous one to that of the Prologue

PATRICK: (*To audience*) You're no doubt wondering why I'm here at this late stage, and where I've been all this time, and why I haven't been telling the story in an orderly manner, and so on ... well, I'll tell you. As you can see, I've got a number of problems back here. It's not only those things you've already witnessed, we've now got the mother to deal with as well. They can be so wearing, these females, when they're over-excited and raising their voices.

We've got them all into the village at last – the mother isn't at all the sort for losing her way in a wood – and we've raised the vicar out of his bed, but he says that he can't possibly begin the service until the morning, this being the proper time for such ceremonies. Well, so we're faced with the problem of how the night is to be spent: and the mother, I suppose naturally enough, feels that her Greta should pass what is to all intents and purposes her wedding-night in the comfort of her own home. All well and good – only the father won't have Bert in his living-room at any price. You can see the dilemma. That's what all this kerfuffle is about. <u>She's</u> accusing <u>him</u> of all kinds of heartlessness, to the point of claiming he's not Greta's natural father – and <u>he's</u> accusing <u>her</u> of encouraging the girl to go the same sinful way she has herself. And there's the threat of violence always overhanging the whole proceedings. So, what with protecting Bert from <u>him</u>, and <u>him</u> from <u>her</u>, and all the while having to keep Angus from running into new troubles, I've had very little opportunity for attending to Winnie's story. (*Pause*) Well, that's all I have to tell you. I heard them saying all those good things about me in the last scene, and I thought I'd put in an appearance. I'll be off now. I come back in the Epilogue.

Epilogue

The morning following the action of the Prologue, in the same wood

GRETA'S MOTHER: I should have known before I married you – my mother always told me – "That Albert," she used to say, "that Albert will die a violent death. He will end up in sorrow and pain, and fall by the sword of his enemy. You are courting disaster", she used to say, "you ..." meaning me ... "You are courting disaster in courting with him. It is his true self you see when he is raging with drink, and, I tell you, he will meet with his doom in one of those rages." Of course, I didn't listen to her. "My Albert," I used to think, "My Albert is a gentle soul underneath, needing only a wife's loving care and calm persuasion to set him on the right path..."

GRETA'S FATHER: But – you silly b....!

G.M: Oh, but don't I know different now! You and your fights! There's not a man in the village will deal with us now for fear of getting his head broken. The women all talk about me as if I was a poor crippled thing to be pitied. For years I've had to put up with creeping about the village bruised and black-eyed, not able to sleep at nights for your roaring and poor little Greta's howls – and now <u>this</u>! You get us thrown out of the church – the <u>church</u>, mind you, the centre of the fashionable world – the very first time we go in there, to see our Greta parted from that Bert – you go and cause a disgraceful scene, right in the middle by that table, and knock the poor vicar about till he can hardly stand, just because he put his hand on Greta's head. I've never known such a stupid, pig-headed, brutish oaf – they'll <u>never</u> let us back in there now – and how do you think we're going to get the wedding done right? No wedding is anything like proper these days without a vicar – and where are <u>we</u> going to get a vicar? It's the end of our life here, I tell you. We'll never see our Greta again. We might as well slink off now through the wood – and as for you, it's perfectly alright with me if you just ...

G.F: Look, I've had about enough of this! You women are all the same – you put all the blame onto us, and you think if you make enough noise about it you're automatically in the right. Don't you think I <u>know</u> by now it was a bad idea to go for the vicar like that? It was just a simple mistake – he said as much himself. The truth is you were making so much racket with your weeping and wailing I couldn't think straight, and no more couldn't the vicar – you could see him screwing his face up, trying to concentrate on his service. Don't you know you're supposed to be quiet in the church? It's you that got us thrown out – they hardly noticed me, you were bawling so loud. And if you think ...

G.M: Oh, that's good. That's good, that is! You can sit there quiet and watch our Greta carried up to that table, in front of all the healthiest people of the village, locked in a lustful embrace with that son of a swineherd, and you accuse me of making a fuss!

G.F: What's the matter with you? Are you stupid, or what? Is it making a noise or keeping quiet you're getting at me for? You want to try thinking before you open your mouth. And if you're trying to make out that I'm in league with that greasy little ...

G.M: You leave Bert alone! He'll do this family more good ...

G.F: He's not having anything to do with this family!

G.M: ... in one week than you've done it in twenty years! When he's your son-in-law ...

G.F: If you think he's going to be ... listen! If you ... what's the matter with you? What is it?

G.M: What do you think that means? It must be a signal or something. The bell. There's only one.

G.F: Well, what of it?

G.M: They always mean something. Something's happened...

G.F: They've just stopped, that's all. They're tired. They can't think of anything else. They can't stop that one swinging. Or it's the end of the piece – that's just the way it ends. There you are!

ANGUS There – what do you think of him now? Just like new! Bet you can't tell him from the real ones, can you? Bi.....i..i..r..dies!

G.F: Angus, what is it you've done, hey? Something in the tree? You've not been breaking branches again? It's the flowers? You've put the flowers there?

G.M: Angus, Angus, why have the bells stopped? Is something dreadful going to happen?

ANGUS: Yes, yes! It's the King of all the Ringers! He's going to sing!

G.F: What's the matter with you, boy? Are you mad or something?

ANGUS: They're waiting for him to begin! They're hung swinging on their strings, they're bending his belfry-branches!

G.M: Albert, make him talk sense! Hit him or something!

G.F: Why don't you hit him, if I'm such a lily breasted milksop?

G.M: Alright, I will hit him!

PATRICK: Here they are, my friends! They're free! The Lord has let them fall apart exactly as ... Fuagh! What is that most uncustomary smell?

ANGUS: Patrick! Patrick! See what we've done for these excitable heathens! You've made the lovers two again, and the bird is back in his tree!

PATRICK:	Angus! Not that poor dead bird, <u>still</u>! What <u>do</u> you want with it, boy! It is not at all a suitable thing for the occasion. Come now and take it down.
ANGUS:	He <u>can't</u> come down. He can only go up. Try to pull him down, he'll fly, branch to branch, you'll fall, break your fingers.
PATRICK:	Angus, do what I say this minute!
ANGUS:	No time, I'm being hunted! Fetch him yourself!
PATRICK:	You know very well I can't get up this contraption!
G.F:	Don't you worry sir, we'll have this boy in a minute.
VICAR:	Here we are, my dears. We have pulled through after all. This Bert is showing little gratitude as yet, but I can only imagine he is intoxicated by his freedom.
BERT:	Let go of me you wretched blatherer!
G.M:	Greta, my little girl! It's true!
GRETA:	Let me get at him! He's not going to drop me that easily!
G.F:	Are you alright, girl? He didn't try anything in the church?
PATRICK:	Father! I'm glad to see you've arrived safely.
VICAR:	Patrick, my dear man, what are you doing up there?
PATRICK:	Oh, it's that boy of mine up to his tricks again. He's put a … oh, never mind about that. Here, can you help me get down?
VICAR:	But of course, my dear fellow.
G.M:	Greta! Come back! It's not time yet!
G.F:	I suppose I'd better…
ANGUS:	Well – a short stay, but eventful.
PATRICK:	This is all most unseemly – it's not at all how the service is supposed to end. We should be kneeling now round Winnie's tomb, singing a song of thanksgiving. If this sort of thing goes on I shouldn't wonder if we were landed with some <u>new</u> misfortune.
ANGUS:	It's Okmar doing it.
PATRICK:	It's what?
ANGUS:	Okmar the ringer. He'll do you a good song, you'll never want to hear another. Look at him shining! I had to borrow half his feathers from the other birds. The peacock was very cross.
PATRICK:	Angus, boy, you know I didn't mean to shout at you –
GRETA:	Where is he? Where's he gone?
ANGUS:	It's that way you want to go. These woods are very confusing for one who's just been freed.
PATRICK:	I'm afraid she's not free yet.
ANGUS:	No.
PATRICK:	It's fortunate for us, Angus, that we understand each other so well.
ANGUS:	Indeed it is Patrick.
PATRICK:	Well, now, if you'll come up and help me down, we'll be on our way.
ANGUS:	Oh, I couldn't do that, Patrick.
PATRICK:	But … you blithering little …!
VICAR:	Here is one of the lost creatures, safely returned. I think it would be as well to start the hymn – what do you say, Patrick? We have at least a

moderate congregation here, and others may turn up as we proceed. Kneel here my boy.

BERT: Look, Father, I can't afford to hang about here.

VICAR: My dear Ogbert, I have repeatedly told you that you can <u>never</u> afford to neglect your devotions, however pressing the situation.

PATRICK: I'm not sure, father, that it would be quite right to begin without them.

Well, now we have a choir. I can do a passable bass, then there's Bert and Angus on the alto –

PATRICK: Angus will you come and do something about this?

VINCENT: It's the boy got you up there somehow, you were saying?

PATRICK: He put the bird in the tree. You see the little bundle of dust above me?

BERT: He shot Okmar. That was the start of all our troubles.

ANGUS: It was fun at first. Now it's getting a bit slow. I'll see you later Pat. There's the other singers to collect. Look! There's the ring-ousel!

PATRICK: Angus! Angus!

BERT: I wish I'd never heard that ...... bird!

VICAR: I suppose the bird has a meaning of some kind, eh, Patrick? It's the death of something or other in Cornwall – pantheism, something of that order? What do you think? Angus must know.

PATRICK: I can't deal with these symbols, father, not in my present situation. Which song is it to be?

VICAR: Certainly it should be one from the special thanksgiving section – number 350, perhaps? You know your part in that one Bert?

BERT: I've rarely felt less like singing.

PATRICK: How does that one go father? You'd better remind me of it.

VICAR: Oh, it's a wonderful great tide of noise! At least it would be. This is the one.

PATRICK: Oh, yes, I know it well. You'll have to pitch it down a bit for me.

VICAR: Try it this way.

GRETA: Oh, Bert! I knew I'd find you! I heard your voice – it was as if you was calling me.

BERT: Oh, let me go, father, please!

GRETA: But, Bert, you can't be like that! We've been a whole night together, in each other's arms!

BERT: Don't you think I know that? You don't smell too good apart from anything else.

GRETA: But you never bothered about my smell before. I've only got two dresses.

BERT: And there were witnesses all night. The father here took over when Patrick turned in, and your mother was hanging about all the time.

GRETA: I think you're very cruel to treat me like this after I've spent a night like that.

BERT: You think you had a bad night? What about me? At least you got to lie on top, God knows how. What do you think my back feels like, after eight hours on that church floor? It's not as if there wasn't all this

	brawling going on still. All I want to do is go and sit somewhere quiet by myself.
PATRICK:	Are you having some trouble with your back, boy?
BERT:	You'd be amazed Patrick. I've never known anything like it. The damp shoots up through those flagstones.
PATRICK:	They tell me Sloane's Liniment is very good, if you can find someone to rub it on for you.
VICAR:	Erm – shall we try the song again, while the two participants are still here together?
PATRICK:	Oh, by all means, father. A very good idea. Now, where were we?
G.M:	They're here, Albert! I knew I recognised those voices. Ah, Greta, we've been looking all over!
GRETA:	Bert! Come back! We were singing!
G.M:	Greta, you're not going again!
VICAR:	I'm afraid that's probably it, Patrick. Still, we've not left Gwinear uncelebrated. I'll just see if I can round them up again…
PATRICK:	Albert, I suppose you couldn't help me down?
G.F:	Eh? Oh – right you are.
PATRICK:	Thank you, that's very kind of you.
G.F:	I suppose I'd better go.
PATRICK:	Oh, yes. Well, goodbye. I hope you have a good day.
G.F:	Goodbye.

Dreamflower

Last night you asked me to bring you a flower.
You didn't say which kind, but I saw a rose
Hanging in the air between us – pink,
Translucent, a ghost flower. Now I realise

It was just the kind of thing you would do,
You were so wayward, even perverse.
You clutched my arm and peered at me, unseeing –
For the place was sad and dark, of course –

And you spoke slowly, as if you were
Forgetting the words. It seems odd, now,
That there were no others around us,
Unless they were hidden in the shadows.

And after all, why a flower? Surely
The whole thing was absurd. You never
Spoke that language, except perhaps to women,
And I can't believe you had found a lover

In that dark place. Besides, I had no flower
To give you. And yet I think something
Passed between us – some message, or sign –
Although I may never know its meaning.

The Farmer and his Son

Crows flew out from trees, making cold cries. Shit looked up but without seeing them. They were miles up across a stream, sent twigs showering that didn't fall, sounded like screwed-up paper. Then they drifted, silent tatters, and a man shooting cracked on the far bank.

Shit crouched with his eyes turned up at the grey sky. Back pressed into the spokes of a wheel, shoulder up against the hub. A long chain curled on the ground about his ankle linked it to the wheel. Head stretched back on top of the hub, he stared into the sky. The gun cracked but he was still and heard nothing. Air played on his taut throat, the hairs and stretched pipes. He saw a black dog crouched silent about to spring and tear. Then he saw a crow perched on his shoulder bend its neck to peck at the lump on his throat. The crow remaining, he watched it peel the skin back from the fibres and stab wrecking into the blood. It bubbled and crooned to itself as it pecked.

Shit closed his eyes on the sky.

He looked down at a hen that made the crooning on the ground beside him. It was taking steps each followed by a pause, by stages lowering its neck, adjusting meanwhile the angle of its head. Shit grew stiff between the hub and the ground, clenching his fists. The hen flattened its body and ran squawking away in a zigzag path. It paused beyond reach of the chain and recomposed itself to its pecking. Other fowls wandered from under a barn-door across the yard, slow-stepping in formation.

A door opened over on Shit's right and a woman stepped into the yard carrying a bucket. From behind her a black dog jogged out across the yard towards the barn. The woman put down her bucket, looking over at Shit. He saw her but did not move. After a time she took hold of a mop that stuck out of the bucket and tipped water into a drain. At the swishing sound the group of fowls broke up undecidedly. The dog pissed against the barn, gazing along the ground at the fowls, then slowly turned its head towards Shit. The woman, straightening herself, looked up at the trees across the stream before she turned to him again. He moved not even his eyes. Woman and dog were far off and indistinct, but he felt their gaze and the fowls walking through the yard did not distract him from them.

The woman decided, went back inside and shut the door. The dog settled down, hind legs tucked under, absently sniffed the ground and raised its head again. Under the wheel was a hole where food was hidden. Shit pressed with his foot on the board that covered it. At length the dog pushed its rump into the air, clumsily standing. The group of hens broke up again to let it go through. Shit unbent from the wheel, feeling under him for the board that hid the food. From the hole he took all the food there was, pastry with custard clinging. He held it softly in his mouth while he replaced the board and pulled himself up against the wheel. The chain rattled up behind his feet, scrabbling over the wheel into a moss-eaten cart. There he sprawled, held by the chain, and let the food fall in hay-coloured lumps among hay. The chain was fast against the edge of the cart, caught in the wheel. He moved round his fixed foot and jabbed the links free from between the spokes. The dog came forward below the wheel looking up at him. Shit crawled on two knees and a hand, picking up his lumps of food. He sat with his back against the back of the cart.

It was a warm place here with a pile of hay on either side of him. The smell was thick and there were no creatures but tiny ones that crawled through the hay when he touched it. He sat with the food cupped in his hands and lowered his head to eat it. Below the cart the dog began to scratch at the edge of the hole. Shit took the lumps of food into his mouth, raising his head only slightly to chew. His eyes were not focused but as he raised his head he turned to the edge of the cart where the dog was hidden. It was moving beneath the cart. With the rattle of its claws on bits of metal there was the struggle it had to force itself under the boards he sat on. In a crack under his feet its nose came snuffling. He had taken the last mouthful but his hands remained cupped and his jaws clamped as he watched this black twitching thing. It roved backwards and forwards in the crack, then snorted, vanished and the dog pushed out from under the cart. Shit crawled like a crab out of his seat, making a circle away from the edge at the end of his chain. The dog put its front paws on the cart. He shoved at it with his foot but it sprang down and stood waiting. Shit crouched coiled at the edge of the cart with his fists clenched, then unbent, fell and sprawled on the ground. The dog waited beyond the length of the chain. He felt for the board under the wheel. The dog jumped and grappled at him with its paws, he swung his arm round with the board, and the board went skittering over the stones of the yard. The dog jumped on him again and thrust with its rump as if fucking him. He closed his eyes and clutched at it hard but his fingers could not close on its fur. He opened his eyes but could see nothing.

A man shouted and came crunching across the yard carrying a shotgun. There was a crow tied to his belt. He stood over them muttering, dragged the dog away and kicked it three times. It ran with its body bent, making circles round the man. Shit went on struggling on the ground, getting the chain caught round his legs. The man lifted the gun by its barrel and brought its butt down in a long curve on Shit's neck. He did so again and again, shifting his feet. Shit shrank as if he were hard and the blows chipped lumps from him one by one. When he was still the man stopped hitting him and straightened up, then untied the crow from his belt, threw it to the ground and with his foot shoved it up against Shit's face.

Through the crow's feathers Shit saw the man move away stumbling. Hens scattered and the dog followed after the man, close to the ground.

Beside the barn was a piece of ground sloping down to the hidden stream. Here there were a tractor and some bushes, and far behind them across the stream the trees. The sky was changing from grey to brown, the trees growing black like the feathers.

The man stopped by the tractor and was hidden against it. After some dim metal sounds he came away, crossing in front of the barn with a bottle. He stopped and shouted very loudly at the house where the woman was. There was nothing but the murmur of the stream and hens' warbling. Then he shouted the same thing again, bent over by the force of his voice.

In the stream's murmur, Shit slept.

When he awoke there was half a circle of yellow light in front of the house, and blackness at the edges of the yard. There were no hens or man or dog. The woman was coming out of the yellow light towards him, she too stumbling with every step. She changed into the man, into something like them both and yet not either, back into the woman. In Shit's nose were the bristle and must of the feathers. She stopped in front of him and he saw only her legs. She peered at the thing in front of his face, stretched out her leg and pushed the thing away. In her hands she had an egg which now she held out to him. He did not move. The hand trembled holding the egg, shook, and withdrew. She got down on her knees in front of him with her head bent over the egg against her breast. She fumbled the egg and cracked it, with trembling fingers peeling off bits of shell. He saw all of her, the legs tucked under, curved hips, elbows stuck out, bent neck, point of her head. He followed the lines twice around her with his eyes, from knees to crown and back. The shell hung in shivering little strings from her fingers. She shook the hands one by one, flicking the shell away. Then she held out the white elastic egg and put it on the ground where the crow had been. He looked at it standing there on its blunt end, pointing obliquely upwards. The crow lay beyond it on the side to which it leaned. The woman was reaching out her hand to him again, one only. With the other she clutched at her dress in her lap. She touched his face with her fingers, on the line across his forehead, down the side of his nose, round the two circles of his eyes. She touched his shoulder, down the arm that hung across his ribs to the ground. She gathered the fingers into her own. He stiffened and would not move, gripping her fingers.

She jerked her hand free and scrambled away across the ground until she was beyond the chain. There she stayed for a long time watching him and even making signs to him. She put her hand to her mouth, the fingertips between her lips. He made no sign. When she left him he was asleep again.

In his sleep he dreamed about the inside of a black egg. In the narrow dome of the egg was a crow with wings and tail curved downwards, spreading out across the sides of the egg. It gazed down along the curve of its beak into the egg's interior. There in the centre hung Shit himself with his arms and legs outstretched. He saw himself naked and white with his arms reaching up as if to meet the wingtips of the crow, and his legs spread wide above the dark bowl of the egg. He wanted to pull the white creature away from the wings, to shrink into a point at the centre, but was held suspended. Below him was depth that caught at his breath; above him the crow overhung the void, and the pattern of its feathers made the law that held all things inside the egg. The feathers spread branching into the walls, weaving forests of barbs that dwindled in dark perspectives. Shit hung miles above the forest and gazed down into its shadows. Through its criss-cross trunks down the wall of the egg, flashing in and out of sight, came another shadow fleeting and distinct. Shit tried to shrink away from it but only his spirit shrank like paper blackening in a fire. Head pressed against his shoulder, he saw down the curve of his ribs the shadow stop below him and look up through the trees, a black dog with blue flames burning in its eyes. His own eyes fixed open reflected the flames. It panted with hunger, slavering bright drips of blue. Loping on through the forest, ranging over the walls of the egg, at every halt it looked up at him as if waiting for him to fall. It vanished into the feathers and reappeared, below him or on the line he pointed with his fingers. It was at once deep in the forest and face to face with him. The blue flames spread and filled the space between them, entered through his eyes and flooded him with cold.

Shit awoke with the night's cold eating his bones. He had not moved, could still not do so. Fixed in front of him still were the slanting egg and, behind and dwarfed by it, the crow, on its belly with its wings half-spread and its beak curved down to the ground. It might have been dragging itself by beak and wings. Above the crow and the egg hung a round moon that froze the world. It had drawn down the crow's beak a metal line, and divided the egg into day and night. The yard had stretched out beyond the edge of the world. Rising out of the earth like an endless flame, the house stood blinded by the moon. He moved forward seeking the face behind its eyes, but the chain made a sound that sent his dream flooding through him. He waited with his eyes fixed on the crow, listening for the stream. Down there where the stream ran was now nothing but the barn's shadow, into which all the shapes dissolved. He crept forward, reached out to the crow and held it by its beak, hiding the line of moonlight. He moved back and the crow came rustling after him over the ground. He stopped; there where the barn's shadow met the moonlit yard was another shadow, moving. It bent its head to sniff at the ground, then pattered on along the edge. A line of blue light slid over its back as it moved. It stopped again with its head in the air. He searched for its eyes but it turned and vanished under the barn. Shit crouched for a long time silent while the dream roared in his ears. He shook his head, waited, shook it again, and went on moving backward, foot by foot, dragging the crow. He reached the cart and with both hands laid the crow in the hole beneath the wheel. It lay on its side, head and tail curved round almost into a circle, claws stuck out like a hawk's about to land on its prey. He looked from side to side as if seeking something, but his eyes were vacant. The board which had covered the hole lay far across the yard in moonlight. He scrambled under the cart among the bits of metal, and there on the ground found a piece of stick which he held in his hand. He crouched beside the wheel and stared down at the crow. Hesitantly he began with his stick to make patterns in the earth beside the hole. The ground was hard, and many times he paused with his stick in the air. He began to make a circle round the hole but stopped before it was done. In the space left open he drew symbols, mysterious and incomplete. In the midst of each he stopped as if forgetting what it meant and who had made it. Each time he made a longer pause before he moved a little to one side and began again to draw. His uncertainty grew, the stick faltered, and stopped. He moved away from the hole, still clutching the stick. Under the cart he crouched and stared down at the patterns on the ground. He did not move but his mouth opened as he tried to understand. He trembled like one shocked. Slowly his eyes too opened wide, and his face took on the lines of fear. Thus it grew fixed.

The Writer's Block

a fragment

24th July: working on 'The Diamond Telephone' (or 'Zibbeldjolvim'?) in Morrab Gardens.

It has become clear that what happened to me, when the machine broke down, was that I lost contact with a kind of inner 'voice' – which could be identified with the 'text' which Proust says is inscribed in every artist's mind, and which is mentioned in turn by Beckett and Bridget Riley. When reading through the story, it is only by disengaging my conscious mind, and letting the words speak directly to the subconscious, that I can be sure of their authenticity.

And it is part of Proust's thesis that the voice or text is accessible only to the subconscious. This explains one of the most puzzling features of the block; that when I was struggling to write, the sentences became more misshapen and incoherent as I went on. The part of my brain concerned with writing had been subjected to such stress that this 'voice' suddenly became inaudible, and I could not write at all. I continued to have ideas, and could still write words, but had no way of connecting the former with the latter. Each word had a meaning, but the meanings did not interact with each other as they must in order to express ideas. The effect of this, at first, was that I could not string together even two or three words without realizing that something was drastically wrong, and having to stop. I didn't understand what had happened, any more than I understood what was happening when I could write.

Writing was something I did, without bothering to understand it. And so I had no way of approaching this problem except to go on as before; to think of what I was going to write, and then start writing, doing everything exactly as I always had, so far as I could remember. In effect I was unconsciously trying to revive my inner voice, or make it audible again. And eventually this effort was successful, in that I began to 'hear' something which allowed me to produce longer strings of words, and even to go on for page after page.

But it was not the true voice I heard – or at least if it was, it was muffled or distorted; more probably it was an imitation, based on fragmentary unconscious memories. In consequence what I wrote was something very different from normal prose. It bore a weird, superficial resemblance to prose, achieved by much hard work; but it was fundamentally different, in that what held the words together was not their meaning, but the power of my will, which inevitably diminished as the writing grew longer, and more unlike what I had meant.

Clerkenwell

I spent my seventh to tenth years in induced sleep on board the ship *IBIS 6*, to be awoken after we had landed on a moon provisionally called Clerkenwell, which belonged to a planet as yet unnamed. The upheaval might have had a more damaging effect on my mind had it not been for the controlled environment of the ship, which had been my home since before our departure from the space-station, and whose brightly-lit corridors and hum of machinery seemed the only surroundings I had known since birth.

Even after we had landed there was no question that any children should leave the ship, so for us the only sign of our new circumstances was a change in the pitch of the vibration, which in our excitement we may have imagined. Our emergence from this period of sleep occasioned a release of energy which compensated to some degree for our deprived condition. It seemed a simple matter to begin life again, and we enjoyed responding to trivial things as if they had been new discoveries. On the other hand the long gap caused some disturbing lapses of memory, and although impressions of certain people – our parents in particular – returned more or less unchanged, there were others, chiefly among our immediate contemporaries, whom we remembered only as participants in some unfinished business whose nature we had long ago forgotten. Though we did not let such problems interfere with our activity, we retained a sense of having been cheated.

One of the most puzzling features of our new life was the formal education we now resumed, in which apparently not even an attempt was made to continue from where we had left off. As I remember, those who taught us had no particular qualification for the task, but performed it when allowed by other duties about the ship, following a kind of rota. I suppose that having pursued a general education up to the level for seven-year-olds, I was now receiving the lessons designed for ten-year-olds without any further preparation. The only means of achieving any progress was to confer with pupils who had been at a higher or lower level when the journey began, and being fairly popular I could make some use of this device, but still I became extremely ignorant. Compulsory subjects included curvilinear geometry, religious instruction, and what seemed most futile of all, palaeontology and the theory of evolution. Rocket-engineering, which most of us would have been only too pleased to learn, played no part in our studies, and it was generally assumed that children showing aptitude in that direction had been filtered into a higher class at an early stage.

An idea given prominence in the history-syllabus, which I met now I think for the first time, was that of a planet called Earth, existing at some great distance in the cosmos, which was supposed to have a particular significance for us, though it was beyond the power of our teachers to explain precisely in what this lay. For the most part we knew where we had been born, and the names of the ships in which we had arrived at the space-station, and in the light of these facts the information that in the remote past certain parties had left earth in certain other ships could arouse little enthusiasm. We accepted the possibility that we had all had ancestors among those people, but the idea that they alone had not had more ancestors in more distant places was evidently one of those obscurities used by adults to veil their ignorance. Equally unaccountable was the fact that no-one could give even an estimate of the time or distance separating us from this event. I concluded that history was in some respects similar to religious instruction.

The teachers tried to keep our interest in the existence of earth alive by showing us messages which, though their form had changed as they passed through the various stations of the cosmos, might have been sent by people living there. These would at least have aroused our curiosity if they had not invariably contained no information, and if they had not been hundreds of thousands of years old by the time we received them. On the other hand, routine communication with less distant places was not discussed in the school-room, apparently on the grounds that the technical matter was too indigestible. Thus we heard nothing of what they thought about our journey at the space-station, nor of any information we were sending back about Clerkenwell and its planet.

We had, however, our own means of filling whatever gaps in our knowledge seemed most conspicuous, and could soon name all the constituents of the soil on Clerkenwell, knew that there was water and the atmosphere was suitable for breathing, although some said the cold was such that no-one could go onto the surface even in a space-suit. In discussion of points like this my own voice had some authority, based on a memory I had of a barren, star-lit landscape which I took to be that of my planet of origin. My sister Clara, five years older than I, said that not only could I not have had this experience, but that the planet had been unlike my description. As she would not, however, either give her own version or admit definitely to having seen it, her evidence was felt to have no weight one way or the other. She was probably right all the same, as there is no report of my having been taken outside the ship in my infancy, still less allowed to wander alone, as I seemed to be in the remembered landscape. I did not defend myself against her arguments, but only described what I could see in my mind, and no doubt the consistency with which I did so led to its being preferred to others' memories, which tended to be confused and may have had to do with large man-made structures rather than planets.

Another point made by Clara was that such memories, whether clear or not, were of no practical use, and that the only way we could achieve an understanding of our situation was by watching the people in control, namely the adults, in particular members of the command-structure and the surface working-parties. In identifying these people we had the help of some of the teachers who worked in administrative capacities near the heart of the ship, and of those of our own number who had parents or other connections in positions of authority. One among us was said to be no less than the daughter of the Captain, though she admitted she was unsure he had not been replaced long ago. It was thus unlikely she could reveal any orders he might be giving, especially as three months after the landing she had received no indication that he was on board.

But we had discovered by now that parties were already at work on the surface, and more important than our uncertainty as to the Captain was the need to keep watch on their comings and goings and so work out the nature of their activity. Fortunately the airlocks, of which there were a dozen or so, were all situated in two groups, near one of the poles of the ship and near its equator, and we knew that during the initial period of exploration the 'A' section or equatorial group was to be used almost exclusively, so it was possible for the watch to be sustained by one person. We might have used more, but to do so increased the risk of drawing attention to our activities and bringing about a stricter confinement to the children's quarters. Alone, a child could loiter in the corridors for weeks, begging food, before anyone thought to make enquiries.

Inevitably there were long arguments about who was to do this work, but in the event it was mostly given to a boy called Otto, who had the advantage that, apart from this name, there was little by which he could be identified. It was said of his parents that they had been killed in an accident, possibly during preparations for departure from the space-station, but Otto himself had no opinion on the subject. He was insignificant in appearance too, being short and thick, with pale skin and hair and a blank expression, seeming somewhere between five and twelve, though he may have been older. Most of us having already been involved in exploration of the ship, he was able to draw on our combined experience. During his absences from school we discussed interpretations of his discoveries, using whatever additional information we could obtain in the laboratories and offices around the children's quarters.

Sometimes in class, if we thought it was safe, one of us would make some reference to what we had learnt, hoping the teacher would respond. There was one in particular we used in this way, who taught us astrology, whether or not astrology was indicated on the timetable (this was the science of reading the future in the stars as they were seen from Earth). This man hinted that he knew what was planned respecting Clerkenwell, not by giving precise facts that we could check, but by mocking our attempts at investigation. He would announce a digression on the subject with a sarcastic remark such as, 'I see Otto could not be with us again. Apparently he believes the celestial bodies have no influence on him.'

Nonetheless at the outset of his first expedition to the airlocks Otto was reluctant to start, thinking we had invented the ideas of a planet and a landing in order to involve him in conflict with the authorities. Eventually, however, we persuaded him and, as he told us later, he found and followed the radial corridor at the end of which were two doors, one leading to the room where the airlocks were controlled, the second to the airlocks themselves. He sat down where the corridor ended in a blank wall, and watched while numerous people passed through these doors, including several groups of two men and two women each who went in through the second. Assuming for the moment we had been telling the truth, he guessed that these were the groups assigned to the expeditionary parties, as they seemed to be in high spirits. Meanwhile he tried unsuccessfully to open the doors with the handful of keys we had collected.

He remained in this spot for several hours, and saw twelve quartets equally divided by sex pass through the door into the airlocks, then being hungry he had to abandon his post for a time. On his return, seeing a man come out of the second door alone, he asked what had happened to the people he had seen going in. The man paid no attention to him and walked off along the corridor. Otto followed, asking for the loan of his key. Since he still failed to respond, Otto pestered him until he refused to give up the key. Otto then demanded to know his reasons, and suggested he was afraid of his superiors' anger. The man denied this, adding that, if he should lose his key, he would simply be given another. When Otto argued that he could in that case have no reason not to grant his request, the man threw the key onto the floor behind him while continuing on his way up the corridor.

With this key Otto got through into another much higher and broader passage where from an open doorway on the right came the sound of hundreds of voices. Just inside this doorway, which led into a vast hall crowded with people, stood a man who seemed inclined to speak to him, but he quickly moved on along the passage. About two hundred yards further on there was a second, unguarded doorway into the hall. Beyond that on the same side were five large metal doors spaced far apart which he took to be the doors of the airlocks. On the left, above the height of four or five feet, the wall was made of glass. Otto walked a little way along this left-hand wall and, jumping up, saw into the control-room which was entered from the radial corridor.

He returned to the main hall and went in through the nearer of the two doors. Here the people sat and sprawled on benches round the walls and on chairs scattered at random in the centre of the room. Some wandered about the room as if looking for someone in the crowd, while others sat eating and talking or playing games. Otto noted several of the groups of four he had seen coming in, and throughout the whole assembly there seemed to be the same equal division between the sexes. He did not try to guess the people's ages, as he had no idea how to do so.

In one group a man read aloud from a printed sheet to three women and another man who listened attentively. Otto approached to hear what was being read. In his further wandering he picked up another copy of this sheet, which he showed us later. It was evidently a guide, though this was not stated explicitly, for those going onto the surface. It began with a very brief description of Clerkenwell and the system to which it belonged, giving little more than the types of planet and star, their size, orbital speeds and distances and so on. There followed a list of rules of conduct, some in the form of advice, some more a matter of precedent which, it was implied, one should not lightly disregard. Of the latter sort was the ordering of people by rank, age, function and so forth with the clear direction as to who in any group and in various hypothetical circumstances was to make decisions of what degree of importance.

Otto found the document hard to follow, but the four adults listened with apparent interest, and at the end fell to discussing it animatedly. At a suitable moment in the conversation Otto asked whether they intended to go out onto Clerkenwell. They now looked at him for the first time, surprised to be addressed by a child, but by no means hostile. One of the men replied that such was indeed the intention of everyone in the room.

Otto asked, 'How will you stop yourselves falling off?'

At first they failed to understand the question, and consulted together as to what he might mean. Then Otto having explained his intention, one of the women described gravity to him as it operated on planets. He understood her to mean that gravity would root one to the spot, and she modified her description accordingly.

After a short pause, Otto remarked that it must be hard to learn how to walk with one's head pointing downwards. But the woman was evidently tired of this exercise and returned to her discussion with the two men, while her role was taken over by one of the other two.

One of the questions that particularly occupied Otto was whether these effects would apply only to those who had been on a planet before, or whether everyone would be in the same position. The women, startled to find how little he knew of life on planets, now began to wonder about his presence in the airlocks. They wanted to hear his story, which he would have been willing to tell, and he explained why he was unable to do so. They expressed their compassion, assuring him that as far as going onto a planet was concerned, it made no difference whether one had had the experience before.

Otto next wanted to know how he could qualify to go onto Clerkenwell with them. They were shocked by the implication of this, and told him there was no question of qualifying, since everyone would be going out in time. Why then, he asked, were they all waiting in this room as if there were no prospect of leaving?

The women replied that although the feasibility of large-scale settlements had been established, it was important not to prejudice the work that was still to be done by a too-hurried descent onto the surface. When he appeared dissatisfied and wanted to know what sort of work it might be, one of them suggested making sure the blend of gases in the atmosphere had no long-term ill-effects, and the other deciding which sites were most suitable for habitation.

Otto, still unconvinced, tried a different approach. 'How did you find out about Clerkenwell?' he asked.

But now they thought he was playing a game, and one of them said rather curtly that since it first appeared its existence had been a matter of common knowledge. When the question was repeated, however, she said that all information came, possibly by a very indirect route, from the Captain. The others all gave him the same answer, and when he asked about the printed sheet, said it came from the administration, whose head was the Captain. As they were becoming suspicious of him, he left them.

One of the features of the room was a small steel door which must have been a side-entrance to the airlocks. However, while Otto was here there was no sign of imminent departure, although several new parties came in. He spoke to a great many people in the crowd, and found that they all had roughly the same idea as to what they were doing there. Finally he spoke even to the guard he had avoided at first, whose function was perhaps to record the arrivals, although he was now eating an orange. He asked Otto for his name, not with the idea of noting it down, but in order to tell him in a confidential tone that Clerkenwell might be an important place some day, and he was lucky to be seeing it at the beginning.

Otto left this room and continued down the corridor past the airlocks into a series of vast interconnected factories, where he saw large metal structures in process of construction. Not, he said, that there was a great deal of activity in these places, but the structures were incomplete, and here and there people were working at one or two of them. They might have been parts of machines, or of buildings. He found his way to the workers' canteen where he was given coffee.

When Otto told us his story, of which this was only a part, it was these machines or buildings I found most interesting, as the only reliable clue to the nature of the operation. I had been sent with Veronica, the Captain's daughter, and Cecco, a boy of seven, to receive his report in the ship's recreation-centre, where it had been agreed he should meet us. His account clearly implied that we had been brought to Clerkenwell in order to live there.

I did not see, however, any likely reason why such a thing should have been undertaken. Veronica and I had heard the idea that the search for a habitable planet was the motive of all space-flight, but we had never imagined it was to be taken literally. If the satellite was indeed to be our home, our first concern should be to convey to the authorities that we were prepared to help with the disembarkation. There were in Otto's story, however, several details suggesting we should not take it at its face-value. The machines, which might have given a clearer indication as to the course we should take, he could not describe more precisely than he had at first. My own feeling was therefore that we could only wait until he returned with drawings, or reported a change in the situation. Veronica, naturally enough, was excited by the allusion to the Captain, which she took to mean that her father might be on board; but in fact not even that inference was justified. Cecco, however, inspired by the devotion to Veronica which was an effect of his separation from his mother, had concluded that the Captain favoured the plan to occupy the satellite, but was opposed by the administration, and that we should look for him in order to give him our support.

Otto, having handed over the sheet of directions, but retaining the key, returned to the equatorial airlocks. In this first report he had described to us how, leaving the factories for the control-room, he had seen there an image on a screen of 'a bit of ground', bare and dark, with little mounds and hollows. There was not much of it, he said, meaning the horizon was close, as if the ground fell away. There had been no human figures in the picture, but only small machines with dishes like telescopes. It was at that moment that Otto had begun seriously to entertain the possibility that the story about Clerkenwell was not a fiction, but represented the true state of affairs. Immediately he had been filled with a desire to settle the question. The value of his work for us was therefore greatly increased over the next few months.

II

Cecco, who had been an infant when we set out and whom I therefore did not remember from that time, had become associated with me since the landing, though I had no particular liking for him. He was notable for his strong convictions and an exaggerated desire for success which had ensured, among other things, his being chosen to go to the recreation-centre to meet Otto. He did not pursue his plan of making contact with the Captain when he found no-one older than himself willing to accept his view of the affair, but it remained a private concern of his. Five or six weeks after the start of Otto's mission he reported to me that he had been approached when on the way to a lesson by the teacher Q. (the teachers did not use their names in school), who had asked him, as if merely curious, some questions about what he did in his spare time – and then, whether he was interested in space-ships. Cecco naturally said he was. Q. had then asked whether he would like to be taken sometime to look at the engines, and to meet some of the people who controlled *IBIS 6* when in flight.

Cecco again answered yes, although hardly believing Q. was serious. Most of us had seen the ship from outside at least once, and vaguely remembered its appearance, but all the parts of its interior connected with its operation were a mystery to us. Cecco wanted to know whether he should accept the invitation, if it were repeated. I gathered from Q.'s proposition that Cecco had been selected as a candidate for the operational staff, whose influence was such that, although the business of flying was for the moment ended, they must still have some part in deciding our fate. I told him to accept the invitation and to keep open any opportunities he might be offered, but to tell me of all future developments.

Accordingly he was absent during the morning of a rest-day in the following week, and in the boys' dormitory that evening he told me where he had been. A woman who was introduced to him as Circe, a worker in material-bombardment, had met him outside the school and had taken him on a journey lasting nearly an hour to a point close to the exact centre of the ship, where she had led him onto a catwalk running around the walls of a vault, at the heart of which was a giant mass of machinery. He had no reason to doubt that it was, as he was told, part of the engine-system. After taking him along the catwalk into other parts of the vault, pointing out the various different types of engine and the places at which the vault was connected to the outer shell of the vessel, Circe led him through a series of rooms where he saw men and women working on computers and other, more primitive types of machinery.

He was taken, Circe told him, into every department dealing with the purely mechanical aspects of *IBIS*'s journeys. In addition to the department where Circe herself worked, material-bombardment, Cecco remembered radiation-bombardment, fuel-synthesis, and especially flight-path construction, which dealt, she told him, not only with mathematical and other problems but with the ideological aspect of space-flight. She gave him a brief description of the system whereby decisions were reached in connection with their work, explaining that although the Captain had the power to impose his own will on the ship, in practice all issues were decided by a complex hierarchy which extended downwards into their own departments. She showed him the room in which communication with the Command Centre and the planet's surface was done. In spite of the multiplicity of departments and activities, he had the impression, like Otto, that the pace of the work was slow. Circe, anticipating this point, said that in the aftermath of a successful landing their work necessarily diminished in importance, but it always continued and would never cease to have some bearing on the life of the ship.

At the end of his visit, she asked whether he would like to come again. Cecco saw that he could lose nothing by accepting this second invitation. She enquired whether the thought of working there appealed to him. Again he realised he must answer yes, although his interest actually lay in using the operational staff as a means of gaining access to other parts of the ship. Apparently not doubting his sincerity, Circe told him he would be in a privileged, and at the same time an isolated position. He would never be able to abandon his vocation, since there would always be a new ship needing his work. He would come to see human development not as depending on the outcome of a single journey, but as a continuous process. Ultimately he might move into the even more rarefied sphere of command. Although employment in the operational staff did not necessarily preclude work on the surface, he might prefer to be more closely involved with the development of Clerkenwell itself – in building, for example, or food-production. Cecco denied that he wished to do either of these things.

Although we did not understand the significance of Cecco's experience, many when told of it favoured making an immediate disclosure to the teachers of everything we had discovered, demanding on the strength of it a degree of control over our future lives. Since he had been forbidden to reveal his dealings with Circe, however, the move was rejected as likely to endanger his position. Clara, who always remained aloof from these investigations, said no doubt if we were kept in ignorance of certain things there was a good reason for it, and we should be careful not to discover something we would prefer not to know. Others, ignoring this warning, and impressed by Cecco's new-found importance, began to agree with him that it was the Captain who held the answer to our difficulties, and suggested we could contact him without implicating Cecco if Veronica were to apply to Q., who acted as director of the school, claiming that she wished for urgent and confidential reasons to see her father. Veronica tried this and was met with an abrupt refusal. The next step which was urged on her was to feign an attack of illness, and again she agreed to give it a try.

Meanwhile Cecco paid his second visit to the headquarters of the operational staff. He was again met by Circe and taken through the same series of rooms, finally arriving in one he had not seen before, furnished with a few desks and a blackboard, where, he was told, he would work initially, if he accepted the position. Here he was introduced to the man under whose supervision he would learn the first principles of fuel-synthesis.

Together this man and Circe gave him an idea of the nature of their work. He did not strictly need to know more than concerned his own function, they said, but it was their practice to let information circulate freely among their departments. They explained that, owing to the complexity of the calculation involved, it was impossible for a spaceship to be designed for more than a single journey. Upon reaching its destination, the ship was little more than a burnt-out hulk, all its resources used, often with vital parts of its machinery destroyed. In case it should be necessary to leave the world on which they landed, their immediate task was to prepare for a future take-off. This often entailed redesigning the engines, and with them the entire structure of the ship, as dictated by the new conditions of take-off and the raw materials and fuel available on the planet. Since the distance they proposed to travel was an important consideration, a new destination was fixed on, and a hypothetical journey to that planet then served as the basis of the necessary calculations. Account was taken, too, of the human aspect of the journey. A prediction was made of the number of people to be carried on the ship, and in connection with this, of the type of community they could be expected to make on the new planet. Out of these details was then constructed the purpose of the journey, which, though less tangible, was as important as the mechanical considerations. A journey could no more be completed without a commonly-held idea than it could without an adequate supply of fuel.

Of course there was the possibility that the journey would never be made, and then this idea would have no existence beyond their own departments. In that case the whole process would seem no more than a prodigious intellectual exercise. But when he had been working with them for some time this would no longer seem strange to him. It was in the nature of their work that it involved much theory and speculation.

Shortly after Cecco recounted this interview, a report came from Otto that he had seen a working-party leave the ship. Observing an unusual excitement among the crowd in the assembly-hall, he had found on making enquiry that four people had been selected for the expedition, had received their instructions and were now being fitted with their equipment inside the airlock. Watching the screen in the control-room, Otto had presently seen a vehicle emerge and move slowly down a ramp onto the patch of ground he had described to us. After a long pause, the sections of a dome-shaped building were lowered from the ship. These were among the objects he had seen being made in the factories; of the others, we had deduced from his drawings, most were either parts of similar buildings or pieces of drilling and excavating-machinery. The vehicle by means of its extensible arms set the sections of the building in position and welded and riveted them together. After it had finished, there was another pause, lasting over an hour. Then it turned and moved away to the point where the ground dipped, where it disappeared from view down the slope.

This suggested we should soon have more detailed knowledge of the work on the surface. At the same time, though the activities of the operational staff, as described by Cecco, had many puzzling features, we felt it would be easy to infiltrate a department burdened with such an unwieldy, impractical system. Unfortunately a difficulty was about to be put in our way. Cecco had been told his informal meetings with Circe were now at an end, and he must decide either to return to school indefinitely, or to take up his residence with his new employers. It was easy to see he did not relish submitting to their authority. If he turned down this opportunity, however, he would have achieved nothing; there was therefore little doubt what choice he would make. I discussed the matter with him in the few days before he was to decide, and he promised if we lost sight of him to convey a message by way of the recreation-centre, where we still held our meetings with Otto. There was an upright in one of the pieces of gymnastic equipment which did not quite touch the floor, and underneath which a scrap of paper could be hidden.

But now a much more sweeping change occurred in our affairs: one morning Q. called us all together and announced that the activities of the school were to cease. We were all to be transferred for an indefinite period to other departments of the ship, and we should in future answer not to his authority but to that of our superiors in our new departments. There was no time to discuss this measure, or even to collect our clothes and belongings. I joined a large group which was led by school officials on a tour of the ship's corridors, stopping every so often while a name was read out and one of us was taken into an office or reception-room. When my own turn came I was led into the kitchen, where, though I disliked the place the moment I saw it, I was to remain until further notice.

III

In the event the work was not as unpleasant as I had expected, though it was monotonous. For reasons unknown to me a surplus of fruit had built up in the course of the journey, and the kitchen was producing mainly fruit-salads and puddings. While these were not difficult to prepare, our attempts to produce a varied menu created a great deal of stress. Also the smell of the piles of rind from apples, oranges and bananas soon became hard to tolerate, combined as it was with the smell of fertilizer from the nearby farming-quarter. The head cook, a surly, greasy person who seemed to be constantly sweating and was quite repellent to look at, made no allowance for the fact that I was unaccustomed to the work; indeed, he seemed hardly to distinguish between individuals at all, but treated everyone with equal inhumanity.

Fortunately I was not alone in this predicament, for my sister Clara and the astrology teacher had both been consigned to the kitchen with me. They were not the companions I should have chosen, but they provided the opportunity to talk. I was working alongside the teacher for much of the time, peeling the fruit while he disposed of the rind. At first a certain reserve persisted between us, but at length it was broken down by our circumstances. We had known him as W., but his name, as I now discovered, was Salazar. I was surprised that the teachers had suffered the same fate as the pupils in the breaking-up of the school. He explained, however, that his was probably an isolated case. He had been working before in the department of births and personal records, and that too had recently ceased to function.

I made every effort to discover the reason for this change in our situation, and to re-establish contact with my friends. In the kitchen, however, there seemed to be little chance of doing so. My appeals could be made only to the head cook, whose response at first suggested a complete lack of mental equipment. After a time I decided he was not completely unintelligent, but had no idea how to answer my questions, and was indifferent to all decisions of the administration. I tried to persuade him he should complain about this latest measure, since it involved him in all the trouble and inconvenience of training new staff. His reply was that it required no training to peel apples.

Although I could obtain no information, I guessed that the new arrangement had to do with the fact that large numbers of the ship's population were idle, while waiting to disembark, in the hall next to the airlocks. I could not understand why, when the same situation must have arisen on numerous occasions, the move out onto a planet should involve such apparent chaos in the ship's administration. I discussed this point with Salazar, who, to my exasperation, had accepted his new role without showing the least inclination to rebel, but only a slightly more marked bitterness in his manner. Why, I asked him, had the work of the school and his department been suspended, when only a trifling revision of the procedure would have allowed it to continue? Were births and personal records so unimportant?

'Of course they're unimportant,' he said. 'Why would anyone look at a list of names?'

'I don't know,' I replied. 'I expected you to tell me. I imagined if they want to enquire at the space-station about someone on Clerkenwell, they send a message to your department.'

'There are no messages from the space-station.' At first I found this hard to believe. 'The journey only took three years,' I said; 'it was perfectly possible to send messages.'

'I didn't say it wasn't possible.'

'They must be sending messages all the time,' I said. 'All the people setting out on journeys – they must want to hear what happened to us, so they know what to expect.'

'There's no doubt of what they can expect – they'll spend years travelling through empty space, then they'll land on a lump of rock. What's the use of our telling them that?'

I returned to my first question, determined he should not evade it. Even if personal records might safely be allowed to lapse, surely the education of the young, who would form the new community on Clerkenwell, was the last thing to be neglected at this crucial moment?

Salazar laughed. 'You didn't expect to learn anything from all that, did you?' he said.

'Isn't that what it was for?'

'It was to keep your minds dulled and your fingers occupied.' He threw a sack of peel into the incinerator. 'If you'd had nothing to do you'd have been under everyone's feet.'

I might have said it had failed, but did not choose to do so. 'What about all the subjects?' I said. 'Astrology and religious instruction – isn't it useful to learn about those things?'

'We're told they were considered important at one time. Personally I don't see how they could have fooled anyone.'

I had never much liked Salazar, and his remarks were not increasing my regard for him, but I persisted: 'Why didn't they teach us something useful?'

'Such as?'

'Something we could have used in our later lives.'

He paused in his activity, and seemed to meditate. 'On a spaceship – you could learn how to fly it, but of course the people who do that have their own recruiting-system. Apart from that ...'

'But we've landed,' I said. 'Isn't there something we could learn about planets, that would help us when we go outside?'

'Well,' said Salazar. 'Planets – they're roughly spherical, and they have orbits. That's all I can think of at the moment.'

In spite of his cynicism I was determined that his experience of planetary settlements should not be wasted, and after repeatedly drawing him out on the subject I suggested he could perform a service by giving a series of talks to members of the kitchen staff, to prepare them for the move onto Clerkenwell. At first he ridiculed this idea, but when I had explained the proposal to him many times he decided he might after all derive some amusement from the exercise, and agreed to give the talks. His pupils amounted to no more than half a dozen pastry-cooks and skivvies, mostly under twenty and none very bright, who assembled for the lectures in the meat-store late in the evening. As it was their responsibility at this time to produce food for the entire ship they were in a state of near-exhaustion when the time for the lecture came round, and had had no opportunity to wash. So far as one could tell, however, they found the process helpful, and Salazar, having accepted the idea, performed his role with enthusiasm.

He covered exactly the subjects which seemed to me most to need airing, namely the psychological and social implications of living on a planet. His basic argument was that a spaceship provided for those living on board an unreal and transient sense of community whose removal after landing could have a severe psychological effect unless a substitute was found. The social structure most suitable for life on the surface, he said, was not a single corporate entity but rather a loose assemblage of smaller groups. He recommended in particular family life, which could give the individual a feeling of security without restricting his or her freedom of movement in the larger community. These small groups, he said, provided a sense of purpose, a focus for the new feelings of personal responsibility which would emerge on leaving the ship, and what was most important, a pretext for activity. Idleness and solitude should be avoided, at least in the first few months.

What most surprised me when I attended these talks was the effect they had on Clara, who listened eagerly, sometimes even asking a question if there was something she did not understand. I developed a new sympathy for her during this period in the kitchen, partly on account of the suffering the work caused her. She had been given the job of baking the puddings, which she found excessively hot and tiring. No matter how fatigued and dirty she was, however, she would appear on time at the evening lecture. I did not know why she felt this sudden enthusiasm for self-improvement, when formerly she had disapproved of our attempts to fill the gaps in our education. It may have been that the particular subject-matter of the talks seemed to her more practical than our probing into the reasons behind things.

She had formed a relationship with a twenty-year-old man called Till, whose work was to take the cooked meals round to the different departments, and who was also an unfailing member of Salazar's audience. They seemed, indeed, to feel a strong affection for each other, and when he returned to replenish his trolley they could often be found in each other's arms in one of the quiet corners of the kitchen. Till was interested not only in Salazar's theories but in my account of the discoveries we had made before the dissolution of the school, and suggested that, as he was allowed to roam freely about the ship in the course of his work, he could serve me as a means of communication with Cecco and the others. His willingness to help was partly due to the anger he felt on hearing about the procedure of the operational staff, which he considered responsible for the increased load of work he had to do.

Concerning our ideas as to why we had been brought to Clerkenwell, and the suggestion that the whole race was seeking a permanent home, he said he had often indulged in similar speculations, and it was in this connection he found Salazar's talks so interesting. He had become convinced, during the constant voyaging from planet to planet of his own childhood, that the problem tending to make this search so protracted an affair was not the uninhabitability of planets so much as the near-impossibility of forming a social structure like the one described by Salazar. Any other structure must necessarily fail, as the sense of insecurity experienced by the people left in isolation ultimately spread and made life on the planet intolerable to all its inhabitants. Thus, he said, the people who were to undertake a particular journey were carefully selected as being likely to combine in stable yet adaptable small groups. But by the time the planet was reached and an attempt was made to build a community, this balance of its parts had been affected by birth and death. At a certain point during the colonisation of the planet, therefore, the conclusion was reached that it was impossible for the community as then constituted to survive. The journey was then resumed, in the hope that a space-station could be found where another potentially stable social group might be selected. Among other things, Till felt, this explained why the people Otto had seen in the airlocks had arrived in groups of two men and two women.

I knew Till's theory was nonsensical, since it clearly could not be avoided that a few people would be isolated. If their feelings of insecurity inevitably destroyed the planetary community, therefore, man would long since have abandoned the idea of living on planets and returned to living permanently on spaceships in the normal way.

However, I gladly accepted his offer of help, and he returned from his round the next day bringing a written message from Cecco. It read as follows: 'Have seen Captin. Have seen Veronika in hospital. He said hed never herd of her. Then he said hed go and see her. He remembered when I said she had a moal on her cheek but said he was to bisy. When I said Id seen Veronika they let me see him. Then he got angry and shouted. Think hes not right, am keeping him under servailance.'

His having been granted an audience with the Captain implied that he had joined the operational staff – otherwise I could deduce nothing from his message. A few days later, however, Till spoke to Otto, and the news from him was more straightforward. He had heard that another party was due to leave the ship, and this time he intended to go out with them. Our idea that the climate was too cold to support life had been unfounded. Two days previously a man had emerged from the dome-shaped building wearing only shirt and shorts, sat on a rock outside the door and remained motionless for two hours. Relieved of the necessity of finding equipment, Otto felt sure he could conceal himself in the airlock during preparations for the next outing, and so slip out onto the surface. There might be some delay before he could effect this scheme, since the disembarkation proceeded as slowly as ever; a second vehicle had followed the first over the brow of the slope, but otherwise this shirted man's appearance was the only activity he had seen. It was in fact about a week later that Till noticed his absence from the airlocks, and when a few more days had passed without his having appeared we assumed he had made his attempt and, all being well, was now at large on the satellite.

I was delighted by his success, and his tale of the man in a shirt removed my last remaining doubt that we were all to follow him onto Clerkenwell. As yet, anticipating a dubious response, I had not discussed our researches with Salazar. I looked forward to confounding him with a full account of our discoveries as soon as we had our first word from Otto on the surface. Meanwhile I was more diligent than ever in attending his lectures, and could talk of nothing but living on a planet and what it must be like. In this connection I recalled my old memory of walking on a planet in the starlight, and felt again the need to believe the picture was authentic. I took the opportunity of raising it at one of the lectures, asking Salazar whether it had been real or imagined. Seeming very annoyed, as always when there was an interruption, he said I couldn't possibly have had the experience, and it was clearly a racial memory.

'What's a racial memory?' I said.

'Have we come to discuss successful child-rearing, or racial memories?' he asked. But Clara also was very eager to hear his judgement of our old dispute, and, as the others rarely spoke, hers was a powerful voice at the lectures. Salazar sighed noisily, and, folding up his notes, put them in his pocket. He explained that, if an intense fear or other emotion had played an important part in the development of the race, it was possible for an image of the object inspiring that emotion, in this case a barren planet surrounded by the emptiness of space, to be stored in the mind of an individual who had no personal experience of it.

'People were afraid of something on that planet?' I suggested. Salazar said I obviously could not understand, so we might as well continue with the lecture. Since we claimed, however, that our faith in his ability and thus our continued attendance at the lectures depended on his explanation of this question, he agreed to try again. It was not, he said, an image of a particular planet but an image of planets in general, in which the awesome qualities represented by the barrenness of the landscape and the empty height of the firmament had been emphasised. As the idea that these particular features might inspire fear was still unfamiliar to me, I said it seemed an unlikely theory.

'I can't help that,' he said, 'I'm indifferent to planets, uninhabited or otherwise. If you believe what it says in the books, people expected to find creatures on them.'

'To find people on them, you mean?' said Clara.

'Not exactly. Other creatures.'

'Hens and cows?' I suggested. I had seen examples of these in the farming-quarter.

'Something like that, yes,' said Salazar.

'Well, they could bring those with them,' said Clara.

Salazar frowned, momentarily at a loss. Then, as if unsure the idea made sense, he said, 'I think they had to be intelligent hens and cows.' I knew from my studies in evolution that there were no such creatures, but before I could tell him so he went on: 'In order that people could discuss things with them.'

'Why should they want to talk to hens and cows?' said Clara. But Salazar, growing impatient, asked what good she thought all this information would be to her. Personally I had decided to take no further part in the conversation, since it seemed unlikely to account for my remembered image.

'If we start being afraid of nothing when we're on Clerkenwell,' said Clara, 'your explanation will cheer us up.'

Salazar seemed to accept this and, frowning again, said he did not know why anyone should want to talk to those animals in particular, but thought the idea might not have been to learn about the lives of the hens and cows so much as to get away from the other human beings.

'What did the other people want to do to them?' asked Clara.

'I don't mean they wanted to do anything,' said Salazar, at last showing some interest. 'Other people bored and disgusted them.' And he reminded her that he was not speaking of individuals but of the whole race.

'Everyone bored and disgusted everyone else?' said Clara faintly. It seemed at first she could hardly comprehend the idea. Salazar was pleased to have shocked her so deeply.

'I don't see there's anything so upsetting in that,' he said. 'It's natural.'

'No it isn't, it's terrible. And it isn't the natural feeling of the race, because there's the reproductive instinct, that you said makes people want to live together, and that's natural.' I had never heard such an intelligent remark from Clara before, even during the lectures. Salazar muttered something about a 'primitive characteristic, soon likely to become dormant', and that this seemed a suitable moment to return to the lecture.

'What do you mean, primitive?' said Clara. 'Are you telling us not to do it?'

'I take it we have come to the end of this highly theoretical digression, and have returned to the subject of the lectures?'

'It doesn't make any difference. You said reproduction was an important feature of life on planets. You said it would give us a sense of purpose.'

'It will,' said Salazar. 'The fact remains that, if our ancestors just felt more lonely as they spread further into space, reproduction is not a good idea.'

'Well, they knew nothing anyway,' said Clara. 'They thought there would be hens and cows on planets.' And Salazar admitted that that was hard to explain.

Two or three days after this conversation, Till brought me another message from Cecco. It read:

'Must see you (Anselmus) imediatly. Come to Command Centre.'

To give me an excuse for leaving the kitchen, Till suggested I take his trolley as if to complete the delivery of meals for the day, while he continued with my work of peeling. The head cook was unlikely to raise any objection to such a scheme. Having helped to reload the trolley, I set out. Till had reminded me of the way to the Command Centre, which was next to the outer shell at about forty degrees latitude. I had not, however, covered more than a quarter of the route when an alarm was sounded and a flurry of purposeless activity began. Although I did not realise it at the time, the disturbance arose from the death of the Captain, killed by Cecco.

Imagining some serious emergency, I left my trolley in the corridor, and as I happened to be close to the sick-bay went in search of Veronica, whom I found in the room she had occupied since failing in her second attempt to contact her father. Apparently no-one had doubted that she was genuinely ill; on her arrival she had been asked what treatment she required, and, as she could not think of anything suitable, had been left alone. She was free to go with me, and agreed to do so. Our first thought was to find Cecco, but when we reached the Command Centre we found it guarded. The guards could tell us nothing about what was happening. Neither did the people we passed in the corridors know the meaning of the alarm. We decided to head for the airlocks, assuming the emergency was connected with events on the surface.

As we neared the airlocks our assumption seemed to be confirmed; there were large numbers of people moving in both directions in the corridors, and from somewhere further ahead came the sound of an excited crowd. Arriving in the corridor that led to the airlocks, we found it blocked by a mass of people. Being smaller than most, however, we pushed our way through to the door whose key Otto had obtained, which now lay open. Inside too, the crowd filled the corridor. On the right, the hall described by Otto was deserted. Only the chairs remained, and a litter of plates and rubbish. We tried the steel door to the airlocks, but could not move the handle.

We returned to the main corridor and entered the control-room, which had also been abandoned. Looking through the glass wall, we could see over the heads of the crowd that the door of one of the airlocks was open. The people were moving through this door, and in two streams past a vehicle that almost filled the airlock, into the open air. We rejoined the crowd, and five minutes later were on the surface.

IV

We looked round for someone we knew, and at last found Otto making his way down the slope. It was night, but the area around the dome was flood-lit. We had seen the tracks of the vehicles going down about a hundred yards away, and at the bottom the vehicles themselves standing side by side. The slope was steep and the ground treacherous, consisting of earth that clung to the feet and rocks that rolled away from under them, so that we often stumbled and fell. Arrived at the foot of the slope, we sat down with Otto out of the light, and he told us what had happened.

On coming out he had found the people on the surface enthusiastic about Clerkenwell, and determined to make it their permanent home. In particular the climate appealed to them, he said. Indeed, as he spoke both Veronica and I, although it was night, were enjoying the effects of the climate. The temperature, though within a few degrees of that persisting inside the ship, was infinitely more pleasant, possibly on account of the humidity. For the moment the sky, which we had expected to be one of the most exciting features of our new home, was obscured by a bank of cloud. The effect of breathing the atmosphere, however, was extraordinary, the blend of gases producing a sensation of light-headedness unlike anything we had expected.

They were doing the work required of them, Otto went on, but without application, their only concern being the foundation of the permanent settlement, which they believed should take place immediately. Then one day he made radio contact with Cecco in the Command Centre. Cecco had made an alarming discovery, did not know what to do about it, and thought the people on the surface should be informed. The Captain had taken a liking to him, and now treated him as an adviser, apparently finding it useful to consult him on the running of the ship. Not wishing to seem ungrateful, Cecco in return had told him about his conversations with Circe and the measures taken by the operational staff in case it became necessary to leave Clerkenwell. The Captain had laughed at his story. The idea of a hypothetical departure, he said, was nonsense – perhaps it was half-believed by Circe; on the other hand, she might have wished to deceive him. Once the process of planning a new journey had begun, the date and time of take-off having been chosen, the journey itself took place as an automatic consequence. There was no possibility, for whatever reason, of preventing the launch. To prove his statement, the Captain pointed out that no-one had left the ship save the few individuals needed to mine the materials for the new journey.

When they heard this, Otto and the other people on the surface had been in no doubt that the plan must be thwarted. Cecco had been unsure what the attitude of the ship's population would be, but Otto and the others persuaded him that the majority would reject such a plan. They decided also, and told Cecco, that the only certain means of preventing the new launch was the murder of the Captain.

When Otto came to the end of his story he said he intended to spend a week or two exploring Clerkenwell on his own, and so he left us. We returned to the top of the slope, wanting to see more of what was happening around the ship. People were unloading equipment through the airlock we had used, from which the vehicle had now been removed. We found later that the murder had been committed at the moment when a party was leaving the ship in this vehicle, in accordance with a plan devised by Otto. Now nearly everyone had emerged, and the crowd divided into groups applying themselves to various purposes. No-one was in charge of these operations, which were conducted methodically, without undue excitement. A few people moved off down the slope into the surrounding darkness. Others went into the dome and examined the drilling equipment and the beginnings of an excavation which were found there. The work was so little advanced, it seemed the launch had been planned in any case for the remote future. People began to lay beds on the ground inside the building.

Dawn was breaking. Looking round at the muddy landscape, Veronica and I felt the desire to visit other parts of the satellite. We did not like to abandon Cecco, but were both reluctant to go back into the ship, where we knew he was held *incommunicado*. Although we did not know whether he was to be tried, or how serious his offence was thought to be, we felt his imprisonment was unlikely to last long. We were proved right, for the last vestiges of authority were soon to disappear. Apparently, with the death of the Captain the hierarchy had lost its ability to act. No new Captain was appointed, and nothing more was heard of the plan to leave Clerkenwell.

The equipment which had been brought out of the ship included a number of small folding structures like tents, intended as temporary quarters for exploring-parties. Several of these had been taken already by people heading for the unknown parts of Clerkenwell. Equipped with one of these structures, we set out on our journey. Three hours later, night fell again.

Life on Clerkenwell soon assumed the pattern it was to follow indefinitely. We stopped about two miles from the ship, and thereafter left that place only on short outings. We soon gave up exploring for pleasure, as all the parts of Clerkenwell we saw were much the same. It seemed everyone felt the same desire to live singly or in couples, and the initial flurry of communal activity soon died down. After a time there was nobody left in or around the ship. An agricultural project had been started there in the first few weeks, and it was sometimes necessary to go there for supplies. Otherwise we spent most of our days basking in the sunlight outside our hut, and the nights in talking about the new possibilities offered by life on Clerkenwell.

At first we found the sequence of day and night distracting. From midnight to midnight was about six hours, but at a certain time in the month the nights began to grow longer and the days shorter, until a night arrived which was sixty hours long. We began by trying to adjust our pattern of sleep and waking accordingly, but found that impossible to sustain, and chose in the end to sleep when we felt inclined, regardless of light and dark. The celestial phenomena were undeniably beautiful both by day and night. The sun was a delicate shade of eggshell pink, though too bright to look at directly. In the shorter nights the planet round which we circled sailed through the sky. As far as I know it never received an official name, though we called it the Navel because of its irregular shape.

Wishing to make practical use of the theories taught by Salazar on the ship, I sought him out in the cave where he lived alone. I had hoped he would be able to advise us further, but he had apparently said all he wished to on the subject, and clearly did not welcome my visits. It annoyed me that he not only left his work of teaching unfinished but acted in clear breach of his own principles by rejecting companionship. After a time, however, I realised his behaviour might have a consistency beyond my understanding, and I left him alone, resolving to put his ideas into practice without his help.

Working in the field beside the ship one day I met my father, whom I recognised immediately, although we had been separated for nearly five years. I greeted him effusively, to his great surprise, then realising he did not know me, introduced myself. Even when I had done so his manner remained slightly reserved, as if he were still not sure of my identity. To save his embarrassment I explained that I had only wished to see him in order to ask his permission to settle down permanently with Veronica. He seemed relieved, and we had quite a friendly discussion before parting, in which he told me that he and my mother had long ceased to think of me as their responsibility. Since Veronica assured me her mother was dead, we decided to become a family without further preliminaries. Quite by chance I discovered that I had reached sexual maturity, and after a lot of work we found a satisfactory method of copulating.

Salazar had made the point in his lectures that the family should not be completely isolated from other groups, but should mingle with them whenever seemed desirable. We decided therefore to visit Till and Clara, who lived together on the other side of Clerkenwell. They too had formed a strong family-group, inside a proper metal structure from the ship's stores. In fact they gave the impression of having lived together for years, and Clara told us she was pregnant. We were delighted by this event, which we celebrated in a day and night's drinking together. When we had agreed on a suitable timetable we had many more such parties, and Veronica and I spent the long walks home talking about Clara and Till and their new-found happiness. It was tacitly agreed that, when the four of us were together, we did not speak of our time on the ship. I did not regret this; in retrospect the principles governing space-flight seemed to have been the result of a long accumulation of misunderstandings, into which it would do us no good to enquire further. At the same time, it felt awkward to be deprived in this way of nearly all our past experience.

This was not the only thing about Till and Clara which had changed since leaving the ship. Clara had regained some of her old intolerance, and it seemed also to have been communicated to Till, for he tended to agree with all her statements. Sometimes when we visited them we felt like intruders, and that they would be happier in each other's company. We decided to suspend our visits for a time. Perhaps, we told ourselves, we were not meant to work so hard to bring Salazar's model society into existence. It might be better simply to wait for some spontaneous development in that direction. After all, in the meantime we had each other, and the many delights of simply living together we had still to experience.

Once Cecco came to visit us, and the thought occurred to me that we might invite him to join our household. He spent some time with us, telling us how he had climbed onto a locker in the Captain's study and dropped a heavy instrument-case on his head. But there was understandably some awkwardness between him and us, and my idea never came to anything. Thus I was left for long periods alone with Veronica again. Then, in spite of their irrelevance to our present life, I would speculate on the mystery of our journey, and the absurd system whereby mankind was doomed to travel perpetually from one planet to another. The point I found hardest to explain was that those who made the system had apparently felt no desire for a planetary existence, whereas it seemed to me then there could be no greater happiness.

Chun Castle

How many times have I climbed this hill?
There was that first time – it must have been
A day of cloud and rain – when I came alone,
Found the path and followed it. On the white stone
Was a plaque which named the relic. The air was chill
And desolate. In my mind, too, a kind of desolation –
An emptiness. I had come here for no good reason.
It was just to see a few stones, buried and overgrown –
A burial mound – that I climbed the hill.

And below the hill, the farm was silent. The people had fled.

Then there were the times when I came with children –
Or was it only one child? She scrambled on ahead,
Still playing a game I'd abandoned. A day of sun, cloud
And wind. Her laughter came back to me, blown
Out of shape, sounding strange in that lonely place.
I remembered the time when I had come through the rain
And climbed until, dimly, I made out the low, humped mass
Of the wall – and beyond, the gateway had issued
Its treacherous invitation. And so I had entered.
Within the circle of that fallen mass, I felt the chill
Heart of time – and yet, outside on the hill
I saw the tomb of someone who had died
Thousand of years before the wall was made –
And beyond hill and field, on either side,
The sea's dull, grey ghost. And now, the sun
Brightened the dark years. Heedless of so many dead
This child played the old games of children.

In the lane a dead tractor, stopped in mid-turn, wheels deep in mud.

(I too had played an old game –
Keep silent…look out for the glint of a spear…
So I had tried to fool time,
Although I had come here for no reason;
I had learnt the paths round the mind,
While climbing other paths, up other hills.)

Now I am climbing with you in the twilight –
End of a clear, calm day. Down below, the night
Has already come. The path is overgrown
And behind me you stumble, cursing like an idiot.
Your voice sounds thin, remote, as if swallowed
By the great stillness. There is still no light
In the farm, or in your car parked in the lane,
Where your wife is waiting. Perhaps, after all, she made
The right decision. In this deepening gloom
We shall not see the inner walls, or the well
Still flowing. And yet we did not want to miss
This chance which might never occur again.
Here the ground levels out. A little further ahead
You will see the wall. We need not walk to the tomb,
Although we see it as a shape in the darkness.
It is enough to step on the path, and feel
The pull of that breathless stretch of time.
If we just stand for a moment on the wall
We may at least see, on each horizon,
The sea showing a different face. And then
We must go back down into the deeper twilight.

A Gothic Tale

I

On this particular afternoon my main concern was to hide my disturbed state of mind from Hardwick. One of the methods I chose was to make a lengthy business of cleaning my pipe, so that I stood facing the hearth, and divided my attention between a collection of implements on the mantelpiece and the blazing fire beneath, into which I threw the flakes of charcoal from the inside of the bowl. Hardwick was sitting in an armchair, watching me, as I sensed somehow, and mocking my occupation with his clouds of smoke, as I suppose the smell told me. He was not to be deceived.

"You expecting that fiancée of yours, Pauwighte?" he said.

"Yes, I am, indeed, I am."

"H'm. I wondered why you'd invited me. I have a meeting of the Society fairly soon, you know."

I must say that this extremely abrupt manner of speech did not signify any real discourtesy or absence of esteem – so, at least, I believed at the time – but rather was the habitual attitude of that very commonplace intimacy which develops quickly, and almost inevitably, among young men in situations such as ours then was. There was so much about each of us, indeed, that was known to the other, that the only alternative to this curtness would have been an intercourse fraught with plumbings of the soul; and there was no other way in which we could go on from day to day, keeping, when we felt it was necessary, small areas of our experience closed to one another. One such area was Hardwick's "Society", about which I knew nothing – not even so much as the extent of its membership, or the purpose of its meetings – and just as he mocked my enthusiasm for outdoor sports by his exaggerated ignorance of every one of them, from cricket to fives, so I treated his Society with a mixture of jocular scorn and frank boredom. Even so, the true familiarity which our social 'familiarity' masked was something quite remarkable, such as I have never experienced with any other person either before or since that period – least of all with Emmeline, whom I knew well, as I have said, but who did not perhaps know me as well, and with whom my conversation rarely if ever rose above the stiffly formal. I was bound to her by something more mysterious than mutual knowledge; what it was I am no longer able to tell.

The time has come to deal with physical appearances, particularly with those of the people involved in my story; it may seem a trivial matter, but its significance will become apparent as I proceed. Hardwick, then, bore witness to that fact which I have frequently observed, that a man's youthfulness is not compromised, but rather enhanced, by the premature development of certain features rightly belonging to old age. Though in fact of a perfectly ordinary height he appeared small, being rather gnarled and bent, and moreover he was heavily bearded and generally dark in complexion; and yet as he lacked none of the vitality proper to his youth, these tokens of age took on the flippancy of caricature, and suggested an irreverent immaturity – in fact as misleading a suggestion as the more superficial one of declining years.

Claude Ammoran, whose letter Emmeline brought upstairs on the occasion of the visit I have begun to describe, was tall and fair, like Emmeline herself. Although I had seen him only once, fifteen months previously, I had read with certainty into Ammoran's lack of colouring a measure of dissipation beyond my experience, and also a rather distasteful vulnerability; but Emmeline, by these simple physical attributes, height and fairness, conveyed nothing beyond an extreme of beauty, which confounded my powers of interpretation, and which elicited no response from Hardwick, when I once approached him on the subject, except a pursing of the lips and raising of bushy eyebrows. It was not by looking at Emmeline – notwithstanding the many hours I spent thus occupied – that I had come to know her, nor indeed by listening to the sound of her voice, which, like Ammoran's, was soft; but my summary of physical appearances is in danger of becoming a eulogy. Suffice it to say that Emmeline shared certain qualities with Claude Ammoran, and that what in Emmeline was strikingly beautiful became, in Ammoran – it does not offend his memory to say so – repulsive. And it pleases my sense of symmetry to remark that there was a similar correspondence between Hardwick and the one person I have not yet introduced – namely Miss Caxton, Emmeline's companion, who was always present during the afternoon visits. She was dark, like Hardwick; but between these two there was not so great an antithesis, for although it amused me to pretend that Hardwick was repulsive, he was in fact attractive to ladies, and Miss Caxton, though somewhat dimmed by my loyalty to Emmeline, was also pleasing to the eye. Hardwick called her "a pretty little girl".

Thus I have made it possible, I hope, to distinguish these people one from another. I have not described my own appearance, as it plays no part in what I have to tell.

The four of us had begun tea, and it was growing dark outside, before Emmeline showed me the letter from Ammoran. So the fire had seemed to increase its warmth, and I had lit the lamp above the mantelpiece. Hardwick, as was his wont on these occasions, had cornered Miss Caxton – quite literally, for they were sitting together in the window-seat, and he was directing her attention outside. This he saw as his role in our gatherings, and he enjoyed himself thoroughly in the playing of it. He would always chide me afterwards for my slowness in taking advantage of the opportunity he thus gave me for private conversation with Emmeline; and while actually diverting Miss Caxton he would contrive to make some kind of ironical reflection, comprehensible only to me, on my own reserve, drowning with his loud monologues the halting confidences which Emmeline and I exchanged. This evening, for example, he was pointing out to Miss Caxton the activities of a number of undergraduates who were disporting themselves below, in the last of the twilight; and although it was in the last degree unlikely that they were playing football, he was explaining to her the rules of that game – with the most grotesque inaccuracies, which I longed to correct.

"Oh, Robert, I found this downstairs," Emmeline said, handing the letter to me. For some reason she had put it inside her muff, and then forgotten about it – or perhaps she had chosen her moment for producing it, as neither of us had said anything for a number of seconds. Hardwick turned round from the window as I took the letter, but Miss Caxton remained peering out; the players had begun to make parting noises, and were obviously returning to their rooms.

II

At the end of term I travelled to Yorkshire by train, via London; I was to be met at Harperby station by a servant from Ammoran's house. My final reason for accepting his invitation was not Hardwick's protestation that "he was a splendid fellow", or the unnamed "problem" mentioned in his letter, with which he felt I could help him; it was simply that Emmeline, during the tea-party to which I have already alluded, had revealed that she was going to spend the winter abroad with her mother and Miss Caxton, and under the circumstances I would have found it tiresome to stay in Cambridge with Hardwick, as I had intended to do. Ammoran's reason for inviting me was not, I felt sure, of the same order of simplicity. I was not blessed with special knowledge in any subject to such a degree that some person of longer acquaintance with him might not have advised him more effectively on any problem that troubled him. Hardwick maintained that I had "made a great impression on him" during the single conversation we had had together: this had been at a college dinner, on the occasion of my coming up, and Ammoran's going down, and the end of Hardwick's first year; the latter had introduced us, and ever since had said that Ammoran would certainly be inclined to renew the friendship. I did not see in this, however, a full explanation of the affair, and it was in a state of curiosity, mixed with a certain apprehension inspired by my recollection of the man's faintly repellent aspect, that I travelled up to Harperby.

The journey took two days and one night, all told, and I arrived at the tiny, isolated station on a particularly dark evening, in the pleasant aftermath of a rainstorm. I was the only person to alight from the train, and as there was no porter to help me with my luggage I carried it myself through the booking-office, where I gave my ticket to a taciturn young man who apparently managed the station unaided. Outside was a completely barren area, where hundreds of puddles had gathered among the cobblestones; there was a single lamp against the wall of the station-building, which was reflected in a semicircle from the pools of water, but which cast no light beyond the cobbled area. I assumed that, as no further lights were visible, the moorland began without prelude. At the very edge of the moor, then, stood a shadow in the form of a carriage with a single horse; I approached, and saw that the driver was in his seat, reins in hand. He obviously did not intend to get down.

"Mr Pauwighte," he said, by no means interrogatively; and as he did not even look at me, I realized that this was to be the limit of our mutual recognition. It was also to be the only help I had with my bags, which I therefore placed on the seats inside the carriage before climbing in myself.

We moved off instantly, through a darkness totally devoid of landmarks. We did not pass a single dwelling on the way, and even when we were approaching the house itself there was no lodge, indeed no gate and no wall, and not even, so far as I could see, any increase of vegetation. The gradient we had been climbing for half an hour became steeper, and then we came out onto a sort of plateau where the house stood, with one or two lights in its windows.

When the carriage stopped, the driver still did not get down; but a butler came from inside the house, and he took my bags as I descended. Then he led me into the hall and indicated a door, saying that if I would wait in the library Mr Ammoran would join me presently. I heard the carriage driving away round the corner of the house.

My first impression as I entered the library was that I had been there before; this must have been in my infancy, I told myself. And although I fully realised that such a childhood visit was as complete an impossibility as any subsequent one, the impression grew momently into a kind of certainty. I found, testing myself, that I knew the titles of almost all the books before I was close enough to read them; and the exceptions to this rule I took as a further substantiation, for the titles with which I was successful were those of the old editions of classical works, whereas the ones which eluded me belonged to recent novel and scientific books with paper covers. Also, as I would otherwise have to say later, when we moved in to the dining-room I was struck by an even stronger, though by then not unexpected, form of the same impression: the position of the table told me instantly at which end of it I was to sit, and that from there I would see the door into the kitchen, which as I entered the room was invisible to me; and I was so intimately familiar with the carving on the fireplace that I expected at any moment to see Emmeline sitting in one of the chairs beside it.

On meeting Ammoran I knew at once that something unnatural had occurred, because he was not the man I had last seen fifteen months before, but someone at least twenty years older. Hence, you see, my insistence on physical appearances: I knew that the present Ammoran was actually close to the age of fifty, though some of the changes in his features suggested an even older man – his pink-flecked eyes, for example, now had bags under them which dragged down the flesh and showed little wet clefts in the underhang of the eyeballs. Also, I knew that in this Ammoran and the one I had met at the college dinner I was not dealing with two distinct souls. However, it was not my place to go looking for a priest, which I would in any case have found insuperably difficult. Perhaps here, too, I had the problem which I in particular was expected to go some way towards solving.

Ammoran was charmingly polite, and spoke in the soft, womanly voice which I remembered. "Pauwighte, I'm glad you could come," he said, as he approached me from the library door.

I remember little about the early part of our conversation, except that it was pleasant. We sat drinking a glass of wine before dinner, and he asked me if I liked oysters. Even the two mysteries – his age and my feeling that I had been in his house before – contributed to my enjoyment of the situation. I could imagine that this charming old man, who had a story to tell, was merely taking his time about beginning it; that when it came it could not fail to be engrossing – meanwhile I was to sit by the fire and drink my wine. My predominant emotion, you see, was still an intense curiosity.

As we were going into the dining-room, however, he did rather startle me with some abrupt questions. "You're thinking of marrying, are you not?" he said, in the very moment that I became aware of the carved fireplace.

"What? Has Hardwick been telling my secrets?" I was preoccupied, as I said this, with the half-remembered movements which took me to my seat at the far end of the table. Nonetheless I felt the impropriety of the question, especially as the butler was present, arranging plates and glasses. My host's next inquiry was even more surprising.

"And you are not too well situated, I mean financially, whereas the lady ...?" At this I rebelled and, oddly, felt for the first time that I might in some obscure way be threatened. I had just recognised the kitchen door, and was not comfortable.

"I really don't ..." I began; but any further heat on my part was prevented by my companion's dismissal of the butler, who had that moment completed the business of setting the first course before us. He departed through the kitchen door, which opened stiffly in a manner I knew well, but crane discreetly though I might, I could see no object beyond it. The butler took a candelabra with him, and the room was now lighted by only seven candles: two on the mantelpiece, and five in the centre of the table; I stared for a moment into the fire, and watched its reflections in the marble, strengthened by the decreased light in the room. It was as if the carvings themselves were flickering, and were about to swell into some larger shape. I had seen fire play on them like this before.

I was roused by the slight sound of my host eating, and looking at my plate, discovered oysters. I was surprised, and took up my glass of wine first. But Ammoran was guzzling, or mumbling, and seemed still to be occupied with food while he drank from his glass; I realised that he was speaking, and caught at the end the word 'society'.

"Society?" I said.

He looked up at me. "Felix Hardwick's Society," he said; and when I produced a laugh which I had thought genuine, but which sounded hard, he continued to stare at me. "I was never a member of it," I explained, lightly, and he continued his eating. I swallowed my first oyster. The fire seemed somehow to have lost its advantage over the candles, and I began to feel rather cold.

Before long Ammoran started a short monologue, staring down always at his plate, and sometimes putting food into his mouth. "I'll never marry again," he said. "My wife was very old; she gave me this house, you know. I can do what I like with it – I'll not have a child now ..." and he said some other things in this vein, until an extended silence made me feel that I ought to resume the conversation.

"You said in your letter that there was a problem ..."

"Ha!" – it was his turn to produce a cold laugh – "that's long since solved, my boy. There's nothing you can do, while you're here, except look around the house. You'll find it's a windy place."

"You certainly seem very isolated." I was watching the kitchen door, which seemed to be standing slightly open; there was a whitish-blue light beyond, and it was growing in strength over the flame-coloured light inside the room. The fire was almost extinguished. I thought I saw the door move, and I certainly felt a draught of cold air; then my host spoke again, and I had to look at him.

"We have a very handsome vault, which you could see." He was smiling at me as if about to burst into laughter again, but there was a sort of fright in his eyes, and a pleading note in his voice which disgusted me. There was nothing I could say, and I shivered involuntarily. But he continued to importune me: "Is it not just the kind of place your future wife might like?" he said, and as his voice rose in pitch I realised that the light in the room had shrunk to a purely silvery glow; I stood up, looking for the candle and the fire. A cold wind was blowing, and the entire shape of the room had changed; moonlight flooded in through the door, though I knew there was no moon. But I could still feel the table, and hearing Ammoran weeping, I looked at him where he still sat bent over his plate. "I am sorry, young man," he sobbed. "I meant you no harm." But they were not tears that dropped onto his plate: they were little shreds of some grey stuff, as if he were silently regurgitating his oysters. I was afraid, and I retreated only to find a cold wall behind my back. When I gripped the table again it had become a stone slab, across which Ammoran was trying to crawl, and I found myself also sinking onto the stone, perhaps fainting. I saw the name 'Hardwick' carved on the stone, and, where the fire should have been, a number of dark openings with objects inside; I was also aware of Ammoran's rotting hand, and someone's high voice which said, "Don't touch me: why do you want to touch me?"

III

You see the wisdom of narrating that first part of the story chronologically: how else could I have justified the effect the metamorphosis had upon me at the time, and then the uncertain feelings, dominated by shame, which followed it? I awoke in bed, attended by a person who introduced himself as Dr Turpin, and although I felt very ill, I knew at once that my most recent memories derived from a particularly grotesque fantasy, or dream, itself based on nothing in reality beyond my own anticipations and (I noted regretfully) wishful thinking – hence the dream-Ammoran's hints that he might bequeath his house to me in the event of my marriage.

When the true Ammoran, summoned by the doctor, entered my bedroom, I could not repress a slight shudder; I was reassured, however, by his appearance, which was exactly as I remembered it from our first meeting, in Cambridge. What he had to tell, too, supported my theory about the dream; he sat on a chair beside my bed, and told me, his soft voice expressive only of kind apology, that on the night I was expected I had not arrived. I had been discovered the next morning, lying on the moor, already in the grip of the fever which had now kept me in bed for two days and nights. The only detail of his story which I found at all disturbing was that the driver who had been sent to meet me, being delayed by a lame horse, was told by the young man who took my ticket that I had already been carried off in another carriage; but this young man, Ammoran assured me, was not entirely in his right mind. I told Ammoran nothing of my dreams; I wished to reflect on it for a little longer in solitude, and besides, I hardly had the strength to talk; I drank half a glass of mulled wine and then fell asleep again.

For several days more I drifted in and out of consciousness, only occasionally talking with Ammoran. One day I apologised to him for my involuntary rudeness in thus sleeping out my visit.

"I am only sorry," he replied, "that your coming to my house has occasioned you such misfortune."

"And I have not even asked you yet about your reason for inviting me. You wrote that I could be of assistance to you in some way."

He laughed, causing me a moment's discomfort. "Oh, you are not to think of that. I am going to make a golf-course – the only way I can turn my horrid garden into a source of pleasure, for some people at least. I wanted you to give your opinion of the ground, and perhaps to map out the course. It was really the shallowest of pretexts for having you here."

Nonetheless, when I first felt myself able to stand I went for a walk on the moor surrounding the house, intending to begin this task of surveying. As I stepped out of the front door and across the drive to the edge of the heath – the prospect of which in this direction was not relieved even by so much as a bush or a naked post, until the village of Harperby appeared many miles away and far below – I was considering, in troubled mood, two new facts about my situation: on my way down I had glanced into the library, and had recognised it; and from a servant whom I had never seen before, I had learned that oysters were indeed served as the first course of dinner on the night I had failed to arrive. I had been greatly shocked by my glimpse of the library, and although I was now trying to comfort myself with reflections on the limited prophetic power of dreams, certain physical symptoms had started to tell me that I was in no state to be out of bed.

I made my way down the hill, however: the day was bracing enough, with high white clouds and a strong wind; when the house and Harperby were both out of sight, I began to examine the quality of the ground. It so abounded in mounds and hollows that I was soon fatigued, as well as dizzy and sick. I noted that there were natural sandy bunkers, and that the variations in the texture of the grass were ideal for the purpose Ammoran envisaged. Greens would have to be laid, of course.

I sat down to rest against the side of a hill, and was for a moment overcome by nausea. Possibly I became unconscious: when I got back to my feet the moisture had soaked into my clothes. But what had alerted me was the sound of voices, very far off and blurred by the wind; the speakers were somewhere over the crest of the next hill, which I made haste to climb. At the top, however, I halted, for to move on would have been to lose sight of them again. They were two women and a man, and their occupation I found at first a little difficult to determine, as they were so far away that even the colours of their garments were obscure. That they were engaged in some elaborate pursuit, however, was beyond doubt: the smaller of the two women bent down, and her companions stood back as if to watch; the central figure made a violent movement, there was a sharp sound followed by a pause, and then their voices sounded again, the women's breathily gay, and the man's jocular and patronising. The man had some burden on his back, to which the taller woman now went. Even at that distance I could see this woman's hair, which was long and light in colour, agitated by the wind.

They were playing golf, and there was something else I recognised about them; it could not be Emmeline, of course, despite the blown hair; but on the other hand, the man was surely Hardwick. I certainly knew all three of them – I ran towards them, shouting, but they did not see me before I had descended into the next hollow, and when I came out of it again they had gone. Rather dazedly, I searched the moor for a further hour, but I did not see them again.

On returning to the house I was as weak and confused as ever. Nonetheless I stayed out of bed until tea-time, and when I was able to speak with Ammoran I asked him about the people I had seen.

"I have no other guests," he said. "You are the only person here."

Darkness was coming again. Ammoran had persuaded me to take more mulled wine instead of tea, to restore my strength, as he said; but something in the situation was having an opposite effect – our surroundings contributed to the process, for we were sitting in the dining-room, and the sight of all the remembered furniture was enormously oppressive to me. There were no candles; the fire in the failing light was making outlines swim again, and the carvings began to put me in mind of coiling worms and reptiles. Not wishing any return of my grotesque visions, I excused myself to Ammoran, and said I must retire.

I was halfway up the stairs before I realised that a man was standing in the shadows of the hall. I confess that the throbbing in my head increased at the sight. The man was watching me; but as he stepped forward I recognised Hardwick, and in my relief I exclaimed, "Felix!"

"Hello, Robert," he replied. "I heard you were ill, and have come from Cambridge to see you."

"But – Emmeline?"

"She is in Italy, as you know."

It is a measure of my confusion that I questioned none of this; forgetful of what Ammoran had said at tea, I proceeded upstairs without another word. Hardwick watched me for a moment, and then went into the library.

IV

I hear the remark, that I am continuing to tell my story chronologically. There is justice in it, if the reader considers only what I have written, and infers nothing from it. But he should have noticed a considerable vagueness in my numbering of the days which followed my first awakening in Harperby, and I must tell him that I am quite uncertain of any sequence governing the remainder of my story, except that supplied by the numbered pages. One fact distinguishing it from what I have already written, however, is that Claude Ammoran no longer plays a part. I ceased to think of him as a participant at a time when the house was full of voices, generally gay, and when I could hear from my bed small parties of people moving up and down the hall and landings, conversing as if a sick person in the house were the last thing on their minds.

When Hardwick came in his expression, by contrast, was very solemn. I saw him often, and still do; he is the only person I see and recognise now. However, I am sure this has nothing to do with any failing in my sensitivity to physical appearances, because I can see that the alteration in Hardwick is an effect of constant trouble, rather than the ordinary process of ageing. More unfamiliar than Hardwick are my own hands, one lying on the coverlet and the other holding a pen; but I accept this as the natural consequence of a period of illness and confinement to bed. No doubt if I could see my face I should be disagreeably surprised. However, I am unable to find a mirror, or any adequate reflective surface, and now I cannot remember ever having seen one in this house.

Hardwick is my host: he has told me that the house is his, and that the previous owner has been dead for several years. He told me that the noisy people were his own guests, a weekend golfing-party. I asked him if Emmeline was among them, thinking no doubt of the group I had seen on the moor; but he did not reply. Instead he busied himself with my pillows, and frowned. When I asked if we should not soon be returning to Cambridge he remained silent: not until I mentioned Dr Turpin did he speak again, and then only to say that the doctor had discontinued his visits, my illness being of insufficient severity to merit further attention.

Now is the time to tell of what I consider the most significant event in my disconnected history. Nothing, so far as I can see, was changed by it, for I am now lying in bed just as I was when it began; but it will perhaps partly explain why I feel so powerless, and why I reflect so much and so despairingly on Emmeline. It was dark then, as it soon will be now, and no-one had come to light my candles. I was not surprised: I thought it might be very late. I had been staring for some time at a shape which I knew to be the writing-desk, against the wall shared by the next room along the passage. I suspect that Emmeline had been in my thoughts, for when I heard a voice behind the wall I immediately involved it with her features although the voice was far too indistinct to be identified and I had no idea who occupied the room. I could hear that the voice belonged to a female suffering some extreme of emotion, and although I knew at once that the event was momentous I continued to lie in bed, listening until there were no more sounds, and I could read into the minutes of silence a sobbing continuation. I was held in bed not by physical weakness but by a general reluctance to intervene in the affairs of others, which had been growing since my first confinement; I had not reacted so strongly to exterior sounds before – not even to those of the golfing-party. My apprehensions about Emmeline, however, proved strong enough on this occasion eventually to get me out of bed, and after another long pause, out onto the landing.

When I knocked on the door next to mine and entered the room, the curtains of the bed were drawn aside, and a woman said, "Felix." The voice was that of Miss Caxton, Emmeline's companion. I could not see her face, but her voice was enough to clarify and reinforce my apprehensions; I rushed forward, and in doing so must have stepped out of the shadow of the door, for she no longer spoke in her tearful tone of welcome for Felix, but screamed in terror, and flung herself back into bed. Propriety, I'm afraid, had no place in my thoughts: I re-opened the curtains myself, and tried to touch her. The bundle of sheets recoiled, and her muffled voice was hysterical: "No, please don't touch me: why do you want to touch me?" Whether or not I did touch her I cannot say.

"Where is Emmeline?" I said.

"She's dead!"

"How did she die?"

"I don't know. I don't know how any of them died."

"Where is she?" I said, knowing from the sound of her weeping that she would soon be incoherent.

"She's dead – in the vault!"

And so I flew through the dark house, and out on the moor I returned to the vault, which I had seen once before. Outside it I met Emmeline, who was standing, and must have been waiting for me; she was doing nothing else: she turned and held out her hand to me. When I first saw her face I was revolted, but then I had accepted the dense network of wrinkles which overspread her features, and I took her hand, which was warm. I thought I could almost remember the contours of its pockets of fat.

"I'm sorry, Robert," she said, "I meant you no harm." Then she walked down the steps into the vault, stumbling as she went against the heavy door, and holding its edge as she took the last few steps into the darkness.

Inside the vault, facing the long tomb on which was inscribed the name "Emmeline Hardwick", I experienced the strange sensation with which I intend to close my narrative. There was a cold wind, like the one I had felt while dining with Claude Ammoran, and it was as if it had penetrated to my soul – not merely my consciousness – and blown it away; so that although I was in oblivion I knew a universal cold and darkness, and felt swift, gigantic changes of place. But then, it was only one sensation among many, and probably it has no more significance than any other fact in my story.

In West Penwith

For Michael and Margaret

There is nothing
older than the stone
beside the doorstep
in the morning garden

there is nothing
older than the morning
passing now from half light
to full noon

Report on our Inquiry into an Unknown Planet*

<u>*From the journal of Captain Lionel Jaffa, M.A. (Cantab): 1984*</u>

June 21st

I am compelled to admit that I deserve no credit for our escape from that particular planet; however, I have resolved to permit myself, during our no doubt brief stay in the world which came into view this morning, no relaxation of vigilance sufficient to allow changes of any kind among us, or more particularly, to endanger my position as captain of the ship. Sir Charles is still, obviously, aware of our situation, and he has been presenting reports in a fairly normal fashion. I think I can assume that his estimation of the planet's distance is accurate. Isobel, too, though I suspect she will never again be as beautiful as she was, has retained all the faculties necessary for fulfilment of her duties. We are making progress, at the rate of one light year about every eighteen months. Isobel has told me that all repairs to the ship's engines could be completed within half an hour, if only we found a suitable resting place.

July 9th

This has been a period of intense excitement and optimism. I was so accustomed to dealing with a space made up of completely unrelated points that it seemed to me a good sign when our position began to display a trend towards simple oscillation between two recurring points, which were therefore inevitably related to one another. Although a borderline was an impossibility, I thought it likely that we were passing by degrees into a new area, and one which promised relatively enjoyable progress. A pleasing alternation could be observed, between the new planet's being a hundred and fifty, and two hundred and fifty thousand million miles away – which was particularly gratifying in that the same course and velocity toward the planet existed in both phases of the alternation, and in that it was interrupted, at less and less frequent intervals, by days in which we seemed to be in other galaxies entirely.

My comfortable anticipation was destroyed, however, when Sir Charles came in one day with the information, delivered, I thought, in rather too complacent a tone, that we had slowed down to about two hundred miles per hour, and would collide with what looked like the West Coast of Africa in two minutes. The situation passed, as it might have been

* I can date this work to some degree: I first read a draft of it in 1973 (as internal evidence also suggests); nevertheless some chapters have the feel of being not only early work but relatively unrevised. Some of the ideas in it anticipate successful later work by others such as Douglas Adams' *The Hitchhiker's Guide to the Galaxy* or Rob Grant and Doug Naylor's *Red Dwarf*; but neither of those shares the depth of literary feel or the unreliable, introspective primary narrator – nor of course the Edwardian, Jules Verne style of spacecraft. The work was left by the author without a conclusion, and I have supplied the material following the last letter by Quincey Horace. *Editor's note*

expected to do, but I have never since been in a position to enjoy the prospect of entering the kind of space I rashly assumed to be close at hand. Our insulation, moreover, functions imperfectly under these circumstances. Several times today, my pen has disappeared from my hand, and on two occasions I have seen it hovering over the wash-stand on the other side of my study, where it has continued for a few moments to go through the motions of writing, before either falling into the basin or vanishing.

July 11th

My principal motive in calling the meeting today was to test my authority: it transpired, however, that any moderately direct enquiries I could have made would have been absurdly embarrassing. Very few of the lower crew-members turned up, and Smallpox, who had been elected spokesman for the contingent, was obliterated from the bridge of his nose down to his shoulders – the mutations having begun invariably in the mouth or the nostrils – with the result that he had to write all his suggestions and replies on little scraps of paper, and pass them round the table.

Sir Charles, showing some of the tact he formerly had in such abundance, though with a slightly exasperated glance in my direction, began to talk about the approaching planet as if a debate on this subject had actually been planned. The information he produced in his first sentence was, in fact, new to me, so I had no difficulty in providing the efficient enthusiasm necessary to play along with his little charade. He claimed that the vision he had had of the coast of Africa, on awaking four mornings ago to find his window filled with the surface of an unexpected planet, had not been, as we had all half assumed (expecting never to need to come to a decision on the subject), a stress- and peril-induced hallucination. The same coast-line, he said, and indeed many other shapes corresponding to the land-masses of Earth, had now become visible on the more familiar planet toward which we were travelling in a reasonably consistent manner. This was not to say, he added immediately, that the two planets were necessarily the same, but on the other hand it seemed a useful supposition to take the near collision episode simply as an exceptionally violent oscillation in a pulse which nonetheless remained relatively moderate.

"I, too, have examined the detail on the planet's surface," said Isobel at this point. "I mean, of course, the planet which we thought yesterday we would reach today, and which today we think we will reach in nine days' time, assuming that these two at least are the same planet. So far I have seen no feature of any kind that distinguishes it satisfactorily from the Earth."

I was plunged into various kinds of confusion by this speech. Its cold formality, though I could expect nothing else after my total rejection of Isobel's altered body, caused me to reflect, perhaps for the first time, on her new position with regard to me, and to think in terms of gauging the precise extent of her resentment. At the same time, my search for a response, or rather an objection, to her actual statement was impeded by the obvious inference I had automatically made, that she had been spending long periods of time in Sir Charles's room (Sir Charles's being the only room with a window) – which inference was disturbing in that it gave rise both to unreasonable jealousy and to objectively horrible speculations about the possibility of a physical relationship between Isobel and Sir Charles.

"What about the other planets?" was the question I eventually managed to organise. "And the stars?"

Sir Charles replied: "Everything is in order, wherever the planet appears in relation to the ship. So far as we know, the planet could in fact be Earth."

"Or a planet identical to the Earth in all, or only some, respects," said Isobel, and a lobe of flesh projecting from her jaw gave the small twitch I have already begun to recognise as a sign of cynicism – a quality she has always had, though it has never before been the dominant feature of her personality. "Or possibly we are oscillating between an identical planet and the Earth itself, in one, or several, of many possible combinations."

During this new and possibly even more remarkable expression of detachment by Isobel, a whispered discussion had been going on among the men sitting on Smallpox's side of the table. They now sat back in their chairs as efficiently as their shapes would allow, and Smallpox produced a note which obviously contained the result of their deliberation. He handed it directly to me. It read as follows:

"Captain Jaffa, Sir. The group of which I am representative wish it to be known that should the planet towards which we are headed prove to be Earth, we would like to be dropped off as close as possible to Mozambique."

This, though it certainly had some bearing on the question of my authority, was a digression from the subject in hand, and had a detrimental effect both on my self-control and on my control over the meeting. Stanley was saying something about several planets identical to Earth, which I ignored, however, quite successfully, as I handed the note to Sir Charles. To cover my confusion I attempted to whisper something inconsequential in Sir Charles's ear, but he refused to respond, merely glancing superciliously at the note before passing it on. He sighed, pushing out his lower lip so that the ends of his fine red moustache stirred, and then he leaned forward, elbows on the table, head in hands, and eyes half-closed. Faced with the necessity of finding a new prop for my composure, I rose from the table and walked over to the book-shelves, from which I extracted an earlier volume of my journal – the very large one, bound in black. By the time I returned to the table Smallpox's note had reached Stanley, and there was silence. Feeling that this was the moment to speak, I laid the book on the table, open, as it happened, at my description of the hole we had nearly fallen into seven years ago, and delivered the speech I had formulated during my brief journey across the room.

"Gentlemen, I do, of course, appreciate your desire to regain what you believe to be your home, and to escape from the insecurity of the life we have been living during the last ten years. And certainly, if we succeed in reaching this planet, and if it bears the slightest resemblance to Earth, we will stay for at least as long as is necessary to repair our engines, during which time every one of you will be at liberty to leave us and make his own way into the world. Indeed, it is our normal policy, as you all know, to remain as a colony in any new world so long as it continues to be habitable. However, it is important to remember that even on the friendliest planet we have found, this has meant a period of only three months. In most cases it is essential to leave within seconds after our arrival, and sometimes even this interval has been too long – many of you received bitter corroboration of this fact when we landed on the White Planet, and still bear the marks on your bodies." (Perhaps it was imprudent to make this reference to our last unfortunate experience – there was a murmur of dissatisfaction, or even hostility, as I finished my sentence – but I felt that once I had successfully destroyed this barrier, I would be well on the way toward subjugating the mutiny. The noise subsided in accordance with my plan, and I resumed).

"The familiar appearance of this planet, at all the distances from which we have so far seen it, should not be taken as a cause for rejoicing. That the universe is capable of deception you should remember as clearly as you remember its apparent capacity for vindictiveness. Moreover, it is when fleeing from worlds of advancing solidity that one stumbles into hidden holes, and when still recovering from the damage caused by inimical worlds that one is tempted with illusory visions of peace and security." (I was going quite well at this point, so I decided to stop while still in full flight) "In conclusion I must say that Earth itself, or a planet identical to it in every respect, would be far from ideal as a permanent resting-place. Earth deserves to be investigated, as does any other planet, and we may find that the situation has changed, but under the conditions which forced us to leave it I personally would remain on Earth no more willingly than I would on the White Planet." I almost added, "or a planet identical to it in every respect", for the further benefit of Isobel, Sir Charles and Stanley, but thought better of it.

On the whole, I believe I conducted myself fairly well, considering the pressure I was under.

Stanley, who still held the note, half-crumpled, in his hand, was evidently disillusioned by the interfering complexities in our situation. My admiration of the boy has increased enormously of late; he shares the pleasure I take in spatial change for its own sake, and I think it was because of a classical love of adventure that he originally came with us. He certainly had no political motives – he is too young to understand politics.

"I suppose the most obvious explanation is mass-illusion of some kind," he said, and he sounded distinctly woebegone.

"I think that's quite possible," I replied, addressing the meeting as a whole, and attempting to give the impression that all such cerebral matters were in good hands. Smallpox's fellows had become completely passive, in any case. I think they had been intimidated by all the polysyllables in my speech. I decided to bring the meeting to a close. I asked Sir Charles and Isobel if they had anything to add about our trajectory.

Isobel said, "Of course not." I ignored her impoliteness, and dismissed everyone in a fairly formal manner.

When they had all gone, I sat in an armchair, lit my pipe, and read for a while the volume of my journal which happened to be at hand. This was, of course, in the main assembly-room, sitting in my father's perfect reproduction of the old library under the portrait of Jezebel. I experienced nostalgia of a quite intense, though indefinable, nature. I am just as excited as Stanley by the prospect of a second Earth, and all the fascinating aberrations it could contain, and I, also, find it depressing that we possibly have only our own minds to explore.

My nostalgia may have been for the time when the appearance of this planet would have occasioned neither such down-to-earth speculations nor such unrest among the crew. Or perhaps it was not pure nostalgia; the idea of an Earth without enough alien features to make it quite distinct from the other, the one we left, fills me with the same claustrophobic anxiety I felt when we seemed to be threatened by an expanding space of solid matter. I have no wish to go home: in this way I am no different from the man who made those entries in my journal seven years ago. And yet, reading that earlier volume, I did discern many stylistic differences; I have certainly lost much of my youthful freshness, though my general attitudes seem not to have changed. As I write this new entry, having come to my own room to go to bed, it is as if I were addressing someone outside myself. Never, in those early days, did I feel the need to mention either my father or my wife. It is a sign of weakness, or at least lack of independence, as is the port of which I drank rather too much while sitting in the assembly-room. Anyone who reads this will think that at this point I realised my life would shortly be coming to an end, and I began to keep a record for those who would follow me.

July 13th

No progress now for two days; we are surrounded by fire, presumably at the heart of a sun. The temperature inside the ship has not increased enormously, but the change seems great to me, probably because of my constant fear that we shall be roasted at any moment. I visit Sir Charles's room only when I feel it is absolutely necessary. His window is a furnace of yellow light, at which it is impossible to look directly; even the opposite wall makes me turn away, blinded and in pain, immediately. In the middle of the room, with my eyes tightly shut, I can see that the light is not steady, but seething, or writhing, with great streams of orange and red coiling through it like vast liquid worms. Sir Charles lives in this environment continuously, and assures me, usually in a loud, hearty boom, that he thrives on it. I suspect that Isobel, too, has rarely left the window-room during the last two days. I went in yesterday and found the pair of them actually fornicating on the floor – the intense light confused their forms, and their movements were also mingled with the flashing activity of the fire, but I was in no doubt as to their occupation. Isobel was on top. The sight of her horribly distended buttocks, with Sir Charles's legs (which seemed to be aflame, but which I know to be white and hairy) projecting from beneath, made me feel physically ill, so I hurriedly left the room. It was largely because of this episode that I did not have the heart to make an entry in my journal yesterday.

July 14th

Still in the middle of our fireball. Isobel tells me we aren't moving, though Heaven knows how she can tell. I ventured into the room today, and they were both sitting on the edge of the bed. Sir Charles suggested I press my face against the wall opposite the window, which, naturally, I did, but when the kaleidoscopic play of light began (the blinds were drawn, so whether it was a direct result of this, or some device of their combined minds, I don't know) I turned back into the room, doing my best to appear nonchalant, and began to ask Sir Charles some serious questions about the kind of progress we might be making in our absence, as it were. He seems to think we shall eventually find ourselves back in precisely the situation of three days ago. When he said this Isobel nodded, or rather her head-region shifted in a laconic way suggestive of a nod, before she lay back on the bed, heaving a bored sigh. It is certainly a logical suggestion. I am not sure that this increases its value, but I will base my future plans on the idea of a complete return, if we should fail to move in some perceptible way before my restlessness gets the better of me.

July 15th

I can hardly suppress my exuberance as I record the fact that we have emerged, and not, as Sir Charles had anticipated, a hundred thousand million miles from the planet, but almost upon it. Sir Charles called me into his room this morning, and gestured at the window, which was no longer a mass of flame, but had taken on the appearance of black velvet, and in it was set, very close to us and slightly above, the great shining orb which is Earth and yet, thankfully, is not. As I stared up at the southern ice-cap I suddenly remembered, in vivid detail, a scene from my childhood, in which I lay in bed with my own private window-ledge above me. On the window-ledge I used to keep a globe, of the old wooden type covered with paper, on which were printed the shapes of the continents in contrasted pastel shades. The paper was rubbed thin, and in places the wood shone through, and the cast-iron pedestal on which it stood was devoid of paint and patchy with rust. I had always refused my father's offers of a new, more up-to-date version, remaining loyal, as children will, to my old battered plaything. My father, I think, respected my motives, but I myself had hardly been aware of them, I realised, as I gazed at this new, glorious globe, not from my bed but from my father's space-ship (on the actual bed in the window-room Isobel lay, as if she had not moved since the day before).

It is always good to see space, of whatever kind, almost filled with a huge sphere like this, of constant volume, and not threatening to fill the extra corners, either with matter, or, as Earth itself would, with grasping and holding tentacles. It is just such a space as this, with something and nothing to choose between, and distinct both from home and from those places infinitely far from home, which I, and, I think, most of the others, are looking for.

Sir Charles asked me what I thought we should do. I said we should have an early lunch, which in my case, as I had not risen till long after eleven, would feel more like a late and ample breakfast – a luxury of which I have always been fond. Stanley already had the pots boiling, so after summoning the crew we proceeded straight to the dining-room. The gladness of the occasion, I felt, deserved to be recognised, so on our table we had a particularly good wine, while in the lower part of the dining-room the crew were served with extra helpings of cider. The food was a goulash of some kind created by Stanley, and was delicious as always. We had cheese to follow, but had it not been a special occasion the cheese would have had to be rationed. I hope there is cheese to be had on this planet.

Sir Charles always insists on a moderate amount of conversation while eating, and today, having excused himself for leaning over my plate to get the salt, he began to comment rather drily on my apparent change of mind since the meeting of four days ago. I had seemed rather apprehensive about our "homecoming", but now I was nothing short of jubilant. This caused me to think rather deeply; it had not occurred to me, and though I now recognised the few minutes I had spent in Sir Charles's room as marking the turning-point in my attitude, I was unable satisfactorily to explain the emotions which had brought about the change. This evening, having devoted some time to meditation, I am more in a position to rationalise my reaction, and I have set down a reasonably clear analysis at the beginning of this entry; at lunch-time, however, I had no real answer for Sir Charles, and I confessed as much.

"Do you think it is Earth?" he said.

"No!" I replied, and immediately realised I had said it much too loudly and quickly. "It is not Earth," I added, "if for no other reason, then because of the nature of the space around it." Sir Charles said nothing – his mouth was full of goulash – but he nodded, non-committally. After a few minutes of uninterrupted eating, he began again: "How do you think the oscillation will operate once we have landed?" Once more, he had raised a subject I had so far ignored. Before I was able to find the words for a reply, he answered his own question, in a way: "It seems to me the existence of a solar system is incompatible with space of this kind." This was the full extent of our conversation during the first course. Isobel could not contribute because she no longer eats at our table.

Sir Charles abstained from cheese, remarking ruefully and rather pessimistically on the shortage; he went to sit with Isobel, and appeared to be talking to her continuously as she laboured at the process of transferring food from her plate to her stomach – which process, I must say, is not nearly as disgusting as that which Smallpox, for example, has to go through when eating.

I was left feeling very conspicuous, alone at the high table, and I ate an abnormal amount of cheese, possibly as a result of my embarrassment. I told myself I could eat Sir Charles's share as well. Before leaving the table, he had hinted that the men should be informed of our situation, which, surprisingly perhaps, I had already decided for myself, and as I spread butter on my biscuits and slowly munched the Camembert I did not really need, I was turning over in my mind ideas for an optimistic speech, calculated, if possible, rather more to increase my popularity than the last one I had given.

When I had eaten every piece of cheese on the table (three helpings, in fact, as Stanley hasn't yet quite accepted that Isobel is no longer with us) and the time had come for my speech, I rose from my seat and coughed, at which there was instant silence in the hall. I will not go into the details of what I said; my style of delivery amply compensated for anything which may have been lacking in the way of content, and the hush which followed must have been benevolent, if not actually reverent. I had achieved a certain degree of lyricism, and I have formerly had occasion to notice that Smallpox and his friends respect this particular manner of expression.

If I continue to distinguish myself so well at oratory, and to keep my normally factious audience in so receptive a state, I'm sure I shall become self-confident.

After lunch, I met Sir Charles and Isobel, in the room with the window. The planet was considerably closer, and we have to decide when and where we intend to land. Since Sir Charles's comment on the uncertainty of the oscillation-effect, I had realised that it would be advisable to wait for a few days at least, and to base our decisions on observation of the way space treated our immobility; I suggested, therefore, that we go into orbit around the planet, preferably in a line which would enable us to see England, if it existed. Isobel went to the control-room to make the necessary calculations, promising to call me when the time had come to press the button. Sir Charles brought out his telescope and set it on its tripod, while I returned to my own room.

I found Quincey Horace waiting for me. He is a thoroughly objectionable man, and on this occasion he made no more attempt than ever to curb either his excessive impertinence or his grimly malevolent sense of humour. He had come, he claimed, to remind me of the men's request to be landed in Africa. This was not what I had expected, after the success of my speech in the dining-room, and I fear I may have lost some of my dignity in replying, for I made it quite obvious that I was not pleased. I told him what we intended to do, and said that no exception to the general plan could be made for anybody; we must all wait together for events to develop.

"Smallpox won't like that, sir, indeed he won't," said Horace. I told him that he and Smallpox could both go to hell, and that he in particular should get out of my room. Ignoring my command completely, he went on: "Am I to tell him we'll be spinning round this planet till you see fit to put down in England?" Somewhat perplexed by his deductive powers, as I had said nothing about England, I simply told him again to leave. "I'm sure he'd like to know in advance, sir, if we're going to end up in England, because he has letters to write to various English people, mainly about his adventures in the last place we visited."

"Horace," I said, "you know as well as I do that this planet is not Earth, and the possibility of your finding someone to whom your blackmail will mean something is very remote indeed. The light in which I consider your request will depend largely on your behaviour and the extent of the moderation it will shortly undergo. Now return to your quarters."

"Thank you, sir. I'm sure you'll find the conduct of me and my colleagues perfectly satisfactory." He went.

Naturally, I found this interview very disturbing. Horace is not only unpleasant, but also quite versatile, and by no means stupid. The style of speech he had adopted, obviously based on his idea of simple thuggery, was of course totally false: in fact, I have never known him to communicate without putting on some performance such as this. He is a cultured man, and I have never understood his constantly demeaning himself by associating with the likes of Smallpox. Another perpetual theme in his acting is that of the unintelligence and general baseness which would lend credibility to this identification with his inferiors, and now I find it more bewildering than ever that he should continue to sustain the pretence. He is acting in direct opposition to his own interests; it is unlikely that he genuinely accepts the simple-minded theory that our destination is Earth itself, and yet he is trying to get himself marooned in the mysterious mock-Africa presented by the planet: and even if it were no illusion and the continent is Africa in every sense of the word, it would hardly be the place most likely to provide him with a congenial future existence. He must know that, with a mind as efficient as his, he has no need of the political asylum presumably expected there by the others, and that, given a certain degree of ambition, which I feel sure he could at least simulate, he would be well-equipped for a fruitful career in England.

I was still puzzling over these contradictions when, later in the afternoon, I was summoned to the control-room by Isobel. She had ascertained that 5.27 p.m. was the time to go into orbit, if we were to follow the line I had stipulated. It was then three minutes past five, and I was faced with twenty-four minutes of private conversation with Isobel, a prospect I viewed with profound misgivings. I began to talk in a technical, business-like way, but fortunately she saw that the effort would shortly prove too much for me, and presumably foreseeing embarrassment as clearly as I did myself, she made her excuses and left. Before going she gave me the accurate timepiece which she had used in her calculations, and by which I was to know when the adjustment to our course should be made.

So I sat down to wait in the pilot's chair, feeling intense relief and a sense of security greater than any I had experienced for many weeks. It was the first time I had been into the control-room since that regrettable incident on the White Planet, and I was very pleased to find that no association had been established in my mind between the place and the occurrence; my sensations were not mixed with any sombre colour or unpleasant aftertaste. I have always liked the control-room more than any other room in the ship. I had thought this was simply a consequence of its being Isobel's domain; I have described in other volumes the many hours I used to spend in there with her, planning our itinerary (which was really just a pleasant way of passing the time, as it rarely made any foreseeable difference which angle we decided to make in our course) and sometimes, when the impracticality of this pursuit grew stale, happily coupling on whatever uncaring bank of machinery presented itself. But now I found that not even these normally painful memories had made any impression on my mind which could alter my conception of the control-room. I laid my hand on one of the cold surfaces, thinking of the increase in its temperature we had sometimes caused, and I was aroused rather than depressed by the reflection; contemplation of the degrading methods I would have to adopt in order to assuage my lust merely served to increase my sense of inner peace – I think I have a basic stability which allows me to enjoy any kind of self-sufficiency.

Of course, it was my environment which enabled me to benefit from this source of strength and independence; I recognised the room's influence in this as I had recognised it in my sudden lack of concern over Horace's paradox. My sympathy with the room was so great that I began to think I had not been regretting lost happiness even when shrinking from confinement with Isobel, three and a half minutes before; I had feared that her presence would compromise, in a perfectly simple way, my relationship with my surroundings.

I will attempt to describe, as I think I have never done before, the room which can bring me such peace of mind. It is fairly small, about twelve feet by ten feet by seven, and the central space in which the pilot can move is further reduced by the instruments and control-panels which jut out from the walls. There is only one chair, comfortably upholstered with black leather; this is bolted to the floor in front of the most important set of controls, those relating to position and direction. I can never look at this panel without marvelling at the simplicity of my father's ideas. In his youth he was a philosopher and poet, achieving great things in both fields, and, unusually, receiving the recognition he deserved; it was not until he began to see the need for a space-ship, in his late fifties, that he turned to practical science, and I have always inclined to the belief that he designed this machine on aesthetic rather than purely scientific principles. There is nothing in the control-room by which it is possible to measure distance or velocity in absolute terms. Instead, there is a large screen in the central panel showing an assortment of black and grey shapes on a white background, roughly corresponding, we have found, to the view from Sir Charles's window. It is necessary, before anything about the ship's progress can be computed, to adjust the position of a small red arrow which is the only feature of a secondary screen superimposed on the first, so that the arrow's point follows the centre of one of the shadow-like shapes. When this has been done, all states and movements of the ship are expressed as if in relation to whatever body, semi-body, or other variation from the general condition of space, is represented by that particular shape. This afternoon the screen was dominated by one large circle, at the centre of which the little red arrow pointed in a more than usually assertive manner. The arrow is the only brightly-coloured thing in the room, floor and ceiling being covered with black carpet and paint, against which the various functioning parts of the room cannot make much visual impact, as they are predominantly of very dark varnished wood and a particularly dull kind of stainless steel. The way in which the eye is drawn to the arrow sometimes makes me think of English street-plans, on which a similar device is used, though the function of such static arrows is to make the observer feel he is 'here', whereas I, observer of this screen, find satisfaction in the awareness that I am constantly outside its field of vision, and that mine is the only place which could never conceivably appear.

The only way of keeping the arrow in the exact centre of any shape is to set a direct course toward the body in question; it is possible for the ship to do this automatically, but I used to enjoy operating the controls by hand, shifting the arrow from part to part of the screen, making minute alterations to our course, and observing the sometimes monumental changes in speed which resulted. I could also sit for hours simply watching the enormously slow movements of the configurations on the screen, becoming convinced that this two-dimensional version of space was a much truer representation than the absurdly detailed and spectacular things which Sir Charles spends so much time watching through his telescope. None of us knows a great deal about the element through which we are travelling, and similarly our experience of the ship has been a continuous and tentative experiment – there is more outside our control than within it, and we can but speculate as to how much the ship itself does, and how much is done to it. Isobel claims to have comprehensive knowledge of the engines, and her analyses and treatment of situations involving merely the power we generate certainly tend to be effective; she had made an adjustment to the engines this afternoon, which, she told me, was directly responsible for the great reduction in our speed relative to that of the planet. It was at sixteen minutes past five that I realised how important this deceleration had been, and the sudden knowledge caused me a certain degree of irritation. I used to be quite happy in my acceptance of Isobel's mechanical wisdom, but my attitude has changed since the White Planet, and I find myself doubting even her central thesis of the moment, that the engines sustained slight damage at the time of her own mutilation, and that repairs are necessary if the ship is to operate at the "maximum efficiency" which she seems to think is a possibility.

I fear I am beginning to ramble; this is neither a description of the control-room nor a straightforward narration of my afternoon. I must concentrate on the button I was going to press, which did actually occupy my mind, or at least hold my eyes, for much of the time I spent in the control-room. Like all the other buttons designed for active interference with our flight, it is a cylindrical stud of black plastic, set in a socket in the stainless steel. It is labelled with the same beautiful simplicity as the rest; "ORBIT-ENTER" is printed on a small enamel plate above it.

I was thinking about the electrical system beneath this button – which must, I reasoned, be either impossibly complex or as simple as the button itself – and also wondering if controls like this could conceivably malfunction (for if it is true that the engines are failing, it will be the first case of faulty equipment we have ever experienced), when, at twenty-four minutes past five, I became conscious of a growing need to urinate. For two and a half minutes I persisted in my resolve to postpone appeasement of this need; but then, when only thirty seconds remained in which to prepare for my task, the need became so pressing that I felt postponement was no longer a practical possibility. Fortunately, there is a toilet in the passage just outside the control-room, so I hurried out with all possible speed. Even so, when I returned I was several seconds late; I lost no more time in pressing the button, hoping that no great difference had been made to our course over the planet's surface. Our speed immediately decreased to zero. I looked at the screen, but no change was visible in the first few seconds, so I came away.

I have now been writing my journal for more than five hours, both before and after dinner, and I think this entry is more detailed and more introspective than anything I have written before. Possibly this is a result of the extreme excitement I feel at being so close to the planet, in which case my urge to express myself is simply energetic and quite commendable; but I am more inclined to think that I have been turned in upon myself by recent events in my relationship with Isobel. I have noticed a worrying number of changes in my day-to-day activity which parallel, in various ways, the changes in my sexual life.

I will make an effort to spend more time on the actual management of my existence, and less on the recording of it.

July 16th

Perhaps thinking that it would help me to keep the resolution I set down in yesterday's entry, I today took Horace into my confidence. Communication of a few basic thoughts and speculations to another person will certainly reduce the need for introspection, and Horace is not such a bizarre choice as at first may appear. I cannot use Sir Charles or

Isobel in this way, having almost completely lost contact with both of them. Horace is at least intelligent, and the blankness of his personality – even my intense antipathy toward him – will aid rather than hinder him in the work of impersonating a page in my journal. He must accept whichever of my thoughts I choose to give him, fully and uncritically.

I was not prepared, however, for the complete lack of reaction he exhibited today. I told him we were still in the same orbit, and gave him my view of the oscillation-process and what its effects would probably be in this case. His only comment was that he would tell Smallpox; I could, I suppose, have predicted this spreading of the information, but I had evidently expected something different, for I found it rather disturbing.

We have seen a shape resembling the British Isles, partially obscured by clouds and somewhat further to our left than we had intended.

July 17th

I know it isn't Earth. In relation to an infinite universe, we have not moved at all; in relation to a universe which is merely vast, we have perhaps been moving in a tiny circle, or a tiny curve with the same effect; however, my senses tell me that we have been travelling at high speeds for ten years. Having travelled in this way at random, I find it easy to accept the conclusion, fallacious though it may be, that we are more likely to find a place identical to our starting-point than to find our starting-point itself. Yet a part of my mind is treating this planet as Earth – and in an obstinate, uncompromising way. I would erase this rebellious piece of knowledge if I could locate it. I am unable to say how my mind sustains this contradiction without losing the stability of total consistency.

I expressed all this, and more, to Horace. He did not react. I am writing it in my journal out of a sense of pure duty.

Isobel and Sir Charles are not affected, as far as I can see, by my strange kind of doubt; Isobel attaches much significance to the position of the British Isles, which I could explain, but I do not feel inclined to.

She expects some kind of spatial shift very soon. I am both expecting and not expecting it

July 18th

We are still in the same orbit. If there is no change by tomorrow night, we intend to begin preparations for a landing.

I will not write anything more for a few days

July 30th

I have re-read my last three entries, and I find them utterly strange, as if they were the work of some other hand; but this is a common illusion among those who express themselves in prose. I was in a very different state of mind two weeks ago, and it is only now, in retrospect, that I begin to realise how confused I was. My sudden desire to communicate with Horace should have told me that all was not well. Of the many changes which have taken place since that time, by no means the least is that we have lost Horace, and I am unable to see his departure as anything but a blessing – a blessing, moreover, whose effect will be as lasting as it is now complete, for we shall never see him again.

I must not confuse my narrative with introductory paragraphs. When I awoke on the morning of July 19th, we were no longer in orbit; we were again approaching the planet, at the speed to which we have always returned after fluctuations caused by space, and it seemed that we would be able to regain our orbit in another four days.

It was at this point that my reaction against Horace began. Our association had developed so quickly, he was in the habit of entering my study, unasked, at a specific time in the afternoon, and sitting mutely in an armchair while I explained the situation, aloud, but as if talking to myself. When he came in on the nineteenth, however, I was aware for the first time of the resentment his privileged position aroused in me. I looked at him as if I didn't know what he had come for, and presently he went away.

I did not see Isobel or Sir Charles at all on the 20th., 21st. or 22nd., and Horace did not return. My only companion during this time was Stanley, who had been told, he said, to take meals for both Isobel and Sir Charles to Sir Charles's room. Not wishing to undergo again the embarrassment of solitude in the dining-room, I asked him to bring my meals to my study, and also invited him to eat with me, if he so desired. He seemed very grateful; I have always known that he sees me as a substitute for his father, and has as hearty a respect for me as I have for him: also, he must have been very lonely during the few weeks before this – an experience he has had many times in the past, although we have tended not to show him any sympathy. In any case, he responded eagerly to my first conscious suggestion of the intimacy which had always been possible, and I began to enjoy the increase in confidence which inevitably followed this transfer of affection, from the intolerable cynic to the youth whose natural innocence had been much increased by the spending of his formative years in a space-ship. He is trying to grow a moustache, and has so far achieved the kind of downy upper lip which Isobel had when I first knew her.

The only other visitor I had in this period was Smallpox, who blundered in at Horace's customary time on the twenty-second. He was in such a state that he actually overturned a small table, and was quite unable to write, so of course he could not tell me the purpose of his visit, urgent though it obviously was. I gently guided him to the door, trying to disregard his grunts and gesticulations, though the degree of disgust they excited in me was extraordinary. Stanley, who was present, having taken to conversing with me in the afternoons, thought I had been unnecessarily harsh. However, I am becoming accustomed to Stanley's compassion, and have learned to treat it critically, for although it is undeniably a virtue, he takes it to extremes on far too many occasions.

We remained on course toward the planet for the predicted four days, after which I felt that my attitudes were sufficiently constant to survive even the repeated ritual of going into orbit. On the morning of the twenty-third, I walked quite confidently into Sir Charles's room and asked him how we were placed in relation to the planet; I did not need to ask, for the world was again near-filling the window. I found, to my slight dismay, that the bed had been moved so that its foot faced the window, and so that the sleeper could absorb the contents of the window in any moment he happened to wake; and the sheets were white with the planet's glow, as Isobel raised from them the upper half of her body. Sir Charles did have something useful to report, however: he said that if we had remained in the same orbit as five days before, we would now be on the opposite side of the planet to the one we were at present observing. I saw that South America was the central feature of the window; I stared at him, with, perhaps, an expression of disbelief; he returned my gaze in a way which suggested strongly that he had suspicions about the course we had been setting before. Not wishing to continue this line of thought, I turned to Isobel and asked her when would be the time to go into orbit, if we wanted, as before, to be as close as possible to England. She drew the blankets up toward her breast as she replied, and turned her serious-face to the wall on the other side of the bed:

"Almost immediately."

I went down to the control-room unaccompanied, feeling that this occasion rather lacked the resonance of the last, and that the remorse brought upon me by my former incompetence had been quite unnecessary. I toyed with the orbit-button for a few seconds, and then, for want of a better time, I pressed it. Everything was as before, except for the insistent unreality of this second run-through, sufficient to disturb even my new-found security.

It was possibly at this time that my mind, though not, I think, my conscious mind, saw the beginning of a process which was eventually to lead to the idea at the centre of this day's narrative. The process accelerated as a result of our oscillation, over the next few days, between the two virtually identical, and yet opposed, orbits we had entered. Either orbit would have taken us over North Africa, through the centre of Europe, down again through Asia, and past the tip of South America. However, if our orbits were in fact two, they were at almost exactly 180 degrees to each other, and while we should have been passing the Russian side of the Arctic in one, we should have been passing the American side of the Antarctic in the other. I gained all this knowledge from extensive observation in Sir Charles's room, where I spent many comfortable hours in the wooden chair near the window, concentrating on the telescope and remaining unaffected by the conversation which went on behind me, usually in undertones and proceeding from the bed. I slept, of course, in my own bedroom, where Stanley had occupied the floor with a pile of his blankets from the galley, and where I would seek relief from the puzzling and increasingly engrossing affairs of the day, in discussion of lighter subjects with Stanley; I discovered that he had been spending time in the library, and had become a keen student of literature, and I happily listened to, criticised and sometimes changed his surprisingly perceptive views on poetry.

All the unpredictable, enormous and (I find) not quite credible changes in our position have so far taken place at night. For a long time now we have all led a completely diurnal existence; only on very few occasions during the last ten years have I found it necessary to keep watch at night, and even on these occasions we have been careful not to lose sight of the twenty-four hour system deriving from noon on the day we left Earth, and the setting of our electric clocks at that time. I did not, at any time during the week I am now describing, seriously consider the idea of staying up all night. It was enough to know that, if we awoke one morning to find ourselves facing, say, Yugoslavia, and I watched, for more or less twelve hours, our perfectly natural course around the sphere, we would next morning be either back in approximately the same position above Yugoslavia, or traversing the Pacific as at bedtime on the previous night; in other words, we had either remained in the same orbit, or had shifted to the other, with which we were equally familiar. We were rather more than twenty thousand miles from the planet, so it revolved completely while we were describing any orbit – the first, the second, or a combination of the two. Isobel had planned this, she said, in order to simplify things; and her planning proved successful, for I was not confused even by the alternating day and night on the planet's surface. My imagination was free to work on the simple issue of oscillation.

The idea, which, as I have already said, is really the central theme of my entry today, developed fairly slowly; I experienced no flash of inspiration. I was contemplating the existence of both orbits, I remember, late in the afternoon of the twenty-seventh, and wondering whether they were simultaneous, or actually alternate, in precisely the way I sensed them. It seemed not to matter very much, as my consciousness had so far sustained a kind of consistency which was quite comprehensible to me. However, I found it intriguing that if the orbits existed simultaneously, there was a ghost-ship of some sort, at a point almost exactly opposite the one we occupied, wherever we happened to be and whatever our relation to previous, present and subsequent orbits. I, personally, attached no great significance to this possible second ship, but it occurred to me that others would see its existence as inevitable, concrete, and, in short, as a matter of fact. I stored the knowledge for future reference, and withdrew my eye from the end of the telescope; I found it impossible as I did so to suppress the loud cough, though I suspected it was becoming a habit, which had been part of this situation's ritual from the beginning. It was a way of warning Sir Charles and Isobel that I would shortly turn round.

No such warning was needed on this occasion, so it must have sounded all the more ridiculous. Isobel was sitting in a chair, positioned so that she could only have been looking through the window or watching me; Sir Charles was on the other side of the room, cleaning his revolver.

"Why are you doing that?" I said. He did not reply, but merely exhaled more deeply than usual, while concentrating on his work. This was always his reaction to enquiries when he was contemplating physical violence.

Isobel, who still faced me, answered for him. "We think your treatment of the crew has been characteristically inefficient."

"How do you know about my treatment of the crew?"

"Stanley."

This was displeasing; her first remark had seemed alarmingly ambiguous, and if Stanley was involved in this situation (though I suspected that his role in it was perfectly innocent) I could consider myself friendless. Wishing to ask Stanley about this straight away, I said I would dress for dinner, and left, trying not to avoid looking at the revolver.

In my study, Quincey Horace was again waiting, and his presence produced in me an almost nauseating sensation with which I have become quite familiar recently, associated with exactly-repeated experiences. His mission was the same as it had been the last time I had come upon him unexpectedly, and our relationship had reverted to the overt antipathy of that time. His mask was rather different; no longer the illiterate bully, or the cold and silent mind-doctor of our more intimate period, he was instead a gangster of a smoother type, with expertly feigned sophistication and even altruism. His real purpose (like everything else in the ship, it seemed) had become more urgent and intense, and it was obvious that he intended me to feel the threat of the crew's numerical superiority, rather as I had felt the presence of the gun in Sir Charles's room.

I was quite nervous, but I found a certain degree of comfort in the pretence, initiated by me, that I was still using him as an ear for my reflections on our general situation. I told him about the second ship whose half-existence I had guessed at, and his face took on for a moment the unsurprised blank which had always so far accompanied his listening to my monologues. It transpired, however, that this attentive imperturbability was now only a part of his assumed sensitivity. After waiting politely for the end of my speech, he reacted in a way which suggested intelligent appraisal of my last statement without detracting from the menace implicit in his own earlier suggestions and demands.

"This would mean that we have twenty-nine more people to think," he said.

"Yes," was all I could manage, being briefly disconcerted by this unfamiliar thought.

"And we would have to take their views into account on the question of a landing-site…"

"Are you assuming," I interrupted, with more dignity and a measure of imperiousness, "that everyone in the ship has an equal vote?" I was evading the subject of the extra people, because I needed more time to think it over. I suppose I had assumed that, even if this second ship truly existed in some way, communication with it must be impossible. There would be a principle built into the oscillation-system which locked an entity in its own strictly limited volume of space throughout any particular vibration, or perhaps (an idea which occurred to me while still speaking to Horace) slipped it into a third, very remote part of space as soon as it began to seek a second. My procrastination tactics worked; as I completed my simultaneous thought and speech, there was a knock at the door, and Stanley came in, bearing my dinner on a tray. I had not fulfilled my spoken intention to dress, but in my own room, out of sight of Sir Charles and Isobel, to do so would have been superfluous.

"For example," I continued, "are we going to ask Stanley what he thinks?"

"About what, sir?" said Stanley.

"About possible landing-sites, Stanley. Mr Horace favours Africa, but I prefer England."

"I don't think I have any opinion, sir, but I'm prepared to accept your decision." I raised an eyebrow at Horace, who had got up from his chair and was preparing to leave.

He was unimpressed. "Your servant's fidelity is admirable", he said. He went, again.

The interview had been relatively comfortable. I tucked a napkin into my collar, feeling quite satisfied, and turned to my spaghetti with meatballs, beginning as I did so my customary mealtime conversation with Stanley. He was sprawled in the armchair Horace had vacated, and he was ostentatiously smoking a cigarette. Our talk was as easy and pleasant as ever: not only did I become convinced, after only three or four mouthfuls, of his complete innocence in the affair of Sir Charles's unexpected knowledge and command of the situation; I was also positively stimulated by his ingenuousness, and was inspired, despite my general feeling of comfort and relaxation, to compensate for the transparent quality of his discourse with an effortless, secret bout of mental activity – activity so fruitful that it at last produced the final form of my idea, which had been so long developing and to which I have already twice referred in this entry.

I am tired, and must go to bed soon; I will try to be as efficient in narrating what remains as I was in precipitating the events themselves, as soon as I had wiped the sauce of the meatballs from my lips. The meeting was held within half an hour, and Horace, Smallpox and the rest were even more cooperative than I had expected. Possibly this was because of my confidence and determination, though Sir Charles's gun, laid on the assembly-room table, may also have played a part; possibly they were abnormally mindless in their acceptance of the ghost-ship idea, or excited into extra stupidity by my promise that my second self, captain of the ghost-ship, would abdicate in Horace's favour when (I did not say "if") they arrived; in any case, they agreed more or less quietly to all my suggestions, and undertook to begin preparations immediately for their departure in the small excursion-craft.

The contribution of Sir Charles and Isobel, and indeed of Stanley, to this meeting (after the initial hard sound of the gun on the table) was total silence. In fact, none of the three has said a word to me about the matter since I first raised it, not even now that the men have gone and we are preparing to leave our orbit. Stanley's silence, I presume, is respectful, though I am sure he disapproves instinctively of my action; that of Sir Charles and Isobel is more difficult to explain, unless it is simply an extension of their general policy of coldness toward me.

All arrangements were made during Horace's private interviews with me, between the night of the twenty-seventh and this morning. At the general meeting he had seemed to become an obsequious fool, thus conforming with the other twenty-four, who had never before been quite so uniform; and he sustained this role, with only one or two maliciously intended lapses, until this morning's exodus. My statement about my other self had been a probe to discover the depth of Horace's new stupidity, and I continued to probe, with promises of increasing implausibility, during our private meetings. Perhaps the climax of the series was a suggestion, accepted as unthinkingly as all the others, that when they had brought the other ship down in Africa he should write to me, using the address, "Captain Lionel Jaffa, M.A. (Cantab.), London".

But I must describe the departure itself, and then have done. It was about tea-time today when we all met in the assembly-room, the twenty-five who were to go standing together just inside the door, silent and listless, perhaps from fear; and we four who were to stay, also silent, but for different reasons, sitting at the far end of the long table. Some of the men carried their belongings, in suitcases and small cloth bags; others were incapable of carrying, and one even had to be supported by his colleagues. The variety of dress was extraordinary: the dominant characters, Horace and Smallpox included, still wore their overalls; but some of the others, out of a bizarre sense of occasion, had put on their "best clothes". Waeldermann, in particular, had produced a hitherto unseen outfit of remarkably fine quality, complete with white bow-tie. I took my leave of one or two men personally, not, I hasten to add, affectionately, but perhaps with a certain degree of respect for the manner in which they had done their duty over the ten years of our voyage. They responded, if at all, sullenly, and I felt regret, briefly, for the loyalty they had so completely abandoned. Horace was among those I ignored, though I was resisting a fairly powerful urge to bid him an ironic farewell.

When this ritual was over, Stanley distributed from a cardboard box on the table the packed lunches he had prepared. It was this more than anything which aroused in me the emotions associated with parting. I remembered all the happy occasions when I myself had eaten from such a grease-stained paper bag, and I compared my excursions with the endless trip my crew would shortly be undertaking; my assurance that it would take them less than a day to reach the other ship, like many another of the excessively contrived arguments I had used in, unnecessarily, persuading Horace to go, had taken on an uncomfortably gruesome quality.

We filed out of the room and turned into the passage which leads past the cellars. Few of the men had ever had occasion to go down there, as we have rarely used the small excursion-craft, and it was very strange to see them all shuffling down the passage at once, in a long single line. Horace's overalls looked particularly incongruous against the dark oak panelling and the rich carpet. We soon came, however, to the launching-bay of the small excursion-craft; here all the surfaces were metal, and the light brilliant, and it was Waeldermann, along with his overdressed companions, who seemed not to be quite at home. Horace now blended perfectly with his surroundings, and he seemed to be conscious of this as he strode over to the craft and opened the door. Sir Charles, Isobel, Stanley and I stood nearby as the men climbed in, through the door which Horace still held open, and we watched their faces appearing in the windows, ranged along the side of the craft as in a bus.

Horace was the last to get in, and before he did so he turned to me.

"See you again," he said, his face twisted in a fatuous grin which I suppose he intended to make him seem debonair.

They were ready to leave, so we four retired behind the glass wall of the air-lock, and after I had closed the door and drained the air-lock I pressed the button which opened the great hatch in the side of the ship. The planet's curve appeared at the edge of the hole, bathed in sunlight. I think I saw a hand waving in one of the windows of the small excursion-craft; then they took off, and I closed the hatch as quickly as possible.

That was eight hours ago. We have now left our orbit – in fact I interrupted my writing, soon after starting this page, in order to perform the operation – and we are approaching the surface of the planet. If all goes well, and if there are no spatial shifts in the meantime, we should land in the equivalent of England sometime tomorrow afternoon. We should have been, and should now be, more apprehensive about the possibility that we might oscillate away from the course we have planned; if we found ourselves back in the same orbit, a disastrous reunion with the small excursion-craft would be virtually inevitable; and yet the departure of the crew has somehow erased the logic upon which this fear could have been built. They have travelled into another phase, I am sure, which can never again coincide with the one where we remain. I cannot imagine how I know, but I also know that they have removed, by their determined and apparently unconcerned quest after others of themselves, the entire effectiveness of the oscillation-system, for at least as long as it takes us to establish our independence of their search and its object's temptations. Our – or perhaps I should say "my"; in fact, I should have been speaking only for myself throughout this rather garbled paragraph – my belief in the temperamental nature of this space is parallel to my belief that it is not Earth below us: I should be apprehensive about landing on an unknown planet, disturbing in its aspect and the echoes it awakes in my mind, yet this, I suddenly know, from my long-stored knowledge of oscillatory space, has been swept aside by the idea that the rest of my life may be going to be spent on this planet, and I am about to climb into my bed for the last time ever on this ship. The crew's silent rebellion against the state of things turned the planet into Earth as it turned the space into Earth's space, and the planet will remain precisely Earth, at least until we land on it.

As for the crew, I should think their destination will be far from what they desire, and it will certainly be beyond their control; Isobel, under my instructions, adapted the machinery of the small excursion-craft so that it is capable only of a rendezvous with the mythical second ship, which it would meet, in theory, by following an orbit intersecting that of the ship at the correct point. Even if one of the crew knows more of engineering than I imagine, they cannot land on the planet, or travel as far as the replica of Mars which no doubt appears in the appropriate place, in a craft as small as the one at their disposal. Unless space, affronted by their negligent daring, has transported them into a completely alien zone, they will probably continue in the same orbit, perhaps with another course in alternation, indefinitely. When they have eaten their packed lunches they will soon cease to be aware of their surroundings, for they have no other provisions.

I suppose what I have done might be considered inhumane; this is possibly why none of my three companions, not even Stanley, has spoken an unnecessary word to me since the crew's departure, though I am sure they share my sudden rather eerie loneliness. But I had no love for the men. My conscience has not disturbed me, and is not likely to; and my lengthy exploration of space has convinced me that I have no higher judge to answer to.

July 31st

Another explanation of Stanley's coldness has occurred to me, and it is more unpleasant than the last in its implications. I have known for a long time that Sir Charles takes a dim view of what he calls my 'eccentricity', but I think Stanley has begun to consider me actually unbalanced – and for all I know this unjust suspicion, which he is, of course, far too respectful to mention to me, may have had some effect on Sir Charles and Isobel. I awoke in the middle of the night, full of a dark, unidentified fear (probably the aftermath of some forgotten dream) and I turned in order to speak to Stanley, who was lying in his sleeping-bag on the floor. I could not see whether he was awake or asleep, though I got the impression he had raised himself to a sitting position and was watching me in the dark. In any case, I realised that I could not speak to him of anything as intimate as my fear; he was keeping his distance, as if from a potentially dangerous animal.

I have nothing else to write. We shall be landing in a little over two hours.

August 1st

It is not Earth. It is a frightful place.

We landed on Hampstead Heath, which I recognised at once, though it was the middle of the night, because we were only a hundred yards or so from West Heath Road, where Isobel's home used to be. The first thing I noticed when we were descending the steps of the ship (rashly leaving our suits behind, as we had seen the trees through the window) was the sweet, evocative smell of dead leaves. I had not experienced this smell for more than ten years, but I knew at once that our calendar had to be put forward about three months, as our clock had been put forward six hours. The moon was almost full, and the night was frosty.

Until we establish what month, or months, it is, I will continue to speak of "August". I am treating the eighteen-hour period, at the end of which we landed, as a whole day.

We were all more or less overcome; it is strange to be plunged suddenly, after so long an absence, into an atmosphere familiar enough not to have been missed. We showed our emotion in different ways. I managed to retain my dignity, but Sir Charles and Isobel were filled with some particularly primitive urge, for they embraced each other with more passion than I had ever previously observed in their intercourse. Stanley, reverting to the Red Indian ways of his very early childhood, began to scurry about in the thick carpet of brown and black leaves, and it soon became obvious that he was gathering wood in order to build a fire.

Being still unreconciled to the sight of Sir Charles's perversions, I wandered off into the more densely packed trees surrounding the clearing we had half found, half made. I had no conscious purpose; I simply went from feature to feature of the intimately-known ground, climbing an occasional small tree, crossing and re-crossing a stream, and at one point urinating into a large, gnarled bole.

When I returned to the ship Stanley had lit his fire, which was huge, considering the time its preparation had taken him, and he was cooking sausages over it in a frying-pan. I sat down gladly by his side, for I had not realised before how cold it was. None of us wanted to go back into the ship, and Stanley, in the intervals between necessary ministrations to the sausages, industriously rushed off to build a second fire in a grassy spot he had found a few hundred yards away, from which the ship could not be seen, and where, he said, he intended to sleep.

Sir Charles and Isobel were sitting on the charred trunk of a tree which the ship had felled in its descent. They silently accepted, and ate, two sausages each. Then, in one of Stanley's periodic absences, they suddenly rose and walked away, arm in arm, out of the circle of firelight. For a moment I thought they were going into the woods to copulate, but then it occurred to me that they would not be coming back. I almost called after them, something inane about having to repair the engines, but after a pause for thought I let them go. When Stanley came back he did not remark on their absence, and indeed he has not mentioned them since then, and they have not returned.

We finished the sausages between us, and then when the fire had died down we went into the ship, got our sleeping-bags, a few bottles of red wine, and Stanley's guitar, and walked over to the place where the other fire was burning. It was a small depression in the ground, bounded by grassy banks, and in its centre the fire was still burning strongly. When we lay down on either side of the fire, we could see nothing but the rim of the basin we were in.

I don't know how Stanley learned to play the guitar, or where he heard all the songs he sings. He sang several melancholy songs to me last night, mainly folk-songs, I think; I remember only one of them, a particularly affecting one which began "Black is the colour of my true love's hair". But I have never had much of an ear for music, and I am unable to criticise his performance of the songs, though I appreciate the purity of his beautifully controlled alto voice.

When the wine and song finally began to close our eyes, we lay back in our sleeping-bags, still not talking, for the strange familiarity of the atmosphere had from the beginning prohibited any protracted interruption of its peace; and we went to sleep, staring up at the equally familiar stars, through at least some of which we must have travelled.

It was during the night that the horrors began. I suddenly became aware that I was in the middle of a powerful, hideous dream. It was not a dream in which things happened, it was simply consciousness of a state, and it obviously had something to do with my rather limited experience of the White Planet. I was suspended in complete whiteness, with no way of telling whether I was vertical or horizontal. And I was not allowed any dimness or vagueness of sensation, such as is usual in dreams, for I was constantly and vividly aware of my dreadful, deathlike situation, and even more urgently aware of my most undeathlike need to be out of it. There was nothing I could do: every muscle in my body was frozen in a state of utter relaxation, my eyes were held open, and if I was breathing I was not aware of it. Sometimes the whiteness seemed to me to be nothingness, through which I was perhaps travelling, at a speed which preserved my body in its limp rigidity; at other times, I thought I was encased in solid matter – indeed, that I was a part of it, for it filled every crevice and blocked every moving part of my form. I realised that both space and solid had inexplicable qualities, but both filled me, in the same way as real space and real solidity, with my recurring horror of the infinite. One infinity pressed on me, threatening to crush out my life; the other dragged at my flesh, as if it would pull me apart and tear consciousness out of my body. The alternation was slow. I don't know how long the dream lasted, but my sense of time was undoubtedly extended, every moment having many times its real length, though the whole period has since been foreshortened by memory. I could not think for long; apart from the whiteness, the only thing in my head was the constant struggle to move, a struggle which no observer would have seen, as it involved nothing but my will. Towards the end even my will failed, and I simply stared at the whiteness, imagining an expression for my face: planting a gape of horror on features which were no doubt blank.

The first and only exterior event in this dream, at the very end, was the sudden appearance of another sense, and an outburst, from some direction I could not identify, of shrill, apparently female screams. I lay still for a little longer, listening in fascination to a terror which was possibly greater than mine, and then I realised that the voice was Stanley's, and that I could move again. I stumbled to my feet, and in the first second, when I was halfway to Stanley and had begun to see dawn-produced colours which, strangely, came as no relief, another sense made itself known with a violent, agonising pain, from the top of my head to my testicles; for a moment I thought I had been cut in two down the middle, then I collapsed in the ashes of our burnt-out fire.

The blackness lasted far too short a time. I awoke to find Stanley's face above me, unnaturally white, with green tinges about the eyes, lips and cheekbones. He had been anxiously trying to revive me, by loosening my clothing, and he showed relief when I opened my eyes. He was sweating, and muttered something inaudible. But his pallor was not all due to his anguish. When I could at last climb to the rim of the basin, I saw a grotesquely alien landscape, still recognisable as Hampstead Heath, but distorted by bizarre effects of light and colouring. The sky was livid violet, as if an unknown kind of electric storm were about to break, and everything had a gleaming halo of some strange, bright colour: the sick, heightened green of the grass was highlighted with blue, and over Stanley's features green played as it does on the head of a mallard.

The pain had gone. It was, I think, another reminder of the White Planet, though I myself had not experienced the pain and mutation when we were actually there. Stanley's screams, I presumed, were a result of an experience similar to mine. I could see no evidence of damage on either of our bodies. So the pain was put into our heads, by the White Planet, either when we were visiting it or when we felt the pain itself.

I could find not even as flimsy an explanation as this for the visual phenomenon we were now faced with. But whatever it was, it seemed to signify that the morning had come, so I felt that however crippled I was by the dream and the pain, I should do something; action would perhaps help to subdue the planet. I turned to Stanley, and spoke for the first time. My voice seemed to be coming from miles away, through a series of closed doors.

"I'm going to call on Isobel, Stanley."

He tried to conceal the fear this announcement caused him. He knew that I would want to go on my own, and he was frightened at the prospect of solitude in this weird environment, but he assented, haltingly, and his voice was as tinny and remote as mine.

There was no need to tell him what I meant by "Isobel". We had both almost forgotten the twisted, secondary Isobel who had walked off with Sir Charles the night before. I meant the Isobel I would find if I found the house on West Heath Road; an Isobel who might prove to be more vile and alien than the other, but whom I was determined to meet, hoping to rediscover in her some of the things for which I had loved the other, before she had been changed.

So far I have not succeeded in finding her. My description of this day's search will be vague and incomplete, and I shall probably not be able to explain exactly what prevented me from reaching Isobel, because I believe I saw her, and my incomprehensible failure to cross the ground between us, or rather, my memory of that failure (though I still seem to be living the experience) has me trembling constantly as I try, back in our relatively homely basin, to start writing about it.

As I left the edge of the basin, and set out across the Heath, I felt absurd rather than fearful. Stanley was watching me, standing quite still; we were both solemnly treating this as a mission of the utmost peril, when in fact it was only a walk of a hundred yards, across what might have been, and in one sense definitely was, our local piece of parkland. But then I looked over my shoulder again, and Stanley had disappeared. He had returned to the basin, he told me later, in order to relight the fire, as he had suddenly felt unbearably cold, and had been unable, not only because of the cold, to continue watching. I was alone, and I began to be terribly afraid, because I seemed to be more completely alone than I actually was. The extraordinary sense-impressions of the place began to take over my whole awareness, for they were not restricted to the sense of sight: the grass beneath my feet felt like so many slender blades of glass, not quite strong enough to pierce the soles of my shoes, some bending and some crunching into powder. Perhaps it was petrified by the excessive frost, which was steadily turning my exposed skin to hardened rubber. I could not stop to examine anything; I felt that if I stopped for a moment, I would be drawn into some inescapable world of a single sense, where the impressions themselves would be strong enough to negate my will-power. Perhaps the most powerful sense was that of hearing: my ears were filled with a rustling roar which I had taken to be the sound of the wind in the trees, until I remembered that there were no leaves on the trees, and that there was no wind. I looked up for a moment at the tops of the trees, and quickly had to look away again, for the black, twisted shapes, perfectly still against the purple sky, had instantly taken on an archaic, deep-rooted significance which was purely malevolent. The rustling, with its strange metallic edge, became the singing of a horde of hidden birds.

My walk involved two successive upward slopes, separated by a dip. At the top of the second was a line of trees, and this was the edge of West Heath Road. I reached the top of the first rise, and caught a glimpse, through the trees, of the road. I saw only one building, and it was not Isobel's house. It was the house next to Isobel's, on the right, distinctive because of the tasteless pink material on its walls, which under the new atmospheric conditions, even seen at a distance through trees, was particularly disgusting; it had a lemon-yellow sheen which flashed twice even in the half-moment during which I was observing it. But the sight served to convince me that my quest would not be fruitless, and as I hurried on, at greater speed and without pausing, I could feel my heart beating in what I knew to be excitement of a sexual, adolescent type, though my fear had by no means diminished.

Down in the dip, of course, I could no longer see the road, and as I began to climb the second slope my excitement and fear mounted together: I would see Isobel's house, but it might be her house in some way I could not imagine. The gradient began to tell, and I was breathing heavily and sweating.

It is here that I lose sight of the motive force behind my actions. They were not my actions. When I was about to emerge over the brow of the slope, something acted upon me, with a curious mixture of sensations, most of which were probably produced spontaneously by my brain itself, to account, however unsatisfactorily, for the occurrence which it could not deny. The strongest sensation was that of a powerful blow, delivered, as if by a man using both fists, to my shoulders; and instantaneously, I found myself back at the foot of the first slope, with no memory of returning over the ground I had crossed. My knees were quivering uncontrollably, and I seemed to have wet my trousers, but I was still standing.

Now, for the first time, I stopped, and I was at once overwhelmed by a combination of shock and the sensory over-exposure I had feared. I was not completely debilitated, however. After a minute or so I resumed my ascent, having shaken off all ill-effects except a general heightening of the senses which might have been simple dizziness caused by exertion. At least, I imagined I had achieved some kind of recovery, but I remember very little about this second attempt to reach the road. All I know is that it ended in the same way as the first: this time I was dropped on the crest of the first rise, from where I could see the pink building, as before. But I was becoming very intoxicated, and the panic, which had started as an irrational reaction to the landscape, and then had been aggravated by the events which justified it, was now becoming frenzy, and working inevitably toward a climax. I was hardly aware of what I was doing as I started off again, but I think I was running, and I think I continued to charge at the barrier before me in a similar animal way until I had been picked up and deposited at various points on my route at least a dozen times. At my last attempt I stumbled on the second slope, exhausted, and I began to fall, but halfway to the ground something stopped me, and I found myself suspended rather as I had been in my dream; I was staring at the ground, which had suddenly become two images superimposed – one of the Heath's grassy floor, and the other of a pavement, which I recognised, from a leaning fire-hydrant sign which I had not noticed since childhood, as the stretch of pavement outside Isobel's house.

In some ways it was like my dream, especially in time's manner of passing; but I was still able to walk, or would have been had I not had to guess, at every step, which of the two versions of the ground (one of which was always some way above the other) was going to support me, and had I not invariably guessed wrongly. I was drunk, staggering and seeing double. The images were superimposed not only on the ground, but throughout my field of vision, and when I looked up I could see Isobel's house, vivid and detailed, but interrupted by trees and blotched with violet sky. Once I saw a female figure pass behind one of the upper windows – a silhouette of Isobel, crossing a violet square. She was the only thing, being black, not distorted by alien colouring, and I could see that she was free from distortion in her body, too. I grasped at the wrought-iron gate which seemed to be in front of me: but as always, I could not make contact with the world I needed. I found that the gate was a dead branch, which scattered flakes of its bark over my already filthy clothes.

I remember nothing about the order of events in this period. I presume that my weariness and disgust grew in a normal, consecutive way, while my terror remained constant; so constant, in fact, that I was hardly aware of it. But at some unspecified point I became conscious of a need to find Stanley, and our fire. The fire was the only feature of this planet in which I saw any stability, and I needed to get back to it. At about the same time, I think, my two sets of visual experience became three, the third being a long view of the Heath with a plume of smoke rising from one place which, I had no doubt, was our little bowl.

The superimposition of three images, I found, was quite impossible to deal with. I had managed to sustain a kind of personal orientation while faced with only two, although I had not had enough presence of mind to examine the relation between the two worlds, or two versions of myself, or whatever the two images had represented. That there had been a relation between them, of an ordered and comprehensible kind, I now realised, though the knowledge was not going to help me to come to terms with this new and triply unsettling species of the phenomenon. Although there had been only two worlds, it had consistently been the case that the one in which I believe myself to be, when I had sufficient confidence to choose, would prove to be the one on which I could in fact make no impression. The infallibility of this rule now led me to believe that the mere laws of probability had had little to do with my spontaneous guesswork and its lack of success. I was screwing my eyes tight shut, in the hope of blotting out at least one of the three possibilities. It was impossible to move any muscle apart from those of my eyelids, as any movement would introduce complexities great enough to remove permanently the power of reflection which this halt had allowed me to regain. I now began to regret my failure to take advantage of the earlier situation's simplicity. I could have applied bluffing tactics, I thought: I could have acted directly against my intuition, as, on a more familiar Earth, I would have done in the case of an unreliable bus-service, which, when treated in resentfully random fashion, succeeded in producing consistent delays of half an hour. If I had treated the two superimposed worlds in an intelligently perverse way, as I would eventually treat the bus-service, I could have forced their natural laws into a corner, and made them confess their dependence on the wanderings of my perception. Now, however, there was no room for intelligence, or for reasoning of any kind. I had, as far as was possible, to ignore my mind's reaction to my eyes, and to find some plan for future action in my memory or my imagination, rather than through my senses.

Seeking in those places, I found something rather surprising: reflection had begun a trend toward calm. Somehow, I had found contentment in standing motionless. Imagination is always calmer than reason, I suppose; in any case, when I opened my eyes it was immediately apparent to me that the world in which I was most interested – the one in which I was facing our little basin-camp, and I could see the smoke of Stanley's fire rising in a vertical line – had begun to conform with my desires. I could now see this image as, in some sense, the centre of my visual world, whether or not I was standing on a piece of ground connected with it directly (I was beginning to develop pins and needles in my feet, and for all I knew they might have been yards above my head); and, even more encouragingly, the pillar of smoke itself seemed to be closer to me. The afternoon was beginning to end, and the sky into which the smoke rose was fading from purple to greyish-blue.

It did not occur to me that time had passed either slowly or quickly, as I could remember experiencing at least two distinctly separate times simultaneously, earlier in the day. Evening was now, however, definitely establishing itself, and the smoke rising into the slate-coloured sky, having as it did a more or less uniform shape from bottom to top of the image, seemed to deny the existence of the other two pictures. Neither the heath viewed from the opposite direction, nor Isobel's ever-fading house, had quite such a dominant or consistent shape; moreover, my favourite image being mainly sky, the other two could be seen as interruptions of this plain background – in short, as hallucinations. While amusing myself with these comfortable reflections, I was overjoyed to see what I thought was the top of Stanley's head, rising for a moment over the rim of the basin, as he changed perhaps from one kneeling position to another. Possibly it was not his head, for a moment later Stanley himself was beside me, dragging me into the basin, by now only a few yards away.

We sat down together on the grass, by a fire which was burning slowly but securely, possibly on account of the heap of white ash which had built up beneath it. I remained for a few moments staring at the ground, in what must have seemed deep depression, though I was merely trying to dispel the other two images, now vastly changed, from the corners of my eyes, and was in fact greatly relieved rather than depressed. I was, however, beginning to recollect the inaccessibility of Isobel, and my attitude continued solemn.

Stanley showed remarkable consideration, and refrained even from speaking to me until he had prepared a pot of tea and placed a steaming mug in my hands. When he began to question me, in a very tentative, gentle manner, I did not reply, and I am not sure that I have spoken a word to him even yet.

It was not long before I managed to shake off the hallucinations completely. I think the tea may have had something to do with this. Also, I found that advancing twilight had as beneficial an effect on the colouring of the landscape in general as on that of the sky: things began to take on the appearance they would have on a relatively normal October evening. The problem I found myself wrestling with, ten minutes after re-entering the basin, was that I had a violent headache (which had begun several hours earlier, though I had not had time to consider it before) and this prevented the rational thought which, I comforted myself by believing, was now the most useful way of passing the time. I still have the headache, but I have managed to make this long entry in my journal, which, I think, has been just as helpful to me in my rationalisation of the day's events as any further chain of speculations would have been. Stanley has fried another batch of sausages, which are as appetising in their cold and greasy state, now I have eaten about ten or eleven, as they were when Stanley was passing the first few, hot and succulent, from the pan; and I have opened another bottle of wine, which is a great comfort to me, although it is doing my head no good.

I think Stanley is asleep. He has been in the same position for a long time now. In one sense, the feelings I have are very pleasant: they remind me of exhaustion after a heavy day on a camping-holiday. But my head reminds me that I have had no pleasure, and although she is probably sleeping a few hundred yards from here, nothing would induce me to go in search of Isobel again tonight. I will now try to go to sleep myself, though I fear one of many things may prevent me, and though I fear that my dream may recur.

August 2nd/November 2nd

I do not know whether to be relieved or dismayed at the complete reversal which has taken place, but the sensations of comfort are still, after several hours, quite overwhelming in their effect. It is fortunate that I brought my journal with me – perhaps I suspected, for what reason I cannot imagine, that we would not be returning to our place on the heath.

When we awoke this morning, no dream having disturbed my sleep, and no pain intervening as I leaned over to shake Stanley, we were surrounded by all the delightful features of a sunny autumn morning on Earth. It was not easy for me to remember the events I had last written about in this book, and I did not try over-hard – I was too much occupied with enjoyment of the compensation this completely incomprehensible world had granted me. Stanley, too, was completely changed. The night before, he had not had the energy to do more than make the tea and supper, ask me a few questions and give me a brief account of his day (a story, for the most part, of sitting in a terrified stupor, and of tending the fire when it was not necessary); but now he was at his most talkative and enthusiastic, full of suggestions for future exploration, and ready to cook yet more sausages, although this time I felt obliged to refuse, taking only a little wine for breakfast, which served to heighten my general exuberance. My headache had completely gone.

Neither of us felt inclined to repeat yesterday's experience, so having settled on a completely different direction, we set off together, Stanley occasionally darting into thickets and returning with more evidence of our surroundings' earthly nature. We were in fact travelling at right angles to my previous course, up the hill towards the Whitestone Pond and Jack Straw's Castle. I had been so lulled by the relatively cheerful and healthy sound of the birds' singing that I felt no trepidation at the prospect of nearing such a centre of activity, but when the first suggestion of roaring traffic began to mingle with the chirruping, the enormity of the assumptions I had been making struck me with the first real doubt of the day, and I stopped, holding Stanley by the arm. Stanley was obviously not affected in the same way for he looked at me with rather a puzzled expression; and having reflected, I decided that there was no particular reason not to continue in the same direction.

The area surrounding the Whitestone Pond had changed, in some way I could not name. We stood at the water's edge, staring perhaps rather stupidly at the apparently normal cars, and at the small boy who was sailing a toy boat on the other side of the pond. We must have looked very strange. I think it was Stanley's first experience of civilisation; he had certainly never before displayed his moustache to such a large audience, and I could see that he was stroking it nervously. My own chin and upper lip were not free of bristles, and I had not undressed or washed since leaving the ship. We were temporarily at a loss. The small boy was looking at us in what might have been a suspicious way. I found myself wondering whose idea it had been to come here in the first place, and for a few moments I was very close to panic.

A sense of duty eventually gave me the power to decide. Stanley was dependent on me. I grunted, and set off in the direction which seemed to lead to the most sparsely populated area. We passed perhaps two or three people, and each one of them looked at us oddly. At one point I realised that I was holding Stanley by the hand; hurriedly letting go of it, I increased our speed as we passed a dignified gentleman with a briefcase.

I think, in retrospect, there was no need for us to feel any discomfort at all. I was continually distracted from my embarrassment by the beauty of this morning's natural products – particularly effects of the sun's light, although the vapour issuing from people's mouths was also fascinating to me – and perhaps the most extraordinary fact was that nothing out of the ordinary had yet happened. Eventually it was inevitable that we should accept our situation as completely worldly, and begin to feel at home in it, for even Stanley had some fundamental memories involving this atmosphere; but meanwhile timidity prevented us from enjoying all these new benefits to the full, and we both perhaps felt an urge to be back in a space at least as private and enclosed as our ship.

I had still not decided in precisely what way this neighbourhood was different from my memory of its counterpart on Earth; but at the point where the road began to slope downwards, we found, on our left-hand side, a small building which I was sure I had never seen before; it had only one storey, its interior was clearly visible through a large, clean window, and it was called 'Stan's Café'. In fact, our main interest now being simple exploration, which could be pursued in any direction, we were nearly overcome and halted several times by the very passivity of the environment – but now our contentment was complete, because this window was so perfect a culmination of the morning's accumulating pleasures that we could easily believe we had been looking for Stan's Café ever since setting out on our walk. The single room contained four or five plain tables, with tubular metal legs and plastic covered tops, each having its own plastic tomato, bottle of brown sauce, and glass salt-and-pepper set, and everything was shiningly clean in a way I had never imagined such an eating-house could be. It struck me that a hitherto unknown transport-café should seem incongruous in this part of Hampstead, but somehow its character was in complete harmony with everything around it. Not even the sauce-bottles had dribbles down their necks. There was a counter with a tea-urn, and under the customary pyrex covers there were cellophane-wrapped meat pies, cheese rolls and sticky cakes; behind the counter lounged the only occupant of the room, presumably Stan himself, who was reading the Daily Mirror. He wore an apron without a single stain.

Stanley and I did not hesitate in deciding that this was where our first contact with the planet's inhabitants should be made; neither of us could then have explained why we had passed the pub, and several pedestrians, without feeling the same urge to communicate, but since then many explanations have occurred to me, and they all seem equally plausible now that we are sitting in this agreeable, soporific establishment.

When we came in, Stan looked up from his paper and said, "Good morning, gentlemen. Would you care for some breakfast?" I was dumbfounded by this approach, but Stanley, despite his having eaten sausages about an hour before, and presumably not being motivated by quite such a watering of the mouth as I experienced, replied with an immediate "Yes, please", upon which Stan raised himself from his leisurely pose against the counter, and courteously leading us to a table by the other window (in the wall opposite the one facing the street – which arrangement of windows was the main cause of the room's light and pleasant aspect) he gave us two copies of the special breakfast-menu.

Stan did not return to his position behind the counter, but stood watching us as we looked at our menus. Strangely, I did not find this disconcerting; I was affected simultaneously by extraordinary sensations of physical well-being and by a growing conviction, notwithstanding my limited acquaintance with him, that Stan the café-proprietor was an incarnation of pure benevolence. I did not, however, wish to establish any kind of intimacy with him straight away, so I continued to study the menu in silence. Finding that it included "Egg, Bacon & Chips" and "Sausages, Beans & Fried Bread" as separate items, my mind instantly leapt to that delicious idea combining elements of the two – egg, bacon and fried bread – which Stanley had never quite understood, and of which I had been deprived, in consequence, for ten years. My experience of similar cafés on Earth had been, on the whole, that combinations not actually on the menu were inconceivable, but my desire for egg, bacon and fried bread, and my confidence in Stan's humanity, persuaded me that I would lose nothing by enquiring.

"Is it possible to have fried bread with egg and bacon instead of sausages and beans, and without chips?" I asked.

"Certainly," replied Stan, in a tone which suggested that he had great respect for my judgment. His voice was very deep, but lacked the superfluous joviality characteristic of, say, Sir Charles's. "Would you like one egg or two?" I asked for two, and before Stanley could place his order I advised him to follow my example; I knew that left to himself he would choose sausages, and I felt that it would be a pity for him to miss this opportunity, for such good fortune could not be expected to repeat itself on an alien planet.

"Two eggs, bacon and fried bread, twice," said Stan, making for his stove. Soon the exquisite smell of frying bacon arrived as the first climax of this extraordinary series of experiences. Combined with it was the faint, ever-present odour of paint, issuing from the radiator under the window, at our side. My left hand is at this moment resting on the radiator, which is turned full on, as the weather is very cold. It is painted white. Perhaps my enormous initial enthusiasm for this place can be partly explained by the fact that I had spent two nights and a day in the open before coming in. Even sitting down on a warm plastic chair was a pleasure in itself. It was some time before I noticed that the window beside us commanded a fine view of the heath, but whether or not my continuous enjoyment, sometimes constant and sometimes growing, had been entirely natural in its origins, I am sure it was nurtured and increased by observation of that part of the heath where I like to think we had been.

While we were waiting for our bacon and eggs, Stanley kept me busy with speculations about our cook. He very much wanted to know whether this was in fact Stan of the café's title; a point which was of considerably less interest to me, and might have caused me some embarrassment had I not been careful to moderate my tone, and thereby also Stanley's. Stan was within easy hearing distance, and I could see our breakfast progressing happily through its various stages as the cook (whose physical appearance, independent of any question of identity, I found quite fascinating) idly handled items of food, and in the later stages plates and cutlery. When the food was ready and Stan came over, carrying a plate in each hand, he also brought his Daily Mirror, and before putting our breakfast on the table he began to manoeuvre a third chair with his foot, saying, "Do you mind if I sit with you?"

In fact he had already more or less sat, and the question, which in this written form seems to require an extra clause of excuse, was lent an air of completeness by the extraordinary richness of his voice. There is an instant acceptability about everything he says. I did not feel any need to reply to his question. I was at once engrossed by the dish which had been set before me. My long deprivation does not in any way account for the orgiastic pleasure which breakfast gave me; the plate which, until a moment ago, had been left on the table, streaked with yellow and speckled with greasy crumbs, held such a banquet of memories for me that I am almost tempted to ask for it to be replaced, so that I can look at it while drinking this apparently infinite mug of black instant coffee.

"Are you Stan?" said Stanley.

"Yes," said Stan. He pretended to read his paper, which was dated Friday, November 2nd, 1973. The headline was "BLACKS INSIST".

"I'm Stanley."

Stan immediately laid down his paper and replied with enthusiasm, "That's funny. You're the only two customers I've had all morning and here's one of you called Stanley. It isn't a very common name, is it?"

"What do you mean?" said Stanley.

This was unfortunate. I realised at once that Stanley was not aware either of the fact that it was possible for a name to be shared by different people, or of the close connection between the names "Stan" and "Stanley". I had many times derived aesthetic pleasure from study of our crew-list, on which, by pure coincidence, no Christian name or surname had been duplicated. But it had never occurred to me that I should enlighten Stanley; nor had I ever pressed him to reveal his own family-name, or any other details of his background. He had always claimed to be completely ignorant of such matters, and to have no name apart from Stanley.

I need not, however, have wasted even the minute amount of eating-time I spared for worry about this misunderstanding between my two companions. In the ensuing conversation, Stan explained the whole subject to Stanley, without himself being further informed about the situation; and his explanation was so lucid that it was a positive pleasure to hear. When he had finished, Stanley thanked him politely, and went on to say that he had been thinking, ever since our arrival in the café, about the similarity between Stan's name and his own, and had begun to suspect something of the truth. Now that all had been revealed, he was delighted to share his name with such an admirable person.

"Is that today's paper?" I asked, my mouth full of egg, bacon and fried bread (I achieved this by cutting off a small piece of each, and forking first the egg, then the fried bread, and the bacon last – a technique long-remembered, which produced mouthfuls far more delicious than the sum of their parts, and large enough, in this situation, to help me feign nonchalance).

"Yes, it's today's alright," said Stan. "I read it every day, though to tell the truth I'm not greatly interested in stuff like this–" and he indicated the front page. "I read it for want of anything better to do, I suppose."

"What blacks are they talking about there?"

"The negroes in Mozambique, I believe. I've read this page, but for the life of me I can't remember what they're insisting on." He chuckled in a warm, grandfatherly way, and began to look through the article, presumably intending to find another broad piece of background information for me. I told him not to bother; that small part of my mind which had so far survived breakfast was entirely occupied with questions of time and dates, none of which I could resolve – but I felt it was necessary at least to retain the questions, until such time as I could give them my full attention.

"You can read it yourself, anyway, when you've had your breakfast," said Stan, propping the paper up against the sauce-bottle.

"Thank you," I said, and realised in the same moment that I had intended all along to study the paper at leisure, though I had had no reason to expect that Stan would allow me to.

I had, until I saw the newspaper, been thinking in terms of 1984, this being the year which my journal, if nothing else, has reached. If we had, during our ten-year voyage, been the victims of coincidence to such an extent that we had actually returned unwittingly to our starting-point – if we had, in other words, experienced in truth what we now only seem to be experiencing – heaven knows what date I would have expected it to be. I have given a little thought to the passing of time in our ship and how it relates to the passing of time on Earth, bearing in mind the extraordinary kinds of space through which we have travelled – the space around the White Planet, for example, where I can only assume we experienced non-existent time as a measurable quantity – but I have decided that it would be quite impossible to compare Earth-time with ship-time accurately, however detailed a history of our voyage we could obtain. Those metaphysical scientists who say otherwise – who think we could not only discover how long our voyage "in fact" took us, but could also explain the origins of the various "illusions" we have suffered, given sufficient data, seem to me to be themselves suffering from sheer lack of experience. No doubt if we had landed on Earth, after reflecting in this way I would have been quite unsurprised to find myself back in 1974, our year of departure; and equally unsurprised had I been plunged into the middle of the eighteenth or twenty-fourth century. I would not have expected our date of arrival to correspond with the date under which I described the event in my journal.

Be all that as it may, I thought it would be 1984 when we landed on this planet. I had been delighted, or terrified, in any case fascinated, by the idea of a more or less exact Earth-replica, and had expected the differences to lie in one all-important feature, such as the nature of space on the planet's surface. The differences, though specialised, I had thought, would be enormous, and of vital importance to us – as if the planet had been waiting for us, and owed its existence to us: so of course its idea of time would agree, at least nominally, with ours. I was, and am still, surprised by this trifling time-difference. It is not even 1974, which would at least have seemed relevant to our history – but 1973, about nine months before we set out. A messy coincidence.

"How old are you, Stanley?" said Stan.

"Fifteen, sir," Stanley replied. He was becoming positively obsequious.

"That's a remarkably fine moustache you've got, for a lad of fifteen. Here am I at fifty-four, and I haven't done much better than that myself." Stan had no facial hair except for a long pair of side-whiskers. Stanley was blushing hotly, and again began to finger the few poor hairs of his upper lip.

"I would grow another moustache, but my wife wouldn't like it," Stan continued. I looked up in surprise, and he pointed with his thumb at a door in the back wall of the café. "She's still asleep, in there. In fact, I'll have to take her a cup of tea soon."

Neither Stanley nor I interrupted breakfast in order to respond, so after a short time Stan resumed his strangely inoffensive patronising of my fellow-eater.

"Yes, you want to be careful when you're getting married." I am not sure to what extent Stanley understood this, as he had, of course, had no contact with more than one female during his acquaintance with me. If his childhood was indeed normal, he must have extended a certain amount of hostility toward the girl-children with whom he was familiar, and his relationship with Isobel had certainly made her seem in some ways a maternal figure, but I think he was still uncertain of the precise difference between her and us, and for all I knew he had never heard of marriage.

Turning to me, Stan said, "Are you married, sir?" I cannot believe that this question was not calculated to arouse in me some powerful emotional response, though I remain convinced that it was intended for my benefit. I had not thought of Jezebel since landing, but now I realised that she must be as much a part of this world as I had found Isobel to be.

"Yes," I said. Fortunately, Stan chose this moment to go and prepare his wife's tea – perhaps discouraged by my curtness – so I was spared further embarrassment. It was only a few moments later, however, that I discovered something which might prove considerably more embarrassing. I had just taken the final mouthful of bacon and fried bread (the egg having been finished some time before) when my eye fell on one of the menus, still lying open, and I noticed for the first time that each item had a price marked against it – for example, "Egg, Bacon & Chips – 35p". Again I was suddenly reminded of something. In establishments such as this, eating was only half the process; payment was just as vital to the café's rituals, if not more so. And I knew at once that we had brought no money with us, though we had cases full of it in the ship.

I waited until Stan had taken the cup of tea to his wife. I needed time to think about this predicament. After a moment's cool reflection it occurred to me that we had two clear alternatives before us, neither of which would be particularly distasteful. I could send Stanley to fetch some money from the ship; the disadvantage of this scheme was that Stan would inevitably want to know what was happening, and I could not think of any convincing destination or mission upon which to base an explanation of Stanley's activity. The second alternative was to claim that we were destitute, and to pay the proprietor in kind – the traditional way, I remembered, being to spend an hour or so washing up; this scheme amply compensated for its own rather degrading nature by giving us a fairly positive programme for another part of the day, and an excuse to remain in this eminently comfortable environment. One disadvantage was that Stan, as he was obviously far from busy, might be rather short of washing-up. However, I decided that this plan was preferable to the first, and when Stan returned from the bedroom I rose from my chair and approached him at the counter, whither he was returning the sugar and milk.

"I find it surprising," said I, "that you don't yet know, after so many years, precisely how much sugar and milk your wife takes in her tea."

"I know well enough, but she ...," Stan paused, and, though I think my features must have shown nothing but my natural and genuine interest in the continuation of his statement, he peered into my eyes, and asked if there was something I wanted to tell him. This put me off completely, of course, and I found myself quite unable to utter the apologies and excuses I had been prepared to offer him. Stan continued, however: "You haven't got any money, have you?"

"No," I said quietly, and staring at my feet, "we haven't."

"I thought that was it," laughed Stan. The violent friendliness of his tone startled me into looking up again. "You don't want to worry about that. You only owe me 88p. Give it to me some other time, if you like. For the time being, just sit down, have some more coffee, and make yourselves at home. It's not often I get people as interesting as you to talk to – that's payment enough, I can tell you. I want to know all about where you've been, and where you're going. I can see you're travellers. And you must meet Mary Bell, when she gets up. Just let me serve this gentleman," – for at that moment, Stan's third customer of the morning had walked in – "and I'll be with you again."

So I came back to our table and began to write this. All thanks and offers of help, I could tell from Stan's manner, would have been superfluous. I knew I should have been more cautious about accepting favours from this man, and more worried about revealing "where we'd been, and where we were going"; but even now I cannot feel anything but the most delicious sensations of security and comfort, and a conviction that if we ever leave this place, it will not be tonight. Stan has been rather busy since the interview above recorded, but he has occasionally stopped at our table and talked with us for a few moments. (He does not, incidentally, favour any other customer with similar attentions). Mary Bell has still not risen, but Stanley has been taken to her room, apparently to be introduced to her while she lies in bed. I continue to be content, and intend now to read the newspaper.

Letter, Mr Quincey Horace to Captain Lionel Jaffa, M.A. (Cantab.)
(never completed)
6th December 1973[1]

My dear Jaffa,

You might think its strange that I'm writing to you after all, but I'm going to tell you about everything that's happened since we left, and then you might understand a lot of things you didn't understand before.

You didn't really think there was a ship on the other side of the planet. I knew that very well. But I also knew that it was more likely than you thought that there really was a ship there. You found out one or two things about the "oscillation", as you called it, but not as many as we found out in our quarters, because, as you know, the ship's insulation didn't work

[1] This date was added at a later stage in the letter's composition, suggesting that the letter was in fact close to completion when it was so mysteriously curtailed by the writer. *The Author.*

as well there as in the parts where you lived, and we made a few experiments when things began to happen like what happened to your pen. You wrote about this in your Journal on July 9th.

We found out, among other things, that small objects really could reproduce themselves when they moved from place to place. There were different kinds of change, and reproduction didn't always happen. We soon found that it could more or less be controlled. The thing we worked with more than anything else was Waeldermann's 24-carat gold cigarette-case, and we finished up with quite a lot of gold cigarette-cases exactly the same.

I still wasn't sure that we'd find another ship when we set out, but I knew it was possible, because the change from orbit to orbit was the sort of change, namely a change which came after a long and steady "oscillation" and fitted in with it, which usually ended with a doubling of the object, though we'd never seen it, of course, happen with a thing as big as the ship.

You probably don't know about the window we had in our quarters. We knew how you felt about windows, so we always kept it a secret from you, and hid it from you when you came round to see us. It wasn't really a window, though that was what we called it. It was a clever, telescopic device, invented by Waeldermann and me, using an extremely small hole in the ship's hull. It wasn't too difficult to hide it, the few times we had to. Anyway, we didn't only watch the planet itself, but also its moon, which is, as anyone with any sense would guess, exactly the same as Earth's moon. This doesn't mean it's completely barren and full of ruins, as you would no doubt expect. Through our telescopic-window we saw the headquarters of an organisation which would offer us help and hospitality if we landed there.

So we weren't in as bad a position as you thought when we left the ship in our small craft. We knew it was useless for landing on Earth, but we almost certainly wouldn't need to. And as it happened, there really was another version of the ship, as you had claimed, on the other side of the planet. We'd been pretty tense until we saw it, but when we did, we opened our packed lunches as a kind of celebration. Waeldermann and I led a discussion about the tactics we should use, and in the end it was us two who made the decision. The others were more interested in chocolate biscuits. But at least we gave them a chance to have their say, if they wanted.

We came a lot nearer to the ship, without getting in contact of course, and waited, and soon things began to happen as we'd expected. We saw the ship's airlock open, and then a small craft came out exactly the same as the one we were in.

This craft was never designed to dock with itself, being the only one of its kind when it was made, but if you think about it you'll see it's possible. The people in craft number 2 evidently got this idea about the same time as we did, because they came very close to us, presenting their hatch in a line with ours. We took the hint, and did our part of the docking operation as well as we could, with the basic equipment you'd left us.

We weren't sure what to do next, but we didn't need to think very long, because we heard a scrambling noise from the other end of the tube, and we knew someone was coming through from the other craft. I made a sign to Waeldermann, and we placed ourselves on either side of the hatch, pressed against the wall. Smallpox came forward to open the door.

The man who came through the door was Pink[2], or someone very like him. We recognised him at once, because he wasn't wearing a space-suit. He stood there for a moment, staring at the men with that haughty expression he has, and then Waeldermann grabbed his arms, I clapped my hand over his mouth, and Smallpox strangled him with a piece of wire.

We'd made no noise during all this, and still keeping silent, I beckoned Waeldermann to follow me into the tube. We went through into the other craft – and there you were, standing all alone in the gangway, looking very worried, and no doubt wanting to know what was going on next-door.

Now, do you want to know how you behave when you're not there to look after yourself?

It amuses me to think how much this letter must fascinate you. Like someone sending you news of absent friends – but I think this is a man you love more than any other friend.

I don't know why you should love him so much. He didn't strike me as a very respectable man.

In short, when I got my knife out you showed all the signs of that "degeneration" you used to talk about at such length. Actually, I was quite sorry I'd shown my hand so soon, because I'd have been interested to hear what you had to say for yourself. This reproduction of you might have been more human than the original, if I'd given it a chance to show any but its animal qualities. As it was the sight of my knife seemed to remove your power of speech. When I finally managed to run you to earth, under one of the passenger-seats, there was nothing I could reasonably do except cut your throat.

In spite of the blood all over the floor, I thought we should all move into this second craft, in case someone had been watching on the screen and could tell which lump was which. I got everyone to move as quickly as possible, and didn't spare the time to move your body. I didn't want anyone in the ship to suspect there had been anything odd about the excursion. So when everyone was in we cast off from our own craft as if it had been just an old piece of wreckage we'd latched onto for a moment. Pink's body is still in it, I should think – there might even be two dead Pinks by now, both spinning round and round your head, and staring in an extra haughtier way than usual.

Your own body is about 150 miles behind me, lying with the remains of the ship in the middle of the desert. It seems it isn't strange in this place to own a lump of rotting flesh while you're still alive. I'm not sure how I'd get used to it myself, especially if my throat had been cut. But I suppose I'd better leave that to you, and get on with telling you how you came to end up in this desert, which is the Sahara, of course.

I needn't waste much time, because it's all pretty obvious. There was no problem getting into the ship because the airlock was still open, and, when we were inside the only people in our way were your woman Isobel Keogh (or was she your woman?) and myself - I at least knew that we'd be meeting ourselves. I hoped I could come to some arrangement with my own soul-mate, so that between us we could control both crews. The only other person with any authority was Smallpox, who was feared, and so long as he stayed feared I could use him, as I couldn't if he was respected.

---

2 Pink is Sir Charles' surname. *The Author.*

Keogh was waiting outside the airlock for the people she thought were in the craft. We used the same strategy as before, waiting with the doors of the craft shut and our heads below the windows, so that in the end she came through the airlock and opened the door herself. Then it was easy – she was dragged inside, screaming about "Charles, Charles" (odd that she wasn't screaming for you) and I left her with the crew while I went with Waeldermann and Smallpox (though Smallpox really wanted to stay behind) to look for the other men.

I never went back to the airlock, but I take it you and she are both lying there now - being baked together – she's more or less got to stay with you. Again, I don't think I'd be pleased about this, though you can make up your own mind. She wasn't very pretty before, but she's a lot less so now.

To get back to the story – we didn't have trouble like we expected with the other men, because they were afraid of us. The boy, Stanley, it seems, had cut his wrists with a razor, whether out of fear or loyalty to you I couldn't say – but I think it was your razor he used. I didn't know why the others were afraid of us at first, but thought perhaps they hadn't realised what living in this place could lead to. Anyway, I've asked Quincey about this since and he says they knew as much as we did about it, in theory that is, but they were shocked when we suddenly turned up like that, just when they were planning to go on the same trip we'd made (events had been more or less the same on Ship 2 as on Ship 1, but they were a bit behind us in time). He says that it looked as though we were thinking more quickly, or moving more quickly or something, and this made us seem superior to them, as if we were the originals and they were the reproductions – instead of the other way round, which was how they'd been looking at it before.

To tell the truth, I got a bit of a shock myself when he said this, because it hadn't struck me that anyone could deny it was us who had the real personalities, although it's obvious, when you think about it, that I've now got two minds as well as two bodies, and each one individually thinks it's the only one of the two with any right to be called Quincey Horace. Anyway, I didn't let Quincey know that he'd surprised me, and I haven't needed to think much since then about the question of "identity" (to borrow a word from your own private store) because we took action at once, seeing that our doubles were knocked off balance for a moment, and put them in a position where we had actual power over them, so they couldn't object if we took charge of our names as well, and called ourselves Quincey 1, Karl 1, etc., and gave them labels marked "2", which couldn't be taken off. Actually, I let everyone decide for himself what was to be done with his double, and though most agreed that this labelling-system of mine was the best idea, some insisted that no world was big enough for two of themselves, so we had a formal execution of eleven men, and burned the bodies with a proper funeral-service when we hit this planet, because no-one wanted his other self put through all the indignities you and your friends went through.

Smallpox and Pete Stuggy had special arrangements made – Smallpox wrote me a long message saying that as this new person looked exactly like him, having the same deformities and so on, he wanted him to be known as Syphilis, and to have that written on his label, just to make sure no-one got confused (I thought he was being funny, but he got very upset when I laughed, so I didn't say any more after that, not wanting to tempt fate) – and Stuggy, who was very disturbed about having a twin, like some of the others only more so (in fact I think it finally tipped him over the edge) insisted on being Stuggy 2 himself, and forcing the new Stuggy to be Stuggy 1. It hasn't made much difference.

Well, in the end we got everyone sorted into two groups, and up till now the 2's have taken orders from the 1's, and done all the hard work, unless the No. 1 of a pair has wanted to carry on doing what he did before, in which case we've got them both doing it, which is fine. I control a small committee consisting of Quincey 2 and Waeldermann 1 (or Karl 1, as he prefers to be known) which makes all the main decisions, and when we were still on the way down dealt with navigation and so on. We weren't much good at navigation, because we were aiming at Mozambique (which is where both 1's and 2's want to go) but we landed here in the Sahara desert. I wouldn't be surprised if this was more than you thought we could do, though. I'm sure this letter's given you quite a few surprises on the subject of how we get on without you, and I haven't finished with the subject yet. Personally, I think I'd make a better captain than you, if I wanted to call myself Captain Horace. I've certainly had a lot less trouble from my crew than you had from yours – and you may argue that I've got all the same ideas as my crew, but I can quite truthfully say that there's only one man in it (whose name I needn't mention, but he's a member of the committee) who gets more from me in the way of fellow-feeling than a pretty basic kind of sympathy. You might not understand this, but I used to think (a long time before I met you or any of your friends) that everyone had this kind of sympathy for everyone else.

We were in a tight spot when we landed, because we hadn't any idea what part of the desert we'd hit, but everyone kept fairly calm, and after a short conference my committee and I decided that we'd have to start walking, in a direction to be decided by further debate. Karl 1 brought out his compass. I couldn't get him to explain why on earth he'd brought it on the voyage in the first place – I think he just likes having things, like his cigarette-case – and I didn't know whether it would still be working, but Karl 1 seemed to think that as his compass and Karl 2's compass agreed, they must both be correct. I still wasn't quite sure, but I decided the best thing would be to pretend I accepted this proof quite confidently. Quincey made the same decision, so the committee's vote was unanimous.

East was obviously our best bet, from what we'd seen through Pink's window, and our own, on our way down, and because Mozambique was where we wanted to get to, though we were a long way off. We loaded as much stuff as we could on the twos' backs (I gave Quincey 2 a specially heavy load, including all the cigarette-cases, in case he started getting above himself) and set out at once, as it was night-time. There were 39 of us – 25 ones and 14 twos – and we spread out in a long line, Karl 1 in front with both compasses, bearers in the middle, and most of the ones bringing up the rear. There wasn't much of the night left, but by the time dawn broke we were all completely exhausted – none of us had ever walked in the desert before – and we collapsed in the full blaze of the sun, and remained more or less unconscious till the next night. This was the start of a horrible time, lasting about six or seven days, during which our number was reduced to twelve, and I couldn't help thinking more than once that it was all up for all of us.

I won't go into detail on the subject of our sufferings – I'm sure a well-travelled man like you can imagine them perfectly well. We didn't run out of food or water, having brought enough for quite a few weeks on the backs of our twos. I'd known from the start that Syphilis would be able to carry huge amounts, and I remember him slouching along under his pile of bags and cases – I'd given him a weight which only a superman could carry – not really a man at all, but a lump of flesh heaving and sweating silently, and bright red all over. Smallpox was more stupid and vicious than ever. I think he enjoyed being better than someone for the first time in his life.

What we suffered from was the heat, and I don't know whether it was normal, but it was only when the heat got really bad that I thought this planet might not be quite the same as Earth after all. Most of the time I felt as if I was dreaming, and we all saw lots of mirages – or just plain delusions, because not many of them were like water-holes or caravans or any of the other usual mirage-subjects. There was one spell, which I think must have been a single day, or daylight resting-period (possibly the first one we had, because this peculiar state of things began straight-away) during which nothing happened which was at all normal, and I can't remember anything about times of the day – that is, I can't say "This happened in the morning, and that happened in the evening", but I remember things like being approached by Smallpox and Syphilis together, where I was lying on the sand, and seeing them, as I looked up into the sun, first like a picture of Tweedledum and Tweedledee in the book "Through the Looking-Glass", and then changing into a huge long line of Smallpoxes and Syphilises, as in two looking-glasses, going on for ever, it seemed, all the way across the desert. I don't even know whether Smallpox really came up to me, that day. I don't want to mix things I saw during that time with the things I feel more sure about.

You might be interested to know that it was Quincey 2 who wrote the last paragraph. I didn't see that particular delusion, though I had a lot which were just as peculiar. Actually, I've told Quincey 2 more than once to take over from me in the writing of this letter, having told him what I'm leading up to (which I don't think I needed to tell him) and he's written two parts of it apart from the last paragraph. I wonder if you can guess which ones they are?

While I'm on the subject, more or less, of these number 2's and how close to their number 1's they are, I'd just like to tell you about some of my colleagues and how they behave in the face of death. You haven't got a number 2 anymore, of course, but you might have met a number 3 by now, and thought it was a number 2. If so, even you will know what it's like to be tied to someone, with what kind of feeling I don't know. I'm only going to tell you about one "fear" of mine in the whole of this letter, and you can decide for yourself if it's the only one I have. It is that by cutting your double's throat I might have harmed you in some way – not that your welfare, need I say, interests me in itself, but we want you to be properly preserved, as you will find later in this letter, for when we visit you. This fear of mine is a result of watching my double friends and seeing how any pain or injury of one half is felt, sometimes just as much, by the other.

Thirteen of us died, as I've said, and of this thirteen twelve were in pairs. Of the six pairs, the 1's in two died within twenty minutes of the 2's, and the 2's in three within thirty seconds of the 1's. The sixth pair was Sgt. Morris, whom we all knew as Bill, and whom I'm sure you'll remember, because he'd been left with only one leg, or one and a fraction, and had to be carried wherever he went. We'd decided at our first conference that we couldn't afford to carry both of them through the desert and as each had suggested at exactly the same time that he should be left behind, having a horrible infectious disease as well as only one leg (Bill having been a hypochondriac ever since his former stay in Africa) and that his counterpart should be carried instead of him, we told them that it was a very good idea, and we left them both behind in the ship, after they'd agreed to light a fire every day in case we could send help. As we never saw any smoke, I'm counting them among the dead. The thirteenth to die was Karl Waeldermann 2, and for a time I thought my old friend Karl 1 was going to go the way of the other six dead men's partners. He spent whole days weeping over his decaying number 2 – I've never seen any grief quite like it – and used to drag the body along behind him during the night. Eventually, we persuaded him to bury it, but ever since then he's been sort of grey about the face, and quiet, and thinner than usual, not that his thinness was strange to begin with – we were all a lot thinner by this time.

The five pairs who died, apart from Sgt Morris, were Pablo and Andrew (these being the 2's who died before their 1's) and Franz, Stuggy (who died very soon, on account of his age, I suppose, his number 1 – from Ship 2, you'll remember – collapsing first at the foot of a dune, immediately joined by my old friend number 2, and clasped in a strong final hug, which was the first sign of affection I'd seen within this pair) and Wilfrid, known to you as Bates.

You will have worked out that apart from Smallpox and Syphilis and me there was only one pair left alive, and this was Raoul Federic Antonius, the powerful man who used to go around without a shirt on, looking black, in charge of what Miss Keogh called "lubrication". Raoul 1 and Raoul 2 are among the seven men out of the remaining twelve (the other five of the seven being me, the other Quincey, Smallpox, Syphilis, and Karl Waeldermann) who will be of interest to you when you've finished reading this letter.

The other five of the twelve were naturally the ones who'd had their 2's executed as soon as they'd found them. There's a definite difference between them and us, and this is probably why they've stayed behind in Africa while we are moving on, making our way to England and in the end to you, though I don't know how long it's going to take us – apart, of course, from what they got up to before leaving England the first time, which might make trouble for them if they went back. They just wanted pieces of land to live on, and it doesn't matter to them whether it's the real Africa or not, now they've been through a lot of the universe and found nothing better. We're not really interested in that kind of thing any more. We know we're free men, but other things have become more important, somehow.

I interrupted my story at a point where we were all on our last legs, dying of sunstroke or something like it. No doubt you've noticed that time is passing quickly while I'm writing this letter – in other words, things are happening more often than either I or my double can find time to write about all the early events in the story. I'll go on with it for as long as it seems to the point, though, or until it looks as though we're going to reach you ourselves before our letter does.

Well, I don't know why it was, but things began to get better on their own, as if something had tried to kill us all and then given up when it was only halfway through. I can't really explain how we first noticed the improvement, but when we finally realised it we knew that things hadn't just become normal, they'd gone further, and conditions were now a lot better than we could have expected if we'd just been crossing an ordinary desert with nothing odd about it. We still knew it was hot, but our bodies accepted it, and we didn't even seem to sweat more than usual. Eventually, I forget precisely when, we gave up our night-walking and instead did our travelling by day, and slept by night.

We didn't have delusions any more, either. At least ten of us, all except Syphilis and possibly Smallpox, that is, were now quite comfortable, and we even began to enjoy ourselves. I don't count Smallpox or Syphilis because they didn't tell us how they were feeling, and Syphilis still looked as though the weight he had to carry was an inconvenience, to say the least.

One day some time after this change had taken place, we were walking the last few yards we were going to do before making camp, and thinking we should try to increase our water-supply, once we'd settled down, by doing those experiments we hadn't tried since leaving the ship. We saw no reason why they shouldn't work again.

It was the end of the day, and we were feeling, or at least I was, the closest thing to exhaustion we'd felt since the change. This was just a matter of the feet and legs, and resulted from walking through dry sand for a few hours. I'm sure you've felt something like this yourself, probably during your childhood, after spending a long day building sand-castles and so forth on the beach. You'll know it's not at all unpleasant, just halfway between an ache and a glow, and it makes sitting down, when you finally get round to it, a lot better than it would have been. Also, I noticed that the view across the desert, it being the hour before night, and the sky being a bit deeper-coloured than usual, was very pleasant to look at. In other words, I was feeling quite content and not at all worried about getting lost in the desert or running out of water.

Then a surprising thing happened. We suddenly came to the top of a dune we hadn't realised we were climbing, and saw first that twilight had arrived, much more suddenly than usual, and second a great long line or caravan, of men, baggage and camels, moving along in the valley below us. They saw us at about the same time, there was a noise of voices and then they stopped, the front camels first and then the ones behind, jostling a bit, until the whole caravan had come to a stop and just stood there below us, evidently waiting to see what we'd do.

We decided straight away that we had to ask them where we were and buy some camels off them. Karl Waeldermann thought he'd be able to speak to them, because he'd been in Africa at the same time as Sgt. Morris, and he said people around here usually spoke one, or at least something like one, of several languages he knew. For some reason, though we were a bit nervous in a general sort of way, we didn't expect them to be unfriendly. We set off down the hill.

Long before we reached them, of course, it was dark. I expect you wondered why I talked about your childhood, further up this page. Well, it might have had something to do with going down this hill. I'm sure I didn't think about childhood just because my legs were tired. Actually, I don't think I thought about childhood, at the time I'm talking about, that is, not the time now when I'm actually talking about it, until I was going down the hill, though now I can see that childhood had something to do with the time just before we got to the top of the hill, as well. When we were going down it I started running, and I noticed that though I was, as I've said, quite nervous, I was also very excited, and the excitement was like excitement I remember feeling when I was a child. Running down a sand-dune is easier for a child than a grown man, because it means jumping again and again, and making deep holes that you have to jump out of, straight away or you'd be bound to stop or fall over. It's the sort of thing a grown man doesn't normally do. But my double was doing the same, and Karl and the two Raoul Antoniuses were more or less keeping up with us, though they weren't putting quite as much energy into it. I noticed that the air and the sand were getting colder as well as darker, and this is what made me think of the sea-side, where children force their tired legs to do things like this at the end of the day, when they're leaving the beach. I'm not really sure why I'm going into detail about this, but I seem to feel that it's the kind of thing I should be telling you about, so I'll just say one more thing that's come into my mind on the subject, namely, that the children's reason for doing this kind of thing, though they might not know it themselves, is that they have to get as much action into the day as they can, and they mustn't waste part of it just because it's the last part.

December 1st

I've put the date here so you have some idea of how things are proceeding as I write. It'll take us another two or three days to get to the port we'll be sailing from.

When we got to the bottom of the hill, we waited for a moment while Karl caught up with us, and then the three of us went up to the man sitting on the first camel, while the others waited at the bottom of the dune. Karl did all the talking, not that there was very much talking, but I noticed that the man looked at me and my double, not oddly, but as if he was asking a question. It was a good job it was dark, otherwise he'd have asked a lot more questions about some of the people waiting at the bottom of the hill. I don't remember what made me think he was asking a question, because his head was nearly all covered with a dark hood-thing, and of course in the dark this meant I couldn't see his face at all. As I said, there wasn't much talking done, and neither Karl nor the man on the camel made any movement or gesture, only at one point Karl went over to Syphilis (who'd taken over the cigarette-cases as his load of food and water had gone down) and went back to the man on the camel with a dozen or so cigarette-cases to show him. I noticed the man on the camel seemed a bit more excited than he had been when he saw them, and he looked at each of them very closely, having called to the man behind him to bring a light. I know he called for a light because he raised his voice and then straight away the man behind him came up on his camel with a candle or torch. I heard Smallpox and the others taking a few steps back when this happened.

Karl and the man on the camel looked very like each other while all this was going on, even though Karl had to be looking up all the time, and had to stretch to get the cigarette-cases up to the man on the camel. The two of them seemed to be set apart from the rest of us – from us two, that is, a few feet behind Karl, and the other nine at the bottom of the hill, and all the rest of the caravan. The eleven of us were completely quiet, and so were the 200 or so, not including the camels and children, who made up the rest of the caravan. A lot of the camels had sat down, not, it seemed, either in accordance with or despite their owners' wishes, and some of them from time to time snorted, as did some of the children, though we assumed, without actually knowing, that their noises were a lot more sensible. I don't know, now, whether Karl's general quietness, mentioned earlier in the letter as having to do with the death of his number 2, was a cause or partly a result of his quietness when talking to the man on the camel. In any case, I realised while watching him talk with the man on the camel that I respected his quietness as much as I respected, and still respect, Karl himself.

When he came back to us Karl said that the man had agreed to take one cigarette-case in exchange for six camels, and had said that we were going in the right direction and had easily enough food and water to make it to civilization, now that we had camels. Karl also suggested that we should sleep at the foot of this dune for the night, because the caravan was moving on to an oasis a few miles away, and he didn't want to accept the man's invitation to go with them. The rest of the committee agreed to this straight away, so while we were laying out our sleeping-things on the sand Karl carried on with negotiations, and the caravan began to prepare for departure.

December 2nd

Some time later, the caravan having gone, Raoul Federic Antonius having lit a fire, and everyone except the committee being asleep, we (the committee) were sitting round the fire, and I asked Karl how he had got the man on the camel to accept only one cigarette-case in exchange for six camels, because it seemed to me a very low price, especially as the caravan evidently didn't have very many spare camels.

Karl didn't say much in reply, as I might have expected. In fact he sighed very heavily before starting, as if the whole thing was a bit boring to him, and he didn't say anything normal like "I said to the man on the camel, in whatever language it was, and he answered" but said it all as a completely plain dialogue, with only about ten or a dozen sentences, each one beginning "Karl:" or "Tuareg:", depending on who it was who'd said that particular sentence, and I'm sure he missed a lot of it out, because even speaking at the rate they did they must have covered a lot more ground than Karl did in his dialogue.

"Tuareg" wasn't the name of the man on the camel, as perhaps you know, but the name of the race of people he belonged to. This particular caravan was on its way to some place not at all civilized, but where it was possible to keep goats or grow oats or something (Karl claimed he hadn't understood everything the man had said) but they'd recently passed very close to a town, and I won't tell you its name, for reasons of my own, but let's call it P—. P— was in that direction (Karl clutched his two compasses, having been holding them all this time) and it was only so many days away on a camel. The cigarette cases were something to do with God, as were myself and the other Quincey. God didn't often visit Man in person, and when he did he certainly didn't return after the first time. The Tuareg, though he didn't have any special love for gold or cigarettes, would be willing to give us six camels in exchange for one gold cigarette-case.

That was the end of Karl's dialogue. My double and I (we were sitting at the other two corners of an equilateral triangle round the fire) turned the conversation to the subject of the six camels, which were sitting quite close to us, all tethered to one long stake (a free gift from the Tuareg) and doing we didn't know what, but smelling very bad. As there were twelve of us, it seemed simple enough to decide who was going to ride which camel. Actually, it wasn't so simple, because of my double's insistence on the right of number ones, or committee-members, to have camels all to themselves if they so wished, instead of sharing them with somebody, which seemed a more natural arrangement. However, I'm beginning to get tired of explaining such things to you in detail. When you hear of us all riding camels to P—, imagine one inferior character, usually Syphilis, or perhaps two, Syphilis with Smallpox or Raoul 2, being dragged along behind the last camel, evidently having a hard time, and being given a lift before long by the riders of the last camel, who were usually Karl and one of the five single men, probably Alexander. Karl and Alexander found they had a lot in common during the last few days of our journey.

Having talked about our camels, we went on to talk about you. You were in our thoughts not because you'd put us in the position we were in (actually, you were only a very indirect cause of this) but because, as I'm sure you'll have realised by now, we'd been reading your diary, or Journal. This was one of the many souvenirs we'd brought from the ship, and the weight of its ten volumes, as well as their assorted shapes and sizes, is one of the main reasons why Syphilis, though he has never met you, has a personal grudge against you. Of course we could only read one volume each at any one time (it never seemed really worthwhile to try and duplicate them, especially as this would have broken Syphilis's already twisted back) and we didn't have much time for reading anyway, only the hour or so before going to sleep, so we didn't all know quite the same things about your private life and inner personality. I'd been reading the most important volume, the 1984 one, which goes up to July 18th, the last sentence being "I will not write anything more for a few days". I don't know what date you thought it was on the day you were killed. The crew thought it was July 30th, but this doesn't mean anything, of course. I don't know what date you think it is now, either, but I'm sure we can meet up with you even if our ideas on this subject are different.

It's always risky to read the private diary of someone who knows you, and I must say some of the things about me, which you didn't expect anyone except yourself to read, seem to me not at all complimentary, and even upset me a little bit. Also, you're sometimes very conceited, and unfair in your descriptions and judgements of other people apart from me. These are the sort of things a person reading someone else's private diary has to make allowances for. I do, and so I didn't mention these things to my two friends sitting round the fire. It isn't these things, in your diary or in your actual way of behaving, that make us all hate you. We don't really mind even that you tried to kill us, because everything you do seems somehow doomed to failure from the start, and we could be insulted by your murderous attempt, without actually being able to resent it properly. It's quite strange that I can say we "hate" you. I don't think anyone could hate you till he'd lived with you for a long time. Anyway, I knew my two friends felt the same way about you I did, and they'd probably found bits about themselves and their friends, in the volumes they'd been reading, which upset them as the bits I've mentioned upset me. So I didn't mention them. What makes us hate you is something to do with the whole, rather than bits. Reading a lot of your journal makes me feel it in just the same way as living with you made me feel it. I must say you express yourself very well in your journal – it's almost as if you were standing next to me while I was reading it.

I did mention some parts to my friends sitting round the fire namely the parts about the "White Planet", as you call it, that horrible place where we stopped for a few minutes, at the "edge" of the region we'd been travelling through in fits and starts for five years (I'm told by Karl that it didn't have any "edges"). Perhaps you don't need to be reminded of it – it was there that Smallpox and Syphilis and some of the others, and Miss Keogh, of course, got those nasty injuries. You didn't write much about it in 1984, but it came to your mind sometimes in connection with something else, and then when you mentioned it it seemed very vivid to you, as if it had only happened a few days before, or as if what happened there was specially important for some reason. I mentioned these parts because I disagreed with some of the things you said. For example, you said you didn't deserve any credit for our escape, though in fact if it hadn't been for you we'd never have left, and also you said that you'd said certain things about it to us, in your speeches at dinner-time, and I didn't remember that you'd said these things at all. The other parts of the speeches seemed a bit unfamiliar to me as well.

"I know," Quincey said. "It's all in this volume – last year's".

"Not last year," Karl said. "1983." He went on to say, after a few interruptions, "Surely you can tell by the weather", but I won't describe this part of our conversation in detail – I've said all I want to say on the subject of time, and anyway, as I've pointed out, it doesn't make any difference to the certainty of our meeting. I want to stay on the subject of the White Planet, because this really was an amazing fact that Quincey was going to tell us.

"He writes about all this White Planet business in here," he said, "and it's so detailed it's silly. It goes on for" (he counted them) "16 pages. And the funny thing is, only about half a page of it is true!"

Straight away I felt that this confirmed a lot of the ideas I had about you. But I had to be sure of the facts before making any definite judgement. So for a long time we talked about possible explanations that would clear you of the suspicion that you'd written untrue things in your diary either because you wanted to mislead someone you expected to read it, or because you yourself thought they were true.

One example of these possible explanations, suggested by me because I thought it was interesting – and I still do, though it's evidently not true, and generally a bit flimsy – was that you'd been writing a fantasy, or story, closely related to actual events, not intended to mislead anyone but purely to exercise your mind and its powers of self-expression. My double laughed at this, and said that even if it could be believed it would be as worrying as the obvious explanation, this being the explanation we were leaving out of the argument just to make it obviously true. Karl said nothing at this stage in the argument. I think he was just sitting on the obvious explanation, making sure we didn't forget it.

When we two Quinceys had run out of ideas, I asked the other to read the passage in question, aloud so we'd all know what we were talking about. This took quite a long time, and I got the impression Karl was asleep during most of it, but I was listening closely, and though I found your style heavy going I was completely fascinated by what you said (I think this was partly because my double was reading it, but let that pass). It set me off on a whole new line of thought, and as soon as Quincey had finished I started the argument all over again.

I questioned Quincey 2 very closely about what he himself had seen and heard at the White Planet. It was exactly the same as what I'd have said. But, I said, strictly speaking Quincey 2 had never been to the White Planet, because he'd not come into being until more than a year after the ship had landed there. Was it possible that, though his memory was an exact duplicate of mine, or had become exact during his contact with me, in other ways the second ship was not an exact duplicate of the first? Was your dead double's journal not the same as your own? Was the history written in the journal Ship 2 had been born with, as true as any other could be?

Quincey got very angry at this, and said he knew very well where he'd been and what he'd done there, and anyway he wished I'd drop this habit of calling his ship "Ship 2", because as far as I was concerned "Ship 2" had been the first to go into orbit round the Earth. I didn't go on to explain my other theory (that he'd had an actual former existence different from mine, but had forgotten it) because this would only have made him angrier. I just said, "Not the Earth", and he retorted, "How do you know?". But this was the end of his fit of ill-temper. We dropped that line of argument, though I carried on thinking about it – after all, the cigarette-cases weren't all the same cigarette-case, because, to name only one of many reasons, all except one of them hadn't been taken away by the Tuareg. And there might be little physical differences between them, too small for us to see.

However, we started talking about you and your "hallucinations", and it was while we were discussing these that Karl spoke.

"He's mad," he said.

We had to admit you were mad. What you did was mad, what you said you did in your journal was mad, and it was mad to say you'd done it when you hadn't. When you deserved to be shot, it was mad to wish on yourself death by some slow torture.

Quincey and I talked for a while about madness in general, and psychiatry, and wondered whether you'd been driven mad by your own inexplicable hatefulness, or whether you were hateful because you were mad. Then dawn broke, much sooner than I'd expected – it was sudden, like the nightfall before, but so much more so that I actually jumped to my feet in surprise – and at the same moment Karl spoke again. We evidently weren't going to get any sleep, but this didn't matter much because we now had camels, and it would be possible to doze, if not actually to sleep, while riding them. It wasn't as simple as that, as I was to find out, but around dawn the idea of shortly mounting my camel (now that Quincey had suggested it, I was set on having one to myself) and setting off at a plod across the desert, filled me with a lazy, luxurious kind of pleasure.

But I'm digressing, and what's more I think I'm imitating the style of your journal, which will never do. I don't share the wish to appear mad which seems to be an essential part of your madness. So "I will not write anything more for a few days".

Before we set out that morning we'd decided to come searching for you, and to ask the others whether they wanted to come with us or to stay behind in Africa. As I think I've said before, Smallpox, Syphilis and the Raoul Antoniuses have come with us, and the other five have stayed behind.

The next important event I want to tell you about happened quite a long time after we'd reached P— , and after we'd travelled from there in various ways to B—, Z—, and other places where we thought we might leave our five settlers. We'd found we had a lot of power, as well as wealth, without ever having tried our duplication experiments again. Eventually we'd left the five, all in one place, in a very advantageous situation. I feel it's very important not to let you know where they are. They're not in Mozambique.

Now we were heading for Tangiers, where we'd be setting sail for England, and we'd stopped for the night in the town of Q—. Apart from the time when we'd run down the sand-dune, we hadn't hurried once since landing, and even on that occasion we hadn't been "in" a hurry. We weren't in any hurry now, and we'd stopped in Q— in the early evening, meaning, after we'd checked in at the hotel and so on, to walk round the bazaar for a while before dinner.

Business wasn't as brisk as it probably had been earlier in the day, and the important event I'm going to tell you about happened when we came to a spot where nothing was happening at all, and where there was no-one about, not even the crowd of children who'd been following us until some more attractive thing had led them off in another direction.

Smallpox and Syphilis had stayed behind at the hotel. The remaining five of us were resting in a shady corner between the square and a street, Karl 1 and I leaning against a deserted stall, Antonius 2 and the other Quincey sitting on a pair of large stones facing us, and Karl pacing to and fro across the street at the point where it opened out into the square. Karl was carrying a large number of figs, but not eating them, and from time to time Antonius 2 would go over to him and bring back a handful for the rest of us to eat. The four of us were talking about you, as usual, and trying to work out exactly why we were going in search of you. Karl was saying nothing, and he didn't seem to be thinking very deeply, but we all tended to keep our eyes on him, because we didn't want to look at each other but there was nothing else nearby that was worth watching.

The important event began when he stopped pacing, and stood looking down the street, at something we couldn't see, though it was evident he'd seen someone coming towards us, and from his expression I'd have said it was someone he knew. We all stopped talking at once, and waited impatiently for the man to come round the corner, but before he appeared we heard him say something to Karl, and Karl replied with what seemed to be a forced smile. Then a European came round the corner, and who do you think it was: – it was you again, though we didn't realise for a moment because you were wearing clothes we'd never seen before.

You looked at us, surprised to see more people, and then your eyes went back to Karl, evidently not having recognised us. You said "What are you doing here, Waeldermann?", like a schoolteacher, and Karl said, "Making some new friends," in a sort of quietly impertinent way, but you pretended you were happy with this reply, because I think you were a bit nervous to be alone with the five of us. You looked back at us four, and Karl said, "Bert and Tom Abercrombie, and Spike and Fred Pine-Coffin – this is Captain Lionel Jaffa, son of the space-ship designer."

You inclined your head slowly, evidently wondering what to do next, and the Raoul Antoniuses muttered polite greetings, also unsure what to make of the encounter. It wasn't only your clothes which confused us. When you arrived, as I said, we'd been trying to work out what it was we were doing, and none of us had so far thought of it as hunting a ghost, so when a ghost actually came and put itself in our hands, I, at least, found my ideas rushing ahead just a bit too fast for me. The other Quincey and I were both fingering the hilts of the expensive Moroccan knives we had hidden in our clothes, and I was going over in my head certain passages from your journal and other parts of your history I happened to know about, and trying to connect them with later events. After a very short time, though, when you had just started talking more seriously with Karl, and ignoring us, I realised that the meeting was on the whole a good thing, and reassuring rather than disturbing. Having worked my knife into a more convenient position, I let go of it, and I noticed Quincey's hand also reappearing empty. I'd managed to distinguish between this ghost-Jaffa and the one we were looking for, and I knew that this one made it more likely that we were actually going to find the other. [*the letter breaks off at this point*]

Letter, Mr Quincey Horace to Sir Charles Pink, M.A. (Cantab.)
December 7th

My dear Pink,

No doubt you are surprised to receive a letter from me, at a time when we should all perhaps be hunting each other down or trying to forget each other; but I think I can convince you that correspondence between us would not be an abuse of the postal system, and even that our respective ideas have been developing in such a way that some kind of community may shortly be possible – developing, that is, in this recent period during which our actions, too, have had their resemblances, and have not in retrospect been all that vindictive.

Not that our ideas have been moving in precisely the same direction – rather, I should say, at the same speed; this will not necessarily make us love each other more than we ever did. It will make us, at the same time and with regard to the same hypothetical situation, stand both closer together and further apart, as if our relationship, like ourselves, had been duplicating itself and creating multiple identities. We have both had to cope with the doppelganger and the more than doppelganger, and we both now know that it is possible to adopt widely differing attitudes to them; I know that you have killed at least one (potentially, perhaps actually, many) of your own selves, and that you would not, except under extreme provocation, allow yourself to take a similar liberty with the lives of someone else: and you know that I, though I have a deep-rooted moral objection to harming any version of myself, feel that the mere abundance of all other life suggests a freedom, or I might almost say a duty, to destroy no matter what being, or being's duplicate (if there is in reality such a distinction), whenever I feel so inclined. The hypothetical situation I mentioned earlier is an encounter between one of my doubles and you, occurring approximately forty days ago, when I would have had, I believe, a strong inclination to kill you, and you, I feel sure, would not have resisted (logically, indeed, you should have been grateful). Thus, although we have, on the subject of the doppelganger's implications for personal responsibility, perfectly antithetical views (as probably never before on any subject), we could be seen as working, in the long run, toward the same end – the peopling of the world with Quincey Horace, and the reduction of Charles Pink, if not actually to nought then at most to one: an end composed of two different and I suppose mutually exclusive ends, each in itself inaccessible and infinitely engaging.

Please excuse me if you find my talk of ends distasteful. All my friends and I have found it constantly necessary, ever since setting out into this world, to think in terms of purpose; we have not been able actually to sustain a single purpose for longer than six weeks, but have always been aware of the need to do so; and we think that the world's influence is sufficiently strong to make you conscious of a similar need. We also think that you are capable of satisfying the need, by sustaining a purpose more or less indefinitely. No doubt you would deny capability of any such thing, and accuse us of vulgar abuse; but we have what we consider evidence of your consistent, if unconscious, tenacity. My letter will be about your tenacity and our conscious present purpose. It would be possible, you see, to combine them; desirable, too, as your own long-lived purpose must needs be short-sighted, egocentric and a waste of consistent tenacity: possibly it is to lift yourself out of the squalid mediocrity suggested by your address, a mediocrity we have ourselves had experience of, over the last month. We will soon be in a position to achieve that end for you quite satisfactorily, and will do so, provided that you then concentrate your unique abilities on the implementation of our large idea, the briefest acquaintance with which will convince you of its worthiness. Quite apart from pertinacity, you see, you are wasting scientific knowledge and technique – acquisitions which had begun to seem irrelevant to all of us, but which we are now beginning to think may again be applicable to our situation. We have no need of your astronomical prowess, being quite content to observe that the sky continues more or less as normal; but we could use your knowledge of more earthbound sciences, particularly chemistry, in which it is comforting to know you are an adept, also psychology, physiology, etc. – you will have realised that our idea involves conducting a series of experiments. The most unusual feature of the series is that we intend to continue it indefinitely – as long, that is, as we can avoid distractions, and if possible either endlessly or until we die. If the idea of immortality has not yet occurred to you, I must point out that increased control over our duplicates, which will necessarily be one of the fields in which we work, may well lead to a situation in which the dying man can reproduce himself with the fatal element left out.

Perhaps it is superfluous to mention that the date at the head of this letter marks nothing but the day on which it was begun. Such discrepancies are among the greatest disadvantages of writing letters, I find. Bearing this in mind, however, I will proceed to give you a summary of our progress in this world so far. Our original intention was simply to settle down, in Mozambique or somewhere similar, and see if we could achieve some kind of compromise between self-interest and the furthering of an ideal society. This plan lasted about three days; I think the immediate causes of its decay were threefold: we had some rather odd visionary experiences in the desert, we immersed ourselves in study of Lionel Jaffa's journals, and our less intelligent colleagues exerted a certain amount of pressure, asking what was remarkable about Mozambique, that we should be trying to find our way there rather than stopping in the first barbaric and fruitful village where we could exploit our superior sophistication. Of course, even if our idealism had not suffered these particular blows, we would quite soon have found ourselves abandoning the social reform plan, if only because of the apathy of the natives. I don't know whether you have tried yet to convey a political idea to someone – from what I remember of you, I should think you haven't – but if you ever should, I think you'll find it a hard task. While wandering through the African states, we naturally received news of a number of revolutions when they were still in progress, and retaining as we did an amateur interest in such things, and needing some kind of direction for our footsteps, we tended to arrive in revolt-torn towns only a few days after receiving the news. Needing, then, something on which to converse with the townspeople, we would ask for more information about the recent revolution; and these strange creatures would... [*the letter breaks off at this point*]

Journal of Miss Isobel Keogh[3]

Thursday, December 6th, 1973

The reason I've waited so long is that I felt we couldn't claim any practical recognition, or expect anyone – ourselves in particular – to consider the contents of this notebook significant, until we'd had some less superficial contact with the people around us than the sort of customer-to-salesman relationship which has immediately established itself in every situation we've encountered except last night's. An example of this was our expedition on Monday, when Charles persuaded me to go to the bank with him; however crazed and unbelievable the events following my decision became, as far as understanding the other participants was concerned they didn't take us any further than the initial over-the-counter exchange between Charles and the other cashier. Monday's adventure and comparable occurrences – comparable, I'm glad to say, not in unpleasantness but in that any active role we took in them was forced upon us by their strangeness – have made me more and more nervous about leaving the house, and, for that matter, going through any door; but now that I know we can do some honest trading ourselves, as well as accepting the callous inertia-sales technique of everything around us, I can see that my timidity is less debilitating than it might have been, and that it has its compensations, especially as regards the stability of whatever emotion it is that keeps Charles from leaving me.

---

3 On the inside front cover of this notebook, the first of the seventy-six lined leaves having been glued to the cardboard so as to form a stiff title-page, Miss Keogh has written, with the same kind of felt-tipped pen used through the journal itself, but in much neater handwriting than elsewhere, the following address: 1,316, Finchley Road, London N.W.2. The remainder of the page is covered with small and intricate drawings, all of subjects either grotesque or repellent, and executed with a neatness similar to that of the address.

The seventy-sixth leaf, also, has been glued to the inside back cover, thus leaving only seventy-four leaves to form the body of the notebook, and, discounting the outer surfaces of the glued-down leaves, one hundred and fifty pages on which it was possible to write. On the stiffened page 150, upside down, Miss Keogh began her second piece of writing, a letter, which extends, upside down, backwards into the middle of the book, and whose purpose is revealed in the journal beginning on page 2. – *The Author.*

A cursory examination of last night's dinner-party wouldn't light on any significant difference between this event and all the preceding ones; it's only by a particularly involved form of intuition that I can see it myself. After all, we only invited Mr Mote, and he brought this extraordinary woman along with him completely unannounced, unexplained and apparently uncontrolled. Also, the various unsolicited happenings were by no means less bizarre than anything else we've been through. The only positive results which might lead to a reasoned optimism about our social life were that Charles did seem to establish actual communication with Mr Mote, even going so far as to reminisce with him about experiences at Cambridge, and to speculate about Lionel's condition; and that by the end of the evening Mr Mote was definitely committed to doing something about our legal situation, which was what Charles had intended to achieve, before anything else, by inviting the man to dinner.

I shall tell the story of the dinner. Mr Mote arrived very early – at about five instead of eight – but Charles, who opened the door, didn't remark on the fact. I was sitting in the dining room, and I remained there, because I always look better when I'm sitting down; in fact, I can convince myself, if no-one else, that in this position I look almost normal. So the first few exchanges in the hall I heard only indistinctly. Nonetheless I could tell it was Mr Mote arriving, from the tone of Charles's voice. It was quite a relief really, because we were both completely ready, not that there was any question of getting dressed up, for me at any rate. If they hadn't come at five we would have had three hours' fairly uncertain waiting together, probably one of us at the table and the other by the fireplace, and stable though our relationship is becoming, I think it would only with difficulty have survived such a period of strain without sustaining at least a few superficial injuries. I could not distinguish words, except "Well, Charlie" (a loud greeting) until they came into the room, but I later found that Charles had made no comment on their early arrival, because he told me he had successfully persisted, from the very beginning, in his resolve not to voice anything like an implied criticism. I was well aware of this resolve, for during the meal he was so careful not to antagonise them that I quite frequently had to introduce the necessary note of aggression myself, presumptuous though I felt this to be even at the time.

Charles's next move, after his self-effacing response to Mr Mote's greeting, was to begin shutting the door, Mr Mote having stepped into the hall. It was then that Charles saw the woman, standing on the step, and that I heard a particularly raucous female voice, as unintelligible to Charles as to me, he tells me. Greatly put out by the sight of this woman, and remaining unenlightened by Mr Mote though he stood clutching the doorknob in overt astonishment for a time, Charles nonetheless had to assume that the second visitor was connected with the first – partly because, had she not been, Charles would have expected a "Hello, hello, hello, what's this?" from his old friend; and partly because the noises she was herself making sounded like a continuation of Mr Mote's opening line, and were ringing with what appeared to be self-confidence. She was somehow entitled, then, to admittance. But who wasn't, Charles asked himself, as he let her in.

I hadn't done the cooking myself, of course; we had employed a man called Dingbrace, discovered by Charles through an advertisement in the local newsagent's window:

"Struggling restaurateur, of prodigious unappreciated talent, requires work in private households, preparing lavish meals for special occasions. Spanish cuisine a speciality. Incredible rates. Apply Mr Dingbrace – 435 2322."

Charles saw this notice quite by chance. That is, he wasn't specifically seeking a cook at the time, but merely scanning the notices in case there were any messages for him. It was part of one of his spells of "walking about" duty, during which spells, in the normal course of things, he has met with equal fortuity the large numbers of old acquaintances who seem to have been looking for him, but who have later proved to have little to offer. Dingbrace, who came into the dining-room at exactly the same time as the others, but from the opposite direction – that is, from the kitchen rather than the hall – had in certain respects anticipated the increased intimacy of this night's proceedings, because he had struck up something resembling a friendship with Charles.

Ever since his arrival on Tuesday, he had been the subject of long eulogistic speeches delivered by Charles, sometimes to me and sometimes to the man himself. Charles knows a great deal about cooking – probably more than Dingbrace – and he would have cooked the meal himself, I'm sure, had it not been for his preoccupation with more important things over the last few days, and for his general preference of theory to practice in the many disciplines of which he is master; what I find persistently puzzling is that he should see so much to praise in Dingbrace, now that it has become obvious, particularly to a man of Charles's expertise, that his advertisement was in some respects an exaggeration. Charles has spent many hours with him in the kitchen, and I feel sure that most of the ideas have come from Charles, though Dingbrace may have implemented them. And yet Charles continues to refer to him, albeit in a tone of affection rather than reverence, as a misunderstood genius. This is an unusually hackneyed allusion, for Charles. Perhaps it is merely a sustained joke. Charles does appear to be responding to a certain superficial jocularity about Dingbrace – loudly urging him on Tuesday, for example, not to go home (wherever that may be, he won't tell us) but to stay here for the night and drink with us in the evening. I don't think the urging was at all necessary. He stayed here last night as well – but that will come at the end of this story.

So this man came into the dining-room, as I've said, at the same time as the others, through a different door, wearing the absurd chef's hat he's never been without, carrying a wooden spoon, his apron streaked with nameless organic matter in the manner of a butcher's. He wasn't coming from precisely the opposite direction, as the two walls and the doors in them are at right angles, but on account of my position by the fire the two entrances were made at opposite extremities of my field of vision. Dingbrace said, "When do you want it, my dear?" and I became aware of the woman, who was leaning heavily against the side of the doorway, and moving forward by revolving slowly round it, her eyes fixed keenly on me. The two gentlemen were entering behind and slightly to her left, and I could see that Charles was looking at the floor, perhaps embarrassed by the slowness forced upon his progress. Mr Mote looked surprisedly at Dingbrace as he came in.

The weather at the moment is very cold and damp, and everything outside seems to be black, grey or brown. It's about four o'clock in the afternoon. I've just come in from the back garden, where I've been resting, observing the potential of our almost empty flower-beds, trying to calculate how long it is since I last considered the front garden seriously; the front garden is a lot smaller, but that's not why I rarely go into it. I don't think there have ever been many large front gardens in London. Except the Jaffas', of course, which I presume is still there. I've also been thinking about the whole question of my deformity, how to become accustomed to it, and so on; the first step being to make myself more aware of it. Not that I don't have a very vivid idea of all the ways in which my body differs from a normal body; I've spent many hours, mainly those immediately before bedtime, studying them in front of the mirror: the problem is that I don't know how they appear to other people, and though I'm naturally frightened of showing myself to other people, I can't get myself to care about my malformity as simple malformity. I think what I must do is write, not in this narrative but after I've finished it, and perhaps somewhere else in the notebook, an account of my abnormality as detailed and accurate as I can make it. 1.) Jawbone. a.) left-hand side. Outer surface, protuberance two-and-a-half inches; inner surface, indentation one-and-a-half inches; increased thickness of bone ... this will involve sitting in front of the mirror with a tape-measure, making notes. And Charles will have to help me; perhaps he'll enjoy it. I'll mention it as soon as he comes home, which I hope will be soon, as I don't like to be alone with a garden and my own writing.

Anyhow, last night I was at once relieved of any apprehension about offending our guests by my appearance, because it was apparent that the woman – whom Mr Mote addressed either as "Belly" or "Stomach", and referred to as "the Virgin", "Maria (the) Beautiful" and other variations on this theme – was considerably more grotesque than I. It was not merely her tendency to communicate by non-verbal sound; we all do so, particularly at moments of high stress, and perhaps for a greater fraction of our speaking lives than we realise. I do so more often and more self-consciously than others, because the new shape of my mouth is a powerful influence on my manner of speech. It is a long time since I said either "yes" or "no". No, the Virgin's strangeness lay in the inescapable impression that her moments of normality were aberrations from an alien consistency deeper than our own; her appearance was peculiar in points which, though not greatly significant to the eye, made even a body as perfect as Charles's reconsider uncomfortably the ideal form behind itself.

Having described about a hundred degrees she began to return round the same doorpost-centred circle, her eyes still fixed on me. I could tell she wasn't drunk because the look she gave me was intense and rational, though incomprehensible. Charles had taken advantage of that point on her curve which was closest to me – as it brought her almost completely into the room, leaving the doorway virtually clear – to step hurriedly past her and move over to the drinks-cabinet by the window, where he was now causing a corkscrew to move in an oscillatory half-circle similar to the Virgin's – but at higher speed – as he seemed to be having unusual difficulty, and wanted to make sure that the corkscrew was properly engaged in the cork. This oddly echoed movement – which, now that it had forced itself upon my awareness, began to appear all over the room in numerous smaller forms such as Mr Mote's gestures with his cigarette – made me think of a dog tied to a tree, repeatedly trying to reach something outside the radius dictated by its rope; it also distracted me from the conversation, which was nonetheless continuing, Mr Mote having said loudly, "Ding-dong, - Dingbry!", and the Virgin at this point having produced her first, perfectly enunciated sentence: "Call him by his Christian name, Algy!". It was spoken in a perfect accent – Oxford (or is it Cambridge?) English – but it had an overtone of stage-insanity. Mr Mote's Christian name is Aloysius.

"Sit down, Belly my pet," he replied, "and stop fidgeting in that absurd manner." He began to question Dingbrace rather circumspectly about his reasons for being here, making the gestures with his cigarette I've already mentioned above, and then, having found he was the cook, moved on to the subject of what we were to have for dinner. Charles said, "Have some of this," bearing an open bottle, for which I was heartily glad, as I had begun to feel both threatened and neglected; and the Virgin, whether answering the call of alcohol or belatedly obeying Mr Mote I don't know – though I'm sure she wasn't drunk – sulkily pulled herself away from the doorway and sat down on the other side of the fire. Dingbrace was saying,

"Fish, if it please you, sir," very pompously, and scratching himself about the dirty apron with his spoon.

I should say at this point that Dingbrace contrasted quite violently with all the other occupants of the room, at least in appearance; I have already mentioned that my dress was not particularly formal or spectacular: it was, however, designed to conceal, as far as possible, the irregularities of my body beneath a sort of neat simplicity, and this it did quite efficiently. The Virgin, on the other hand, was positively resplendent, her costume having a mass of elaboration which was far too opulent, excessive and interesting to be considered simply bad taste, and which was obviously intended, moreover, to accentuate rather than to hide the few visible peculiarities of the Virgin's anatomy; she had an ostrich-feather boa, for example, which she twirled and twined very fluently about a protuberance from the centre of her sternum. The protuberance was thus made to seem both more natural and more mysterious, and was certainly guaranteed a proportion of every observer's attention and curiosity. At first I took it for a third breast, but later I decided, on account of its apparent consistency, that it was more likely to be the stump of an amputated third arm. Charles and Mr Mote were wearing dinner-jackets, as they have done on such occasions, it seems, ever since forming their three-cornered friendship with Lionel at Cambridge. So Dingbrace's heavily daubed apron excited more disgust than it might otherwise have done. He was returning to the kitchen, in any case, and I said, "In about half an hour, please, Dingbrace" – a reply which had been delayed by all this rather confusing observation of simultaneous occurrences – as Mr Mote came to join the congregation round the bottle, saying, "It's not Friday, is it? I thought you were a Jew, Charlie-boy."

"It's Wednesday."

"Well, I must say I never expected to find you in a hole like this. Thank you."

"Me? You think it's me? I? Well. Thank you."

"Damn fine wine this."

"Yes, I don't know what it is, it came from the shop at the bottom of the road."

"I can see perfectly well it's you. I'd know your D.J. anywhere."

"But didn't you – er – read the reports of my murder? On Monday, outside the National Westminster Bank." I hear someone opening the front door. I hope this is Charles, returning.

Later

It was indeed Charles, who is now asleep in the chair which was occupied last night, during the preliminary drinking at least, by the Virgin. He has been dropping in and out of sleep ever since he got home, poor boy, but this time it looks more deep and lasting, so I return to my labours. He has been to see the Jaffas, as arranged – Lionel's wife, Jezebel, and surprisingly his father, Charles, but not Lionel himself, as he, it seems, is in Africa. Charles has been telling me the story of his visit to the house – "Yes, my pet, it has a beautiful garden, which I think must be the one you remember; a tarmacadam drive, with white pebbles set in the edges – and a very green lawn – and I believe I saw that large swinging couch you've told me about, though I'm not sure of it. I was rather preoccupied at the time."

I have been taking very detailed notes, in order to preserve his exact words – aided by my rudimentary shorthand, and by Charles's frequent dozing – and as one passage seems oddly relevant to the tale of the dinner-party, at the exact point I have now reached, I intend to transcribe it here. Of course, the Virgin and I were not completely silent during the first conversation between Charles and Mr Mote, but for some reason I chose to write about the gentlemen's conversation first, and add the ladies later, and as it has turned out this chance arrangement is greatly conducive to unity in what from now on will be a double narrative.

"She's a very handsome woman – very handsome. Not particularly elegant, you know, but handsome, in an elfish way – not that she's very small. She makes one feel protective; not a bit like you, my dear." (A rather lecherous chuckle.) "She let me in herself, after I'd told her who I was, and she introduced me to the old man almost straight away, over the tea-table. If you really want every single detail, I think she made some pleasantries about the times of meals, how I was too late for lunch and too early for tea, and so on. Then she led the old man in, and it was a complete surprise, of course; I didn't even know she'd left the room until she was back in it with this old man. He was bending over a stick, and trembling, and complaining about having to eat his tea with other people and moreover at this unprecedented hour, and so on, and so on; he was behaving, in fact, like a very expert buffoon, and I leapt to my feet – I have no idea what my motive in doing that may have been.

"Mrs Jaffa said 'Sir Charles, this is my father-in-law, Sir Charles Jaffa. Sir Charles Pink, father, you remember.'

"He said – oh, and his state of mind seemed to change, and he put on a silly grin – 'Yes, I'm Sir Charles too.' Charles did a very amusing imitation of the old man's voice, and sustained it throughout the story, though he left Mrs Jaffa unmimicked. I can vouch for the accuracy of the imitation, but will not attempt to commit it to paper.

"I had lost so much of my *sang froid* that I blurted out, 'I thought you were dead, sir', and then he began a long speech, not entirely unprovoked; I can't remember his exact words, but the gist of it was something like this:

" 'Well, young man, we often think our fellow-creatures are dead, don't we? Sometimes we're proved wrong, that's all. Someone told me *you* were dead, if it comes to that, but I believe little of what other people read in the papers. I think if you begin by stating your business, you'll find you can proceed in full confidence that I'm alive – without even thinking about it, indeed – and I'm prepared to take it on trust that you're not completely dead yet yourself, provided you accept ...' " It was at this point that Charles fell asleep for the first time; I became aware of a pause, which grew longer as I caught up, on paper, with the ended speech, and then as I stared, pen poised, at the space waiting for the next word: it didn't come, and I looked up to find Charles sunk in sleep, head on chest and hands in lap, his drooping form surrounded by fire.

That's it, in any case – all that's relevant to the dinner-party so far. Neither Mr Mote nor Sir Charles Jaffa questioned Charles's existence, though he'd supposedly been murdered, on Monday outside the National Westminster Bank. When he started talking again it was at a completely different point in the story, and I never heard the end of Sir Charles Jaffa's speech, because I didn't like to interrupt. Why everyone should have been so blasé about Charles's charmed existence I don't know, though I can think of several facts any one of which would be an adequate explanation. I could reveal a number of things to these people about the alleged murder – the actual murder – and ask them if the information made them think differently; but the fact that it probably wouldn't is one of my explanations. Perhaps such incidents are common here. We certainly haven't been visited by the police yet (a point made by Charles about five minutes ago causing me more alarm than reassurance) although they are investigating, it seems.

Poor Charles (I say it again) – he gets just as frightened about things as Lionel ever did (I say it in the past tense, perhaps because he's "dead" to me; but I'm sure he still exists, if only because people here seem to exist rather more than people elsewhere). The difference is that Charles tries so hard to hide his fright, while Lionel used simply to cover his with an automatic bestiality. And I used to be excited, I'm afraid, by his occasional sadism; but ever since the period of these horrible changes in my body – the White Planet, the place came to be called – I've shrunk, for some reason, from anything suggesting cruelty. I don't actively resist it, but I try to avoid situations where it might arise. Not with complete success (which is hardly to be expected) for Charles committed an act of cruelty about ten minutes ago, shortly after raising the question of the police. He is capable of cruelty, but his tends to be cruelty of omission, rather than well-planned and minutely designed torture. Perhaps it is immodest of me not only to have reached for his fly-buttons but also to write about it; his reaction, however, was significant, and perhaps I only imagine that I'm actually choosing events to include in this narrative. Having just said, "I think I also saw…", after which he lapsed into a brooding silence before mentioning the police, he pushed my licentious hand away with a disgruntled noise, left his chair and went upstairs, presumably to bed; all this happened about fifteen minutes ago, and he hasn't come down again yet.

Friday, December 7th, 1973

It must simply be worry which makes him behave so strangely (worry as opposed to fear, the concealment of which is one of his sources of worry). He isn't conscious of his cruelty. I remember now that he reacted in much the same way to my suggestion that he help me catalogue my deformities; not in quite the same way, though, for in this case he seemed positively shocked.

But I mustn't make today's entry a mere continuation of yesterday's digression. Nor must I wait so long again. The point at which I intended to start this morning's entry was this morning's edition of *The Times*, the steps by which I approached my actual starting-point being as follows: today is Friday, and, tomorrow being Saturday, I won't be able to read *The Times* tomorrow (though I became interested in it for the first time this morning) because it is only delivered five days a week; the reason for this is that Charles is worried about money; I wrote yesterday about the fact that Charles is worried; I must re-read yesterday's entry in order to guard against repetition and stylistic irregularities.

Something else from yesterday's entry, which I can now use as an introduction to the real matter of today, is the speculation about everything's relevance; as I believe I've said, I never interested myself in *The Times* before this morning (though Charles had told me that previous editions represented the Mozambique business as something rather different from the Mozambique business we were used to at home): however, having read it all the way through this morning, from what motive I don't know, possibly boredom, I can now speculate about little save the standing fact that every article in the newspaper appeared to be about us and our history – whether directly or indirectly, every reporter seemed to be addressing his disclosures to my deserted breakfast-table. I exclude those interested solely in sport. I intend to transcribe two articles from the edition of *The Times* in question, the two articles being those in which I feel I will continue to take an interest as events, and my narration of them, develop; I don't expect to be able to preserve this copy of *The Times* for ever, though we have nineteen back-numbers piled neatly in a corner of the kitchen. The most striking feature of these articles is their unfamiliarity; although an edition of *The Times* for 7th December, 1973, was certainly available to me on Earth, before we left, my memory tells me that if we were to return to the same place (absolute impossibility) and I were to go to the offices of *The Times* or the British Museum, I would never find anything remotely resembling these articles, either in content or in style.

The two are not associated by the editor (or editorial team, I suppose), one being a small item of "news" at the bottom of page 3, and the other a relatively long passage on a Subject of General Interest. There is at least one possibility, however, by which the two could have been more or less journalistically linked – namely, that the ship mentioned in the former is the one on which Lionel, son of the protagonist of the latter, is returning from Africa to England.

STRANGE OBJECT SEEN FROM SHIP

Liverpool – Thursday. A report has been received from S.S.Nabucco, sailing from Tangier to Liverpool, that this morning, after a storm of such unprecedented violence that some anxiety was felt for the safety of the ship, though it is a solid craft, an unidentified object was seen to fall from a great unspecified height, and to plunge into the ocean at a distance of some one and a half miles from the ship. The object was witnessed independently by a large number of people, including the captain, members of the crew, and several distinguished passengers, over a period of time suggesting that the object came from the outer reaches of the atmosphere; it was reported to be of enormous size, to be made, apparently, of metal, and one of the theories put forward by the witnesses is that it was a space-craft or satellite, formerly in orbit round the Earth, affected, in some unexplained way, by the atmospheric disturbances of the previous four or five hours.

THE CLAIMS OF SIR CHARLES JAFFA, SPACE-SHIP DESIGNER

The long drawn-out legal wranglings between the Crown and Sir Charles Jaffa, which began almost immediately after the discovery on Hampstead Heath of a space-ship, on the morning of August 1st., have finally come to a conclusion with a decision in favour of Sir Charles, who is now free to do with the space-ship whatever he wishes. The question, as all readers of this article must know, was one of the property; the space-ship, though it showed signs of recent use, was found utterly deserted, and if no-one had come forward to claim it, its discoverers having shown a marked lack of interest in possession of such a bulky object, it would have passed into the hands of Sir James Baconbury, the Scientist Royal.

Sir Charles claimed the ship, however, immediately, he tells us, after reading in this journal of its discovery; and he made, moreover, such a convincing display of ownership, that he not only managed to sway public opinion at the time, but also engaged in the already well-documented court-battle with an assurance which perhaps anticipated, and has now most certainly been rewarded by, a complete and much applauded victory.

Jaffa's career was most notable for the almost picturesque lack of seriousness with which it was regarded by his fellow scientists. "I believe that that frightful man, Arnold Schoenberg, once said of that equally frightful man, John Cage, that he was less an artist, or something, than an inventor. I am afraid that I must do Herr Schoenberg the courtesy of echoing his statement, with regard to our revered colleague, Sir Charles Jaffa, who has, I am sure – and let him not think for a moment that this is an adverse criticism – considerable less in him of the inventor, which is what, I believe, he would like us to imagine that he is, than of the artist, and, to be more specific, of the poet, which is what, I believe, he has tried his hand at being, and is what, I suggest, he has been with far greater success..." Here I will cut short the speech of Sir James Baconbury, given at a 1971 dinner of the Royal Society, which is by now sufficiently well known to merit no further quotation than is absolutely necessary. Sir James's description of Sir Charles's métier was, I feel, accurate, and it is largely this pleasing vacillation between the introvert and extravert qualities (to put it very simply) of the poet and the scientist respectively, which has earned for all of Sir Charles's works, few and diverse as they have been, their quite extraordinary popular appeal.

Perhaps the rumour about his creative activity most potentially damaging to his reputation among those as single-minded as Baconbury has been that his space-ship, which, he tells us, has been on the drawing-board and the "construction-pad" concurrently for more than seven years, and which, if only because of his phenomenal age (he also tells us) is likely to prove his magnum opus, is not in fact a space-ship at all, in any real sense of the word, but some kind of poetic or otherwise fanciful idea, which is no doubt being worked towards some kind of artistic or otherwise practical expression, but which could never conceivably materialise as anything quite so concrete as an erection of metal and plastic capable of making an assertive motion in the general direction of the stars. The arguments in favour of this theory were many; not the least convincing was that although a number of journalists, myself included, had infiltrated his private domain (a large house with extensive grounds in the south of London, where he now lives alone with his daughter-in-law, Mrs Jezebel Jaffa), not one had ever caught a glimpse of workshops, "construction-pads", or mechanical operations of any kind. It was possible that Sir Charles had engaged some manufacturer in strict secrecy: however, even then such speculations were fruitless. Now, if we are to accept as just the judicial decision which has just been made, we must reject all such rumours and perhaps a few other things to boot.

I will refer to two main bodies of material as used in the trial: the evidence of one Miss Isobel Keogh, introduced as Sir Charles's chief engineer; and the various statements of Sir Charles Jaffa himself. The former was significant in that she proved, beyond any reasonable doubt, that the design of the craft found on Hampstead Heath was identical to that embodied in certain very numerous blueprints in her possession, and that these blueprints were associated very closely with a project undertaken by Sir Charles Jaffa, during the execution of which she had been engaged by him, at an enormous fee, to deal with certain mechanical details which he felt incapable of adequately managing for himself.

The latter adopted a blustering style from the very beginning, and sustained it throughout the proceedings; such a style is not entirely consistent with his customary public identity, but it was probably calculated as the attitude most likely to achieve success in this particular case, about which Sir Charles certainly felt very strongly. He made few concessions to any ideas other than his own preconceived notions of the truth of the matter, even though some of his assertions worked very strongly against him in purely legal terms. He claimed, for example, that although this space-ship was identical to his, as he and Miss Keogh had designed it, and identical, moreover, in details of which someone who had merely stolen the designs would not have thought, yet it was not the machine upon which he had been working. "The principal difference between this craft and my own working model," he says, "is that this one has been used for space-travel, whereas mine will not be used in such a way for at least another three months. It incorporates, I admit, certain refinements which have not yet been worked into mine, but anyone who examines intelligently our designs will see that these refinements were always the logical conclusion of our operations, and that they will now be their actual conclusion."

I find myself unable to comment, ultimately, on the rights and wrongs of this case; I will leave you, instead, with another statement made by Sir Charles – not in the trial itself, this time, but in answer to a report which appeared in one of the less reputable dailies quite recently. The Press, indeed, has been unusually active over this matter – especially the science correspondents – and I would not be surprised if you were to find something rather more pertinent and interesting on the subject in one of our other pages today.

"I wish it to be made known among all journalists that Mr Baconbury's asseverations are absurd to the point of offensiveness. I would not dispute that he has been "examining the problem of time" for as long as he claims. Nor am I about to raise any objection to his working as hard as he likes on whatever imaginary notion he pleases. The imagination is capable of greater work than the intellect. If I personally, however, lacked either of these two faculties, I would be rather cautious about undertaking any work at all. Imagination and intellect both work best in various combinations with each other and with other things. But to return to my tolerance of Mr Baconbury's imagination. It remains as complete and magnanimous as I describe it only so long as he does not indicate one of my possessions, indeed of my creations, and claim that it depends for its pattern of behaviour on the random working of this rather isolated function of his own brain. I thank him for conceding the fact that my space-ship did not depart of its own accord (abandoning its created purpose without the assistance even of a crew) on a simple "journey along the time-dimension". I thank him also for his deduction, which does not follow but which is nonetheless welcome, that the ship on the Heath and the one in my back garden have separate existences. They do. These existences, however, are most definitely not "two different points on the time continuum made simultaneously visible by the action of a warp"; and it is for this reference to his silly "warps" for which I do not thank, but curse, Mr Baconbury. In one sense, at least, the two are facets of single existence, but neither has anything to do with time. They do not bend things, or pass from our universe into some other and then back into ours again. They are developed and used, and they decay, just like everything else, more or less independently. Only if these particular things are in any way dependent it is on me that they depend. The simple fact is that I have made at least two space-ships (perhaps not entirely in accordance with my original conscious intention) rather than a single one.

"And now, two final notes on related subjects. First, the name which I prefer to use at present is "Sir (and I thank yet again the person responsible for this noble addition, which improves the rhythm immeasurably) Charles Jaffa, Space-Ship Designer". The parenthesis is not included in the name, of course. It is a name designed, partly, for the journalists I address. I know their penchant for the kind of dramatic poetry which also appeals most to me, and although the more conventional critics will probably take exception to the identification of my name with any kind of dramatic poetry, it is as a line from this particular type, which it will be convenient to call "journalese epic", that I have always seen it. The line is composed, more or less, of four different feet: an iamb, a trochee, a dactyl and a spondee. That is how I would describe it, anyway, and I should know, as it is one of my favourite "speech-rhythms" for use in dialogue. Why has it been composed? Like all such things, to make a simple statement monolithic, thus persuading its audience to attach to it an exaggerated significance. Why have I mentioned it here? Because my audience of journalists, ignoring my poetic effect, has failed to contradict Baconbury when he asserts that I, having been spared a certain amount of "less spectacular" work, which might otherwise, he claims, never have been done, by the appearance through his time-warp of the completion of my designs, will shortly myself depart on a much publicised space-journey. I am Sir Charles Jaffa, Space-ship Designer. I am not an Astronaut. No doubt my space-ship will be used by someone. My son Lionel has expressed an interest, but recently he's become mixed up with all this political nonsense, and gone off to Africa, and if someone comes along in his absence I have no intention of reserving my space-ship for him. He seems incidentally, to be deserting his wife Jezebel, the woman with whom I am now living, and you can make of that whatever you will. My dear friend and engineer Isobel Keogh may not be totally irrelevant to this fact.

"Secondly, the "hairy man" certain witnesses claim to have seen at the scene of the discovery was quite obviously displaying an intelligent interest in my invention, and doubtless in its contents. If he, or it, has used the former to travel here from an alien planet, then good luck to him (or it). As to the latter – another group of my possessions by no means less interesting than the ships themselves – I can assure him, if he is reading this, that all items of value were transferred to my house long before their removal became a "criminal" act."

I will now resume my transcription of the narration by Charles (to whose murder the newspaper also refers, in its by now habitually bored manner) of his visit to the house of Sir Charles Jaffa, yesterday. The moment of embarrassment at which this section begins was caused by his passing, but I'm afraid typically indiscreet, reference to Lionel; upon which Mrs Jaffa, it seems, was so disturbed that she could hardly restrain herself from bursting into tears on the spot, and very shortly afterwards she hurriedly left the room and did not reappear.

"Well, you can imagine how I felt, but old Jaffa didn't seem to mind, in fact I think she has quite a lot to put up with from him, not that I saw him persecuting her or anything like that. He seemed to be going to say something, though, and something told me it wasn't going to be something likely to make me any happier, if you see what I mean, and I felt obliged to change the subject anyway, so I asked him what he'd been working on recently, knowing that he's the kind of chap who'd like to talk about that kind of thing, and also hoping to hear something about the ship, of course. Well, he didn't say anything about the ship, but I did seem to have diverted anything in the way of unpleasantness. I'm afraid I'm not making this very coherent for your diary, am I?"

"That's alright," I said, catching up in the meantime. "You just tell it as it occurs to you, and perhaps I can rearrange it later."

"Well, alright, he jumped up, or rather rose rather more quickly than I would have expected of such an infirm man, and went over to a large brass-bound chest standing in a corner, which, I could tell from the way he shuffled through its contents, he uses as a filing-cabinet, and then he turned round with a very large piece of paper in his hand, his whole manner having changed and become rather theatrical and jokey, and he intoned, 'A small poem, egg-like in structure'.

"Then he handed it to me, also in a very pompous way, and naturally I took it and looked at what was written on it, and then I'm afraid I must have smiled, because it was just a title and four lines, exactly in the centre of this enormous piece of paper – I've got it here, actually..." and Charles reached into the inside pocket of his jacket, from where he produced a piece of paper so large, indeed, that it had been folded five times before finding accommodation in the pocket; and its contents were exactly as Charles had described, except that an unnaturally large signature had been added below and to the right of the poem. He tossed it onto my table as I continued to write. "...because," he continued, "the last thing I said on this subject was 'Yes, I like it', because that's the kind of thing you're supposed to say in these situations, and then Jaffa immediately said 'Well, keep it, dear boy, I've got lots more copies in the library, and besides I know it off by heart', so I showed all the proper gratitude; then he said 'Here, I'll sign it for you', and he did so, and then I put it in my pocket."

I wrote for a little longer, marvelling at Charles's imitation of Jaffa's voice, then I unfolded the paper and studied it. Charles seemed to have been stumped by the time-warp in his story. "What else did you say about it?" I asked, at length, and Charles rearranged his knees – he had been staring into the fire again – and resumed.

"Well, it was very difficult, of course, because I don't know the first thing about poetry, as you must have realised, but after suppressing my smile I tried to consider it intelligently, and the first thing that came into my head was 'It's a kind of reply to T. S. Eliot, isn't it?', because of course I recognised the allusion; and he said 'Yes' as if he was disgusted by something. Then I considered at greater length, because he didn't seem to want to say anything else on the subject of T. S. Eliot, and the next thing I said was 'What inspired you to write it at this particular time of year? It seems to me to be about the Spring' because, as you can see, it is definitely about the Spring.

"Well, this was when the extraordinary thing happened, because for about half an hour or forty minutes – ever since, in fact, Mrs Jaffa had taken the tea-things out – I had been aware of sounds coming from the room she had originally brought the tea-things from. It was about eight o'clock by now, and she had lit a standard lamp in one corner, and a smaller lamp on top of a chest of drawers in the other corner near the brass-bound box, possibly quite some time before, I don't remember exactly when, now; they were the sounds of washing up, anyway, and at first I had assumed it was Mrs Jaffa herself who was doing it, as she'd only just gone out with the things; but then five minutes later she came back into the room, and from then on I suppose I must have assumed it was some kind of house-maid who was doing it, because the sounds continued, but I didn't give any thought whatever to it at the time. It – or they, rather – the sounds, I mean – just increased the domestic atmosphere of the place, which was really very comfortable indeed. Then after Mrs Jaffa had run out in a state, and we'd started talking about poetry, I associated the washing-up with her again, because I was wondering where she'd gone and what she was doing, though in retrospect I don't imagine that she took over from the maid. Anyway, the extraordinary thing was this. I'd said 'It seems to me to be about the Spring', and if I was thinking about the washing-up at all it was a sort of cross between Mrs Jaffa and one of her maids that I imagined to be doing it. Then a woman's voice from this room, which I took to be the kitchen, said 'We're going to put it on all our Christmas cards this year, aren't we, Charles?' I hadn't heard any conversation between two female voices from that room, and I then realised that Mrs Jaffa would have said something even to a maid when she had taken the tea-things out. But it wasn't Mrs Jaffa who said this, because of course I'd become used to her voice over the last two hours or so, and there was something in the way this unseen woman said 'aren't we, Charles' which made me wonder for a moment whether she was addressing old Jaffa or me, myself.

"Anyway, I said 'I think it's rather more appropriate to Easter being egg-shaped and everything,' but he didn't seem to enjoy my little joke at all, and he said something obscene which he thought was much funnier, and after the last bit I've already told you about, I thought I'd better change the subject again."

There is some mystery about Charles's whole story, perhaps most succinctly expressed in the questions, "Who was the woman in the kitchen?", and "What (or whom) did he think he 'also saw'?", but it is a mystery, like that of all these people's attitude to Charles's continued existence after his murder, which has so many perfectly plausible solutions that any written summary of it would necessarily be inaccurate and absurd. For example, the woman in the kitchen was some old flame of Charles, whose employment as maid by the Jaffas was partly the cause of Charles's becoming associated with Jaffa's project in the first place, and who had been hearing Charles's voice while she did the washing-up, in the same way as he heard hers, as a singularly evocative echo from the past; and she, being unable longer to suppress her desire, and having become accustomed to Jaffa's habit of giving copies of his poems to all visitors, desperately attempted to re-establish communication by using this insignificant quatrain, which she knew Charles would eventually possess, as an excuse for the pretence that she and Charles still had a household together, which she hoped would move him, and which did in fact vaguely remind him of something, but was not precise enough to evoke a response from him, so that she could not, of course, follow up her initial bold step. But as to the other mystery, there is a solution more straightforward and assertive, which I hesitate to write down; it was Sir Charles Jaffa the woman addressed: and my certainty of this one small fact leads me to believe that for myself (that is, for Isobel Keogh) the entire episode of the poem and the washing-up was, not quite as indirect an experience as Charles's recounting of it to me would suggest.

The second mystery is more significant than the first, and there is a third which is more significant than either, being perhaps most succinctly expressed in the question "Where is Charles today?". As always, I use the word 'significant' to mean 'significant to me', and in this instance of the mysteries the particular significance, with its three different (large) quantities, lies in the quality of unnaturalness: just as I could apply a scale of general significance to all things, without exception, in my universe, I can and do apply a scale of unnaturalness to that world where the quality is universal, and even so appears to be increasing its range; the world, I mean, containing only all mysterious things within my relationship with Charles, the man who supposedly loves me.

The third mystery is the largest fact I have yet found in this world. I have for a long time been reluctant to leave this house, oppressive though I find it, and ever since I first felt this reluctance Charles has understood it and done everything possible in the way of making allowances for it, taking me out, for example, only when he felt it was necessary for my welfare; and when, after the murder on Monday, I resolved never to leave the house again –

until, that is, things had become much less uncertain – Charles accepted and respected my resolution. Always – and this week more faithfully than ever – he has kept his promise to bring comfort into my isolation, by telling me, before his customary departure in the morning, precisely what he intends to do during the day, and by giving me, on his return in the evening, a minute account of the degree and manner in which his intentions have been fulfilled; and this has been consolidated since yesterday by the occupation of writing in this book one of my greatest compensations for being alone in this house. And yet now that the book has become more necessary to me, Charles's essential confidence and frankness seem to be slipping away.

Or perhaps I've written this cause and effect the wrong way round. We bought the book together on Monday morning, before the more dreadful event; and it is possible that any new changes inherent in our situation stem from these two most memorable events of the single day. Having thought, I must admit that they are not the most, but the only, memorable events of that day; and even the murder now appears to have been a less immediate experience than that, say, of the washer-up in Charles's story, about which I know more actual facts, and of which I have more than vague, drunken impressions. Concerning Monday, I remember a furious fight, in a narrow alley beside the bank, between Charles and a person identical to him – like Tweedledum and Tweedledee, right down to the clothes – and leaving a dead body behind us, our least intense and acknowledged fear being that of retribution for the crime. Again, perhaps there is a most obvious solution of the mystery (that of Charles's not being himself), to which I have made the nearest possible approach short of writing it down. But this time I feel that the solution, instead of being simply right, is simply wrong.

And right or wrong, even if I could grasp it, it would not help me with my present problem: where is Charles this morning, and why should he not have told me where he intended to be? So complete has our understanding in this matter formerly been, that the day's mission has never had to be an idiosyncratic plan, or its announcement an autocratic dictation, understood by Charles alone; I have always seen the necessity and meaning of such activities as "walking about", and he, equally, has treated any suggestion of mine as indicating a necessary task, and has invariably acted upon it.

Today was to have been devoted, at least in part, to a commission suggested by me, and one, moreover, which is more obviously necessary than most – namely the shopping; we have completely run out of eggs, butter, bread, cheese, bacon and potatoes, and will very shortly be in need of toothpaste and various other things. I'm afraid I'm a very poor housekeeper; living alone for so long in West Heath Road taught me negligence rather than competence. I am hardly capable of cooking anything, omelettes and the even simpler egg-dishes being all I can manage with any confidence, and although I am now constantly trying to increase my repertoire, no new addition to it has so far either done it any credit or remained a permanent part of it. Charles has, on every occasion, performed a supremely convincing imitation of one faced with a delicious meal, so unfailingly and automatically that it could be nothing but play-acting; it is, however, deeply felt – his own attitude to cooking, although he is an expert on the subject, has always been that it must be left, in practice, utterly to servants; and he therefore has unlimited tacit sympathy with me in my plight.

I remember, in the early stages of my relationship with Lionel, adding increasingly huge quantities of garlic to every meal I cooked for him, at first in search of some exotic and impressive variety, and later in order to conceal all the deficiencies in which the dishes themselves abounded. Lionel's attitude was, as I now see it, the exact antithesis of Charles's; instead of supplying benevolent solemnity, implying reverence, he revelled in cynical humour, talking of all the ingredients in the abstract – expounding, for example, on garlic as the "purest form of food" – as if to imply that my cooking was a subject unable to bear any discussion other than the metaphysical.

Sometimes, when meditating on the reactions of these two different men to my cooking, I begin to wish that Charles and I had brought Stanley to this house, so that I could give up the whole messy art, and leave everything to our "cabin-boy's" incomparable expertise; however, quite apart from the facts that it would have been most unfair to Lionel and that Stanley would never, apparently, have left Lionel in any case, I don't think I would have been comfortable in anything even remotely resembling a triangular relationship at this stage – Sir Charles and Mrs Jaffa and myself notwithstanding – and I think the introduction of Stanley would inevitably have resulted in such a triangle. Of course, complete solitude is even more objectionable, and now that Dingbrace has at last left complete solitude is my lot.

Dingbrace was another inimitable cook, I have begun to recognise, but I was by no means sorry to see him go; he has been treating our house as his own for the last three days – much encouraged, I must admit, by Charles – the most insupportable impertinence having been, in my estimation, his ostentatious display of an intimacy, apparently of even longer standing than Charles's, with Mr Aloysius Mote. He could be described, quite simply, as a very vulgar man. His behaviour this morning was no more acceptable than usual: having come down for breakfast so impossibly late that I had since Charles's departure read the entire newspaper, washed up and begun to write this entry in my diary, he took my very generous offer of a cup of coffee as an invitation to sit with me and talk as if we had been old neighbours. Not content with monopolising Charles's friend and acting the part of gigolo in the Virgin's disgusting scenarios, or indeed with having stayed in our house a full day and night after we had dispensed with his services, he was now intent on establishing some kind of intimacy with me, and he sat and talked to me for hours on end, never ceasing to address me as his "dear", and constantly trying to set himself up as a confidant to whom all my troubles might be safely told. In the end the sheer monotony of his paternal tone began to tell, and I made certain disclosures, after which he put his arm round me and began to paw at my unusually protuberant hips – which have been more sensitive to touch (rather than less, as might have been expected) since their extension – all the while continuing his hypnotic condolences. When he started pulling at my dressing gown, however, as if to coax it up over my legs, and squeezing the flesh of my thighs through the material, I was sufficiently shocked to leap up and tell him to leave, which he did immediately, carrying his case of cooking-utensils, and amplifying his confessor-tone for friendly goodbyes, reassurances, and anticipations of further meetings, to which I did not reply.

And now that he's left, my lot, as I've said, is complete solitude, in a house where the continuous sound of traffic from Finchley Road, the occasional glance, quickly withdrawn, of a pedestrian through the window, and the claustrophobic quality of the bare and almost silent garden, merely serve to accentuate all forms of isolation. Possibly Charles will be back soon; it may be that he is doing the shopping now, in which case he will be back for a late lunch. Having told him last night that some shopping must be done, I made a list for him, and although he ignored my request for suggestions, I think I made it a fairly comprehensive list. However, when he went upstairs so unexpectedly, he left the list behind him, so I took it up to bed with me, and brought it down again this morning. Over breakfast I tried to draw his attention to the list, but he was reading the newspaper, and I was so disturbed by his general uncommunicativeness that I forgot to present it among the last things he took possession of before leaving the house. So here it is in front of me now, and I can't help feeling that his lack of interest in it, his forgetting to take it with him, and his reluctance to reveal what was actually occupying his thoughts, all indicate that he has not gone shopping at all, but is engaged in some other pursuit which he is not inclined to make known to me. Of course, he may simply be worried about money again, in which case, having read my list and found it too uneconomical, he has gone out, slightly embarrassed, to buy only those things he considers absolutely necessary.

I have had a very frightening experience, and am not sure whether to attribute it to the strange conditions on this planet or to agencies such as might have been called "supernatural" on Earth. I am by no means imaginative or fearful – less so than ever since the climax of the dinner-party on Wednesday night – but still the effect of this house in its more normal states (when I am able, for example, collectedly to count the number of rooms) has been to make me feel very lonely and nervous, sometimes so much so that I have had to break into a run (or the quickest gait possible to me) when passing a certain point in the hall, or when leaving the bathroom after having brushed my hair. Perhaps it is the effect of certain combinations of darkness and shadows, or the cumulative effect of the silence and indifference pervading all the furniture which surrounds me; in any case, it is now for me as never before the necessary result of being left alone: a reversion to childhood fears, which are momentary, but which may be inspired simply by the way light falls on certain objects at certain times of day. It is to the bathroom I have just been – to the lavatory, actually – and while sitting, staring at the dreadfully familiar arrangement of wall-decorations and window, I began to feel the advent of a fear such as I have been describing. So I hurried the last stages of my toilet – inadvisedly, as avoiding glimpses of myself in the mirror is one of the activities most likely to bring me to the pitch of hysteria – and rushed out, as yet with no sense of relief, onto the landing.

I stopped outside the closed door of the bedroom Charles and I sometimes share; I had heard a sound from within, which had the effect of both rationalising and intensifying my fear. As I waited, I heard it for the second time, and realised that it was the groan of a bed-spring. Then I began to hear voices, obviously those of a couple about to move on from foreplay to consummation, both being subdued and urgent; I recognised the male at once as Charles, and didn't for a moment consider bursting into the room: I was motivated both by common discretion and by a wave of horror, which made the door-handle seem the darkest and most odious thing, never in the wildest nightmare to be approached, far less touched. For I also knew at once that the Charles I heard was not the one I had been waiting for, anymore than the one I had been through space with; the Charles murdered outside the bank could have been any one of them. What I heard, I can tell from my reaction, was a pair of ghosts – possible I knew at the time (just a few minutes ago) by the conventional, well-worn trappings of the supernatural experience – if I had pushed the door it would have been unnaturally fixed, or would have opened on a scene of stillness in all but the audible; a perfectly well-made bed – or bedclothes tossing unaided, accompanied by the voices. Or perhaps even the voices would have stopped, leaving only an open window and blown curtains. They were rising now, as I shrank, the man's into rhythmic grunts and the woman's into sharp cries, and the bed was swaying noisily through three or four inches; I had never heard these sounds objectively before, and for a moment I was interested. She was any woman, her sounds becoming louder and more anonymous as she approached obliteration; but when it came, it was not annihilation, it was explosion of identity, for I recognised the rushing descent of nonsense-words, the ecstatic sentences of gibberish, as my own language, which no men but Charleses and Lionels have ever heard, and even they through the veil of their own orgasm, and which no-one but myself has ever spoken. The sounds, his and hers, were cut off in mid-moan like a broken tape.

That was my frightening experience. Should I tell Charles about it, when he comes? It all depends, I suppose, on how intimate I am with my own Charles after new differences have been created by the day's events. I know now that he hasn't only been shopping, because I've had my lunch and lit a fire, and it's already getting dark outside. Whatever his new identity, I could always love something in the image of Charles; it's of no importance what all the other images, or even the image in question, might do. I'm sure he doesn't know how much his position in the world depends on his moustache; I've almost come to pity Lionel's clean-shavenness. No doubt even the most sympathetic and rewarding Charles would attribute my story to the influence of the empty house, and surround me with equally empty reassurances; he knows very well himself how depressing this particular house can be. And it may be, of course, that I still share at least one natural relationship, in this all-important place. Christmas is coming, and at such times isolated pairs of lovers can easily feel the hostile pressure of a very, very temporary secret. It may be that Charles has gone out to buy me a Christmas present. I don't mind the ritual; I'm sure he will get me a very nice present.

I was sitting in precisely this chair, though without my notebook on my knee, with precisely the same levels of darkness and fire seen in the window and grate, on Wednesday night, when I wasn't alone. It has begun to snow! I can see the flakes melting on the window; and a bus has just stopped outside our house – there is a bus-stop just outside our house.

It was when Charles and Aloysius Mote were discussing the quality of the wine, at this fireplace, that I cut short my narrative of Wednesday's dinner-party. Then I said it would have to be a double narrative. Unfortunately, it has become multiple; there is too much to write: I will have to deal with the dinner-party less exhaustively. Still, it is good to have something with which to occupy myself – such a self-assured occupation, too! – and if I should be left alone here all night, God knows how much of all I have to tell will be written down. Perhaps, though, I should be designing a space-ship of my own – which might eventually be made – in this time, instead of pondering on the effects produced by (largely) someone else's; I'm not sure that I am capable, especially now, of such a creative step. But I think I'll avail myself a little longer of the comfort provided by this more introspective pursuit. If I need a space-ship I can always go to Sir Charles Jaffa, who has at least two.

I said I would say what the Virgin and I had been saying, while Charles and Aloysius Mote were beginning their conversation. As I've decided that other things are more important to my story, I won't write it out in full, but one remark which I will relate as direct speech is the Virgin's.

"How quaint to have dinner half an hour after tea-time! It won't be a bit like this, you know, when you come and have Christmas dinner at our café."

Upon which I explained in startled fashion that I'd forgotten it was only that time, as indeed I had, and justified myself by the drawing-in of the evenings, and said that perhaps I'd better tell Dingbrace to delay his preparations.

"Oh no, it's perfectly natural to him, he has dinner at all times of day."

I was doing my best to entertain, an activity of which I've had little experience. Nonetheless I got up (with a slight hobble, I'm afraid) and started for the kitchen. I was anxious to change my position not only because it would almost certainly be polite to amend the bizarre mealtime, but also because the Virgin was bouncing up and down in her chair, and her voice seemed to have risen to a shriek, which I wanted to hear from the other side of the room, just to make sure. Even as I turned my back, it burst out again:

"It's no good, as soon as a thing's said, it's done, as far as he's concerned!"

Now, there were several questions in my mind, raised by this small exchange, and I was turning them over rather incoherently as I took my first step toward the kitchen.

Had the Virgin forgotten that Mr Mote had arrived three hours early, or was her failure to apologise for him, given such an opportunity as discussion of this obviously related topic, actual conscious perversity? For all either she or I knew, my own lapse of memory might have been caused not by the early darkness, but by the prematurity of the dinner-guest.

Had Charles and I been invited to have Christmas dinner with the Virgin and Mr Mote? Or with the Virgin and someone else?

If so, were we to have it in a "café" intimately known to the pair as a good place to eat, or had she used the possessive pronoun literally? Had Charles's old friend, a graduate in law, taken to managing an eating-house?

Was the Virgin really so well-acquainted with Dingbrace's eating-habits and peculiarities of temperament? If so, how had she become so?

A general question, covering the specific questions already enumerated, and several additional, less pressing questions: the strange, slightly insulting tone adopted by the Virgin, her apparent willingness to consult just as readily the hired cook's desires and convenience as her hostess's, her enthusiastic references to a system of relationships whose very existence I was only beginning to realise – were these things all parts of some behavioural norm, into contact with which I had not previously come? Perhaps the idea of the planet was to enliven such modest entertainments as our own with an atmosphere of insecurity and uncertainty – in which case I was failing in my duty by not reciprocating.

Fortunately I didn't reach the kitchen. Suffering from a certain degree of mental turmoil, I had missed the last few remarks made by Charles and Aloysius Mote. The latest of their words I have actually recorded, "National Westminster Bank", were in fact being uttered at about the time I was making my apology to the Virgin for our unconventional timetable. On my way past the men, I was unexpectedly accosted by Aloysius Mote, who said, indicating that there had been a fairly hurried change of subject, "I hear you've been Lionel's bedfellow". Charles claims that he can't remember how the topic arose. At the time, with a dry but tolerably dignified giggle, he said, "No, Mote, it's not about that," but Aloysius Mote was already continuing, with the words, "Don't you think he's potty?"

Charles chuckled, this time, and took a sip of wine. Humour was obviously the note.

"Definitely," I accordingly said.

"And he broke it off because he's against plastic surgery?"

'No, Mote, that's not the point," Charles bravely began again, not in a spirit of censure, but as if vastly amused by Mr Mote's digression – however, at this point we were interrupted by a tumultuous noise of armchair-springs, and all three looked round, to find the Virgin sitting perfectly motionless, apparently waiting with all attention for the next utterance, although she had probably only just that moment come to rest.

After an instant she altered the angle of her head, and said (in her original voice, I was glad to hear), "Well, Charles, what *is* the point? Can I have some more wine?" She presented her glass. Aloysius Mote took the bottle from the mantelpiece and poured some wine for her (saying, "Here you are, Stomach"), an act which Charles perceived with relief, as it released him from the necessity of performing it himself, and left him free to turn away, which he did, feeling still, no doubt, that the best course to take with the Virgin was to pretend as far as possible that she didn't exist – as the words of his own invitation had implied.

"Well, Mote," he said, "I don't really like to broach the central issue right at the start like this. Shall we sit down? Pour some more for yourself."

I don't want to go on with this. My attention to detail is giving it all the outward appearance of a laboured attempt to be farcical – and surely no criticism could be levelled against it with less justice. Lacking in proportion, and in the end needlessly sensational, it may well turn out to be. But after all, it isn't intended as a short story, or for publication. I am writing it purely for my own satisfaction, insofar as such a feeling is possible to me in my present circumstances. Perhaps it is because it concerns my own behaviour and situation so closely that I suffer from this conviction that the whole thing is unbelievably sordid. I remember from my designing days that products of my pen were even more likely to excite a sense of responsibility in me than such things as speech and social activity: so when my social and authorial ineptitudes are working together in this way, it is only to be expected that I will be virtually crippled with embarrassment. And yet I can think of no other style or manner in which to treat the issue of Wednesday's dinner-party. I will let the subject rest for a spell, and write about Charles's Thursday (or even Monday?) instead.

I find I can't examine the notes I took from Charles's story last night without dwelling dangerously on the change in his attitude to me, discernible even in so short an interval. It is becoming very dark outside, and the snow, from what I can see of its effect on the window, has turned into a very unpleasant kind of rain. Could it be the weather that is delaying Charles? The clock on the mantelpiece has stopped, and I don't want to go into the kitchen to find out the time. I think it must be very late, though – there is a singular lack of activity out in the street, and now I come to remember, I haven't heard a single motor-vehicle pass since the bus I mentioned a page or two ago. Is it so late that the bus-services have stopped? The rarity of pedestrians might be explained by the weather, but the complete absence of road-traffic can't be easily dismissed; people tend not to be deterred by sleet when they can step into heated mobile cupboards. In comparison with theirs, my willpower seems sadly deficient – for a moment I intended to walk over to the window, though what I can have hoped to establish I find rather difficult to write. Did I expect Finchley Road to be swarming with silent cars? A very sudden technological advance, presumably involving also a reduction in the level of exhaust-fumes.

Instead, I merely leaned forward and placed some lumps of coke on the fire. My finger-tips are black in consequence, and the unpleasant sensation in my single nostril is lingering, as all such sensations have lingered since the accident. Exhaust-fumes always remind me of the White Planet. (N.B. I must remember to catalogue the inefficiencies of my organs as well as their distortions.) There is a useful project for me, as I'm wasting so much time: design a silent fume-free motor-car. I could easily make such a thing, probably with materials from the dump behind our back garden. Of course it would have to be a legally acceptable design, and no doubt there would be complications over insurance and licences; but at least I would be less reluctant to move about – rain isn't the only thing a driver can ignore. And a car would be more practical than a new space-ship. Space-ships are far less useful than people imagine, in any case; I think my situation is sufficient proof of that. I'm beginning to think that there is more likelihood of being plunged into a really worthwhile interstellar journey by chance, while sitting in an armchair by the fire, than by design, after months of preparation. Here is a possible explanation of the silence: I'm sure I've heard of sitting-rooms, or whole houses, launching themselves unexpectedly into space. It would be a relief, after the monotony of waiting for Charles, to find my surroundings changing of their own accord, as I seem to be unable to change them myself.

But enough of this wandering – let us have some genuine events. Back to the story, at a slightly later point.

The three of us, at least, had sat down at the table, as yet empty of everything except cutlery and a rather pathetic vase of flowers. Whether or not the Virgin was still in her armchair I can't remember, which is surprising, considering the confidence with which I set out to relate this episode in all its detail. I have a number of separate recollections which disagree over the question of the Virgin's whereabouts at this point. Some suggest that she came to the table with us, and some that she didn't join us until a little later. It may be, of course, that she came with us only to leave us again for a few minutes.

Omitting the first few commonplaces exchanged in this new situation (Charles at the head of the table, facing the window, with his back to the kitchen door, and Aloysius Mote and I side by side, facing the hall door, with our backs to the fire) I will resume at the point when Charles, after a certain amount of coaxing from me, did in fact broach the central issue.

"Given that you accept that I'm the old Charles Pink you used to know – you do accept that, don't you? Yes. Good. I want you to help me set things in motion, you know – to get my true identity publicly acknowledged, and ..."

"Why, what is your true identity?" blurted Aloysius, interestedly enough but unhelpfully; and then, observing Charles's glare of disturbed concentration, "Oh, I see."

"...and to get all my rights restored, you know, because there are certain things I want to do..."

"Like the time you wanted to prove you had nothing to do with that ceremony in the chapel."

"For example, I want to get out of this place..."

"I can understand that. Do you remember?"

"Well no, I don't, actually."

"When they had that ceremony in the chapel, and one of them dressed up as you? With a pillow and a false moustache?"

"No, I have no recollection of that incident at all."

Naturally, I found this quite intriguing, though Charles didn't seem to share my curiosity, being put out, rather than encouraged, by the continued interruption; and although I hoped to resume the subject of the ceremony in the chapel at a later point, I, too, felt that this was the time to concentrate on the present problem, if any progress was to be made. So I entered the conversation and drew both men back to the topic of Charles's identity.

"Easiest thing in the world, old boy," said Aloysius Mote. "I haven't seen any obits yet – all you have to do is write to all the papers, tell them to keep the obits in cold storage, and put a special letter in the Times, saying whatever you like."

"It would help, wouldn't it, if we could find out who the – er – the two people involved in the incident really were? I want, you see ..."

"Oh, the police'll have some chap in the dock before long, and you can always invent a demented twin brother who's been kept in a tower. Very convincing, that kind of thing. I could manage that myself, if you like – set myself up as your lawyer, produce a few wills – child's play."

"I want, you see, to get all this done as quickly as possible ..."

"What? A fine game like this? It'll give us months of happy ..."

"Because there are certain things I want to do ..."

"Yes ..."

"For one thing, we want, Isobel and I, to get married."

"Ha Ha!" said Mr Mote, after a pause, gaily but rather grossly. "Ha! You're going to make an honest monster of her!"

I must say at this point that it was the first I'd heard of the question of marriage; neither has Charles said anything on the subject since. I was sufficiently shocked at the time to meet with silence both Charles's statement and Mr Mote's gross reaction to it. In retrospect, especially as Charles himself seems to have forgotten the question, I can recall this discussion of it with more or less indifference, although for the rest of the evening (until, that is, far more terrible emotions began to take over) my understanding was rather blurred by the conflicting joy and rage inspired by this prospect of virtually permanent union with Charles and by his offensively archaic attitude to our respective rights of initiative and confidence in relation to it. I have now realised that marriage would have little or no effect on our relationship; were this not the case, the idea, at least, would have crossed my mind before Wednesday night. I now sustain merely a dull hope and expectation that Charles will not mention matrimony again, thus avoiding any renewed shock, embarrassment or anger.

"That's a bit more complicated, you know," Aloysius Mote was saying, before I had summoned enough energy to go and compose myself. "There's no doubt about you, but – who did you say this lady was?" That was the point at which I chose to leave, dimly recognising the tacit pretext that the conversation was turning to questions of myself, and that it would be vanity on my part to contribute. Mr Mote, of course, was intimately acquainted with an Isobel Keogh living in West Heath Road, resembling me in certain respects, but perfectly formed (and apparently of the type best suited to Mr Mote's sexual inclinations, despite his connection with the eccentrically-formed Belly-woman); he had, in fact, called at her house that very morning, on legal business connected with her blueprints, and had been slightly surprised to find her ready to receive him. All this I did not learn till later; while Mr Mote was discussing the issue with Charles, I was climbing the stairs, and meeting, in descent, the Virgin, whom I would have confidently sworn I had left sitting at the table with the others.

Charles is home again at last. I've asked him to tell me his story, so that I can write it down here, and he has obliged, but for some reason his talk tonight has given me far less material than its fellow of last night supplied. The latter, expressly made as full as humanly possible, nonetheless seemed a little sparse beside the apparently inexhaustible stock of detail I possessed concerning Wednesday night; and now the thinning-process has extended itself, and I am left with a paltry three pages of notes concerning the events of today. The particularly extraordinary thing is that there has been a parallel process, working in reverse; these diminishing volumes of information have embraced increasingly long periods of time, from some five hours on Wednesday to a period so intent on expanding far enough to consume the whole of Friday that not only did Charles leave slightly early in the morning (as I believe I've said)[4] but Saturday had already been trespassed upon by the time he returned. The shopping remains undone; he's had dinner, he says, failing to ask whether I'm in the same happy condition, possibly on account of his extreme wetness and the urgent necessity of taking his clothes off. Normally he would have performed this operation in front of the fire, but tonight he went upstairs and returned later in his dressing-gown.

He's been to see the Isobel of West Heath Road, in whom I'm beginning to develop a profound interest. His purpose in going there, of course, was more or less the same as his purpose on Thursday in undertaking the more premeditated visit to Sir Charles Jaffa: to discover what stage, if any, plans for a projected space-flight may have reached, and more particularly, what part has been or is to be played in such a project by Lionel Jaffa. It must be said immediately that he has gained no more concrete information on this subject from Miss Keogh than he gained from Sir Charles Jaffa; where the latter managed to avoid the subject, aided apparently by indifference rather than by any well-engineered plan of secrecy, the former openly professed ignorance of anything beyond the design of the space-craft itself – a profession which loyalty and memory persuade me to take for truth. The one other real disclosure Charles has made about today's visit is that, whereas Sir Charles Jaffa was sufficiently vague about Charles's identity, history and demise (all of which attributes he would no doubt be prepared to consider variable factors in anyone's life) to render explanations unnecessary, Isobel, on the other hand, greeted Charles as a wholly new acquaintance, having heard little of his history and nothing of his death; she accepted him as a friend of Lionel, and he explained that he had been invited to assist in the project, about which he had not as yet been told much (both true statements, if regarded in rather different lights).

So after the more or less formal self-introduction, the welcome, the expression of justifiable curiosity, and the regretful confession of inability to satisfy it, there seems to have been remarkably little intercourse during the long period which Charles and Isobel presumably spent together. What I know about the meeting Charles told me while sitting in the chair opposite mine, in his dressing-gown, occasionally rubbing his head with a towel. He successfully cleared up a small number of mysteries which had been bothering me earlier in the day, by explaining that Isobel had been close at hand during his interview with Sir Charles Jaffa, washing up the tea-things, and once, while walking in the garden, passing the window of the room in which the interview took place; also that this triangular household (Sir Charles, Mrs Jaffa and Isobel) was, as suggested by Aloysius Mote, an arrangement of a regular, semi-permanent nature, in which relations were more intimate, and roles more interchangeable, than the nominal position of each member indicated. Again, my memory seems to support these assertions.

"Everything Mrs Jaffa did," said Charles on Thursday night, "made it look as though she was the real mistress of the house; arranging everything, you know, and trying to make me feel at home, and so on. I suppose it's only natural, with an old man like that, you know, that she should take control. But it's not as if she'd been there all that long – she lived in Chiswick with Lionel, you know – yes, of course you know. So it looks as though *she* left *him*, instead of the other way round, and went to his father, instead of her mother (whoever that may be) which would at least mean she's pretty resourceful.

"I don't think that can be it. I suppose *he* might have left *her* while they were both on a visit. They used to visit quite often, didn't they?

---

[4] She hasn't. *The Author.*

"Anyway, she brought the tea in, and I can't imagine how she got it ready so quickly, because Jaffa and I only said about three things each while she was out, about you, as it happens – or rather, the other. Jaffa had just said what a charming girl you were. Then Mrs Jaffa brought the tea in, and he said, "Both charming girls," so of course I agreed audibly, though I thought it was an odd remark to make. Then when she started pouring out the tea he came out with that old chestnut about being mother, and even after that I managed to stay fairly calm and solemn – just clasped my hands and sat forward (he'd been sitting forward all the time, with his hands on the head of his stick) – but she treated the remark with the proper shock and disgust, went quite red, and said, "Really, father," and "Take no notice of him, Sir Charles," In fact, he lowered the tone of the whole conversation, and it was all horribly suburban – it'd sound right in this place, but it didn't there. There were lots of little sandwiches and cakes, though, all delicious, especially the anchovies. I enjoyed that part."

But in clearing up some mysteries Charles has merely replaced them with larger, less welcome ones. Any gaps in the story from which I have just quoted an episode must be small, as my necessarily inaccurate sense of time tells me that I have almost enough events to fill the corresponding portion of Thursday; the gaps were left, moreover, through the accident of sleep – Charles was genuinely fatigued on Thursday night, and I feel sure that his pauses were involuntary. While telling the story of his visit to Isobel, however, the longer spell of wakefulness preceding his commencement of the narrative rendered him beyond fatigue and considerably further from sleep, his condition in consequence resembling the lassitude of the insomniac. The pauses in this tale coincided with his frequent applications of the towel to his head; and I must say that the degree of detachment which may be induced by or feigned while rubbing the head with a towel is considerable. The pauses were therefore lengthy and significant, and when I accused him directly of wilful omission he became irritable and said that it was very tiresome having to remember every single detail of his day merely for the sake of my damned silly book. It has occurred to me before that he must regard most forms of writing as more or less silly, and not really fit occupations for a responsible adult; but his statements on the subject have hitherto been more tolerant.

I have followed his regrettable example, and revealed to him nothing of what has happened to me today.

Saturday

I am about to go to bed, though I did not get up till late evening, and found Charles gone. It is midnight, and he still hasn't come home.

Sunday

A letter came this morning, correctly addressed and stamped, etc.; as soon as I heard the faint sound of the knocker I rushed into the hall, and seeing the letter on the mat I hurriedly picked it up and then opened the door, in the hope of seeing the postman, with whom I have exchanged words before (assuming it was the same one), and asking him why there should be a delivery on Sunday morning. He was not in sight, however. The envelope was postmarked "Cricklewood – 8 Dec – 1973 – N.W.3" and contained a small piece of paper, on which were written the words, "Busy. Back Soon. C." (which I think is an amended quotation from *The House at Pooh Corner* by A.A. Milne, though I have no means of verifying this, as there are no books in the house apart from this notebook).

Monday, December 10th

Dingbrace came, with a huge box full of groceries, behaved with exceptional politeness (except for one or two occasions, when a mere hint from me restored his decorum instantly) and refused to be paid. Perhaps I should have insisted, but I am convinced that the gift was not intended to oblige me to him.

I have been for a walk in the garden, feeling rather aimless, as always, despite my various occupations. But at least there has been no return of quasi-superstitious dread; and Dingbrace's visit has cheered me, not only because it has provided me with the material for my first square meal in four days – perhaps I could eventually revise my opinion of the man's character. And some contact with humanity is necessary, though I would be happier if he were a woman.

I might go for a walk in the street one of these days.

The following section, though obviously written after the above, is not dated. At a still later date it was crossed out, with a dense network of roughly scribbled lines, which nonetheless left an occasional space in which a legible phrase or sentence can now be found. This explains the fragmentary nature of the entry. It should also be mentioned that the three entries preceding this (those for Saturday, Sunday and Monday, December 10th) as well as a considerable number of those following, are interspersed with intricate diagrams and calculations, in a similar way imperfectly obliterated, but of such a highly technical nature that they have been omitted, by – The Author.

HEAD.

Cranium unchanged. I can only assume this means the brain…however …

Left eye … the socket …

…… as left except fingers … 3:3/4"; 4:1/2"; 5… grasp things with left …

… elbow …

Right shoulder, angle increased 12 degrees.

Both breasts reduction in diameter and …. quality of skin … closer together, hang … left nipple half … will this change? Since … third month.

… consequent reduction in volume of rib-cage, 1.74 cubic feet.

Waist measurement …

LOWER TORSO.

i. Coccyx …

…interior width reduced … tremendously increased pleasure also mentioned by … delivery more difficult.

…obviously related to difference between arms.

Right thigh, increase three inches less.

…. limp …

Tuesday, December 11th

An even more startling visit than the last; this time LIONEL came, asking for Charles. The visit began happily, as he failed to recognise me – in fact, when I opened the door he indulged in a little start of horror which quite lucidly conveyed the impression that he hadn't before been aware of the existence of people with shapes like mine. Also, of course, I couldn't produce Charles for him, which simplified things. Determined to keep my identity a secret from him, I coined a false name for myself on the spot: "Christabel Cook", chosen for its alliteration and, I think, because its two parts both name roles which I would like to see myself acting. I invited him in for a drink (Dingbrace had included a bottle of brandy in my supplies) and he accepted rather absently, as if hoping to leave his exit clear. I said that I expected Charles at any moment, and he showed some interest at this point, but he continued to behave like someone about to depart. He walked around the sitting-room, drink in hand, examining things and asking an occasional question about Charles – how he felt about the murder, how he was filling his time, and so on. All perfectly easy to answer. For a few moments the conversation became a little more personal, when I asked him if he'd enjoyed Africa, and he asked me if I enjoyed living in this house. He said, "You don't appear to have any books." I agreed, and then he commended himself to Charles, invited us both to drop in on him at Chiswick, and left.

Wednesday, December 12th

This being the day on which the following was written, by me, Christabel Cook, in my diary, although the events of the day play no part in it, and will themselves probably never be written[5].

It may well be imagined what disgust this encounter with the Virgin on the stairs occasioned me, when I repeat that although she might for all I knew have been either at the table or in an armchair, I was positively convinced that I had just left her in the dining-room. Add to this her repellent appearance, and the fact that she was advancing down on me with a bony three-fingered hand extended. Being confused, I had mounted the first two or three steps before seeing her, and quite apart from the implausibility of retreating from such a position, I had no desire to return to the room where I was being discussed in a manner doubtless of the frankest, where my hand in marriage was being bandied about freely, and where my arrival would certainly prompt some remark from Aloysius Mote about the speed at which I urinated. Cornered, therefore, I continued upward, eyes lowered, and presently, though I had hoped I might avoid them, I felt the two fingers and thumb close on my shoulder – in fact I almost felt them meet in my sparse flesh – and heard a voice (which was completely new to me) like gravel, or possibly vinegar; in short, she had dropped the stage lunatic and become the pantomime witch.

---

[5] The occasionally detached attitude adopted by Miss Keogh to her own writings is probably best explained by her fear that the power she has over her destiny, already grossly diminished, is being further eroded and will ultimately slip away from her altogether. This growing fear, which on Thursday and Friday drove her to write voluminously in her notebook, from Saturday to Tuesday induced her to seek reassurance as much in re-reading what she had already written as in composing new material. Reading one's own life is even easier and safer than writing it. Picking up her pen, therefore, after a lengthy bout of reading, she is inclined to see herself almost in the third person: referring to herself thus as "Christabel Cook" (the name she invented upon meeting Lionel Jaffa for the first time, in order to simplify, or alternatively to confuse matters for him, and to make possible, as it were, a fresh start) she is doubtless attempting to ensure a sufficient distinction between herself and the Isobel Keogh already known to Jaffa; a distinction made for the convenience of the reader, so that the reader, that is, herself, will always remain as far as possible in control of the situation. It is possible that the continued presence of Isobel Keogh in her mind, which presence amounts eventually almost to an obsession, has been magnified on this occasion by some mention of the woman during her interview on Tuesday with Captain Jaffa – mention which, as many other things from now on, she omits. *The Author*

"I'm glad we're alone, she said. "Dingbrace and I have met some friends of yours, you know. I'd like to talk about them with you."

I whinnied, or yelped, and her clutch tightened; the plight of the wedding-guest, in Coleridge's poem *The Ancient Mariner*, occurred to me.

"One of them is a lovely young boy called Stanley: he is so beautiful and innocent, I hope you will be able to tell me how to captivate him. So far I have done little but tell him stories of my youth" (was she going to tell them to me? It might be more comfortable) "and I find that they are of no help in getting him into my bed. He sings to me most delightfully, but alas, I cannot reciprocate," and she raised her free hand, whether to reveal the unsuitability of the hand itself for grasping a conventional musical instrument, or to indicate her admittedly erratic throat, I could not tell. Availing myself of the instant's pause, I moved my feet down one step, but her only physical response was to let fall the raised hand. "Were you not going upstairs?" she said. And, "Perhaps," she continued, as, finding myself forced by her grip on my shoulder to stand at a slight angle, I returned my feet to the higher step they had previously occupied, thus regaining verticality, "my life has not been sufficiently titillating. I might try to arouse him instead..."

"Where did you see Stanley?" I asked, feeling at once the need for an alternative means of cutting off the woman's flow, and compassionate interest in Stanley's welfare; but she went on, "...with lewd fiction dressed as autobiography; I have never had much experience of these matters myself, but I know some excellent stories about them. There is one in particular which I might tell him, concerning two shepherds and two shepherdesses, in which the first shepherd and first shepherdess, growing up together and falling in love, investigate one day the possibilities of each other's bodies; the shepherd finding that these possibilities are as immense as their reputation, but that they involve in proportion labour and embarrassing pitfalls, through and over which he is painfully driven by the promise of still greater and more beautiful forms of that which he already feels, is surprised to find that his lovely partner, on the contrary, has been transported apparently without delay to the utmost visible summit of what they mutually desire, and that even while her limbs are convulsively clutching him she is able, by the most ingenious caresses imaginable, to help him in his strivings, and to remove at least some of the obstacles that separate him from her."

"Look," I said ...

"Here, of course, the teller of the story can dwell on the details of their intercourse, and try to evoke for the listener a vivid picture of their bodies and their organs. It might even be possible, if the time is at all ripe, to introduce a few small demonstrations, naturally of a very tentative kind." She moved down to my step from the one immediately above, without letting go of my shoulder, so that I had to press myself against the banisters. "Do you think it will work? Do you have any better ideas, or know any better stories? I think this one is admirably suited to Stanley, somehow, though of course I'll have to change the setting if he's to find it at all convincing."

"Well," I replied, "I think you're right – it's a very short story, isn't it? – but really I'm more interested in when and where ..."

"So the first shepherd, several days and many experiments later, while tending his flock in another part of the hills, finds himself thinking rather deeply about something whose initiation cost him absolutely no thought at all. He is worried, as you will have guessed, about the source of his darling's expertise: can it be that shepherdesses are born with this phenomenal aptitude? It would be a natural state of things tending to great harmony in sexual affairs; but something leads him to doubt it. And he is unwilling to approach the girl herself on the subject, for fear that she will think he has unjust suspicions of her. So later in the day, while testing his new-found power on his other childhood friend, the second shepherdess, and discovering to his astonishment that she is immeasurably more skilful even than his own first lover, bringing him, while herself enjoying the most violent conceivable spasms of pleasure, so close to his desired goal that only the constantly self-exceeding heights of his joy convince him that he has not already arrived, he determines, even as her slim hips push against his, to ask of this freer and, he begins to think, even more lovely young girl, that explanation which he is not able to ask of his heart's possessor. "Meanwhile," said the Virgin, slyly placing her arm round my erstwhile waist in what I soon saw was an attempt to draw me upstairs, "the narrator has another opportunity to arouse her audience's lust with salacious detail, and some at least of the second shepherdess's extraordinary techniques may be put into practice in order to give the story depth."

"Weren't you going downstairs?" I said, levering myself out of her clutch, upon which she grabbed me by the wrist, and continued: "At first the second shepherdess takes no notice of the first shepherd's enquiry, beyond laughing up at him for a moment, and then, still with a smile on her face, applying her mouth to that part of him which hard work has exhausted. But even as it revives under her ministrations, he repeats his importunity, and at length, after a decent spell of renewed fondling, tumbling and rather heated repose, his frequently breathless reiterations of the same question persuade her that it would be wise to give him this small degree of extra satisfaction. So having resumed her single thin – and short – garment, laughing at him still, she leads him by the hand to my story's fourth character, the second shepherd."

"Look," I repeated, and this time, possibly because we had arrived at a natural break in the story, was able to continue, "your powers of story-telling are really quite astounding, and with all your facial expressions, and gestures and so on, I must admit it's very exciting, but I can't interest myself much in your plans for the future until you've told me something about your meeting with these friends of mine – at least tell me who they were."

"Oh, the other, my dear, was Captain Lionel Jaffa," and, as I blushed violently without knowing why, she nudged me painfully in the ribs, and leered. "He's a handsome fellow, isn't he, my pet? Of course I didn't see him myself, it was only Dingbrace who saw him, but I've seen his picture in the papers, and Dingbrace said that he wants to be my assistant in my fortune-telling work, so I hope I'll meet him soon. I think it's so clever of you to have had a man like that, which is why I think you'll be able to help me. After all, we're about the same shape, aren't we, my dear? Stanley seems not to be afraid of me, I'm happy to say, but when Dingbrace told me that Captain Jaffa wanted to come in to see me I panicked, and didn't want him to see me in bed, and so forth. Stanley is too young to be frightened, but Captain Jaffa might not have found me attractive – I've been told that he's not entirely in his right senses, and you know how susceptible these mental cases can sometimes be. Anyhow, I'll need to collect my thoughts and prepare myself thoroughly before I can approach him in any useful way, and frankly I'm surprised that a nervous little thing like you ever got so far with him, because, you know, you nearly always find that bodies like ours appeal in some obscure way, but you never know which way in advance, and then the appeal is always more likely to turn into something nasty; it's not as simple as it is with these shepherds and shepherdesses, who all have perfectly conventional anatomies, of course. The girls are so careful always to sit in the shade, although they're half naked, that their legs and arms are as white as their breasts: the first has a plump little stomach, and dimples in the small of her back, and wrinkles in all those hollows and creases where the flesh of one part joins that of another; the second is all slender, long-limbed, and light to manipulate and lift. Their skin, unlike yours and mine, is as smooth as liquid – and so is their lovers' firmer flesh than the first, and greater experience, and a taste for the soft, fresh and untried.

"When the first shepherd and second shepherdess acquaint him with their purposes – the former's to find the source of the latter's knowledge, and the latter's simply to enjoy herself further – he has them strip before him, and demonstrate together how much progress each of them has made. The sight of the charming pair's eager coupling – for their abstinence has not been so short that they are not both more than ready for this new trial, though each of them, for by no means the same reasons, might have welcomed by now a different partner – excites him so much that even as she cries out in her pleasure he begins to handle the girl's trembling hinder parts (these being uppermost); and, coaxing her onto all fours above the newly sated first shepherd, mounts her from behind – for the last time, as it proves, ever, or at least in so many years that she has by that time cast off the charms of youth and assumed attractions of quite another kind. Then, having told her to leave him alone with his spent colleague, and having watched her depart ..."

Voices burst into laughter somewhere downstairs, and she saw that I was listening hard to the sound. She watched, in fact, as closely as I listened. It was the first time the party down below had intruded since I had shut the dining-room door – not, indeed, on account of any merit in the story I was being told; it would be ridiculous to imagine that I had been carried away by the narrative to such an extent as to be unaware of any sound, above the level of a normal utterance, which had in reality issued from the dining-room. Having pointed out that she had either an excellent memory (far better than mine) or extraordinary spontaneous control over complex, if not particularly attractive, syntax, I would indeed have been at a loss for any further comment of a favourable kind to make on the Virgin's story and her telling of it. Besides, even had it been momentous in content and riveting in delivery, my anxiety would not have allowed me to listen with more than the dazed retentiveness I did in fact afford it.

No, the only explanation was that there had in truth been no sound during all this time, apart from the jagged continuo of the Virgin's voice, which might have reached me in my imprisoned condition on the stairs. The laughter which now quite unexpectedly beat at the door of my cell was mixed both with the clank of glass and with the rattle of cutlery, which told me that in all probability dinner had been served almost immediately after my departure from the room, that the silence had been that of communal eating, and that now the pressure was beginning to relax: it was possible to be frivolous again, and people were growing careless with their spoons and eager with their glasses. This would have been the one obvious conclusion, had it not occurred to me that the actual setting of the dinner on the table, which had certainly taken place, would have made sounds very similar to the ones I heard. It was either the beginning or almost the end I heard. But if the former, what had the silence been? And if the latter, why had I not heard the former? Had there been time for the consumption of Dingbrace's extensive dinner? And would my guests, however unconventional their manners, really have eaten the entire dinner, from end to end, without me, their hostess?

But it was the laughter itself which concerned me in particular. During the three moments it lasted I rummaged through it, and afterwards I tried to hold it together in my mind, while peeling off the extraneous mineral sounds. I recognised the cavernous guffaw belonging to Charles, and it was around this that the other vibrations grouped themselves; but in scrutinising these latter I experienced the auditory equivalent of a horrifying visual effect familiar to me from childhood: the effect produced, that is, by staring fixedly at a single, unique object, for so long as to annihilate all certainty of its uniqueness. I had done this many times, I remembered, with the television set in my parents' home. Whether the screen were blank or animated, I would gaze at it until convinced that I had, at the very least, two similar television sets to deal with: that however small the space it occupied, the thing had a plural significance. When the sensation became intolerable it was a temporary relief to cross my eyes – to squint, that is, voluntarily – the double image thereby produced seeming closer to a representation of the true state of things, thus less deceitful and less evil. A very temporary relief, however: for when I had sustained the squint only so long as to become accustomed to it, I would begin to see in each of the two television sets a potential for plurality equal to that of the single, original one – and thus would have double the number of disembodied machines to accommodate. To extend the comparison to a third sense, the effect was not unlike that involved in the ancient game of rubbing one's nose with crossed fingers – except that touch is obstinate, slow to yield the sensation and quick to efface it, rarely suggesting more than two noses; whereas sight and hearing lie in wait for the smallest opportunity to multiply their products, love to confuse and overwhelm.

In short, I could not tell how many people were laughing. In relation to Charles's contribution, the rest was harsh and high-pitched, and might have been made all by Aloysius Mote, or, improbably, by him and Dingbrace in duet. Within the group there were either two or three laughers altogether, including Charles, but the ambiguity between two and three has always been one of the hardest to resolve; and the concentration involved in arriving at this estimate of the integral sound's constituents, making my ears swim, engendered a doubt concerning the uniqueness of the whole sound itself: were there two, or three, or four identical groups of the same laughing people?

But over and above, and intimately connected with all these questions of number, was the question of quality, or timbre – and here I approach the central issue in my explanation of the trouble caused me by this sound. I have already said that the accompaniment to Charles might have been provided either by Aloysius Mote or by Dingbrace and Aloysius Mote: but was it conceivable, on the other hand, that one of the vocalists was neither of these two, but a female? To be explicit, here I was on the stairs with the Virgin and a lingering belief that I had left her in the dining-room. Could I rely, at least for a delay in the confirmation of my surmise, on some feature of the human voice which was invariably, immemorially, unequivocally and eternally feminine? In the presence of the Virgin and myself, and of our voices, which were both capable at the very least of a Wagnerian tenor's gruffer spoken emotions, I doubted it extremely. And of course the Virgin's voice, although something insidious told me that it was indeed, by a certain unmistakeable but unnamed sign, present in the sound I heard, could hardly yet have exhausted its repertoire of the perverse and exotic colours which had already alarmed and taught me so much.

She wielded it. "Perhaps Aloysius has brought his girlfriend?" She had seen the trend of my listening; she was clairvoyante, naturally, as she had intimated, but she would only use her power to distress me. "Or do you imagine that Dingbrace is married, and that his wife comes to help him with the dishing-up?"

"Excuse me," I said, "I must go down", and I pulled at my wrist.

"But you haven't been up yet."

"I haven't got time for that now, really" – but she placed her other, seven-fingered hand on the back of my neck. "You haven't heard the end of my story," she said – I was firmly fixed at the two points, and I struggled – "or told me whether you think it will do. They'll be alright downstairs, there are quite enough of them. As I was saying: when the second shepherd ..." At this point, I'm afraid, I started crying, and although it was only a brief spasm of helplessness, it obscured for me the opening of her story's continuation; I was aware only of the liquid flowing down my nostril and around the corners of my eyes. I have, however, worked out exactly what she must have said during this pause.

"...has watched the second shepherdess depart, he turns to the first shepherd, who, on account of the unusually hectic day's fornicating he has had, is still prostrate. The second shepherd, having merely impregnated a single young lady a single time, is relatively sprightly ..." Here I was bringing forth the last few anticlimactic sobs, and having wiped my nose with my free hand, I began to absorb more sullenly than ever what the Virgin was saying: "... and although he follows his companion's example in neglecting to put on again his smock, or girdle, or whatever they wear, he shows himself able to deliver a monologue, which goes as follows: 'Come, my friend, we must attend to our sheep, for some of them will have strayed during this pleasant interlude. We have found that the enjoyment to be had from women is so easily procured that one sometimes revels in it almost involuntarily; and that it seems so great at first tasting that one can for the time think of little else: but it is for all that the thing of the least importance in the world, and it must not be sought after. In your enthusiasm you wanted to embrace what you saw as a composite mystery, and to that end you enquired whether any further power were to be had from the stockpile whence your girls had gained their knowledge'".

"This isn't going to be very exciting for Stanley, is it?" I said.

"I'm coming to that shortly. 'I can tell you,' the second shepherd proceeds, 'having seen you at work underneath and inside her who was formerly my mistress, that you have all the knowledge and power you are ever likely to have, or, I am sure, anyone ever profits by; indeed, merely by looking at your body I can tell that you have no cause for this nervous investigation. I was the first to unveil both the nymphs of our acquaintance, and to show them the inconsiderable details; you begin to know by now where I, myself, discovered the power to do this. Thus you now have the full account of what you have earned by visiting this part of the hills, and you know whether or not it will be worth your while to return to your own home and to your own loved one. Come on.' So they go off together, still naked, and gather their sheep all into a single flock. The first shepherd is not yet absolutely sure how to take his friend's patronising pessimism: his exertions have left him with a languid, purely physical yearning for continued pleasure, while reducing his power to requite it. Anyway, after a suitably primitive supper he is introduced by his wise companion to an entirely new pastime, and to wholly new sensations; with the result that from now on the two shepherds are inseparable, and neither shepherdess, so far as we know, is ever again plumbed by either of their tools, now reserved for quite other uses."

Another gust of laughter rushed up the stairs, as if one or two males and a female found the story pleasant. "Is that the end?" I said, desperately hoping that she would let me go, and just as desperately determined to humour her for however long she wanted.

"Yes. You can imagine," she said, "the state of mind the listener, I mean Stanley, will be left in, male and female having been distinguished for him as potent and negligible respectively; the idea is, of course (perhaps I should have said), that long before the end of the story the reciter will have achieved her desire – at about the stage, to be precise, of the copulation witnessed by the second shepherd, when a mirror might be brought into play."

"It's a very *moral* story, isn't it?" I said, having worked out by now, you see, some good things to say about it, though they did not necessarily increase its worth in my own eyes.

She was exasperated by my irrelevance. "It has a moral, yes, but really you can read some moral significance or other into any fiction you like, as I believe the Duchess in *Alice in Wonderland* pointed out, though I'm not conscious of having borrowed the remark from her. This is a *utilitarian* story, *applied* fiction, which is a different thing altogether."

"Well, thank you, I've enjoyed it very much. Now I think we both ought to be joining the others, don't you? Otherwise we won't get any dinner at all."

"Why, don't you trust your friends to save some for you?" she said, and her six fingers and a thumb tightened on my neck, as they had been doing, I believed, gradually since the end of the story. "Surely Sir Charles Pink is the soul of honour? I, personally, can vouch for Aloysius and Dingbrace, and fortunately Captain Lionel Jaffa isn't here. I certainly wouldn't eat your dinner myself, and as for Isobel Keogh – oh, but that's you, isn't it, my dear?

"She is certainly welcome to eat anything of mine, I must say," I replied, and on paper it looks rather cool and self-possessed. At any rate, it was the signal for a third, particularly powerful uproar of good-humoured appreciation from below; and this third noise did not, like the other two, carry its number-secret unfathomed into almost instant silence, but prolonged itself, each component part starting afresh, with more breath than before, after every little pause, and no two ever pausing together: so that the three voices were beautifully set in relief against one another, the bass relieving the tenor, the tenor the contralto, the contralto the bass, and so on.

"The party's going well," said the Virgin, and it was as if the leading lady of a vocal ensemble had commented on her own group's recorded performance of a laughing-song. I didn't like it: in fact I shuddered, and it may have been this movement which caused me to lose for a moment my grip on the hilarious counterpoint, and to imagine that with the spoken part the voices amounted to six plus one; otherwise it may have been the seven pressed indentations in my neck, caused and filled by the Virgin's left fingers. It was only a momentary complication, in any case, and after it the simpler sound resumed in a manner which suggested to me that, leaving aside the Virgin's prose solo, there were some literal repetitions in the piece: the return of some central idea, perhaps, after the brief thickening of the texture; or, more simply, a circular tape? But no, they were live performers, and one of them was doubling on the solo instrument.

"I'll bet it's Jaffa they're laughing at," she said. "Actually, I know it is. It's his self-importance that's so funny, you see, and the way he's making such a fool of himself (or will do, anyway) over this Isobel Keogh – not you, of course, another girl of the same name – and patronizing Stanley all the time, as if the boy couldn't give him lessons in virtually anything involving knowledge of the world..."

"How do you know...?" I began, not quite sure which question to ask first, or that either answer would help me.

"It's being rich and mad that counts; anyway, it's not very interesting, and I'm sure you don't want to join in the conversation" (which was still the same absolute noise, by the way). "There's a sequel to my story, by the way, concerning the two shepherdesses and how they got on after their desertion"; her right talon was bound for my shoulder, and the cluster of tentacles round my neck fidgeted as if about to move down to my middle, to effect a new double embrace and restart the cycle of clutches. "It at least provides the conventional happy ending..." but I had foreseen the moment when both grips would be slack, and now I wormed round and started downstairs on my toes, showing her my heels in my haste. Where I intended to go I didn't know, though the dining-room didn't repel me entirely, containing as it did at least Charles, whoever else might be there[6]. The concert continued, Charles being still the resonant, prominent, optimistic element in the accompaniment, but whether the Virgin on the stairs was proceeding with her spoken arabesques, had fallen silent, or sang along with the general motif of laughter, I did not hear – the number of laughing Virgins was obscured by the body of the orchestra.

Enough of this musical nonsense: when I got to the door of the dining-room there was something about the sound of Charles's laughter not quite so comforting as I'd imagined, so that I didn't want to go in, and I kept on down the hall towards the kitchen, speeding up somewhat in case the Virgin should be following me – though I believe I could see her still standing on the stairs (of course I couldn't stay in the kitchen for ever – perhaps she was waiting to slip into the dining-room after I'd disappeared, in order to get me more confused than ever, when I went in from the kitchen, about how many of her there were. I'd go quickly from the kitchen to the dining-room, I decided).

The first peculiarity, as I scurried along the hall, was that the sound of laughter didn't diminish: just outside the dining-room door it had been no louder than anywhere else; it had in fact been constant in volume ever since I'd first heard it on the stairs. And now, more unpleasantly than by any of my previous problems with this sound, I was struck by the impossibility of fixing its source. I had assumed it was in the dining-room, but now found that it covered my entire aural range; the sudden encirclement made me stop and almost faint, or at least fall down, as I wondered what direction I was following, whether this was the hall, and where it went. The Virgin spoke – she was still on the stairs (and I set off again) so I could get to the dining-room before her and be quite sure where we were – "You're going round in circles, my dear: you'll find it's not quite what you expect."

I was there; I pushed open the kitchen door, and at once – at quite the wrong moment – the sounds made their first, enormous crescendo. It was not the kitchen: although at first I saw Dingbrace and his stove superimposed on them, what I finally focused on was the group of laughing people round the table in the dining-room (who were all at right angles to the positions they'd occupied in the dining-room I'd previously left, thus proving conclusively that our sense of direction – or at least mine – is absolute, not relative, and can work in a vacuum). They were Charles and Aloysius Mote, not Dingbrace, leaning exuberantly over the table towards each other, and a woman, deformed and silent, who stared in my direction as I entered, and who, though at first I saw the second, dreaded Virgin superimposed on her, in a moment changed her outline and became (this will not be the first such revelation in these pages) myself – and not Isobel Keogh, but me, Christabel Cook.

---

[6] Her low opinion of the Virgin's technique notwithstanding, Miss Cook is herself no expert storyteller. The following passage, up to and including the Virgin's speech, will be found to be of greater effect (that is, "closer to a representation of the true state of things" and thus presumably to what Miss Cook intended) if read at varying speeds, and twice: once in order to establish how your final reading-speed will vary, thus slowly and analytically; and again at the varying speeds established, but on the whole more quickly, without bothering too much about the sense. *The Author*

She was not looking at me, however, only in my direction by chance. It was the men who made an event of my entrance, both actually rising in their seats and turning towards me, their laughter developing into boozy greetings. I couldn't divide my attention in proportion to the attention paid me, however hard I tried: I had to study Christabel, to know whether, now she had seen it was my direction she stared in, she stared at, or still, as a moment ago, through me. But the damned men diverted me before I could tell.

"God, you're a slow pisser," called Aloysius, happily, quite as if he knew I was more privy to the joke than he...

Charles's "The girl herself. Hello my dear" overlapped with the beginning of Mr Mote's statement, and his "We were just talking about Lionel" with its end: both in the end more sedate remarks, not to say tedious, but to me in my condition as inflammatory as they well could be. Settling my eyes' indecision whom to settle on, I glanced back into the hall; had it changed I would have run into it, turned right, and out through the front door; but as it was it remained the same dark passage from the kitchen, where I should have been, dead straight to the front door and the street. I turned back and shut the kitchen door behind me, committing myself to the dining-room's ninety degrees of change. I even started towards a chair, staggering a little, as I was still fully conscious of the differences involved. It was instantly vacated and thrust under me by Aloysius, and I found myself sitting at a long side of the table, Charles at the short end on my left, Mr Mote having moved down the parallel, to my right, and my quiet but conspicuous new friend – as quiet as me – further on down the same line, and round a right-angled corner to the other short end, so that she was sometimes hidden by my mobile neighbour Aloysius. I was facing a door which should have belonged to the hall, and through which Dingbrace now came, bearing things which unmistakeably belonged to the kitchen. Christabel wasn't in the position I'd occupied in the previous dining-room, if I took the table as a point of reference; but during this time I idly wondered if it mightn't be actually the same space, being at right angles ... impossible to work out, of course, without knowing the dimensions of the rooms.

"You're not eating your fish," said Dingbrace, pointing at me – as I thought, almost politely – and so leaving me in no doubt, though when I looked at my plate I found that instead of the innocent fillet of some English fish I might have expected earlier, there were whole bodies with eyes and tails, fried but distinct individuals, looking up in expectation of my fork. One was a shrimp, I noticed, and one an octopus, but mostly they were fish of different sizes. I glanced reproachfully to my right (after all, why should Mr Mote in particular have left his main course untouched? Everyone else, including him in his new place, was on the dessert) and caught, over his nape, a reproachful glance cast by my semi-reversed double, not at me, but like mine and similarly misdirected. Perhaps she sympathised with me, if aware of me at all.

Meanwhile much was being said, to me and perhaps to the other Miss Cook, some of it about what had been said on the subject of Lionel, some similarly about Charles's country home, Near Step House, in Westmorland; I am not going to write it all down, and at the time I left the answering of it to her, as she unfortunately left it to me. Dingbrace the cook said to one of us, I think to her, that he'd brought the cheese in, a remark whose superfluousness justified us both, I thought, in our silence. But the real cause of mine was that I was listening to hers, asking myself if the cause of hers was the same. The question was whether she felt cowed or superior, or not at all; if she did not know me, did I have the advantage, or had I been snubbed?

Aloysius, returning to the vertical from verifying a legal point for Charles, found me staring through him and said, "Did you see Maria?" But Dingbrace came between us, and I was aware of having said my first say since entering the room, the accent, I noticed, on the "is": "What is this, Dingbrace?" He was putting board, bread, cheese, butter, knives, item by item regularly onto the table, watching his work with a servility I had never seen in him before; and without raising his eyes or stopping, he said, "It's called *pescado variado*, Miss." Charles said, "He's seen Lionel, you know," and, confident now of getting a reaction, though by no means so confident as I was to become later, I said, "Have you?", a question which appears not to have been interrupted, though I have to report, with regret, as I have to report so many interrupted questions, that it was, by my own voice, again not connected with my will, and in fact from the far end of the table: "Where did you learn to make it, Dingbrace?", which obscured my addition (by coincidence, "Where?") but in any case Dingbrace, raising his eyes across the centre of the table to the wall, replied: "In Spain, Miss."

"You see," Charles said, "on Friday," referring back to Thursday, "I was misled all along by her being so different from you, you see, it was her I saw walking across the garden, and the window being all little diamond panes – also, of course, because I had to pay attention to Jaffa – I didn't see her nearly clearly or long enough for such a slight resemblance to stir my memory. You being so far off in her future, and she in my past, and a long way over the garden, if you see what I mean. I just assumed they'd got a beautiful stranger in the house – because beauty often strikes you in that way, you know, and I think I was a little struck. But it wasn't till long after I'd heard her voice from the scullery that I saw the connection."

She'd been walking across the garden towards the summer-house, I remembered and still do, intending to do some work there, and had spent one of the happiest afternoons of her life so far; three-quarters enclosed thus with the beautifully successful, and still smoothly working, written evidence of her own mechanical brain's mechanical products, she had sat and watched through her open quarter the distant, big swinging couch, at the side of the house, hardly working in the almost frozen wind, herself allowing her own work to proceed just as passively, adding a line when gravity took her pencil, and in spite of the cold she had listened to the stream at the bottom of the Jaffas' garden. She had not, of course, thought about Lionel Jaffa, except insofar as he was present in the garden, and the minutes had passed gratefully until his fearful wife had called her to the washing-up, thus marking the start of the evening and a blacker period. They had told her later (the wife still not knowing to whom she owed her husband's absence, the father affectionate and delightful) that the man who'd visited had been a certain Sir Charles Pink, and had seemed extraordinarily interested in the ship, which to the father and Isobel was an excellent hope. Then they'd gone to bed, Isobel and the wife tending to the father's wants – the first slightly sick but reverent, the second prim but martyred, the third like a shepherd, but the whole not so simple as the Virgin's story.

"Jaffa said, 'She's resilient as reinforced rubber, like hard rubber, armoured and bony' and I just agreed, because I wasn't quite on his level when it came to similes (or alliteration, I think it's called) and I didn't think then that I wasn't supposed to know you, you know – he didn't seem to notice that, anyway, any more than he cared about who I was, though he certainly pretended either to have met me or to have heard about me before – and anyway, you know, I remember that you were generally *harder* before" (I don't know what punctuation mark he would himself have chosen here) "It must be something to do with beauty – of the run-of-the-mill kind" (the last clause hurried). "I treat you as quite strong because I remember the other Isobel, and you remind me of her sometimes, but really I'm sure it won't be like two copies of the same person."

Thursday, December 13th

"Then Mrs Jaffa brought the tea in, as I've said[7]; and he said, '...,' – ah – I'm afraid I can't remember quite what he said just then. Does it matter?"

"No, my darling," I said, "you've told me this part already. Why not start again, at the point where you've just finished criticising his poem, and you've started talking about politics."

"Oh, very well, I thought I'd better change the subject again, as I've also said, and as ill-luck would have it I chose the government – the Queen and so on. I can't remember quite what suggested it to me."

I've had enough of this already. I haven't been able to apply myself to anything useful all day. I have to confess that I spent most of the morning in front of my mirror, and not attempting an objective self-appraisal, as the other day, but quite the reverse: I have a big pot of foundation cream, and another of face powder, souvenirs, retained by inertia in my bag and on my dressing-table; and the transformations I attempted and effected this morning, with these materials, were quite astounding. They also used a startling quantity of the cream, though not of the powder. Had I been touched by any but my own sculpting hand I might have been found to be far less substantial than I appeared. It was not a pleasant activity in any case, and this reflection did not add to it appeal. It was not in any way a return to Miss Keogh, of whom I was not conscious: and now I do not know whether avoidance of her was intentional on the part of the hand, which here overcompensated for, overfilled a depression, there allowed one to remain, where it was acceptable, only surprising. It was intentional avoidance of her or merely an aesthetic force, a sense of balance working against the protuberances. My hand and cream could not affect the protuberances, of course, only a knife.

I had done my hair, too (which is not at all bad), at the outset of this venture into the plastic arts, and in short, from the time of rising and washing right through to the afternoon period I will shortly tell of, I found myself more and more deeply immersed in a developing image, which sat in front of me and steadily drank in, with me, greater and greater quantities of the cream, the furniture, the room, the light and the time. It stared at me with a growing interest and intelligence, until I was not aware of adding to it myself, only of watching it grow. Its hair was beautiful and dark, becoming darker as the face took on more and more uniformly the colour of the powder, paler and paler with emotion at the sight of me. Its surroundings grew darker, and its lips paler: it might have been on the point of speaking.

So I had quite a close relationship with it when at about five the doorbell rang; and mixed with my panic was a strange resentment of the interruption. Who knows what intercourse had been prevented? But during my repeated attempts to brave the stairs, and my simultaneous, equally nervous, spasmodic dressing, I found my opinion of its desirability as a friend on the wane. Was it not, I asked myself, simply too *brash*, a failed voluptuousness fitting in Las Vegas but foolish in Finchley? Perhaps this was one of the whore's customers at the door. But in that case, I knew, it would be capable at least of a certain coldness, well

---

7 He had, though not at quite the same point. *The Author*

endowed with the power to refuse – entry or anything. With that knowledge I gained a grip on the stairs, and scuttled down them.

It was LIONEL, again, bearing under one arm a large parcel and in the other hand a bunch of flowers; and for the second time his feet all but rose from the WELCOME doormat in a visible testimonial to my appearance. Having returned, as it were, to earth, he said, "Miss Cook" in a tone nicely graded between enquiry and greeting, and came in, thrusting the flowers under one arm and the parcel further under the other. He was not prepared for presentation ceremonies, which had not, I remembered, under any circumstances been his strong point. It was on the whole, however, a far more satisfactory visit than his Wednesday's; he was not interested in Charles – whom I too have more or less given up – except to the extent that he snorted rather aggressively whenever I mentioned his name. He knew all about Charles's whereabouts and doings, but I didn't ask him about them. He had come to see me in particular (I would hardly have believed, indeed, that the flowers, initially prominent and almost proffered, had been for Charles) and when he began to say what appeared to be at the worst some peripheral things of those he wanted to say to me, it was with an earnestness which had been lacking entirely from his Wednesday's manner.

At length he got round to the parcel, the flowers still lying on the floor beside his chair: and placing it between his knees (for it was a longish thinnish parcel) he began himself to remove, apparently for want of a less awkward approach to the problem, though causing me much disappointment and frustration, the brown paper which I originally assumed he had himself wrapped round it. As it proved, though, it might have been the bookseller. Twelve discreetly shining red volumes, rose out of the paper, about five inches by eight all the way down the pile, and Lionel picked up the top one, addressing the spine: "*The Invisible Man* – that's a good one. I saw you didn't have any books, and I thought I'd get these for you."

"Oh, thank you very much," said I. They made up, of course, as I eventually forced him to admit, and much later, having impelled him to give them up to me, as I established conclusively for myself, a selection from the works of H. G. Wells – a volume of short stories, large quantities of novels, and an occasional non-fiction piece – the sort of selection which can give the impression of containing all that it's really worthwhile to read of a man's output, while in fact amounting only to a tiny fraction of it. I had seen single volumes of the same edition before, humbly priced in second-hand bookshops, without even pausing to look inside. I had read all that was worthwhile of this man's output. Nonetheless, the degree of pleasurable anticipation which Lionel's present roused in me was quite extraordinary, and the degree of gratitude, it seemed, greater than any I'd felt before.

Well, when I'd pushed the thing so far that he'd acknowledged my (in the circumstances) feeble acknowledgement, there was no corking up his renewed youth. I'd read some of these books before, then? Not all, he hoped? And I was familiar with the idea of space-travel? – holding up *The First Men in the Moon*; I smiled, while wondering if I had yet further alterations to make in my notions of history, and – a slightly greater start – of the books, because it pleased me to find myself able, after such a long time, to use the simple affirmative, "Yes." *The Time Machine*, I remarked, wasn't represented.

"Oh, don't worry about that," he frowned. "It's only space we're interested in."

"We?" I questioned.

"My father and I."

Then I made some progress with a discussion of the relation between time and space, based on Mr Wells's proposition in the book just mentioned, but Lionel wouldn't have much of it. He orated lengthily, instead, on the general desirability of escaping from the world, and yet more lengthily on the necessity of finding exactly the right sort of people to escape with. He didn't actually mention his father's space-ships, or invite me to cross the galaxy with him, but it was my own lack of response which prevented him. I might at least have mentioned that I'd read the article in *The Times* about his father.

But the only contribution I did, in the event, make, was to get up from my seat (remembering at once that my face and parts of my body were in immediate danger of dropping off) and to say, indicating the flowers, "Shall I put these in some water?", to which he replied, "Oh; yes," before continuing.

It was as I bent down to pick them up, feeling as if I had a tea-tray balanced on my head, and walked with them gingerly out of the room, that he reached the section of his speech which concerned the possibility of founding, if only for a single generation, the ideal society based on a certain complex design of his own, in which power would be ... his voice did not falter as I passed along the hall, feeling free now to glance over my shoulder in case I had dropped anything, and gained the kitchen complete. Presumably he imagined that my hearing was such as to follow a mere raised voice through two open doors.

When I returned he had begun to recommend *A Modern Utopia* (which appeared with *The Food of the Gods* in the seventh book down) as an aid to comprehension of his own utopia's final form – though not, I would of course understand, as an exact representation of it – and I accordingly promised to read it first of all, assuring him that I had, indeed, understood. He appeared satisfied with that, and content with the amount he had said, though it was difficult to tell whether he had made any progress with me. Having finished for the day he became restless again, and began to walk round and round the room as on Wednesday, even echoing a remark he had made then: "You don't appear to have a telephone." He didn't mention the flowers before leaving. I have been reading *A Modern Utopia* and find it very entertaining, although the political ideas seem to me to be rather naïve and wholly impractical. I have also been peeping at *The Food of the Gods*, which looks a good deal more interesting.

Friday, December 14th

DINGBRACE came with the groceries again today, and apart from the tins of meatballs and frankfurters, the onions, peppers and potatoes, he included a HUGE bottle of cheap perfume – not, I hope, a hint – a young lady's complete kit for the making-up of the eyes, a set of new felt-tipped pens in thirty different colours, three boxes of *Lion Brand* white writing-paper and envelopes, a pair of high-heeled patent leather shoes (one of them the right size) and an extra large envelope, stuffed haphazardly with bank-notes of different values. The last item, for reasons incomprehensible to me as to anyone, I refused to accept, but for the rest, he appeared to me as a corpulent, familiar delivery-man, from whom it was quite natural that I should accept the things. We had a dialogue rich in sexual jokes, at the end of which I was actually hoping that he would slap my behind or squeeze my breasts, but he didn't. He told me not to forget to come on Christmas Eve, and for the moment after that I positively jumped at him, telling him that I had to be somewhere else – or perhaps I didn't – and anyway, where did he live? Where did he live, anyway? But he said that he'd come and collect me, and if I wasn't here, never mind.

Saturday, December 15th

Addresses:

Us (or me) : 1,316 Finchley Road, London N.W.3

Charles in the Lake District : Near Step House, Step, Near Rydal, Westmorland

Isobel Keogh : "Le Bienvenu",
154 West Heath Road,
London, N.W.2

Sir Charles Jaffa : The Launching Pad,
Outwood Lane,
London, S.E.13

Lionel Jaffa : Bidesloe Mansions,
155, Stopcombe Close,
Chiswick, W.4.

Aloysius Mote?
Dingbrace?
Maria (the) Beautiful?

Dear Isobel,

I suppose you will have recognised my handwriting – that at least hasn't changed much – and you will by now have looked at the end of the letter. I, of course, don't know how that will look yet, but do you recognise the name? I don't even know yet whether I'm going to put my address at the top.

So for the moment this is no longer a letter, or even the draft of one. It's very difficult to write for an audience, after all this self-directed scribbling – can you, for example, make anything of this? It might perhaps be easier to begin in one of the new writing-pads, but then there would be all the business of the clean first sheet and the firm block of paper to be gone through again. One of the delights of this notebook is that more than a quarter of its thickness is thoroughly crinkly, and the remaining block has been pressed irregularly so that its edges are curling over; thus you are slowly continuing an already well-established process, which it is easy to imagine directs all your present steps. Before setting out into a new white expanse, on the other hand, it will be necessary to know precisely where you are going; and this notebook will provide as good a plan as might be hoped for.

So: it is Sunday tomorrow, and if all goes according to the pattern, I should have another letter from Charles. It will be an important letter, this time, and may even include an address, but I haven't left a space in my list, as I'm sure that the address in question is already on it. I am also sure that the letter I am at present engaged in writing will be, in some sense, a reply to the one I shall receive. Should I, therefore, mention Lionel and Dingbrace? Lionel's activities will be of too much interest to Isobel, Dingbrace's of none at all. And do I, after all, really want to communicate secretly with Charles? He will be less likely than Isobel to recognise my name, but certain to recognise the address. Am I sure that Charles will see the letter, or understand it? Perhaps Isobel will not read it herself, but leave it entirely to him.

I will include both my name and my address, and thus remain a mystery to both of them.

1,316, Finchley Road,
London N.W.3
15th. December, 1973

Dear Isobel,

This, though not a threatening letter (and covering, unlike the average essay in blackmail, a wide range of topics), will almost certainly prove to involve, under every distinct heading, a distinct warning. And to proceed directly to self-justification, it is not the feigned benevolence of the blackmailer or the viciousness of the deformed pleasure-seeker it will display; rather, if you like, the complacency of the befuddled astrologer, disturbing by its eccentricity but in the end merely bone-headed. It will reveal an intimate knowledge of your concerns, but I don't suppose that that will bother you unduly: let me assure you, in any case, that it is merely a part of the general derangement, and not at all a major theme in the letter. I will begin, for example, by revealing that I am known to that Sir Charles Pink whose acquaintance you recently made; and this is true – here is a disturbing part – *however strenuously he denies it*. And then, to prove my point, I will go on to say that this should in no way affect your opinion of him, because so far he has not lied and knows nothing about this letter. But you will be dominating him by now in such a manner as not to need advice of this kind. I flatter myself that, although my material so far has resembled that of the blackmailer, I have succeeded in sustaining a sympathetic tone. I will now attempt to go further and evoke pity, using the same kind of dubious stuff, but still in an unsensational, objective and rigidly moral way. I live at the above address, not out of choice, and am not at all sure just at present how I'll ever get away from it. I am the woman whom Charles, so to speak, deserted here (though by the same token I've been adopted by your own new beau, Captain Lionel Jaffa) and deserted, be it added, only when I had begun to suspect that he was an impostor, and possibly the murderer of the real Charles – oh – it is difficult to be unsensational. As I write this it rests on the draining-board (carefully wiped dry beforehand, though that will not concern you) and I leave it from time to time – as now – in order to attend to my dinner, a packet of pea soup, which has, on account of my concern for this sentence, boiled over: the consequence being that I will have less than a pint. Not that it's a question of material want; no, sensationalism and riches aren't the same thing, and this isn't a begging letter either. Start again.

It has been an uninteresting day. I spent the morning altering a pair of shoes – not on account of material want – and over lunch transcribed all the addresses of which I'm reasonably sure into my notebook. I was convinced that letter-writing was precisely the activity I inclined to; but then somehow I lost a number of hours, and ended up with a greasy plate and no inclination. Nonetheless I have spent the evening writing what I have written so far, which shows that I retain a degree of persistence, and am correspondingly less deserving of pity.

And now, to complete my display of horrid importuner's devices honourably used, I have read about you in the newspaper, in connection with Sir Charles Jaffa's spaceship. How is old Sir Charles, by the way? I hope his gout is not troubling him as much as it used. And poor Mrs Jezebel, for whom no doubt any solicitude you feel is as purely polite as my own? The Jaffa household is my central theme, as it might have been that of any blackmailer who had read the same newspaper articles; but although I have not seen the Jaffas for more than ten years, the recent news alone I have had of them justifies, by its detail, the warnings I shall give you. I have a dreadful feeling – don't you? – that this letter is going to turn into a perpetual introduction, summarising its business in advance until it discovers that it has stated everything without having begun, and then perhaps continuing without either summary or statement. There are too many self-criticisms used as fresh starting-points.

The exaggerated sensibility of Charles Jaffa led him, and still leads Sir Charles, through an interminable series of contacts with multifarious young and more advanced ladies, both on account of his rapidly shifting spiritual affinities and in pursuit of a sexual ambition, polygamous but otherwise uncertain in outline. During the first half of his forty-second year he was seen in the public company of three now celebrated women: Gabrielle Roseata, Rachel Orange, and Maria Klapperpost; singly and in groups, on many separate occasions. This was not remarkable, of course, even in the sense in which I suggest and you and I know that Jaffa's sexual life is remarkable. Gabrielle Roseata was an opera-singer, Maria Klapperpost a vendor of tickets, often for Gabrielle's performances, and Rachel Orange a prostitute with a taste for art, supplied with all that her taste necessitated, and with all other necessaries, for long periods solely by Charles Jaffa. What could have been more likely, then, than that the poet and scientist should have found reasons for appearing in the company of each? Many years later, when the four had set up house together, Charles and Rachel would still go to meet Maria at the box-office, and then at the tail-end of the audience the trio would go up to hear Gabrielle sing; it is hardly necessary to add that a quartet was formed in her dressing-room, and later crowded into the last bus home. I mention these three in particular because it was during his period of housekeeping with them that Sir Charles brought forth his son Lionel: the household closed itself up for several months, only the man, no woman, ever going out; one of the three must have been a midwife, another a mother, and the third a good lover of Charles, or a keeper of secrets. How many people know as much as I, and whether even you know more, I don't: the point is that the offspring of Sir Charles Jaffa and of any of these ladies, the histories of all four families being known, must be treated with extreme circumspection. I am not deriving my conclusions just at present from the stars: I know that no-one but you or I could have borne Sir Charles Jaffa a reasonable child. My knowledge must be greater than yours, in one respect, and in another yours invalidates mine. To steal Captain Lionel Jaffa from his wife was a foolish action, and to accept him as he rebounded from his stealer would be yet more foolish. What do you think, then, of Charles Pink? I would value your opinion, being almost as new to intimacy with him as you are to knowledge of him.

I have finished my dinner, and feel horribly full of reconstituted pea soup. I have re-read the letter so often that to have told you every time I did so would have made it twice as long (exaggeration). In the end I probably won't send it to you. I'm going to bed.

Horrible, deceitful, ungrateful bitch! I've found your letter to Charles, and he kept it under his pillow. Did you suggest to me that I go and sleep in that room tonight? Not content with scaring me out of it by getting yourself – (you know what you got done to yourself, and if you don't you can guess – I heard you) – now you tempt me back into it just to get me feeling sick with reading your horrible gushing. Here it is, you can have it back, and you'll find that I've marked it and added comments where I think you might have been less effusive[8].

Sunday, December 16th.

Unable to wait any longer for Charles's letter, I went out at nine o'clock. I was wearing my new shoes, which hurt me about the balls of the toes. I wasn't at all nervous: I was so confident that I shut the front door with a single hand, so as not to be obliged, as I had been obliged when opening it with both, to clutch my bag of articles with an elbow as if nervously to my ribs. I had seen, when opening the door, a very cold section of Finchley Road, but without rain, snow or pedestrians; now I turned and looked at it again, and found that a pedestrian had begun to traverse it, from right to left – peering of course over my hedge, especially as she had heard the sound of the front door.

I hope you find it as interesting as I do, that there is in general a good deal less traffic up and down this road than I remember (for I had frequented it long before I moved into this house, as you probably know). There is one particular phenomenon of which I would welcome an explanation, from you as from anyone: Monday is so quiet as to be practically dead, and over Tuesday, Wednesday, Thursday, Friday and Saturday there is a gradual increase in the flow (uninterrupted at night) until on Sunday a small climax is reached, this being the busiest of seven quiet days. I am sure that this is the case, and trust may be placed in my conclusion, as I have had several weeks for initial observations under good conditions, and two for systematic substantiation of my theory under perfect; both at day and at night.

It being Sunday now, then, this pedestrian was the first of a fair number. I could already see more on the other side of the road, passing from left to right. She was old, but no-one I knew; even so she stared at me only for a moment, without the least surprise, before turning away with the air of one who hasn't looked at all. This was by no means what I had expected. I congratulated myself, as I had spent the night in a hard chair, and retouched my make-up in the few necessary places before coming out, largely in order to make myself less noteworthy. There were cars passing also, I noticed, though not continuously; a second-long pause was not an uncommon thing: not a completely silent pause, of course, but one containing only diminishing sound and less obviously growing sound – no immediate, constant sound, that is. The intervals in which the constant sound was approximately halved (contradiction) – when traffic was continuous in only one direction – were frequent, but, I found, impossible to gauge. I might possibly go into the business of how the roughly-halved sound was greater when it was the opposite side that paused, and how the pausing side's diminishing and growing sounds had to be taken into account; but there would be very little point, as I don't feel inclined to, and the information would be rendered insignificant by the absence of accurate statistics. I wasn't, in any case, expecting reactions to my appearance from the people in the cars; they no doubt had other things on their minds. I was pleased by my old female pedestrian's non-reaction, however, because I had been working, after all, in something of an isolated situation, cut off from outside influences, when creating the new me

8 There are approximately twenty blank pages from this point on – suggesting that Miss Cook was intending either to transcribe the letter here, if it existed, and enclose the original with the letter she was herself writing, or to affix the original to her own pages, and transcribe, etc. However, there is no sign of her having begun to execute either plan. *The Author*

(the make-up I have mentioned, as you perhaps aren't aware, is a very extensive application of foundation cream and face powder, which transforms my appearance completely).

All the same, at the gate I turned so as to walk away from her, that is to the right; and was at once disillusioned, because there was approaching me a man whose reactions to something – and I was directly in his path – were demonstrably extreme. He was old, with a stick, and his movements were so wild that I will not describe them (except to say that he flailed with the stick in what appeared to be furious gestures); his staggerings from side to side of the pavement (description) were such as to obscure for me virtually all details of his appearance and behaviour save those I have already imparted to you. However, as I advanced I absorbed, one by one, further points of information concerning him: he was advancing; he was in an extreme hurry; the extremity of his movements might have been accounted for in part or even solely by the extreme hurry he was in. When we met he stopped, and I was disillusioned again, because I had thought for a moment that it wasn't me he was reacting to. I stopped also. He was Sir Charles Jaffa, and he stared at me very madly, but then I realised, from the way he was balanced on his stick, that I hadn't caused the madness in his stare, only augmented it. I was pleased again, and almost spoke. But he looked away, returned for a final disapproving glance, and then carried on, his sideways motion gathering momentum over about ten yards and seconds.

I moved away from him, too, knowing that it would be foolish to speak. But as it became increasingly plain to me that I was going in the same direction as a week last Monday – was approaching the National Westminster Bank – I stopped, increasingly for longer and with greater frequency, to look behind me after the receding Sir Charles. I found that I could still see, also, the original pedestrian I had seen passing my gate, though as yet no-one apart from her or Sir Charles going in either direction along this stretch of pavement, even though it was extremely long, stretching to a distant vanishing-point below a very tall building. This isolation of the woman, Sir Charles and the tall building suggested that the immediate destinies of the three were in some special way connected; certainly they were all catching up on one another, the building being motionless and the woman progressing even more slowly than Sir Charles. Whether the converging was happening in such a way that the three would meet, I couldn't calculate.

In the other direction, I had almost left the row of houses in which my own was included, and was coming to a little growth of shops, the first being a newsagent's, whose newspaper-hoardings I could see edge-on outside. It was, in fact, when I had stopped alongside this first edge of the hoarding that I turned to look again at the progress of Sir Charles and the woman (noticing that more pedestrians had appeared beneath the building and were walking in my direction); and as this retrospective study was the longest yet on account of the novelty, I was very violently struck by a quick male pedestrian who'd been walking towards me from the shops without looking where he was going.

I realised at once that part of my face was falling off, and clapped my hand to my cheek as I looked round at my interceptor. I was in time to see that he had been looking at the newspaper-hoarding, which was what had caused our collision; and to catch a look of shock entirely different in character from Sir Charles Jaffa's, and more intense. Lionel Jaffa's was mostly to do with the collision itself, of course, but he had been shocked beforehand, and now was shocked for the third time by my appearance, all of which I heard in the way his doubly-concerned "Oh, I'm terribly sorry! Do exc..." changed to the treble "You! Miss Cook!" He had grabbed me by the elbows – the first time he had touched me – and it was far from being an unwelcome grab: it was not imprisonment, like the Virgin's multiform clutch of eleven days previously, but on the contrary freed me for a moment from the desire for physical contact which I had felt with Dingbrace the anteprevious day, and even transcended that desire; but it was all the same an inconvenience, as one elbow was unnaturally raised by the necessity of keeping my cheek in place, and it looked impolite to force unevenness thus on Lionel's gesture, which should in essence and therefore preferably in execution have been spontaneous and natural.

The hand on my cheek must at first have looked like a shock rather self-consciously echoing his own, but as it persisted in this perverse situation Lionel began to cast other interpretations. "Have you got toothache?" he said, perhaps protecting himself from the more insulting suggestions of my unbendability. "Are you looking for a dentist? Look, I could show you one, just a little further down this road." I gently shook my head, and in that moment had the answer: I closed my fingers on the detached feature, squashing it into an inside-fist shape of aromatic clay, and unbent, leaving one cheek convex and the other cavernous, the latter perhaps smeared with five rough bands (from my four fingers) of cream, though by the time I found a mirror it certainly wasn't.

Lionel appeared satisfied with this, and felt that he could now devote the time to his other troubles: "Look, I can't stop, have you seen an old man?" "Your father?" I said, forgetting for a moment (he did too – how famous his father was, I mean, himself to a lesser extent: he'd imagined he'd had the advantage over me, but really it had been quite the other way round; and accordingly his shocked looks continued) "Yes, he came past me a moment ago; in fact," turning my head to substantiate the point, "he should still be in sight." He was, though sometimes obscured by the new pedestrians, who, coming from underneath the tall building, had now passed him. He had stopped on the horizon, having caught up with the woman, who had stopped also, and he was now apparently addressing her in violent terms, gesturing with his stick.

Lionel looked in their direction; "Tchah," he said (I think that's about the best way I can put it). "Look," he then said for the third time, turning to me and I to him, "I can't stop, but I must see Charles. Can you tell me when he'll be in?" "I don't..." I began. "I know he doesn't spend much time at home, but hasn't he arranged to meet you some time?" He was watching his father again. "I've written to him," that was the end of his piece. "So far as I know," I replied, extraordinarily proud of myself, "Sir Charles is dead." He gripped my elbows painfully, and seemed on the edge of tears; his shock had brought him to this point: "No, no he isn't. Tell me when I can see him. Where are you going for Christmas?"

I at once took control of the situation: I removed my elbows from his hands, and would have held both his wrists, had I not found one of my hands to be full of sticky stuff; as it was I held one, and tried to push it over towards the other, in order to make a show of holding both with one hand, and perhaps to rest my closed fist on top of both. "I'm going to a party with a man called Dingbrace," I said, "or perhaps with a woman called Maria." "The Dingbraces – both of you?" he said, but the next moment he had run away, and I, looking after him, observed that his father had disappeared.

Well, what do you think of the way I dealt with your young man? You can see that there is no cause for jealousy, I hope: indeed, in the way he was so anxious to steer me to the dentist's chair, perhaps there is cause for gloating. You should not, however, be quite so complacent about his anxiety to see Charles. The seeking-out of old college friends cannot possibly be healthy for the later adjuncts to his life, among which you must number yourself, and in this particular case I know that the influence of Charles on Lionel would be especially pernicious, especially for you. If you think I am saying all this in a round-about way, I, alas, can only agree; but at least you now have nothing to fear from my influence on Lionel.

As for me, I went three short steps on my way, at least two of them backwards, as I still had an interest in the opposite direction, and then found myself compromised, with my back to the road, facing the newspaper-hoarding. I, too, was nearly crying now, but desisted on account of the damage this would do to my remaining cheek. The one I had removed I flung into a litter-basket which stood beside the hoarding.

There had been a very sudden increase in the number of pedestrians (some of them, doubtless, those who had obscured Sir Charles Jaffa) and they passed both behind and in front of me, and would have obscured any sight I tried to get of Lionel. The newspaper-hoarding said "Charles – Inquest Begins Tomorrow". Fortunately, my ability to interpret such things had been entirely revived by my walks with Charles in the period preceding the last Thursday but one; I instantly thought of Prince Charles, the Queen's son, and only when I had rejected him did I associate the notice with the Charles previously uppermost in my thoughts, who happened to be Sir Charles Pink. Looking more closely at it, I found that there had been a Sir at the top, now obscured by the way the paper had been fitted into the wooden frame. This confirmed the reading for me, though I still did not see how the general public was expected to distinguish between Sir Charles Pink and Sir Charles Jaffa; the latter had recently featured in legal proceedings, whose end doubtless had been more obscure than their beginning; but none had so far as I knew been heralded or foreshadowed, concerning the former, since the day of the murder (thirteen days previously). I had, in any case, to buy the newspaper (as none is delivered to our house on Sunday) and make absolutely sure.

Have you heard anything about an inquest? Why haven't I been invited, if there is to be one? I should have thought I would be the principal – no, the only witness. I can't imagine how they're managing it – or would manage – at all: but then my ideas of what inquests in general might be are, at best, rather hazy. I certainly have no idea how or when the people concerned are summoned. So, unhappy though I was about having to play the customer again, I clutched my money (inside my bag) and strolled into the shop.

The hoarding had been entitled, *The Guardian*, but as no such thing is published on Sunday I knew it would be futile to ask for that particular newspaper. Instead, I had to ask whether the advertisement was in reality connected with some other journal, and if so, which. He was at bottom, I think, an intolerant man: I had to repeat my enquiry many times before he would understand it, and ironically it was he, not I, who became angry during this period of confusion. In the end, however, he overcame his choler for long enough to drop a heavy wad of paper in front of me, say "You'll find all about it in there", and demand from me a quarter of all the money I had in the world. It was the *Sunday Times*: I paid for it, of course, and lifted it out of the shop, but once I had it on the pavement I didn't know quite what to do with it. I looked to the left, but neither Lionel nor his father was in sight. My first idea was to take it to a pub, so that I could sit down to deal with it: it didn't immediately occur to me that a pub might not be open at that time in the morning, and indeed, I have since discovered that there was no reason why it should not have been; the law having no say in the matter of opening-times on this planet. I'm afraid I may sometimes write as if I imagined I came from another world. Please take no notice of this: look on it as another quirk of the mad astrologer.

I went on my way, then (to the right) more hurriedly than before, having an object in view; I can't say, however, that I kept it very plainly in view, as I judged the possible courses through groups of pedestrians, and became more and more minutely aware, as I did so, that I had followed more or less the same route in quieter circumstances, thirteen days ago. It became particularly vivid when I passed the very shop where I had bought this notebook (not the writing-pad from which this sheet is torn, you understand, but the rough-book in which I sketched out the letter) on the day in question. "We" had bought, I should say.

It is perhaps this, especially, that I want to warn you against, though I sometimes despair of making anything plain to you when things concerning no-one but myself follow on from one another so irresistibly. This – the thing I want especially to warn you against – is the power of perfectly familiar objects (by which I mean the ones of which you are now hardly aware) to absorb, and later to regenerate, a seemingly unlimited quantity of unpleasant suggestions.

This shop, which I had gone into and out of many times without retaining the knowledge that it was a single distinct shop, now offered a constructed index to my isolation. It contained, among other things, the absence of Charles and the invisibility of Lionel; the utter strangeness (or inversion) of my environment; the vicious circle between myself and my notebook; and primarily, the source of all the other connections, a thirteen-day-old bloodbath.

You are saying to yourself that this is not the promised centre of my letter, all bound up as it was to be with the Jaffa household. No, indeed, this isn't the centre, but I'm sure you can see how it might make an alternative pivot – the inner rod, as it were, of the cylinder formed by my (or your) relationship with a particular family. The trouble is that there must always be a practical, working order for anything of this nature, which can do nothing but distort the original design. The further we get from the address, absolutely, the further we get from the plan. It's obvious that I'm going to start again: the only question is, at what point shall I stop the present process, and begin the next?

It all became rather too much at about the time I reached the entrance to an underground station. As there was still nowhere to sit I leaned against the nearest pillar, which was not a part of the portal proper, but the edge of a preliminary alcove containing a very narrow-fronted shop – a tobacconist's, I think. I looked inside what appeared to be the heaviest section of the *Sunday Times* – the relatively shiny colour-magazine, which was also the easiest part to open and to keep from closing. The cover had been very evocative of Christmas, but in spite of this the interior seemed mainly concerned with dogs, and was not what I needed. I shut my eyes, trying hard to compromise between relaxation and looking like an outcast; in the dark I tried to remember what (if any) part this Underground station had played in the events of the last Monday but one, and whether I had noticed it on that occasion, and wondered if, when (if ever) I opened my eyes again, I would prefer to be seen in this uncertain state only by strangers, or the series of (as I saw them) coincidences to be continued, dubiously blessing me with the company of more people from my past and yours. Although this is always a doubtful issue, I believe myself now in a position to assert that they were not coincidences, but only one coincidence; that the original female pedestrian, Rachel Orange, possibly Lionel's mother, who happened to have travelled from Surbiton to Frognal that morning, had begun to pass my house at the moment chosen by me for leaving it.

When I opened my eyes, however, I did not know whether I was faced with a new coincidence or not: Lionel was coming out of the station and turning left, thus towards me and in the same direction as before; but otherwise transformed. He was wearing the same clothes, but had now slept in them every night for a month, and his pseudo-military peaked cap had been pulled down over his ears, stuffed into his pocket, and sat upon so many times that it had entirely lost its shape; it looked, indeed, as though it had been consciously converted from a uniform-fragment, with the function of placing its owner in a certain group, to the exact reverse of such a thing. It did suggest the bohemian, but to do so was obviously not its purpose. I had seen many styles of hat worked into such pliability – even a policeman's helmet – but never a peaked cap before. He had also grown, in this short period, an eighth of an inch of black beard (a change I was almost happy to see) and more than ten years older. He carried a stick, was generally swarthy, and walked past me without looking in my direction; he looked at the nearest clock as he passed. Whatever his new identity, I could never love anything in the image of Lionel; it's of no importance how much facial hair the new image, or even all the images, might grow. I'm sure Charles doesn't know how his special position in the world depends on the special quality of his moustache; I've almost come to pity Lionel's ragged covering of unshavenness. Lionel passed, and I remained in position, observed by many anonymous people who thus cancelled out anything resembling a coincidence.

An unknown, but probably small quantity of time passed before Charles, in his turn, rose out of the Underground station, and looked up, down and across the street, as if still half-blind from the twilight. This was just what I needed: I dropped the *Sunday Times* into my bag, which is very large, and then delved underneath the newspaper to make sure that I still had your letter to him. Whether or not he had seen it before, I intended to show it to him before sending it to you. While I delved he continued to stand indecisive, either seeing me or not; before I'd found what I sought he spun round in fright, and re-descended into the Underground station. I followed him, still delving. I found that I had automatically regained the ability to go into Underground stations while completely absorbed by the contents of my bag. By the time I reached the ticket-office I'd found the letter and lost Charles, and had to start a new search for what money remained to me. I bought the most expensive ticket for twenty-five pence, leaving myself with fifteen, and chose a line (as I saw it) at random: Metropolitan.

It was as I plunged into the labyrinth, possibly wondering if it mattered to me whether or not I found Charles on the platform in question, and hearing a train leave from another, that a helpful way of restarting this letter occurred to me. Not that this will concern you: it may have been merely that I felt peaceful, as if all the personal problems which had interfered with the beginning of its composition had now been resolved, leaving the way clear for untroubled thought and an unbiased view of past, present and future; or that I perversely associated my descent to the underground – a more complete change of place than any I had envisaged on leaving the house – with a reversal, instead of a mere deepening, in the state of things, thus hitting on the idea of reversing the notebook in order to write an upside-down letter from the last page on, and realising that it would be better not to worry about reversals in time and so on, but to deal with the most important events whether they were causes or effects. In any case, all that is what I intend to do as soon as I get home.

Letter from L to Isobel Keogh, no date

Dear Isobel,

You may not recognise yourself in this. Even so, the names are not altered, and the writing is not consciously disguised.

It was the middle of the tenth year of the voyage, when the people in the ship were going through one of their spells of animal routine. All thought about tasks and pleasures was avoided, so that one day would seem as much as possible like all the others. The activities themselves also were reduced to a minimum. No-one amused himself in the control-room, as some had done in more optimistic periods, by manipulating the red arrow on the screen until the ship's speed, while the engines merely idled, became almost inconceivable. Most of the travellers, and certainly those in the upper hierarchy, spent their time in their own cabins, lying on their beds. When communication was necessary they did not look into each other's eyes.

Only Sir Charles Pink ever went into the control-room. He did so twice a day in order to check on course, speed, surroundings and so on. Others may have occupied themselves spasmodically with calculations and other writing, but these were always of a remote, impractical nature. Isobel, for example, was certainly working on the problem of the total distance they had travelled – or, more particularly, of whether they had travelled any distance at all. She had in front of her the details of the supposed journey so far: all the bearings which had been taken on whatever object – on the stars which had been visible from the Earth, and on those other bodies which had appeared during the flight – however futile and capricious the manoeuvring of the arrow had been; and with these innumerable recorded trajectories, some of which, of course, had been negative, she was trying to perform an enormous calculation in which they all cancelled out. The question of angles very shortly became meaningless, but also in terms of the given trajectories she began to draw a map in which the course of the ship was a small repeated circle, and, having abandoned this, another in which space was shown to involve actual absolute values of place and time, and to be made up of connected immovable areas, apart from which the ship was the only motionless thing. These mathematical and diagrammatic projects, however, were not the major part of her work, which frequently degenerated into the lengthy compilation of an account, in prose, of her tortuous reasoning on the problem. This was unreadable (not that she contemplated showing it to anyone) and had a tendency, being guided by no plan save that of the sentences' individual connections, to become involved with her personal affairs and mental condition, over which admittedly it had a great influence. Even when writing this she would sometimes be overcome by idleness and would stare at the page without writing – and not in thought; her resumptions after hours-long pauses were the only points in the whole where she made faulty connections.

This apathetic spell, experienced by her as by the whole crew, lasted longer than any had previously done, and its intensity grew. It was not uncommon in the morning to push one's legs out of bed, sit on the edge, and at once feel so weary that one had to lie down again and go back to sleep. A reason for this intensity and extension, though not the cause of the fit itself, was discovered when its effects had long been evident. Sir Charles had been in the habit of entering the control-room, glancing at the panel and then leaving again; one day, however, he was suddenly so tired that he leaned on the panel, and raising his head to take a deep breath, saw the pressure-gauge. The pressure inside the vessel was several degrees higher than normal. In the following days he recorded the readings, and found that a very slow, very regular increase in pressure was taking place, in accordance with the growing general lassitude. He also changed the setting of the steering and speed mechanism, which had been set to select at random its own course and power; he chose what was apparently the most distant object on the screen, a pulsating white spot innumerable light years away, and steered towards this, turning on full power. Setting the red arrow also on this spot, he found a resulting speed of around five hundred million miles per hour. In inverse proportion, however, to the growing pressure and apathy, this speed decreased by several hundred miles per hour per day.

He reluctantly visited the cabin of Lionel Jaffa, in order to make an official report. He found the captain, however, crouched in a corner, quite naked, hands dangling over his knees, humming to himself. Isobel too was naked and apparently unoccupied, but she at least was sitting at the desk, which encouraged Charles to relate to her instead all the contents of the above paragraph. He had not had the presence of mind to leave, but in speaking to her he avoided with his eyes her thighs and nipples, and so found her face. Although the eyes were vacant, he was no doubt happy to see again at least an indication of another person. When the two of them left for the control-room he reminded her to put some clothes on, which she did not at the time understand, although she complied. Later, she was embarrassed to remember how he had stood beside her while she dressed.

The reaction to his news about the pressure was apologetic: she had devised nothing, she said, which could neutralize all conceivable high pressures. On hearing of the diminishing speed, however, her state approached excitement, and she took from Sir Charles his record of the decline, saying that she would study it. Her conclusions were simple: if such a regular, continuous process existed (as opposed to the customary lack of change or jumbled, random switches) it followed that the medium supporting it, speed, was real. Whether the ship was moving through space or space around the ship was of no consequence. She returned to the control-room with Sir Charles in order to try a further experiment: the ever-diminishing speed, still little less than 500,000,000 m.p.h., was the maximum now attainable; she wished to find the minimum, hoping that this would show a similar mathematical behaviour.

The way to reduce speed was to move the arrow to an area of space which was blank on the screen: with a little finer shifting in the apparently empty space the needle would suddenly plunge, and a point would at last be reached where a light flashed, indicating zero speed, or a very close approximation to it. Isobel, sitting at the screen, head bent, placed her sheaf of notes on the panel. The paper was stained, and her fingers were shaking.

"Why is the arrow in the centre of the screen?" she asked, only half-turning to Sir Charles.

"It was a white spot there. Indefinite distance. It seems to have gone." He, having submitted his findings, from which he had not been able to deduce even the faltering facts Isobel was now pursuing, had subsided to the role of assistant, and was sitting in a chair at right angles to the panel.

She, gently pressing the arm which controlled the arrow, was exploring by fractions of millimeters an area of black space, with the needle trembling on the zero-mark. Every so often the arm would yield in a way which told her the "speed" had diminished still further. The needle had long since passed any calibrations the eye could discern, but the light did not flash. For a long time, Isobel pushed the speed further and further down, following the yielding of the arm, never letting it tighten, dealing in smaller and smaller pressures of the hand, wiping the hand, which still shook, from time to time on her leg; but zero was not reached.

"Turn off the engines," she said. It had no effect at all, except that the floor of the room seemed more inert. It could not have been expected to affect the speed. They waited in silence for a time, then Isobel, as if giving up, although in fact quietly triumphant, raised her head.

"We are almost certainly moving," she said.

"Look, the white spot is back." It was there in the exact centre of the screen, visibly pulsating. "Do you think it's that we're heading for? I'll make some studies of it through the telescope."

"It doesn't matter *where* we're going. Leave the arrow where it is, but don't change course. I should think the speed will keep going down, for as long as we let it, without reaching nought. Of course if you find something interesting ..."

"I thought that by changing course we might relieve the pressure – then Lionel might wake up, and we could talk about finding somewhere to land."

"It was only when you noticed the rising pressure that you set this course; I really don't think there would be any point in changing it. Lionel will be able to make a decision when it's necessary."

So the young engineer made her way back to the captain's cabin, clutching her battered notes and a new set of suggestive data which only complicated the whirling in her head. She left Sir Charles with nothing fruitful to do. She knew that nothing would be done, either, in the cabin she occupied with Lionel. This was often a place of frenzied activity, but of only one sort: however deep the captain's stupor or the engineer's, one of them was likely to turn at any moment and caress the other, stroking or probing in an urgent way, after which they would be lost in a long fornication, whether standing, lying or kneeling, which could fill with hard work and sweat the best part of half a day. It was not uncommon, after a hot night, for Isobel to set out from the bed toward the desk, only to be overtaken after two steps by Lionel, who reached out from the bed after only a moment lying quiet, dragging her down by the waist as he spilled out of the bed, and at last sprawling with her on the floor in a mess of blankets, often until Stanley came in with the dinner. After such a debauch, when they lay even more vacant than usual, she sometimes tried to engage her eyes with his, and said, "This white spot we're approaching – it appears and disappears," or, "Have you recorded the speeds in your journal?" His response to these attempts was always intelligent, suggesting complete control, but short and dismissive. Having made it he rolled himself into the blankets, away from her.

Sir Charles, after what had followed his last discoveries, was less willing than ever to enter Jaffa's cabin, no matter what he saw through the telescope. He began to be convinced of the worthlessness of what he had at first considered important, and like the others would simply sit for long periods, following mournful, self-deprecating trains of thought, expecting Isobel at any moment.

His depression and her absence drove him at last to the dining-room, where he hoped to find that the crew's mood had changed, and that he would be told the full value of his discoveries. This room, despite its size, was full of smoke and mixed smells. Among used dishes and bottles sat and sprawled the crew, largely silent, exploding locally into laughter or violence only once in a while. At one long table sat Quincey Horace, Karl Waeldermann and Raoul Antonius, Karl at the mid-point of a long side, the others at the ends; they were playing a card game of extraordinary, futile complexity, although based on very simple rules. The single complicating element in the game was that each hand dealt to a player affected the hand dealt to him in every subsequent round, its role constantly diminishing but never ceasing entirely. Thus by the hundredth round each man was effectively playing with a hand of eighteen hundred cards, every one of a different value. The game was not designed to end, although after, say, a week-long cycle, there was sometimes a mutual agreement to return to some sort of starting-point. Even then, no previous card was completely forgotten – all the hands thus far were simply reduced to a greatly inferior range of functions. Beside each man was a tremendous heap of papers, entirely covered with figures in a code unknown to either of his opponents, which he lengthily consulted before playing any card. Horace's pile was neat, weighted with a cleanly-picked leg of lamb, and still more than a foot and a half high; Antonius had an extensive system of piles, interlocking, laid cross-wise, fanned out; Waeldermann's papers were simply strewn all around him, on the floor, on the table, on neighbouring chairs, sandwiched in piles of dirty plates, indefinitely lost under the carpet. When a card was at last played it was a long throw, for the men at the ends, into the centre of the table. The man in the middle, in addition to his personal documents, had charge of a series of notebooks in which he recorded all the common knowledge, that which was public in the progress of the game itself. At the moment Sir Charles came into the room, this man, as stated above, was Karl Waeldermann.

The other members of the crew, further down the room, were doubtless pursuing similar complexities, although Sir Charles did not at the time investigate what they were doing. Superficially they appeared inactive, possibly drunk; among them Stanley moved with a tray – it appeared to be a meal-time. In fact it was always meal-time, and Stanley's job was endless. At the moment none of them was eating. Sir Charles felt out of place; no-one took any notice of him, and he walked twice round the room before deciding to sit at the card-players' table.

He occupied the fourth side of the table, opposite Waeldermann. The men looked at him briefly but did not speak. Waeldermann was writing, Antonius studying his notes. Sir Charles saw that it was Horace's turn, as he consulted papers and cards alternately, seeming both more hurried and more organized than the others. It was the first part of a round: only two cards lay face up, the King of Spades on the Three of Clubs.

Horace was in difficulties. He frowned, returned to his topmost paper, asked to see the book in which Waeldermann was writing, and seemed no nearer to playing a card. At last he said, while still in the midst of working something out, "Well, what do you want? You can't join in the game, if that's what you're thinking."

Sir Charles denied this and made two or three attempts to apologise for his real object, although none of the players seemed interested. What he finally said was, "I need to make sure that you will be ready to land soon, if necessary."

There was a pause before Horace said, "For God's sake," possibly reacting to something he saw in his papers, then, "You know damn well we'll have practically nothing to do even then. Is there a planet or something?"

Sir Charles welcomed this question and answered it fully, describing the white light-source in the screen. "It's impossible to tell how far away it is. Signals don't return, and the size of it changes from a pin-prick to a football and back again."

Meanwhile Horace had not looked up from his papers, but now he spoke harshly to Antonius: "I suppose you had no idea that King was fifteenth magnitude?" Antonius slowly raised his head, revealing a shy, toothy smile which quickly turned to a laugh. "What do you think?" he said. "Either I'm a fool or I'm not. Anyway, there shouldn't be any talking, as you know."

Horace continued to glare at him for a few moments, then appeared to forget him, and spoke almost as bitterly to Sir Charles: "That doesn't sound much like a planet. We're not doing anything to help you land on that."

"I really can't imagine what else it might be, unless it's a meteor, which comes to the same thing. The surroundings of it are extraordinary: they're never the same for two days running, which I suppose means that it travels very quickly while we are still locked onto it, although it can move away from us and towards us independently. It must keep stopping and starting, too. Oh, and there are white flickerings and patches round the edge of the screen which I can't explain at all." Horace had returned to his studies, but Sir Charles assumed that his explanation was sinking in. "The planet looks exactly the same through the window as it does on the screen, which is unusual again. It might be possible to explain the changes in size by an expanding and contracting atmosphere, but I think we are definitely moving towards it, at quite a speed, too, although the instruments say we're hardly moving at all. Miss Keogh is working on that at the moment."

Horace now threw the book back down the table to Waeldermann, as if unbearably frustrated by his calculations. "I want another break," he said.

"You are in a mess, aren't you?" said Antonius. "We might as well not play at all, the length of time it takes you to sort yourself out."

The remark was good-humoured, but Horace replied angrily: "At least I can still think. At least I don't play cards at random, like you. It'd be easier to follow you if there were the least vestige of intelligence in your game."

"Oh, come on, we've all got the same problems."

Waeldermann interrupted this potential fight, having consulted the book. "It is permissible to have a break now, if you like. Will twenty minutes be alright?" Antonius got up from the table and stretched, sighing, before wandering down the room towards the other group. Waeldermann looked from him to Horace, who quickly selected one or two of his papers and some blank sheets; with these he went to an empty table, where he began to read and write alternately with great intensity.

Sir Charles was troubled by this card game and the situations it brought about. He knew that the atmosphere in the ship had affected both his ability to command and his conception of the flight's ultimate purpose, and that the captain was for similar reasons unable to perform his task as figurehead and coordinator of the enterprise, but this frivolity and petulance in the crew was a deterioration greater than any he had anticipated. In particular he was worried about Horace, who now seemed at once the most deeply involved in the game and the least accomplished player, whereas formerly Sir Charles had seen him as a useful influence on the crew, the most intelligent and least excitable man.

He looked over Waeldermann's shoulder at the book. Waeldermann smiled up at him rather bleakly and offered the book for his inspection. Like Isobel's scientific work, this progressed from pages squarely filled with figures and obscure symbols to a paragraphless flow of untidy prose. The early pages were flat and brittle, and the painstakingly-formed figures in their dead-straight rows had an authority about them, as if this were the text all the rest was a clumsy attempt to interpret. The pages on which Waeldermann had been writing were warped with the deep scoring of the ball-pen, studded with crossings-out and nearly illegible. Waeldermann answered Sir Charles's questions: the entirely imaginary object of the game, he said, was that a round be played in which the total value of each player's cards in the order in which he chose to play them should be identical to the value of the cards of each of the others. This, virtually an impossibility at the outset, had with all the ensuing rounds and the complex alterations they had made to the cards' values receded further and further into the astronomical realms of chance: hopelessly attempting to work out the odds was an amusement favoured by those who tired of the game itself. The present passage in the book, which Waeldermann deciphered for Sir Charles, dealt briefly, and he hoped scientifically, with the speculation that the moment in the game where the object at last became an actual impossibility might also paradoxically be that in which it was achieved. This was not, he hastened earnestly to assure him, the most important question at present: on the contrary, he had merely touched on it in proving the validity of an idea of his own, which was to switch from all the values with which they were now playing to their negative equivalents. He had recently spent nearly all his powers in explaining to the others how this would immeasurably improve the game, but they were both in their different ways utter blockheads who could not step back from the web in which they were involved to see its entirety. Look at the way now they were using this break from play to indulge in private reflections, instead of discussing reasonably that teamwork which, always given the degree of secrecy enjoined by the rules, was the essence of the game. Quincy went to another table because, he claimed, he couldn't deal with his personal code at this stage in the game; Raoul refused to say anything about his play, and very rarely even looked at his notes. Waeldermann wondered whether they had really lost sight of the hypothetical simplicity towards which, by piling complexity on complexity, they should all be working, or whether they had perversely abandoned the idea to pursue instead their own facile, crippled notions, leaving him lost and deceived. He laid the book among the scattered cards and papers, and rested his chin on his hand.

At this moment there was a tremendous rumpus at the far end of the dining-room. Stanley, in the absence of orders for food, had been valiantly attempting to clear up, tray held high, delicately stepping between the crew's sprawled legs; he had just achieved a pile of soiled plates about equal to his strength when Franz Mister, sitting against a table-leg, raised his own leg a little too high for the step Stanley had begun, and sent the poor boy plummeting to the floor. He landed utterly flat on his face and the plates shot out in a straight line, the first knocking Smallpox senseless, the others shattering on the wooden tiles. The crash and the laughter that rose were the main part of the noise. Leo Nodroyen at once sprang up – it was the first movement he had made for over three hours – and held Stanley's arms, shouting all the time in foolish joy, while Mister was apparently trying to get Stanley's trousers off him. It was not clear whether Antonius was still among the men or not. Horace ignored the sounds. Waeldermann lifted his head and winced; Sir Charles asked him if this usually went on, and whether they should not do something, but he replied, "No, it would only break out in some other way."

At the same moment Isobel had entered the room, and as Waeldermann was speaking she reached the card-players' table. She, like Horace, took no notice of what was happening. It was not good for him, this sort of isolation, and it happened to him rather too often in those days. Isobel went straight to Sir Charles and grasped his arm, speaking excitedly.

"I've just come from the control-room. I think I've been making a mistake. Have you looked at the screen?"

"Not since this morning."

"We've arrived – I mean, the white spot is filling the screen, there are only black flickerings at the edge now and again. I think it must be that white spot, mustn't it?"

"Sounds very like it. It was quite far away this morning."

"That's where I think I've been wrong. As I've been working it out, even the greatest relative speed and the smallest distance I could admit between the object and us would have meant more than a thousand years to reach it. And according to the instruments we've been travelling at virtually no speed in a different direction. It seems to me that in fact we haven't been travelling in the conventional sense at all, as I thought in the first place."

"You mean it's come to us, by a short route, as it were?"

"Rather I think normal space and time, assuming they exist, or as we imagine them, haven't been operating."

Waeldermann, who had been looking up at them, at one and then at the other, and blinking very often, now spoke: "How are we going to land if there's no space or time?" Isobel turned to him and replied without changing her tone, for she did not consider her knowledge exclusive: "Obviously we must have some indication of something solid first. I shouldn't think we'd be able to stop without gravity. The speed is still going down, but the deceleration is diminishing.

She paused and looked at the mess on the table. "What's all this?" Waeldermann at once began to collect his own papers and put them in neater piles, while nervously beginning a very complex explanation, but Sir Charles broke in with a brief description of the game as he understood it. He seemed to be apologising although indeed he had not condoned the playing of the game. Waeldermann was silent and embarrassed. Isobel, openly incredulous, spoke as if forgetting them both: "But it's absurd! The ship's resources must not be wasted like this. We may have a great deal of paper, but it's not going to last very long if it's used at this rate." She picked up a stray sheet to study, but Waeldermann, quietly saying, "No ... please ...," held out his hand for it, and after a moment rose from his seat and snatched it from her. She picked up the book. "Surely this is one of Lionel's notebooks?" He took that from her also. Finally she strode round the table to the pile of blank sheets, which she held firmly against her breast. "Did you let them into the cupboard?" she said to Sir Charles; then, to Waeldermann, stressing many words, "There's important work to be done on this – work that means finding somewhere to land. You might at least have used pencil."

Waeldermann at last spoke: "But this is important too. Quincey will tell you. It's already taught us a lot about space – about infinity, you know – and this is a crucial stage."

He had pointed at Horace, whom Isobel now sought, wheeling round. She saw for the first time the tangle of bodies at the room's further end, from which there came at the same moment Stanley's hysterical cries, "No, Franz! Listen ...," and other less ordered noises. Realisation of the crew's state was coming to her all at once. Still clutching the blank paper, exclaiming to herself, she set off down the hall.

Sir Charles had been troubled further by all this. He was not used to Isobel's showing such authority; it embarrassed him, making him uncertain what to do. He had no doubt that her prohibitive attitude was right, but whether to confiscate the playing-cards or to follow her and part the strugglers he could not decide. He admired her new strength; he would not like to offend her by implying that she needed help. Formerly she had quietly been a good example to everyone in the ship, making, indeed, authoritative statements, but never in an aggressive way, and nearly always in response to a question. Her suggestions had always been acted on, but she had never assumed this would be so. Apart from her effect on his own power of decision, Sir Charles could not at once isolate that which worried him in the new Isobel. He watched Horace as she passed him, who was still furiously scribbling, oblivious of everything that happened in the room, as indeed she was of him. Once he rose suddenly, eyes still on his paper, as if he might have the answer; but after a pause he sat down again and resumed his work.

Happily for Sir Charles, indecision and Isobel were taken from him. Lionel appeared in the doorway, stooping, dressed in stained trousers and a ragged vest. From the noise and the intertwined bodies he recoiled, holding his head, but before going he beckoned to Isobel, who stopped a few yards short of the rioters. She called, "Stanley!", looked back once at Sir Charles, then went out.

It was not, you will say, as she would have said herself, that Lionel alone was immune to her new power, that he alone could still command her. She did not see these questions of personality in terms of domination and submission. She was not aware at the time of the change which Sir Charles detected in her. It was Sir Charles himself who told me of this, as he told me of more than half the events I have so far described, in that intimacy with him which followed. She knew her own love of Lionel – love which fed, certainly, on his pallor, his weakness, his lack of self-knowledge and of general awareness, although she would not then have chosen these words I now choose. Neither would she have described as power that beauty in her body which she knew. I do not deny that she was prettily made: all her skin was smooth, her breasts round, her belly flat, her mound thick with hair of uncommon softness. You and I both know the pleasure this gave her, and the strange shivering as he (is it Lionel now?) uncovered it, the blankness of his face, the feeling that she was both herself and him. I know how this comes to you when, in your bedroom over the Heath, you undress in front of the mirror, watch yourself lie on the bed, legs spread, and stroke your sides with crossed arms, turning and arching your body. Many times I have surprised you like this, and even of late myself, although what it gives me is different, and the positions I favour are different. My body is wider, I stroke long, hard humps, and I am able to see that power played its part in the ecstasy. It is power I feel now in writing to you, for of the three of us I am the only one who sees. My world is darker then your long windows and your long mirror, darker than her bright corridors and the whiteness in the screen; I sit humped and shrouded at a table with a candle, scribbling, but I know the two of you and can make you do whatever I wish.

Later in the same day came the first of those phenomena which were to be known as shifts. It came when this Isobel and her Lionel had been alone for an hour or so, playing the parts they did not understand, in the old way and in others which were less familiar. At this moment Lionel was sitting at the desk and she was kneeling beside him. Both were looking at the book in which he was trying to write.

She encouraged him: "What about when you came into the dining-room just now? Can you think of anything to say about the crew? Hadn't they changed since you'd last seen them?"

"No, look, it's alright. I must finish what I'm saying here – it's only... only a few sentences now. I've just got to wait for the next one." The pen was trembling over a little dot it had made where the next sentence was to begin. The skin of his thigh was streaked with blue where he had put his hand when in wider-ranging thought.

"But I don't understand what you've put there. Is it about this white spot? Because you can look at my notes if you like, or I could write..."

"Just be quiet for a minute, would you? If you'd stop talking for a minute it might come. I know what it's about, it's just the style that's peculiar. The style takes over, the writing takes over." His hand moved stiffly to his forehead, putting a blue mark there, hiding his face from Isobel. "It'll be quite clear when I get to the end of this bit."

"But Lionel," she said, then sank back onto her heels and put her hand on his leg. A moment later he started to write, and she rose again, but at once he hid with his arm what he was writing, and put his head down almost onto the desk. Then he suddenly stood up, threw the pen down and went over to the bed.

"I'm not going to do it if you're watching. You shouldn't watch this sort of thing. It's just between me and the writing. It's my journal, after all."

"That's silly," she began. Then followed a long process of persuasion in which her hardest task was to allay his sexual excitement; she had also to talk him out of a genuine terror he felt at the thought of writing, on account, she finally made him admit, of the impression he had already mentioned, that the writing itself took control. Her motives in persuading him to write can now easily be worked out, although her action at the time seemed instinctive. Ultimately he did manage to fill a page or so, although to do so upset him. This is what he wrote:

"January, 1984. It is all around the ship now. We exist on its terms, the ship and everything inside it, although our minds have not yet accepted the new conditions – they perpetuate the old illusions, as defence or through inertia. As yet we feel only increasing pressure, but in the end all the elements of our old universe will have collapsed. Except, perhaps, life – although it is hard to imagine in what sense this continues. It is certain that we are completely enclosed by it, and that neither space nor time exists either outside or inside the ship. It is impossible to use the terms "inside", "outside", "enclosed". [It] – you, who have not yet conquered our minds (or rather, who already have, although they can still imagine a continuity of events in which there is a time when you still have not) do not exist in space, and space cannot exist inside you. Space therefore cannot exist inside the ship."

Here he turned the page, to find that a gaudy spider, realistically drawn with red and blue wax crayons on tissue-paper, had been inserted between the leaves. He started, and for a few moments trembled violently, again putting his hands to his head. Then he handed the spider to Isobel, saying, "Did you do this?" She truthfully denied it, taking it from him. A little later, he resumed his writing.

"The pressure is the beginning of our acceptance of this idea. I write this to show you that my thoughts are ahead of you, and will always be so – are always so. You have already taken control of my existence, but I have already understood you, although I think I am thinking you out as I write. I imagine I am writing, and breathing, although what I am doing is in fact utterly different, something impossible in space, impossible to one who has a body. It involves a direct connection with you. You understand. We have been part of you since you appeared in the screen. Perhaps then we might have got out, but we did not understand. We followed you helplessly; there seemed to be a diminishing area of space between us, and you seemed to flicker wildly through space, travelling inconceivable distances instantaneously, while we seemed to hold our course towards you. Change was still just possible then; doubtless we did, in some sense, come to areas of space whose distance from our place of origin would have to be measured in infinities of infinities. We retained some connection with space. Now, however, the last change has occurred. We cannot get out. We are locked into the processes by which you exist. It is impossible to speak of processes, but there is something in you corresponding to such things, and I must tell you that many things appear to us as processes which are not. Consciousness is one for which you perhaps have an equivalent. We have found your equivalent, but imagine we have not. Do not think that your action on us is to you exactly what it is to us. Wait a moment,"

These were the words on the page when the shift began. There was no noise; Isobel was watching the word "moment", feeling that at last this strange paragraph was making sense, when a sudden violent pressure behind her eyes caused the words and the book itself to explode, and everything in the room to bend, shatter or otherwise lose its spatial relation to everything else. There was a plunging throughout her body as if she were in a free-falling lift, and it seemed to her that the floor of the cabin was rocking and lurching. Although it was as still as ever, and she and Lionel knelt and sat throughout the shift, surprisedly looking at each other's eyes, she felt that she rose involuntarily to her feet, stumbled against him, and swayed through the length and breadth of the room with him in a shambling dance, ending flat on the bed or against the wall. The sensation, so far as they could calculate, lasted three seconds.

In the aftermath, when they found themselves motionless as they had always been, and for the first time moved slightly towards each other, an extraordinary dizziness persisted: for Isobel, the captain's face glittered white and flickered against the wall behind, as if she had held her breath for too long, or for the first time in twenty years inhaled some tobacco-smoke. "Oh hell," he said, and the frightened tone was to her tinny and grotesque. For hours afterwards, when she had begun to think her perception had returned to normal, some small thing would remind her of this change – especially the tone of someone's voice, or an expression on his face. It was not that the strangeness eventually left her, but rather that she forgot in what it had consisted.

They left the room without thinking of dressing – which on this occasion was not noticed. The long, brilliantly-lit corridor had never seemed to her such a hostile place before. Along it, towards them staggered Sir Charles, who had just emerged from the dining-room. A great uproar of voices and clattering furniture came through the open door. Reaching them, Sir Charles leaned against the wall and tried to explain what had happened, but was unable. His clothes were torn and he was bleeding about the head. He managed only to tell them not to go into the dining-room. In his attitude to Lionel, through his feebleness, that reserve could still be detected which had presumably survived from the recent period of apathy. Isobel had to help him into the captain's cabin, where he was laid on the bed and his wounds were treated. When he was able to speak, he explained that everyone had had an experience similar to their own, although it had affected some members of the crew remarkably. Horace, for example, had fainted, whereas Antonius had shouted and become violent, upsetting the card-table. Sir Charles himself had the feeling that everything still looked slightly different; even as he said this, Isobel saw a particular curving of his lips and moustache whose unfamiliarity could not be entirely ascribed to his position and state. He did not mention the wounds on his head, but left them to assume he had been hurt in the general confusion.

It was not long after this that the second shift occurred, while Sir Charles was still sleeping on their bed. Isobel had immediately, on his falling asleep, begun to write in her notebook her theories as to what the first shift might have been, kneeling as before, and resting the book on the carpet. She consulted the last entries of Lionel's journal during this work. Lionel himself was silent; she did not know what he was doing. She had written little, however, before he came up behind her, knelt with his legs against hers, and took her breasts in his hands. She put down the pen and leaned her head back against his shoulder.

'What are you doing there?" he said, in an absurdly small whisper. "I was getting lonely on my own. Lionel mustn't get Lonely, must he? He wants his Isobel."

She merely said, 'Yes," and put her hands back to touch his hips. He pushed himself against her and caressed her from breasts to thighs, while continuing to speak: "Lonely wants

Isobel – he doesn't want to know about that nasty jolt. He thinks she should leave it alone and stay with Lonely all the time. Then he wouldn't be lonely, would he? He likes his Isobel, because she's so pretty and soft. He likes her arms and her tummy and her legs and her… does she like him?" He was trying with his hands to make her turn round; she did so, without completely standing, and sat astride his legs, saying, "Yes, she does," and kissing him. When her mouth moved down to his neck he began talking again: "He doesn't like to know all about what's going on – that doesn't matter, if he's with Isobel. He likes to forget all that – he thinks she should, too. He likes just lying with her all the time. He likes to get inside her."

He had indeed been inside her since she had turned. She looked briefly at Sir Charles, who was snoring slightly. The rising and falling of his chest for a moment matched her own slow movement up and down. Her position with Lionel on the floor meant that she was the more active of the two; she started to bite his neck and shoulder as she moved, and he went on talking without pause, varying more strangely the same theme, while his words came to her less and less clearly. It was not unusual for him to talk in this way, and her own participation in the game was often more extensive than on this occasion. Since the whispering had begun, however, it had had a thin, sharp tone which was foreign to her and which she could not dispel by concentration; neither could she accept as familiar the name "Lonely", although it had surely been used before. At length she could only stop trying to recapture the ritual, and had to accept the strangeness of the voice and the name, especially as her mind began to give way to powerful (also subtly changed) sensations, and Lionel's thrusting inside her became more violent. An awkwardness remained, however, which she felt partly as physical cold on her shoulders and arms; Lionel's whispering might now have become shouting, and even while she began to speak bizarre words herself she noticed that Sir Charles's sleep was disturbed, that he was contributing his own snorts and groans to the concert. She was vividly aware of her sweating face, which now hung over Lionel's shoulder, and of her bucking hindquarters. It was just as Lionel stiffened and dug his nails into her back that for the second time she felt herself plunge as if down a deep shaft, and her eyes again seemed to be bursting from her head. The sensation of violent turbulence in the room came too, but this time she knew that she was locked to Lionel on the floor. The sensations were distinct and simultaneous: she felt Lionel's eruption inside her as a tiny and insignificant version of the explosion going on around them. Nonetheless she automatically pushed herself down onto him, triggering her own orgasm, which for a time fought against the falling sensation that still surged down through her. There was a moment in the centre when she was entirely clear-headed and could have resumed her written explanation of what was happening. Lionel fell back onto the floor, and she went with him; for a long time she lay on him, trying to sort out the after-effects of the shift from those of their copulation. Sir Charles had made a tremendous lurch in his sleep, and as Lionel's frantic breathing and her own subsided, his spluttering intruded with increasing force. She could not, however, identify with confidence anything she felt or heard. Her perception was tinny and confused, as after the first shift. She could feel with her hands Lionel's chest and shoulders, and with her body the rest of his, extending down to the fitful touching of their feet; but this became for her every moment something different: a mountain-range, a pile of rubbish, a herd of sheep, or simply a hole, a nothing that held her up, that pushed her flesh into its particular curved and bumpy shape.

Sir Charles, it seemed, had slept through everything. His face was haggard and his sleep continuously troubled, but as he was not disturbed by the others he slept for a further twenty-seven hours, occasionally crying out. By the end of this period his condition was causing anxiety, but he awoke safely, the only change in him being a decline in self-assurance: he spoke more hurriedly, with frequent false starts. He did not remember the shift, but had had very vivid dreams, the only account of which he could give was a confused ramble involving "damn tiny little living snowflakes". To Isobel his face also seemed greatly changed: she could hardly recognise him, she said, he was so thin. That this was likely to be an illusion of light and shadow was shown, however, when she felt his cheeks with her fingers, finding them as corpulent as ever, though much smoother.

The subsequent shifts began, naturally, to lose their surprise effect; on the other hand they lost none of their violence, and those people who were suffering cumulatively degenerated more rather than less rapidly. Isobel's record of the shifts was kept in greater detail, and she spent much time seeking a pattern in their occurrence. Their frequency was very irregular: the interval between the first and second had been two hours; between the second and third it was one, between the third and fourth eight, between the fourth and fifth three, and from the fifth to the fourteenth all intervals were fractions of one hour, after which there were again eight hours between the fourteenth and fifteenth. The first indication she had of any pattern was that over fourteen days the frequency of the shifts had on average increased. She did not think it likely that they were controlled by either speed or pressure, which during all this time continued steadily on their downward and upward curves. The speed was already a fraction of one mile per hour, and diminished by regularly diminishing intervals. The pressure according to the gauge was correspondingly enormous, far too high, in fact, for the continuance of human life; no-one now felt any abnormality in the atmosphere, however, which meant either that their metabolisms had impossibly accustomed themselves to the increase, or, as Lionel's journal suggested, and as Isobel began to believe, the ideas of pressure, measurement and atmosphere were all now invalid, and the gauge was connected instead with some alien system which none of them could understand.

With the sensation of high pressure, also, had gone all the listlessness and indifference of the period before they had entered the white spot: in their place came the effects of the shifts, different for each person. Lionel had become cynical, obsessed with his personal struggle against the extra-spatial environment described in his journal, and at the same time convinced that it was an eternal (or rather instantaneous) stalemate. He was active in the struggle, doing a great deal of research in the control-room. Long study of the screen was one of his techniques, although it had been completely white since the day of the first shift, and Isobel could find in it no detail except that supplied after a time by her tired eyes. The two of them worked together, on slightly different lines, occasionally accepting ideas from one another, and although they spent less time on sex Lionel was still insistent when he felt the need, meeting mild resistance from Isobel rather more frequently. She was less willing to accept his strange third-person monologues during intercourse, and could no longer respond to them. Ironically she found it disturbing that this did not matter to him, that he still chattered without expecting a reply – sometimes without even referring to her, but speaking exclusively of Lonely and the White Thing. "The White Thing knows what Lonely's doing," he might say, while pushing into her, "but it can't stop him, no, and he's going to get inside the White Thing too."

It was impossible not to notice that these effusions invariably came before shifts, as the experience of near-simultaneous orgasm and shift was often repeated. This was partly what led Isobel to accept one of Lionel's ideas about the shifts – that they should seek the immediate cause of them not in such spatial functions as speed and pressure but in the moods and attitudes of the people on the ship. At least it seemed to her a useful working theory; she undertook a preliminary investigation, which consisted in asking Charles how he had been feeling at the time of each shift. He studied the list she showed him, and at last said that he had recently been falling asleep rather frequently, and must have missed the last dozen or so, as he had been under the impression that there had been no shifts for several days. The only connection between sleep and sex seemed to be that both often took place in bed, although Isobel felt that there must be something less obvious, which could be shown to have significance in her investigation. She wished to inquire further, and, as both Sir Charles and Lionel agreed, it was decided that they should venture again into the dining-room to question the crew.

Their entrance into the dining-room was remarkable: where before they had been met with indifference, everyone who now saw them come in registered some degree of surprise, and the news of their arrival very quickly spread around the room until everyone had looked, although many returned straight away to what they were doing. Everyone had looked, that is, except Bendacker, who was walking continuously around the edge of the room in deep thought, Klein, who was sitting with his head slumped on a table, and Stanley, who had been stripped and tied to the other end of the same table, face and torso flat against the top, ankles tightly fastened to the ornate wooden legs. Ivansohnn, having looked, screamed and ran into a corner. Most of the others were clustered in a big group round the card-table, where the three principals were engaged in play. When the three intruders had been accepted as the genuine, original versions of the expedition's leaders (I assume this is what was in question) they were eagerly beckoned over to the table, where something exciting was about to happen. According to the pace of this particular game, however, it might still take a matter of hours actually to happen: aficionados of the game watched with interest the changing face of the next player as he calculated. Realising that the newcomers might find this tedious, however, Andrew Ampole spoke to them about the reason for their strange reception, which was simply that no food had been taken to their cabin for over two weeks, and most of the crew had imagined them to be either dead or dying. The three looked at each other: it was true, they had not eaten. To forget to eat for one or two days was not uncommon, but such a long fast was unheard of. None of them had felt the least twinge of hunger, or appeared to have undergone physical change. No-one, however, was as surprised as might have been expected – the story came as confirmation of many theories, including Lionel's and Isobel's. Why, however, had no food been taken to them? First, Ampole explained, because Stanley was, as they saw, unable to get up; and secondly, because various rather frightening ideas had gained currency in the dining-room, all variants of the notion that everything outside that one room (except the adjoining lavatory) had ceased to exist.

As this explanation proceeded, Nodroyen, trousers around his knees, had addressed the upturned buttocks of Stanley; with a hand on the table either side, he was slowly pushing into the boy. Lionel, however, now seeing him, rushed over to him in a fury and thrust him away from the table. Nodroyen, hampered by his trousers, fell backwards onto the floor, and Lionel leaned over him, still red with anger, striking him about the face and kicking him. Sir Charles and Isobel hurried to take the captain's arms and restrain him, although she for one felt a revulsion almost equal to his own. He hardly seemed aware of them, but bellowed, "Get that man! Take the rope off the boy and tie him up!" His orders were obeyed; after a slight hesitation Smallpox dragged Nodroyen to his feet and twisted his arms behind him. The two held men faced each other, Lionel slowly cooling and Nodroyen seeming very conscious of his erection, which was only just beginning to subside. Meanwhile Franz Mister was untying Stanley, and chafing his limbs perhaps more thoroughly than was necessary. Stanley said, "I don't mind being tied up, sir, really," but Lionel shut him up and told him to put his clothes on.

'Right," he continued, finally freeing himself from his two colleagues, "there are going to have ... there are obviously a lot of things to be said in here." He realised, however, that the men around the card-table, after an initial glance at the disturbance, had returned with undiminished attention to the game, and were not listening to him. He pushed between two spectators and leaned over the table, demanding that play cease. The players continued unperturbed, but again began to discuss the possibility of a pause. Waeldermann, having the book, announced that it was not theoretically permissible, but under the circumstances he felt that an exception might be made (Ampole whispered in Lionel's ear that this being the hundred and sixty-second round made a difference, but Lionel shouted, "I couldn't care less about that"). Antonius said, "We'd better make bloody sure it comes out this time, or we'll be at it for another six months." They had decided to pause; there was a gathering together of papers, and Waeldermann wrote the state of play in the book.

"Now, go down to the other tables," said Lionel. "I'll speak to you from here." There was no objection to this: Horace and Waeldermann wandered slowly away, still studying their notes. Antonius was making for the door into the main corridor, but on Lionel's "Where do you think you're going?" silently turned back into the room. Lionel completed his preparations by calling Sir Charles and Isobel over to him; the latter also brought Stanley, who had not yet completed his dressing (it was not entirely that she felt he should be protected; as you can guess, she avoided the role of ship's matron, and as a rule eschewed anything likely to accentuate her femininity. Neither was it entirely a sexual attraction, although she can now see that she had been excited by his nakedness and vulnerability. Rather it was that she anticipated some acrimonious exchange between those at the card-table and the other occupants of the room, and felt that her own side needed an ally taken from the heart of the opposition. Please excuse this self-analytical aside: I know that an urge to analyse is one of those masculine characteristics which have remained with both you and her, just as you have both continued to pursue your perversely chosen occupation, engineering; and as a result neither you nor I can read without exasperation the self-analytical words of any other person. I, however, am perhaps more pardonably introspective than either of you, being deprived just at present of that outlet for less strictly controlled feeling which you have in your Lionel, and which she and I found ultimately in our Charles).

"Gentlemen," said Lionel, then paused lengthily, while leaning forward and pressing on the edge of the table. At last he said, "Does that man have to keep on walking about like that?" There was an immediate spasm throughout the room, universally imagined or real: all felt the long-familiar pressure on the diaphragm, and turmoil, after a brief interval of frenzied stillness, erupted in truth, sound and motion at once filling the hall. Isobel, I think, merely turned her head, repetitively, from side to side, savouring the electrical sensations thus caused, and senselessly taking in some of what had taken hold of the others. Bendacker's walk had changed to a stumbling run, interrupted by collisions. Most of those he hit simply fell back over people or furniture; some put up a fight, but none could change Bendacker's course. Ivansohnn, still in his corner, was screaming again, shielding his head with his arms. Smallpox lay on his back, groaning, and Klein, head still on the table, was bouncing up and down on his chair. Many simply shouted, with or without apparently reason. Nodroyen, stimulated anew despite his tied wrists and ankles, had finally ejaculated, and now squatted against a wall, unable to pull up his trousers, evidently confused and upset. Sir Charles and Stanley wept on each other's shoulder, squealing, "Just the same, just the same!" Antonius had run into the corridor, and Lionel staggered this way and that as if uncertain where to go. Only Waeldermann was completely still: he sat with his hands flat on the table, back straight and eyes closed.

Lionel, a few yards from where he had begun his speech, fell to his knees and yelled, "Listen!" Instantly there was silence from all but Smallpox; a second passed, then Nodroyen fell forward across the prostrate man's face, quieting him too, and stayed there, not knowing how to rise. In the stillness no-one could measure the next pause, but at the end of it Antonius returned, and his feet could be heard on the polished floor. He found them all frozen in their positions. Isobel's eyes were on him, and saw that he did not falter.

"Everything is as it should be, sir," he said.

Lionel's response for a time was incomprehensible. He was staring at the floor, and from his throat came loud, high-pitched noises, rasping and then slipping into drawn-out whines. At last one of the whines contained words, which Isobel slowly understood:

"You must stop doing this to Lonely! He won't have it! Is it you, or someone else?"

His complaint died away, and she then expected it to resume, but an answer came, in a low, steady voice:

"No, this time, it is I sir."

The voice belonged to Waeldermann. Neither speaker looked at the other, Lionel still bending toward the floor, Waeldermann keeping his eyes closed, but the dialogue continued, and Isobel, silent with the others, listened.

"Well what do you mean by it? What's Lonely done to you? What's going to happen to him?"

"You must accept, sir, that this is the only way in which we can get through unscathed. These patches of turbulence come as acknowledgement from the forces around us that we are going in the right direction."

"We have no direction, you ninny, we are outside direction. Do you expect the Captain not to know that?"

"Nonetheless this is how we must reach the centre, where we shall stop and it will seem that we have regained control of the vessel, and where..."

"And did you put that thing inside his journal, too? That horrible drawing on toilet paper? He can't go to the toilet any more – "

"No, no, that was someone else, working in his own way toward the same end, no doubt genuinely misguided. The only true progress is achieved through the Game, and at the moment I am the key to the Game. I understand all the moves which are necessary for our victory, and all those which are unimportant, yet must be played one way or the other. I guide my fellow-players without their admitting it, and perhaps I in turn am guided. The shifts coincide with my small intermediate successes. This is the hundred and sixty-second round, as has been explained to you. Already, in the fifty-fourth and other rounds, our scores have corresponded so closely that we have been able to make enormous reductions in the value of our cards. Now there are nearly nine thousand cards in play, and we shortly expect a closer result, and a greater reduction, than any we have experienced before. Naturally, each round takes longer than the last to play, as we have to deal with more and more of the decreasing values, always with greater numbers of decimal places; but in the three hundred and twenty-fourth round we shall pass the peak, when the rounds' totals, as well as the individual cards in play, all of negligible values, we shall reach nought: our scores will be equal. The medium in which we are all travelling, and of which we consist, is Chance. If you wish to see it in this way, we have utterly unlimited choice as to what form our future existence will take: we would be able, for example, to shrug off humanity by the merest effort of will. On the other hand, the consequences of our actions are correspondingly more far-reaching and irrevocable. Each shift is like a nail knocked into the fixed fabric of events. There is in any case no time here, for revoking or repeating. An action and its effects are instantaneous. To a certain extent I am able to see the effects of all our actions. We shall eventually regain the more limited degree of control to which we are accustomed: it is necessary, however, that the Game be played correctly. When the resolution has been achieved, which under normal circumstances would have been impossible, we shall have passed through this perilous area."

During this speech Lionel had managed to rise, and Waeldermann had turned to look at him. The captain's composure was returning, and he began to walk down the room, between the tables. His voice, however, was still high and excited.

"Piffle!" he said. "You're not making any sense. How can anything be made of Chance? Anyway, it wasn't you that did it this time, it was that man with his filthy semen all over the floor." He pointed at Nodroyen, who could not move. "We can't stop, we shan't stop while we're in this, Captain Lonely knows all about that – and you certainly won't stop us by playing that silly game, which you won't be playing any more, anyway. It's not space, no, but it's made of unrelated areas, or cells, and the shifts are when we go from one to another. That man did it this time by trying to bugger the cabin-boy. When the time comes he will be the first to go outside, and test the place for the others."

There was a moment of silence, and of slight shock, before Waeldermann said, "That would be unwise, sir. He is not intelligent enough to understand his new potentialities. He would break into pieces."

"He can undergo some tests himself before he's put outside. Pick him up and put his head in the drinking-water."

This time it was Mister and Perran who obeyed. Smallpox, when Nodroyen was raised from him, at once started groaning again and calling ecstatically for "More – more of that buzzing." There was louder shouting, however, from the trio above him, and it was seen that Nodroyen had escaped: he stumbled rapidly over a remarkable distance, squealing, with his arms and legs free; then fell, screaming in shock and terror, and began to disappear – or rather, to sink through the floor. Mister grabbed him again and pulled him out: the prisoner then collapsed, his right hand and foot horribly crushed and bleeding. He had become for a moment intangible, and slipped through his bonds, his trousers and his captors' hands. It was found that the crushed hand and foot were not his only injuries; in many places his vest and jacket had sunk into his flesh and become inseparable from it.

This did not affect Lionel's decision. While Nodroyen was still unconscious, his head was thrust into the bowl of drinking-water and held there. There was no struggle. Lionel made sure that the experiment continued for ten minutes, during which he explained that, if the speed of the vessel continued to decrease at its present rate, it would within the week have become too small to appear on the scale (that is, it would be less, in miles per hour, than nine over ten to the power seventy-three); and that he had chosen the moment for Nodroyen's forced exit from the ship. Then, having told Sir Charles to supervise Nodroyen's immersion for a further two hours, and to confiscate all the equipment pertaining to the card game, he left, accompanied by Isobel and Stanley.

Although she had noticed in herself a developing resistance to the shifts, her attitude to her surroundings had been badly affected by what she had seen and heard. Stepping into the corridor, she was not altogether confident that she would land on something solid; when she did, she doubted that its outlines would prove constant. Her sense of all objects' existence had been undermined – indeed, by rational argument. Consciously, she admitted that this new sense was well-founded, and that reality was in truth no more than a selection of illusory sensations. At least, she admitted this of her own experience. Whether an essence nonetheless persisted she could not be sure.

The corridor in this part of the ship was not oak-panelled, as in the control- and communication-areas, but plated with a dully reflecting metal of irregular surface, and brilliantly lit by concealed strips along the tops of the walls. It caused a prickling of the eyelids, the more so after a shift. Between the hall and Lionel's cabin there was a ninety-degrees turn to the right: in the facing wall, after the exit from the dining-room, I see the three approaching, distorted by the metal, and it is not possible to say which is which, although I am on the right, and Stanley in the middle. They are all silent. I wonder what Charles is doing in the dining-room. Will he follow his orders?

Thus, on entering the cabin, she was able to continue her history of the shifts, although she had already begun to destroy the first pages (her calculation of distance travelled), complicating my position as narrator. Fortunately, she remembers much of this. She wrote with a ballpoint pen. Lionel, however, sat at the desk with quill and inkwell, trying to write in his journal, "February, 1984". When the ink would not properly mark or dry, he sprang up with a small scream of frustration, crying with childish emphasis, "Bloody hell! The ink won't bloody work!" Although herself not innocent of irritation, she went to help him, and was surprised to find that he was right. They blew on the ink, blotted it, smelt it, finally poured it into a glass and tasted it. They agreed that it was not ink: she gave her opinion that it might be blackcurrant cordial.

Meanwhile Stanley had crouched by the skirting-board, and was absorbed in examination of something. Finally he called, "It's there in the hole! I can see its legs!" Lionel still pursued the ink question, investigating his big bottle (which also contained the sugary stuff) until Stanley's continuing commentary brought from him an angry question. When Stanley said, "A spider," his attitude changed. The two crouched over the hole together, prodding with the pen. But Stanley could not understand his captain's perturbation. "There are millions of flies in the kitchen," he said. "There are bound to be spiders as well." "What colour was it?" asked Lionel. "Sort of red, with stripes," said Stanley. "They're peculiar in this part of space."

When Charles came in later, Lionel was still there, although Stanley was bored and had given up. Charles seemed tired and worn: she gave him a glass of wine. He reported that after an hour and a half Nodroyen had begun to struggle, but under restraint had become quiet, and remained so until his head was lifted out of the bowl. Now he was utterly helpless, and given to spasms of shivering, but ready so far as they could tell, for the next part of the experiment. Investigating this story, I wanted to know why there had not been more questioning of the experiment among the crew – in particular, I wondered whether Charles himself had been threatened. He confided to me, when we were alone, that he had intentionally devoted all his attention to the experiment, and tacitly allowed the card game to proceed behind his back; the crew, in consequence – or those members who were able to show interest in anything – had very shortly become as absorbed as ever in the game, ignoring what was happening to their colleague.

She had, in fact, to listen very often to his telling of the incident, and to his justification of it. She would sit on the edge of his bed while he lay, talking apparently to the ceiling. Meanwhile she looked at the window, across the room, and sometimes hardly attended. In the window was the intolerable whiteness of which they were a part, and which, with the droning of his voice, induced in her states sometimes approaching trance, in which the whiteness would turn black, and the edges of the room, fuzzily perceived and apparently in motion, white. While the white in the window remained, it was impossible to hold it still for long. I remember one night in particular – it was two o'clock in the morning; Charles would perhaps soon sleep, although she now found sleep impossible, and had not for more than a week even tried to attain it – when the blank white became gradually a system of dots, travelling downwards in swarms. They were agitated as if by a fitful wind; suddenly a curve in the vertical would belly out from the left-hand edge of the window: in the centre it became a clockwise spiral, then suddenly dispersed into a horizontal stream back to the left. The falling of the specks in the top of the window was slowed by this turbulence below, and increasingly they were dragged into whatever trend was going on there, geometrically accelerating as they approached correspondence with the pattern. The slowing and quickening created spaces between the dots, which grew darker and began to hold tall, looming shapes, made of lines that seemed constant, letting the dots wind their curlicues around them.

"... could I?" said Charles.

"No, no."

"If he did, and I tried to explain it to him, he's so excitable now, he might see it as some kind of threat, and stop the game himself."

"Charles, have you seen in the window tonight? It's peculiar, it reminds me of something. It's a bit like the faces, but there's something else behind it."

"I really don't know what to do. If Nodroyen dies, it probably won't affect their plans at all, except that they'll be more resentful than ever about any interference. But to me it would mean that I'd been wrong, and they were probably wrong too."

"I don't see why ... yes, it's like winter. It's the snow coming down, and the country behind it. It must be very heavy snow, or else it's night."

"Yes, you must rest. It's just whatever you need to see – especially if you're not sleeping. You should try to sleep." Charles still did not raise his head. "Do you think it's possible that he'll die? Is it possible to die at all?"

"No, I don't think so." She turned to him for a moment, and put her hand on his arm, but very soon turned back to the window.

"I often think I should try a final experiment – or not necessarily final. I mean, if you cut your throat, would the blood come out? Nodroyen bled when his fingers got stuck in the floor. What would happen when you hadn't any blood left?" She did not react, and he raised himself, saying, "Where's my razor?"

"It's a village, look," she said. "Those are houses there, and the big shape on the left is the church. You can't see the moon because of the clouds."

"Good Lord, yes," said Charles, and his suicidal urge was for the moment forgotten. "Either I'm seeing what you tell me to see, or it's been put there."

"Do you think we could go out? We'd need some warmer clothes."

"Don't talk nonsense, old thing. Look at those flakes at the bottom, the way they're growing and flickering, and moving about like people. They're eating away the hedge there. It's pretty though – like a Christmas card."

Meanwhile Lionel had much work to do, and never appeared unoccupied. He did not ask about her absences, merely noting her presence when she returned, and sometimes asking for her assistance. He had borrowed her pen in order to continue his journal. Also he had set traps around the floor and walls of his cabin – pools of glue baited with living flies collected by Stanley – so far without result. His most important project, however, was Nodroyen's second ordeal. The unfortunate man had been buried under four feet of earth in the nursery; at first he had repeatedly broken out, but now he lay quiescent. Lionel spent many hours searching in the encyclopaedia for stories of men who had been buried alive for long periods, and frequently cursed the limitations of the ship's library. He remembered modern tales in which men had been underground for several months, and he suspected the ancients of having taken the experiment even further; the cases he recalled, however, had always involved a coffin containing food and drink, with an air-tube to the surface. Nodroyen had been buried in the bare earth, and it had been packed tightly on top of him. Perret, who was in charge of the nursery, had thoroughly stamped it down, and guaranteed that no air could possibly get through. During his last interment, at which Lionel had himself wielded a shovel, Nodroyen had been unconscious, with his eyes open.

Lionel at last decided that the precise length of burial would have to be decided solely by the rate at which the speed decreased, and that after all it was not of great importance. Charles and the crew agreed on this last point, and reminded Lionel that it was the development of Nodroyen's mind which mattered, rather than his power of (physical) endurance. Stanley, whose duties at least nominally included those of ship's doctor, was charged with the immediate supervision and documentation of Nodroyen's progress; in this period he was often to be seen crouching on the requisitioned potato-patch, muttering with his lips close to the earth, and always his reports to Lionel included the information that Nodroyen was quite ready for his ejection. Little attention was paid to these reports, however, as no-one accepted that Stanley could learn much of his patient's condition from the surface.

So Lionel for a time did not concern himself with Nodroyen or with the question of landing, but assiduously hunted spiders and checked his cabin for those trifling, seemingly mischievous changes which he found so disturbing. Many times, when she was there, he took her to bed and made love to her with renewed enthusiasm; but at these times her sense of incorporeality was at its strongest, perhaps aggravated by the prettiness of his talk, which concerned his traps and other small objects. After their coupling and the consequent shift, she would lie still for a long time, firmly grasping the iron framework of the bed, trying, often vainly, to assure herself of such things as its roughness and the pain its edges caused her. Returning to Charles's room, she would slip almost gratefully into his tortuous arguments on duty and other abstractions, while gazing at the white window. Agonisingly boring it certainly was, and Charles's new self-searching aroused in her nothing but contempt; but the endless argument seemed to her the medium in which she could best live. When she touched him the movement was always swift, and she at once withdrew, or he did. This she found comforting; it invariably launched them into further expanses of rationalising. The fact is, she was by no means sure what she was doing at this time. The writing she did then is a labyrinth of words almost devoid of meaning. It is hard to sort out any intelligible story from this material.

One day, as it were, shortly before the ejection, when the speed had all but disappeared from the scale, Lionel, sitting down to write his journal, his mind perhaps running on measuring-instruments, discovered that all his timepieces had stopped, and left his cabin to check the time and date on someone else's. A closely-watched system of mirrors warned the men of his approach, so that by the time he reached them all signs of the game had disappeared – in fact, he found no signs of any activity at all. It was foolish to look for a functioning clock here: there was only a stop-watch, which Waeldermann at last produced from his locker, saying that it had been used to measure the intervals in the game. Not, he added, that they imagined they had thus learned anything about the intervals. Lionel, persisting in what for them was like the pestering of a young child, then asked whether anyone happened to know the date, or had a sense of the time of day. They could think of no lawful activity to turn to, the better to ignore him, but neither could they dream up any response to his question. They looked at him in silence, and he left.

When he opened the door into his cabin, the pot of glue fell on his head. It was a large plastic pot of liquid glue, which had been punctured in several places; gushes of the stuff ran down him, down the door, over the carpet. He did not pause, however. As if he had known it was going to happen, or it had not happened, he shut the door and came over to the bed, streaming with glue, thinking of what the men had said. "They are letting it all have too much influence on them," he said. "I suppose the Captain must go to Sir Charles next. Or would you go for him?" Only when she drew his attention to the glue did he speak of it himself, but then as if he had reacted normally all along, shouting in surprise and anger. She tried to rub the glue off his face for him, holding him while he squirmed with rage. She found the task distasteful, but she restrained him even when he wanted to go and interrogate the crew. He was going to torture them, he said, until he found out which one had played all these tricks. She took him to the wash-basin instead. She could not tell whether the water was hot or cold, but it had no effect on his face. It seemed not even to wet it, whereas the glue in his perpetual light stubble remained precisely as wet and sticky as it had been. It was light-duty glue, intended to stick only paper, but she could find no way of removing it.

Inevitably, in the succeeding hours, which Lionel counted night-hours and passed largely in bed (although he did not sleep) he analysed the case at length, reviewing the evidence against each person in the ship. It did not take him long to work out that she was herself an important suspect, having been alone in the room when he returned, and unable to say whether anyone had come to the door in his absence. Again and again he returned, while she passively listened, to the theory that she had set this and all the other traps for him, either consciously or otherwise, as a consequence of sexual frustration; at other points in his speech he said that the spiders had put the glue there. When perhaps five or ten hours had passed like this, and he was again talking about members of the crew, he suddenly got up and went to the door with the intention of carrying out his interrogation. The door seemed jammed, however. He tugged at it with increasing violence, but caused not the slightest vibration in any part of it. Finally, investigating its edges together, they found that there was no longer a gap between door and wall; so far as they could tell, the two had merged into one continuous piece of material.

There followed a period of hammering and battering, which produced no result. Lionel kept up these efforts after she had gone to lie down in exhaustion, hearing nothing of what he did. When she raised her head, however, he had succeeded – or rather, he was no longer in the room, while the door remained whole and in place. In fact it had undergone no change, but Lionel had gone through.

Almost at once she was nervous, feeling a threat in the sealed, windowless room. She could easily convince herself that suffocation was not a danger, but solitude was for her like a progressive physical contraction, a prelude to immolation or absorption into nothingness. She had an immeasurable time of this solitude to survive. At first she tried, by concentration, to experience the time as the nothing it actually was. This exercise achieved only an urgent, surging panic. By the end of the time she was moving rapidly round the room on her toes, touching no object for longer than a second, and making continuous high-pitched noises with her mouth. She saw dark stains spreading out over the door, as if from a flame applied to the other side, but they always shrank back in exactly the same way, leaving the wood unblemished. Her rescue was finally effected when the door melted like plastic, buckling and falling away at exaggerated speed, dissolving into air before it hit the floor, and leaving a great irregular hole at least twice the size of the original doorway. In the opening Lionel, Charles and Waeldermann were disclosed, crouching over three dice which they had thrown on the floor of the passage.

Lionel no longer spoke to her. He had decided to forget the persecution of himself, and to get on instead with the main plan for assault on the White Planet. Before she had recovered from her incarceration, Nodroyen was disinterred and examined by Stanley. He was alive but suffering from lassitude. He could not close his eyes or focus them, and his brain seemed to work disjointedly, moving forward and then leaping back, so that his speech was minutely repetitive. The most remarkable observation Stanley made was that his flesh had been eroded. He had been buried naked (Stanley had cut with scissors round those parts of his garments which had amalgamated with his skin) and was now dark brown all over, entirely covered with pock-marks, and had here and there much larger, rougher indentations which were black at their centres. His stomach, for example, was hollowed out so that he looked emaciated, although on closer examination the wasting appeared more like corruption than starvation. There was no smell of decomposition, only a tang of the earth. The brown stain, like the glue which still glistened on Lionel's face, could not be removed. Stanley questioned the man, but learned little except that the hallucinations on which he had relied had changed from scenes in which he took an active, even violent part to others in which he merely observed, motionless, and shrinking from his extended state to a single point somewhere outside the action.

The ship was still in measurable motion, but Lionel was not now going to wait for the event he had chosen to fix the time of landing. He considered Stanley's evidence sufficient proof of Nodroyen's readiness, and intended to combine the third test with the expulsion itself, pinning all their hopes on the one experiment. The card-players, while the captain was so active, suspended their game, and he remained unaware that it had been continuing in secret. They, and all those others who were convinced of the Game's importance to their safety, were nonetheless horrified by what they imagined to be the inevitable consequences of Lionel's premature action. They talked earnestly and quietly in the corners of the dining-room while Lionel and Stanley conferred at the old card-table, Lionel sometimes rising to make an announcement or give an order concerning preparations for the expulsion. They had expected that the device used to break down the door, suggested and executed by Waeldermann, would change his hostile attitude to their ideas, but he had not once referred to this successful throw of the dice since it had been made.

At the last moment, when Nodroyen had been led down the dark wood-lined passages to the airlock where the small landing-craft was kept, a party of crew members approached Lionel and tried to change his mind. The explained the working of the dice-trick to him – the many preliminary throws, and meditation on them, which had narrowed down, as Waeldermann expressed it, the co-ordinates of the event in which the door broke; and the importance of announcing, as he had done, these co-ordinates at exactly the moment they appeared on the last throw of the dice. Lionel, expressionlessly watching the men, said they had just virtually admitted that the door would have broken whether they had performed the trick or not; if this was not so, let them do the miracle again now, and prevent him from ejecting Nodroyen; and finally, he was after all risking the essence of only one man – if they tried to prevent him, by whatever means, he would forcibly eject them all. The result of an issue decided by force, he added, would always be unpredictable in this environment, but probably disastrous for all concerned. His arguments were powerful: telling themselves that the only chance of the vessel's survival lay in submission, they retired to watch from outside the airlock.

How do I know, you ask, what they felt? Stanley and she had some sympathy with them: they also watched outside, and heard the talk. Only Lionel was prepared to set himself rigidly against their theory about the White Planet. Charles also, she knew, felt that they were groping towards an important discovery (which they claimed to have made and verified). But he was helping Lionel in the airlock.

Nodroyen was not to be put inside the landing-craft; it had been turned round, so that its engines faced the exit from the ship. He had been denied even a space-suit, no-one believing that such a thing would make the least difference. While Lionel sat inside the landing-craft, setting a timing-device on its engines, and on the exit, which could be controlled from there, Charles busied himself at the back with rope, tying Nodroyen upright against the outlet of the main engine. Having done this he came running across the airlock, followed seconds later by Lionel. For a few moments all stood watching: Nodroyen was held against the great circular opening of the engine, his shoulders being perhaps a third of the way toward its upper rim; his feet dangled about three yards above the floor, and his chest was slumped forwards toward the exit. He did not raise his head, but in the last seconds he made one or two fitful movements with his arms and legs, so that he swung slightly in the ropes that held him.

There was little waiting: Lionel had closed the door and turned to watch, and at once the exit began to open: it had hardly been seen to move, although it opened quickly, when the engine fired, and the airlock disappeared in a white blaze. Even so it was plain to them that the explosion was abnormal. The thrust had been in both directions, outward and inward, and it was not a simple wash of light that engulfed the room, but a turmoil of light in collision where the two forces had met. The conflict continued, and was still spreading. The door and windows into the airlock had vanished, and the audience was backing off. Lionel had stood still for less than a second: already he had pressed the switch to reclose the exit. But the retreat accelerated, and he pushed through the others to get away from the billowing light. There was no sound except that of feet and voices, but it seemed that the passage away from the airlock had become a river of white-hot molten metal: one caught only glimpses of the other people running, and they too were dazzlingly white, open-mouthed and stumbling at the head of the stream. Smallpox was swallowed by it and began to howl, but then came out again on all fours, scrabbling along at great speed like a monkey.

At a certain point the rush of light began to break into splinters. Lionel shouted back to close all doors as they were passed. One could not be sure who was last in the panic, but remembering no-one behind, slammed the doors, and with each new barrier the deluge was weaker, becoming intermittent streams of bubbles and flashes, as if of nothingness, which rushed overhead or through one's body. Once in the main part of the ship, the retreat itself, too, began to splinter, each man seeking what he thought the safest corner. It was hard to follow Charles and Lionel, who were together at the front, but Stanley appeared, coming back, and understanding, led on behind them.

The four reached the control-room, far from the airlock, and this time Stanley shut the door. There was no exit from here. One had to turn and encounter what persisted of the invasion. The only defence, however, was to sit and be calm. Streaks and bubbles remained, floating or resting in corners of the room, but they appeared like a malfunction of one's eyes, moving with one's glance, as after a shift. With agitation and rapid movement they increased, so that larger areas of wall became invisible: it was best to close one's eyes, although they penetrated even that darkness.

There was no speech. Charles and Lionel sat to the right, on the control-panel; Stanley in front, against the door. There was no speech, that is, as they were in these positions – only meditation, eyes closed, on what led to these positions, the positions themselves, and what followed them. What led to them was the flight of many people through narrow passages, what followed the return of one or more of them through similar passages. The extending of these passages was the same as the extending of cause and effect. Try as one might, as I think one did, one could not distinguish them. They extended on either side of the mind, in places obscured by the streaks and bubbles of nothing. The passages on one side, leading towards this room and the situation here, would, if one tried too hard to recreate them, be engulfed by the whiteness, and then one could not remember. On opening the eyes there would be nothing to see. Stanley's hand was there to touch, even to hold, but I cannot tell whether it came with this blankness of the eyes, or only with the flickering seen fragments of Charles and Lionel. One was aware of the others in the room: there were three of them, in the positions I have described, but one counted them, with eyes and mind, without ever reaching the total. There was speculation about the number. Each number suggested seemed inadequate – four seemed wrong, so did six, so did three, so did one, so did eighty-one. In counting, one could neither reach the total nor start again at one, in case there had been a mistake. Perhaps the others outside the room confused the counting of those inside; but it was not possible to think this. If there were others, they must be inside the room. In the passages leading to one's positions in the room there were others, running, but their not being here meant that they had never been and would never be. Still they confused one's thinking, existent or not, because one owed them something, had a duty to them, which could not be identified. It caused great anxiety, trying to identify this duty. One of them, perhaps, was injured – melted, burned, blown to pieces – in pain; but then one could do nothing about pain. It was a question whether pain existed. If it did, it was in oneself, a burning, unchanging agony against which struggle was impossible. But it did not change, so struggle was unnecessary. Or it might be that two of them were injured, or all of them. This is the kind of sequence in which anxiety might grow, multiplying on itself. But it did not grow; to try a logical step such as this was to know that one was really not anxious at all, had never been anxious. But this in itself was a cause of anxiety: if anxiety did not exist, what was it one was feeling, and what did one have to feel for the others outside the room? Perhaps they were not injured, but it was the question of existence which made them so dependent. They did not exist, and yet could not be said not to exist. One had to help them to exist, by continuing to think of them. It was important to sustain one's anxiety about them, however hard this was.

The positions were not as I have described them, or rather not entirely so. This must have contributed to the difficulty of counting the people in the room. Lionel stood in the centre of the floor, looking at the ceiling. It was not certain why he did this. There was speech, also, but it did not come from any of the people in the room. It came partly from the floor, partly from the ceiling. Lionel was able to answer this voice, or rather to speak while it was speaking, as if it were his own voice. There were at least two voices, however, I am sure. He was not able to speak to anyone in the room. One could not answer anyone who spoke in the room, not that anyone spoke in the room. Therefore one of the voices came from outside the room. This did not mean, I thought when telling the story, that there were necessarily others outside the room. It was not possible to follow the dialogue, or to think of it as a dialogue, but in telling the story, without knowing of saying whether it is really what passed, or how it passed, I put it in this way:

Lionel: Nodroyen!

The Voice: (screams, howls, growls, groans, in widely varying pitch, volume and intonation, with short pauses, the changes being always extreme and unpredictable, so that there seems no change at all: the Voice is reacting to some external stimulus, illogical in character, of which we know nothing).

Lionel: Nodroyen!

(The exchange, if it can be called an exchange, is repeated many times, so many that it is impossible to listen every time. Every conceivable combination of the two speeches is used: that is, Lionel must repeat his address once, twice, three times, etc., before the response is heard; and also the response, if it can be called a response, comes unasked, and is extended so long that Lionel must again call "Nodroyen" when it is not necessary, when the Voice is still making its response. These repetitions, or variations, are not in any sequence. They all appear simultaneously. The Voice uses every interpretation which my description of its utterance will admit. Lionel calls "Nodroyen" in every tone which is consistent with a loud voice, that is, imploringly, in despair, ecstatically, etc...)

The Voice: Can't see him. Go away!

Lionel: Nodroyen!

The Voice: (screams, etc., as before. It is to be understood that the Voice's last speech before this, and every speech which follows, are not unique events occurring at particular points in the dialogue, but as it were ingredients in the mixture, which appear many times, in every possible combination with all the other speeches. Thus if an attempt were made to transcribe the whole dialogue in a sequence, the result would stretch to many thousands of pages. I am making this transcription now from memories of the dialogue, and from memories of memories, for none of this was written previously. One was unable to write. A memory deals with sitting before a sheet of paper, pen in hand; one could get no further than this, however. There was nothing to say where the pen had come from, or why; and to seek the ideas for writing which were certainly present, somewhere, was to become involved in another logical circle like the one anxiety had created – which had not, by the way, stopped its spinning. In this transcription, therefore, selection and ordering of speeches has been dictated largely by the pattern created in the tunnel of multiplying memories.)

Lionel: Nodroyen! Are you in the airlock?
The Voice: Can't see him. He's lying down, like dead.
Lionel: Are you in the airlock? Are you dead?
The Voice: Like dead. Nothing but white.
Lionel: Are you dead? Can you see yourself?
The Voice: White, shifting. Has to shift to see him.
Lionel: Nodroyen! Are you in one place?
The Voice: Can't see him. Not him calling.
Lionel: Who is calling? He wants to know.
The Voice: Not him, the voice. He can't move.
Lionel: He wants to know, can you move?
The Voice: Has to shift to move, then see him.
Lionel: If you can move, you're in one place.
The Voice: He's underneath. Has to shift to get to him.
Lionel: Nodroyen! Can you hear? If you can hear...
The Voice: Move down through the white to tell him.
Lionel: Nodroyen! He mustn't move, mustn't move too fast.

The Voice: (screams, etc., as before. The speeches do not alternate as I have suggested; they all appear simultaneously. The most audible tone is panic. The voices seem to fluctuate wildly in space, in volume and in quality, becoming more and less metallic, as if involving themselves with the walls of the room. Lionel beats his fist against his head, to make thought easier. Here are some longer speeches, in which I have used yet more freely my power to arrange the memories, making the syntax more explicit, sometimes even clarifying what I judge to be the subject-matter. The first speaker I have named "The Second Voice"; by this I mean to imply that the Voice mentioned above – or the First Voice – concerns itself exclusively with permutations of those speeches already transcribed, and the Second Voice is superimposed upon it.)

The Second Voice: He's here now. He's not dead. The white doesn't have to shift for him to move. The white is like treacle – he can feel it. He's moving through it, half crawling, half swimming. He thinks he must be sinking through it as well as moving along, but he thinks there's no reason why he should sink. There's no reason why he should move along, but he feels he is moving along. He's here now. He can move because he has a body. His hands are moving up and down, his feet are moving backwards and forwards – or it's the other way around. The white gets in the way of some of his body, but it's here alright. He can see some of it. He doesn't want to lose his body, because if he had no body the white would have to shift for him to move, and that makes the pain worse. He's frightened of the shifts. He has to concentrate very hard to keep his body. He mustn't try to move too quickly

(The Voice has been given statements, Lionel mainly questions. It is convenient to use a sequence in which the one apparently answers the other, although there is nothing to indicate that answers were intended.)

Lionel: Listen: the Captain wants to know, if you can see him, what does he look like? What else can you see in the white? Is there anything else to say he is moving? If the Captain can move, can he get to you, or to him, to help you? Should he try to move?

The Second Voice: He's brown, like burned, with holes. When the white shifts, he changes. He wants to get out of the white, but there's something in the way. It gets inside him, changed him. It hasn't got a shape, but it wants to get inside him. Go away! It's trying to get into his back, but he can't turn round. He'll lose his body. No, he'll keep it! He's stronger than you! Go away! (screams, etc, as before.

There were not four people in the room, as I have said. On opening the eyes there was nothing, only white, as if the eyes were closed. The voices were there, describing the things that happened.

There was only one voice, which was everywhere. It did not speak, but only wept, sobbing almost inaudibly, or else howling and choking. One's own body was there, in parts: the white swallowed some of it, but parts were still there. It was moving, all the parts independently. Something tried to get into it. In the room there were not three other people: one saw parts of others, but not of three. One or more of the three had not come to the room, as I have said.

There was no end to the dialogue: one could go, now, as far as one wished into its complexities. One was moving, not necessarily in the room, but the voices were everywhere, and one could hear them everywhere. Moreover, in a sense the room was everywhere: if one moved very far, there was nonetheless the possibility of seeing part of the room, which had not been swallowed by the white.

Here is a third phase of the dialogue. It is superimposed on the other two.)

The Third Voice: There are two of them. One of them has got his body, the other one is trying to get inside. He's changed. He's bent in the middle, his legs are too big. He's trying to move along by leaping like a frog.

The Fourth Voice: There are two of them. One of them has got his body (etc.)

Lionel: (as if himself involved in the drama; one cannot tell which if, indeed, there are more than one, of the voices, if any, he is addressing) Don't think that because he's moving slowly, he can't move at all. He's only moving slowly so that the white doesn't shift. You can't move more quickly than he can. You haven't got a body, he has. He's stronger than you. If he moved more quickly than he's moving now, he'd escape from you, you wouldn't get inside his body. He wouldn't even have a body any more. If you move quickly, you don't have a body. Without a body you can't move at all. You can't get inside him. (Screams, etc., as before.)

The Fifth Voice: There are four of them. Two of them have got his body, the other two are trying to get inside. He's all tangled, like a ball of wool that's melting. The pain tangles him up. Can't see which parts of him are moving.

The Sixth and Seventh Voices: There are four of them (etc.)

Lionel: He's all tangled (etc.) Can't get inside him. Can't see the Captain, but he's moving, must split in two. He can untangle himself. Must move quickly and think. Can't see the Captain, but he' here. Everyone's here, must think.

There is no end to the dialogue. I go further into its complexities as if down part of the ship's labyrinth, as the visual impressions of the things before me seem to grow complex: for now the white faults in the scene, though they fluctuate wildly from continuous uniform whiteness to mere streaks and bubbles, seem in some grandly-conceived sequence including all the stages to grow in number, increase their influence, work from being only little faults towards being parts of a total whiteness; and the spaces between the faults are filled with things seen in different parts of the ship, the more spaces the greater this variety. The control-room is here, so is the passage with the lavatories outside it, so is the passage with lavatories outside the dining-room. There seems no purpose in distinguishing between "is" and "seems"; for "seems" I will write "is". These fragments of different parts overlap, providing composite places containing, say, half of Lionel talking to the ceiling, who somewhere about his waist becomes the metal wall outside his cabin; and as these impressions are more complex, so they are more heavily veiled, with thicker white gauze, so that utter complexity will be whiteness. For "will be", too, I write "is" from now on. The memories do not distinguish, and I cannot afford to mistrust the memories.

"You imagined you were moving," as Charles said to me when we were alone, "out of the control-room, through the ship's passages. On the other hand, you could not distinguish between moments in which you passed through different places, because there was no such distinction. Moments and places were all present simultaneously. The progression from simplicity to complexity you are now imposing on the memories. You imagined it as a journey to the airlock because of your supposed duty to Nodroyen, who was thought of as being outside the ship, although you could not, of course, have any awareness of motivation."

The voices are everywhere, but they do not follow the course of the journey, for the visual impressions are now like a dim and intricate kaleidoscope-pattern, whereas the voices are very few, only three, or only the one, sobbing and weeping as before. Myself involved in the drama, I speak to one or other of the voices, or in the voice. The Captain is trying to move; he is trying not to split, I say. The voices describe what is happening to me, or what I see. There are people in the pattern of fragments: at the bottom-right, far along the corridor, impossible to say which corridor, I see Smallpox inching towards me like a caterpillar, head held stiffly above the invisible floor, eyes staring, mouth open. Also I am at the corner between the dining-room and the Captain's cabin, before turning it. I can never turn it. Part of my reflection is in the facing part-wall. It is the Captain reaching out his hand towards me. I too am reaching out a hand to the reflection, but I cannot see my hand, only that of the reflection. Indeed, in examining this particular memory I find no concrete evidence of movement – no sensation, for example, of my own feet on the floor. This bears out what Charles said. It is not enough to assume that this memory deals with some other person.

But after that I remember no more, until later. And then the persons involved were different, and in a way, if you like, normality had returned. You remember that.

L

<u>*Report on the Inquest into the Death of Sir Charles Pink, Bart.*</u>[9]

The inquest was held for arbitrary and official reasons at Chiswick, and not far from the private residence of Lionel Jaffa (to which he was in the habit of retiring when disgusted with his father). A coincidence, I repeat. It involved a large number of (and virtually no-one

---

9 This section, again, is undated, though obviously later in composition than the preceding letter from Ms Cook, and, I believe, from the letter from "L", which I have inserted at this point although it does not, as do both the preceding and subsequent documents, appear in the same notebook. Its point of view, also, is puzzling, again so far as time is concerned, rather than any question of person. My purpose here is to state that, in spite of the diverse confusions into which this may throw the reader, the author is justified in considering it a consistent and integral section of the whole "Report". Although undated, it is the same length as the last day's entry of Ms Cook's letter; thus I cannot look on it as a mere appendage, or enclosure, such as Miss Cook has seen fit to include in other days. It has, moreover, I believe, an effect of summarising, or at least of concluding what has gone before; thus I for one accept the author's denials of all such accusations as that it "departs from the original design" or "indicates that Miss Cook had given up the idea of writing a diary, and now devoted her notebook instead to random jottings". *The Author*

else but) people who have figured in this journal, and who will do so again: who constitute, in fact, this journal's entire material. It was a modest display of reasoning, whose starting-point might well be said to have been Sir Charles's mangled corpse and the report of the doctors who performed the post-mortem upon it. These claimed that the direct cause of death had almost certainly been strangulation, although the body was positively peppered with tunnels and hollows, any one of which, given time, would have proved mortal. The body had been found outside the National Westminster Bank in Finchley Road, at 4-30 in the afternoon of Monday, December 3rd, and would have been awash with blood, had this substance not either congealed, seeped into the pavement, or found its way down twenty yards of gutter to a drain. It (the corpse) had been one for about two hours, and it has continued to be a source of amazement for me (though apparently for no-one else) that such a gross piece of carrion – surely an unfamiliar object in Finchley Road, even now – should have remained unnoticed for so long. I admit that when the living body was actually being converted in the manner described I was aware of no-one's presence but our own, and that I even went so far as to remark to myself on the unusual dearth of people. I admit also that the reaction of many a passer-by to the carnage down the side-street may well have been "Ah, a tragedy. No doubt the police, like Fortinbras, will soon come and add the finishing touches to the scene." I can even conceive as a possibility that someone made a proficient attempt at concealment – whether an innocent or guilty man or the murderer (for I didn't follow closely his every move) – and that the first few gouts of blood were lent an innocent aspect by the tarpaulin or motor-car from under which they flowed. I do not, however, consider any of these half-explanations sufficiently convincing to justify the complete silence on this aspect of the affair which the inquest itself maintained. Be that as it may, it is with the aspects the inquest made a noise about that the present Report concerns itself. My own opinions have little or no significance, as I played little or no part in the inquest.

One of the first things it dealt with was a list of suspects, in case the verdict should prove to be murder or manslaughter. This included – to my surprise – Isobel Keogh, on the grounds that she has had the opportunity, and Christabel Cook, because she had a motive; Sir Charles Jaffa, it claimed, might have objected to his son's elevation of the victim, his old college friend, to the status of participant in the father's designs for the son: and Captain Lionel Jaffa might have clung to the thunder which, assuming his father to have been initiator of the victim's inclusion in their plan, he saw this potential rival as likely to steal. This last suspect (Jaffa's junior) might also, it suspected, have been engaged in some powerful rivalry with the victim long before he (the victim) had encountered either Sir Charles Jaffa or his plan. The one remaining suspect was Sir Charles Pink, for whose selection it was felt no justification was necessary. Where the police, and thereby the coroner, had obtained the information they did consider necessary, was not entirely a mystery to me: I had had to submit a long written statement, and when it came to light that I was given to writing in any case, also the manuscript of my journal. Both the Jaffas concerned would doubtless have been equally happy to oblige in the same way: and possibly Isobel too, though about that I'm not sure. Many things had come into the open, in addition, during the dispute over Sir Charles Jaffa's spaceship.

The first moot point in the hypothetical case against Sir Charles Jaffa was whether it would have been necessary, in order for him to have done the deed or to have had a motive for it, to have met the victim beforehand; and the second was whether he had done so. In the event of his not having done so, you see (and not having communicated with him in any way), it would undoubtedly have been less likely that Captain Lionel rather than Sir Charles had been the jealous person. However, it was decided that the first point could not be decided; as to the second, the Coroner addressed Sir Charles Pink as follows:

CORONER: You claim, then, to have met Sir Charles Jaffa for the first time three days after Sir Charles Pink's death, and accept that you thereby possibly release him from suspicion?

PINK: Yes, sir, but I don't quite see...

CORONER: Very good; but we have here a statement by Captain Lionel Jaffa, in which he states quite clearly that you met his father on a certain afternoon in Cambridge in – what was the year? – thank you – nineteen sixty-one.

PINK: If that is so, sir, I have absolutely no recollection of the incident whatever.

CORONER: Mr Mote, perhaps you have something to say at this point.

MOTE: Well, sir, as Sir Charles Pink's legal representative it must be borne in mind that I have a certain interest in the weight of evidence against his fellow suspects; however...

CORONER: You carry professional ethics too far, Mr Mote. As you are on oath, the statement is irrelevant.

MOTE: ... however, it is indeed the case that I also was present at this meeting in Cambridge between Charles Pink and Sir Charles Jaffa.

CORONER: And what happened on that occasion?

MOTE: I find that my own memory is almost as fallible as my client's; but so far as I remember, the two were drawn to each other, and during the evening became very friendly. I think they spent some time alone together at a table in the bar, while Sir Charles's son...

CORONER: Pink or Jaffa?

MOTE: Jaffa, sir. My client had not as yet come into his title, nor did he have any children so far as the court is concerned.

CORONER: "Come into" it, you say? Into his "Sir", you mean?

MOTE: Yes, sir.

CORONER: And this "coming in", when was it? What did it entail?

MOTE: Er – it occurred automatically on the death of his father; but as for the precise date of this event, I think, with all due respect, that it would be advisable to exclude from the case as much information as possible concerning only the parents of the principals.

CORONER: Don't worry, Mote, I'm not trying to make your client out to be a multiple murderer or parricide, or anything like that. It's just these "Sir"s and "Captain"s that interest me. I think we ought to know exactly whom we're dealing with before we start. Now, in my own case it wasn't a question of anyone's death, something positive had to happen.[10]

I believe this is also true of Sir Charles Jaffa, and certainly it is so in the case of my friend Sir James Baconbury[11], who discovered something in the field of astronomy.

MOTE: Shouldn't that be "Baconbury"[12], sir?

CORONER: Now, while we're on this subject ... do you have any further questions for Sir Charles Pink, Mr Mote?

---

[10] This is Sir John Corunna, in whose career no event has any bearing on this narrative save the events of the present inquest, and perhaps the one or two events which led to his being knighted. *The Author*

[11] Pronounced "Bunbury". *The Author*

[12] Pronounced as written. *The Author*

MOTE: I have no questions at all.

CORONER: Then let's call Captain Lionel Jaffa.

(This was done, Sir Charles Pink standing down. It should be mentioned here that the "principals", as Mr Mote had called them, including those designated "suspects", were all sitting in the front row of seats, and could be called into and out of the witness-box with great ease and rapidity. Mr Mote had a seat among them, but frequently rose to stride about the area between this front row and the Coroner, particularly when cross-examining a witness. Sir Charles Pink, who had now been standing in the witness-box for more than an hour, habitually appeared in every imaginable sense decrepit. He was pale, hirsute and confused, rarely answering a question with any confidence; he seemed constantly on the point of making some significant revelation, but was never given time to bring it out. He glanced often at Captain Lionel Jaffa, who on the contrary displayed an enjoyment of the proceedings which would have been cynical had it not contained a youthful happy negligence. His self-possession during this ordeal (which must have heightened, after all, the anguish he felt at the loss of one who was possibly his dearest friend) savoured as much of the heroic as of the callous.[13] He now stepped elegantly into the witness-box and swore in the customary manner on the Bible, after which:)

CORONER: Are you Captain Lionel Jaffa, B.A. (Cantab.)?

L. JAFFA: Yes.

CORONER: Of Bidesloe Mansions; son of Sir Charles Jaffa and of some woman unknown?

L. JAFFA: Possibly not unknown to my father, sir.[14]

CORONER: We will deal with that possibility later.

MOTE: With your permission, sir, the relevance of the witness's parentage does not go beyond certain general facts which are readily obtainable, no cross-examination of his ...

CORONER: Captain Jaffa, do you serve in one of Her Majesty's Armed Forces, or have you retired?

L. JAFFA: Neither of those is the case, sir.

CORONER: Then you must be master of some merchant vessel.

L. JAFFA: No. If, as I think, you wish to know whether my "Captain" performs the same function as your "Sir", I have to tell you that it does not. "Captain" was bestowed on me as Christian name, by my parents, much as "Sergeant" and more often "Major" are given as names to dogs by their owners. "Lionel" is thus my second name.

CORONER: Do you have any more questions for Mr Jaffa, Mr Mote?

L. JAFFA: I'd rather you didn't ...

MOTE: Lionel - (or[15], as his friends sometimes used to refer to him) – Lionel, Captain Jaffa: I have met you on only three occasions since our university courses ended, ten

---

13 Miss Cook is of course entitled to her own interpretation of the difference in demeanour between Pink and Jaffa, and certainly something of what she says must be true; however, it should be noted that Sir Charles had many miles further to travel than the younger man, in order to reach the court-room every morning. *The Author*

14 Certain members of the audience laughed here, upon which Sir John frowned, first in their general direction, and finally in that of Sir Charles Jaffa. *The Author*

15 Aside, to the audience. *The Author*

years ago, whereas Charles – Pink[16] - and I have taken advantage of every opportunity which offered to renew our friendship; I remain convinced, the ten years having passed, that of my two friends you are the more likely, in a case such as this where memory is all-important, to have both the ability and the inclination to recall the past with accuracy.

PINK: I say …

MOTE: Therefore I ask you, whether you can say with certainty that your father and Sir Charles Pink met, ten years or more ago.

L. JAFFA: It must be remembered that, at about the time you mention, my father tested for the first time his scheme for launching and perpetuating news of his own death, the idea being that in this way he might make far more money than he had when "alive", like most dead artists. In the light of this, there is the possibility that, although I remember distinctly that Charles and my father talked together for several hours in Cambridge so far as Charles is concerned he did not at that time meet Sir Charles Jaffa. My father never required any help from us …

CORONER: Us?

L. JAFFA: From my mother, Jezebel or myself, when preparing his aliases or performing, disguised or otherwise, his impersonations of anonymous other people.

MOTE: Your wife, then, was present at the function in Cambridge? I remember that she was, of course, but you understand that I'm just coaxing you into giving your own version of the story.

L. JAFFA: Yes, though she wasn't my wife at the time. I'd bought two guest-tickets for the Advent Carol Service …

PINK: Look, I'd just like to say that I don't remember this at all. So far as I can remember, I went to the Carol Service in 1961 with …

MOTE: You say that the two spent time together *in the bar*, thus implying that both you and they took alcohol?

MOTE: Yes, and alcohol is notorious for producing complete lack of recall, so don't take this statement too seriously. When you met Sir Charles Jaffa, three days after Sir Charles Pink's death, did you recognise him?

PINK: Well, I must say that I was never, from the first, in any doubt as to his identity. But Captain Jaffa had spoken of him, and even described him to me, so often that it is hardly surprising…

MOTE: Did you think you had met him before?

PINK: No.

CORONER: Was your father disguised in Cambridge?

L. JAFFA: I don't remember.

MOTE: You, too, took alcohol, I think?

L. JAFFA: Almost certainly.

CORONER: Was there anything distinctive in the appearance of Sir Charles Jaffa, when you met him on the sixth of this month?

PINK: Only that he was old, and walked with a stick.

MOTE: So it is possible that no disguise was necessary, and that twelve years of ageing had made all the difference?

---

16 This in anticipation of Sir John's query. *The Author*

MOTE: In any case, it is futile to speculate when all those concerned had been drinking, probably to excess. Was there anything peculiar in the behaviour of this person[17] when you met him on this recent date?

PINK: To be quite frank, I thought his behaviour peculiar throughout – but, you know, if I'd met him before, perhaps I'd have realised that for him, it was quite normal. For example – erm – when I was being shown out, by Mrs Jaffa[18], he called to me from his bedroom, where he'd gone on her advice, or at her command, I should say – erm – "You've had her before, I can tell. You fascist prudes don't fool me."

CORONER: Why do you choose that remark in particular?

L. JAFFA: If I may make a remark, I don't think that any significance should be attached to any remark made by my father.

MOTE: Well, we shall all have to decide that point for ourselves a little later on. Meanwhile, I would like one small gloss on this particular remark: did it refer to your wife? She was, after all, showing Sir Charles out at the time.

L. JAFFA: I can only repeat my last remark. It is impossible to answer the question helpfully.

CORONER: To whom did it refer, Sir Charles?

PINK: To – a young lady, I think, whom I had seen crossing the lawn. I wasn't sure that he'd seen me looking at her, but I believe she was Miss Isobel Keogh.

MOTE: Whom you had indeed had before, eh? I feel, sir, that we are approaching the crux of my argument regarding the fallibility of Sir Charles's memory for faces. If I may be allowed to take the stand?

MOTE: It must be said, however, that we shall need a small digression first, or rather to refer to yet another recent event which has a bearing on the case. We find it pertinent, as it involves yet more anecdotes of Sir Charles's inability to identify people accurately, and of his consistent, or some would say compulsive, indulgence in alcohol.

(The Coroner shrugged, and Mr Mote was allowed to take Captain Jaffa's place in the witness-box)

MOTE: Now, the effect which alcohol has on me – when I take a sufficient quantity, which is not frequently – is to obscure, or to blacken experience, at the time; and to perpetuate the same blackness in my memory of the experience, until I am reminded of what the experience was. Then the blackness can be almost completely dissipated. Now, in relation to Sir Charles Pink's repeated statements about his experience in Cambridge...

MOTE: Your statement is more closely related to an experience of your own, which should be considerably fresher in your memory. Do you remember having dinner with Sir Charles Pink, two days after Sir Charles Pink's death?[19] Sir Charles himself has already admitted that the dinner took place, so bear in mind that your version will be compared with his.

---

17 Mr Mote paused in front of Sir Charles Jaffa's seat. *The Author*

18 Another glance here at Captain Lionel Jaffa, whose complacency seemed to have been actually increased by his elevation to the witness-box. *The Author*

19 On hearing this question Mr Mote gripped the front of his witness-box, white knuckled. No-one who did not know him well could have decided whether this indicated some profound emotion, inspired by the question, or mere exasperation at having been interrupted. *The Author*

MOTE: Yes, I think it might be said that I remember it. I remember, oddly, the earlier stages more clearly than the later, even when reminded.

MOTE: The reason for which may be simply that, as you yourself have suggested, the blackness is never quite completely dissipated.

MOTE: Yes, or that another part of the effect alcohol has on me – which I was proceeding to describe – is to make me doubt my ability to reason, not only at the time, but for a period which extends further and further into the past, beyond, eventually, the point at which I began to drink. Thus while I continue to drink, and afterwards, an increasing proportion of the time is taken up with reflection on an increasing portion of the past, increasingly to the exclusion of the present.

MOTE: You might be said, then, to be living in the past, or, even better, in a world of fantasy, where you try to impose the drunkard's inflated view of his consistency on acts already committed?

MOTE: Yes, I remember that the sweet course at Sir Charles's had something of this quality. There was some doubt, was there not, as to the identity of the young lady who was still eating her main course at that time?

MOTE: Yes, and as you have told me, yet more doubt as to your earlier apparent ability to distinguish her from the other ladies, and to reject confidently Sir Charles's claim, presumably flippant, that she was Isobel Keogh?

MOTE: Either flippant, I had thought, or part of a complicated imposture, later to be explained to me in private, and perhaps intended to help in the general legal deceptions which Sir Charles expected shortly to become necessary.

MOTE: You began to feel that your reason had already been clouded when providing for you this dual interpretation of Sir Charles's claim, and were astonished at the impertinence with which you had treated the ladies while still assuming them to be parties to a conspiracy.

MOTE: Yes, and although more and more inclined to burst into drunken humour, I attempted simultaneously to atone for my impoliteness and to make certain of the various ladies' names.

CORONER: I don't see that this is getting us anywhere, Mr Mote. You accept the statement made by the lady in question in her diary[20], that Sir Charles told you she was Isobel Keogh?

MOTE: Mr Mote had also been told by Captain Jaffa – whom, incidentally, I must compliment on the tremendous improvement he has made in his appearance for this inquest – that he should expect to meet Miss Keogh when visiting Sir Charles.

CORONER: And then at some point during the evening you were not sure how many ladies were actually present, and assumed that they were a group, befriended by Sir Charles, who lived under the same roof because of their unfortunate physical disabilities.

PINK: I must speak, sir. I certainly did not claim that Isobel Keogh was present. The lady responsible for the dinner was Miss Christabel Cook.

CORONER: You are not, I trust, *living* with Miss Cook?

PINK: No, indeed, I live in Westmorland.

CORONER: Then I think we may adjourn until tomorrow.

---

20 The Coroner took this notebook from its place in front of him on the bench, and displayed it, while leafing through it. *The Author*

In the morning of Monday the 24th of December it was raining, but a small crowd of enthusiasts had gathered at the door of the court-rooms before the central characters arrived. They stood with streaming umbrellas, passively split into two groups by the presence of two caped policemen. A number of people, Aloysius Mote among them, sprinted one by one up the steps to the door, unhailed by these reticent fanatics, whose only reaction was to the water thrown up by departing taxis. Isobel Keogh arrived on foot, wearing a shiny black macintosh and an archaic clear plastic rain-hat, and had to step into the road in order to skirt one of the groups of spectators. She walked up the steps without acclaim, and once inside shed her macintosh to reveal a smart suit, the skirt just below knee-length, of navy-blue with a pattern of large white circles. The temperature was still high for December, and the room set aside for the inquest was well heated. Christabel Cook, in contrast, was driven to the door in a large private car – not a Rolls Royce, but ostentatious, and painted black – and sat for a moment with her driver (both their faces were hidden by veils) before rushing (to avoid a soaking) up the steps, followed from the back seat by Dingbrace, who held her bag at near-arm's-length from his body, and an umbrella directly over it. The crowd did not respond. Miss Cook was wearing a shapeless pale-blue smock with dark-blue smudges, the black veil lying oddly over its upper half. No footnote here, please.[21] The audience continued silent until a white Aston Martin made its way to the kerb. Sir Charles Jaffa, in common with Dingbrace, had sensibly arranged to be driven to court by a member of his family, so that he had no parking-problem. Neither Christabel Cook nor Isobel Keogh, I should like to make clear, had any relation near enough to be called on for such a service, even had he been able to drive. As Sir Charles walked across the pavement and up the steps with his son Lionel, a single spectator on the edge of the crowd uttered a small cheer, which was followed by some muttering among the remainder. Sir Charles turned to acknowledge this vague salute, whereas Lionel merely looked puzzled.

It was Sir Charles who answered the greatest number of questions on this particular day. He did not have to stand; someone suggested that a chair be taken into the box, but he declined. Towards the end of the cross-examination he slouched, with his elbows on the front of the witness-box, his forearms projecting stiffly into the court, and his hands drooping or flapping independently at their ends. One reason for the length of his interrogation was that he persistently introduced unconnected issues, especially that of his space-ship and of the hairy man who was supposed to have been seen beside it on Hampstead Heath. When taxed with the irrelevance of these things he would claim to be within seconds of establishing their connection with the question, only then to go on with his subject until again stopped. It was not senility, as Aloysius Mote and others asserted; on the contrary his logic was impeccable, and there can be no doubt that he would, given time, have reached the connecting-points he claimed to be able to reach. They were also, in a sense, connecting-points from which he departed. Thus:

CORONER: Was it in Westmorland that you last saw him before November 1st?

JAFFA: He is a rather short, heavily-built man of thirty or forty, with thin red hair pressed flat against his skull, and a protuberant moustache of the same colour. Of course any

---

21 It is hard to believe that Miss Cook actually <u>knew</u> her manuscript would eventually fall into authorial hands. This plea may have been a result of general nervousness engendered by dealings with the police. *The Author*

of these details may change or have changed. He has a very resonant voice, and nearly always wears a waistcoat, often dark green. His feet ...

CORONER: Sir Charles, Sir Charles is present, and those of us at the front can see him quite easily. There is no need to describe him in such detail.

JAFFA: But as the proceedings initiated by him in order to establish his identity are not yet complete – unlike those concerning my space-ship, which you were perhaps more justified in considering a closed affair – I thought I should begin by making it as clear as possible which person I was referring to.

CORONER: The trial's being still in progress is, I'm afraid, yet another reason for its not being mentioned during the present inquest. I think that all other legal proceedings might be successfully avoided if you confined yourself as strictly as possible to the questions put to you in connection with the particular issue before us.

JAFFA: You may claim that there is something particular about the issue before us, but it must not be forgotten that I, apart from my successful struggle for my property and Sir Charles Pink's as yet undecided battle for his identity, am involved in two yet further cases with which it is possible for me to confound the present one: I refer, of course, to my son's prospective divorce from his wife Jezebel, and the action which has been brought against me for the devastation of an area on Hampstead Heath.

CORONER: It is understandable that at your advanced age you should have difficulty in keeping all these things separate in your mind. Many of those present, particularly the people in the front row, have an involvement as deep as your own in all the cases you have mentioned – Sir Charles Pink, indeed, is possibly even more heavily committed than you – and I am sure they would all agree that a proliferation of court hearings tends to confuse. We must all make allowances for each other, and strive for simplicity whenever there is the least chance of attaining it.[22]

Letter, Mr Quincey Horace to Sir Charles Pink, M.A. (Cantab.)

My dear Pink,

You might think it's strange that I'm writing to you after all; but I'm going to put a proposition to you, and when I've told you the story of our voyage towards Liverpool, which we're at present engaged on, you might be in a position to understand it and therefore accept it. The reasons for our being on the way to Liverpool at all are fairly simple, compared, at least, with the new reasons for action we've come across since embarking.

We'd been hoping, you'll remember, to buy some native women in the desert or elsewhere in the surrounding regions, and thus to found a new and ideal town in Mozambique – ideal, that is, so far as our general lack of satisfaction guided us towards the ideal. We soon found, naturally enough, that we were all dissatisfied about different things,

---

22 There can be no reason for pursuing the inquest in any detail beyond this point, although Miss Cook's account of it does continue. The next important event is an unsuccessful attempt on the part of Sir Charles Jaffa to implicate the mysterious hairy man. A final note for the fashion-conscious: the smock worn by Miss Cook was of the kind which gives the illusion of pregnancy. This particular smock, however, served to conceal the fact that Miss Cook had indeed been carrying a child since October or September. *The Author*

but that's beside the point. I've no doubt that Jaffa has found an opportunity, somewhere in his travels, to show you the letter I sent to him a few weeks ago; if by some peculiar coincidence he hasn't, it doesn't matter too much (I may say that, although I've had a lot of contact with him over the last three or four days, I haven't shown him any of the drafts of that letter, or the parts of this one that have been written; I haven't even given him any idea that I might be writing to you, and I hope that you at your end will show an equal discretion and keep this out of his way). If, then, as seems most likely, you have seen my letter to him, you will remember some of the things which made us feel a bit uncertain about the idea of settling down, and set us thinking instead about finding a ship to England: our peculiar hallucinatory experiences in the Sahara; our readings from the copy of Jaffa's diary which we found in the second space-ship (successfully landed by us); our meeting with the crippled and insane vendor of bananas and figs; and the wretched village of huts and rotting tents where we finally left Alexander, Ramon, Jose, Butch and Klein. I will only add that, as the remaining seven of us made our way towards the port from which I suppose we all saw ourselves eventually leaving for England – and our choice of caravan-transport rather than the quite convenient train shows that we needed time to get used to this vision – we went on indulging a sort of amateur interest in the political ambitions of the country's many oppressed people.

Often, travelling in our solitary caravan, with the modest load of objects and commodities we'd decided to bring with us, and our few Arab servants, we heard about riots and upheavals in nearby spots only a matter of hours after they'd taken place. We went without fail to investigate the scenes of these happenings – in fact we always welcomed the digression, as if this sort of holiday sight-seeing was much more the sort of thing we should be doing with our new wealth – but the reception we had at the town of W— was more or less typical: we entered along a battered street, and had to pass through two or three more, all empty of life, before coming to the heart of the town and meeting the usual babble which meant that our affluent and eccentric appearance had been noted. We had offers of pots and carpets – fairly singed and bloody articles, most of them. People were clearing mutilated bodies off the streets all this time; the population of the town must have been reduced by a half or more. When we made it clear that information was the only thing we were prepared to pay for, the survivors began to look blank. Some of them gave up at once and went back to sitting in the rubble. We asked the more persistent tradesmen about the recent revolution – who was now in power, what changes had been made, and so on – and though it was obvious that they tried very hard, they were quite unable to understand our questions. We used our own Arabs as interpreters, so it was not a problem of language. Some thought we were trying to buy severed limbs as souvenirs – one of them waved a foot in my face aggressively – and others thought we were trying to buy the whole town. They seemed to have no doubt that they could sell it to us, whether or not that was what we wanted. W— was the one revolt-torn town in which we spent a night, maybe with the idea of getting to the root of this political ignorance once and for all. We found three households which were prepared to put us up in groups, and they gave a pretty fair social cross-section of the place. Quincey and Karl and I, for instance, had as host a relatively wealthy and important man called Ahmed, with whom we spent upwards of seven hours eating, drinking and smoking. It was obvious that he held us in great respect, for one reason or another, and as well as the courteous desire to be of help in any way he could, he felt a need to answer our enquiries satisfactorily so that his declaration of kinship with us would have more conviction. We didn't get any further, though, than such hashish-turned dialogues as this :

Q. Is this such a place, then, as could sustain any number of men in a condition equal to that enjoyed by you and your wives and sons?

A. There are indeed many beautiful women – my daughters, whom you have seen, and whom you will see again before long, are neither the most nor the least attractive. Also there are considerably fewer men than there were yesterday.

Q. I think my brother means to ask whether, of those few who are left, all will have an equal power to acquire the women they want. I am delighted by your couscous.

A. The couscous is, I am afraid, only the everyday dish which we find sufficient for ourselves. Your arrival was unexpected; if you were good enough to stay indefinitely, however, we would be able to treat you as your exalted state demands. The wealth of the dead is available, of course, to all.

Q. We are pleased to find that the trouble has not at least affected your own state, and it will indeed be most agreeable to stay in this happy place. I am practically asleep, I fear.

A. I am deeply affected by the interest you have shown in our welfare and what you are pleased to call my enlightenment. You and your friends may sleep without fear, in this or any house in W—. The bloodshed was without cause, and will not be repeated.

Q. Thank you, but we are travellers by nature and have not been immobile for many years, so you must forgive us if we leave you. Come on, wake up. Thank you, just a little more, perhaps. You must allow us to give you some gold, as much as you like, or anything – we can get you some more of this wine, if you like.

In the morning we wandered rather dazedly into the sunlit square, and were just in time to prevent Smallpox and Syphilis from allowing themselves to be exhibited for money. Having set out again on our camels we conferred with Raoul Antonius and his double about the results of this excursion, and found that they'd made about as much progress as we had ourselves. Raoul wasn't terribly well – he'd been lodged in a poorer household – and he was very dark and silent. None of us thought about where we were going, or tried to draw any conclusions out of our observations. We concentrated on remaining upright on our beasts, and just resumed our course where we'd left it off.

It's now the third day of our voyage, and I'm sitting on the deck in the sunshine, which continues. The chair beside me is empty, though it was occupied until a minute ago by a girl called Mabel, about whom it is possible, I think, you will know quite a lot by the time you and I have finished this letter. I have just been talking with her about Quincey, and it seems the two have formed something of an attachment already. I have about a quarter of a pint of pink gin in which the ice has nowhere near completely melted yet, and although it is on the deck I can easily reach it on account of the lowness of my chair. The sea is sending gentle pulsations through my stomach, and the breeze is twitching bits of my hair (so curly nowadays you would hardly know me) which reach below my hat (white, like the rest of my clothing, and bought before I realised that Lionel had one almost identical to it. The coincidence was not of my making). In short, I am very comfortable, positively enjoying myself, as so often since the turning-point in the desert.

I only hope you too are having a good time, but I don't think you can be. This letter is supposed to improve your state of mind. The opening wasn't, perhaps, very successful in that way: there's no great sense of purpose in it, and if it was meant only as a light introduction there should have been more about feasting and less about blood and severed feet and so on; I know these are painful subjects to you. I feel not only comfortable but also powerful, as if I am going to be able to make what is to come both more straightforward and pleasanter than anything which has been written by us since we set out. It's a long time since I in particular was allowed to use the pen, and now is a very good moment in our story to have the privilege.

So, on with the present: directly in front of me Lionel is leaning over the rail, and the sight of his buttocks and sloping back tell me that he wants and expects me to start a conversation with him, but I haven't any intention of doing so. The wind, stronger over there, is twitching his hat also, which I can just see, but I happen to know that it's fastened with a string; his hair, too, but his, of course, is still very short, and a lot lighter than we've known it on account of the sun. He doesn't know me well enough yet to start the conversation himself. I can also see that from the bar where the steward gets my gin, Karl and the two Raouls have just emerged onto the deck, and are making their way fairly steadily towards us. Karl is holding a glass of lager, which is heaving slightly like the sea. I should mention that since getting onto the ship Raoul seems to have been revelling in the new element, as if he's been out of his spiritual home for years; they're both shoeless and shirtless, wearing identical jeans, and have taken to wearing a single gold ear-ring, one on the right and one on the left. One has grown a very impressive black moustache and beard, but goes on shaving his cheeks and jaws; the other has only the usual darkness of the jowls we both know, but has found a telescope somewhere which he often applies to his face – in order, he says, to see things in the distance, but also changing the way he looks himself.

It is now obvious to me that the three are approaching Lionel without making it obvious to him. We all like to talk to him from time to time, but if we seemed too eager it would cause a lot of awkwardness, when we reached Liverpool if not before. They want him to say the first words, and indeed he has seen them out of the corner of his eye, and is turning round, and is talking to them as if they were only strolling: "Good morning, Karl, and Antonius, and – er – it is Antonius, isn't it?" "Yes, indeed." I haven't got time to describe all their actions, or even to say who it is who's talking most of the time, I expect, although it look as if Karl is going to do most of it, on our side at least. Fortunately at the moment he is letting Lionel think of the next thing to say, and Lionel seems to be finding it a bit difficult: I have time to say that Raoul is playing with his telescope, and directing it at a point rather foolhardily close to the sun. "I'm not yet quite sure I can trust you in this matter of names, Karl. I hope they aren't going to change again." Karl is drinking his beer. "Surely you know us all well enough by now not to need to worry about that any more. You must do, if Raoul knows *you* well enough..." "Which..." I'm having to miss some words out, not many though. "I envy you your stomach – I can't light my pipe till the middle of the afternoon. The strange thing is – I knew there was something strange – I've never known two brothers keep the same Christian name before, and now..." Bearded Raoul is picking his teeth. "It's really very calm, isn't it?" "Why do you pick brothers?" Raoul is saying this. "If we're cousins it's alright." "There are lots of cases, I should say, if you think about it. If they each have more than one

Christian name – most people do. It might be both their middle names, or one middle and one first, or both first with different middles. You can use whichever you like. People have favourite names, it might be their father's name – is it Raoul? – it might be the name of all male relations of both of them. Same with Quincey." "Quincey?" I suppose Karl'll now point at me, but I'm busy writing, not looking up. "Oh yes, is that his sister?" "I don't think so." My mistake – it's the other one they're talking about.

The chair is still empty – I can look up. He's playing one of those stupid deck games with Mabel, flinging rubber things over a net. How he can make such an ass of himself I don't know. I know I've never been the least bit inclined before to fight against my dislike of all these types of organised prancing. It's an opportunity to see Mabel in motion, of course. Not even Ahmed's dancing daughters had such an effect; the sweating round stomachs were almost too much, whereas Mabel's legs have just the right degree of self-consciousness. Playing this ridiculous game, too, is a way of expressing the desire to touch them, and makes it more likely that she'll let me. I don't suppose she's any happier about silly ball-games than I am, so it's a sort of mating-dance, purely a matter of instinct. It doesn't occupy my whole mind; not even Mabel does that. The others are obviously enjoying it – all looking, without really knowing it, in the same direction. Raoul at the back with his telescope – what efficiency! They've all just noticed, and there's a pause in their talk while they take it in, but they'll be embarrassed when they start again, because it's too long to be silent.

Karl spoke next, as he had spoken last: "No, it's not his sister." I could see why he said that. It was afterwards that Lionel turned round slowly to face him, and began also slowly to speak: "Yes, well, it's just that when someone new comes into the world – " "Not new." " – one feels obliged to give him a name which shows one wants to distinguish him from the ones who've gone before, so it's customary to choose a new name – " "Not new," Raoul repeated into his beard. " – not that I've had any children, though I have a famous father, of whom you've probably heard, and brothers – and preferably something which draws attention to a physical differentiation, or a peculiarity of behaviour – these things are very slight at first, of course, almost imaginary..." Raoul interrupted him, though not quite at the point where I have, and changed the subject completely.

"What's that?" he cried into his telescope, which is pointing almost straight into the sky. The other three all looked up, of course – so did I, for a while. I thought at first he meant the new clouds which had appeared, sailing across the sun without affecting the temperature or the light. It was fascinating to watch: the clouds seemed to be moving to the right, that is towards the stern (as this is the starboard side), but it occurs to me that as what wind there is is blowing in the same direction as the ship (north, I should think), trying to turn the pages backwards, and being to Mabel's disadvantage in the game, this is probably an illusion and the clouds are travelling with us too, but more slowly: not reading the letter Chinese-fashion, but being a few pages behind. Watching them go to the right, having excluded all things on the ship from your field of vision, and knowing that they're actually moving to the left, gives you a sort of sea-sick vertigo; you would expect the sun to be a fixed point by which you could judge all these different movements, but it, too, is moving north. You can never trust the sea, of course. The sky is white, and some of the clouds are moving faster than others (or perhaps I should say more slowly); when one veil passes in front of the sun there's sometimes still another behind it, moving past. The white light of the sun blends all the layers in front of it into a continuous vortex, like a pit with the sun at the bottom of it. There are no shadows. I thought at first that what Raoul had seen, if anything, was a cloud more clearly defined than the ones which had gone before, magnified into something strange by the peculiar narrowness of his field of vision. We all stared into the sky and watched the clouds, and went on watching them as Raoul didn't say any more.

"My father is a famous explorer," says Lionel's voice. The light still washes the deck, the same colour all over, and the sound of rubber hitting wood travels over the wood. I look up: yes, he's still staring into the sky, even though he's spoken! "You've obviously been a sailor in your time." I should think this makes Raoul smile – the one with the beard, at least. He's pleased, but will try to make his smile mysterious. "Perhaps that's how you came across Karl – in some ship or other?" They were looking at each other again by this time – all except the man with the telescope; but Raoul wasn't going to be drawn out.

Mabel is losing the game by five points to nothing, but although she seems to strive to get the rubber thing over the net (bouncing on stretched legs until her shorts make little ridges in her flesh) she is totally engaged in the much more subtle task of losing while appearing to play her best. The clouds all try to be last to reach the north, while appearing to race each other to the south; the page fills up while appearing to you to be already full.

"By the way, Karl, have you given any thought to that project of my father's that I told you about?" This is the big moment – "by the way", indeed! "Yes, I have, I'd like to hear more about it." ("Thwack!" from the rubber thing.) "It occurs to me – no disrespect of course – that you can't possibly be sure of the thing's getting off the ground." "My father..." "Yes, but what about you, personally? Have you ever been more than half a mile above sea-level?" "Yes, when climbing, in Switzerland – and I suppose in New York, not quite half a mile, perhaps." "But you've never been in an aeroplane?" "No, I always travel by ship. It's something to do with the windows in an aeroplane – I've seen them in films of course – views through little circular windows of the sun floating in great burnished expanses of blue, and down below nothing but a mass of white stuff, unbroken and unmoving, like potato salad..." ("Oof!" says Mabel, and staggers).

He's becoming emotional, and Karl is enjoying it. So is Raoul. "Yes, one of the frightening things is that although it looks so crisp and sustaining, you know that you would fall through it like a fork, through the blue and then through the white, without noticing the slightest increase in resistance, or being able to measure your fall either. I don't use aeroplanes any more than you do, and you can't be absolutely sure they'll work until you've been in one. I prefer a boat, and a good slow one at that. We chose this one because it goes a long way round. None of us likes changes of state coming just like that, without a long intermediate period – every state being boundless, or alternatively so short as not to exist, it seems unnatural to go from one to another as if you'd just jumped over a wall. My God! Raoul, give me your telescope! Hold my drink!"

Mabel has fallen. In a clatter of wood and a squeaking of rubber, she went down, having thoughtlessly got her limbs into a position where balance was impossible, or where the natural course of one interfered with that of another. She lay panting on the deck, thus not dead but possibly injured beyond repair, or suffering great pain. Some of us rushed towards her – not Karl, as it was something else entirely he wanted the telescope for, the fall happening an instant after he'd started to look through it – and offered to assist her. I got there first, being closest to her and quickest to observe her fall, and it was I who, relishing the warm white cotton, picked her up and helped her to a seat – one hand in a moist armpit – while she limped, probably from lack of imagination, at an ankle. Quincey wasn't far behind, however, and he stood over us, offering ineffectual hands and glowering at me, while we went through our little performance. His notebook lay blank on the deck twenty feet away, the breezes turning the pages as they wished; the pen lay by the gin he'd got to replace his sweat, ink drying and ice melting; the racket he'd bought at the ship shop in order to impress Mabel was abandoned elsewhere on the deck, warping in the sun.

Mabel leaned against me, flattening a breast and pressing with her bare good leg, and murmured, "Penelope". This was her sister, who, when I'd been in the bar persuading Mabel to play deck-tennis and that Quincey was a novelist of genius, had been sandwiched between Smallpox and Syphilis, apparently enjoying their conversation. I ought to say that these two have been developing a means of communication other than the written notes Smallpox used before they met. They can both make certain sounds with their twisted tongues and lips, though neither has the right ones for English, and the way in which they've been using the sounds they can make of late suggests a conscious purpose and, in short, a basic sort of language. I don't think anyone has taken any notice of this, except Penelope, or come to the conclusion I've just come to while writing; we've been vaguely aware only that the noises issuing from Smallpox and Syphilis, whenever they've happened to be near, have been growing in fluency and now sound much less like instinctive ejaculations than a sustained dialogue, in which certain combinations of sounds, whose obscurity suggests the working of intelligence, frequently recur and chime together like the refrain of a song. I'm sure we've all found ourselves repeating senselessly at odd moments one or another of these combinations, subtly conscious that it belongs to our twin friends but failing to attribute its order to their minds. Now that I've seen the pattern I can say it isn't like any other kind of speech, and couldn't be expected to make sense to an outsider. One peculiarity is that the language is different for each speaker: of the sounds they have at their disposal, Smallpox has command of the consonants, and Syphilis uses the vowels. Thinking of the separate words they form, I'm becoming convinced that two I especially remember, one of consonants and one of vowels, are their names for each other. Smallpox often makes, in a tone that suggests he's addressing Syphilis, a sound that might be "Irrked": and similarly frequently produces a noise which is quite close to being the written word, "Yaiyer". These are only rough attempts to spell the words, of course; "Irrked" (Syphilis) is a lot more guttural, and "Yaiyer" (Smallpox) more of a sing-song sound. Whether they have names for themselves I can't say - there wouldn't be as much need to use these - but they can't, anyway, be the same words, unless Smallpox uses "Irrked" to mean both Syphilis and himself, and Syphilis uses "Yaiyer" in the same way. Or – but it's too complicated. I must pay more attention to them, and write down what I discover. As I was saying, down in the bar the musicality of their speech was colouring my enjoyment, across the table, of Mabel's conversation, and as always by-passing my conscious recognition: but for the first time it must have been rising towards that recognition (possibly through the stirring-up influence of Penelope's sitting between them) and preparing in the absent parts of my mind that revelation which came on the last page before this. They were long bench-like seats, though with comfortable padded back-rests, and as Mabel told me what Quincey had been saying to her from his deck-chair I was turned completely towards her, with both hands on the leather in between her and me. I saw Penelope and her companions with my right eye only, and Karl and the two Raouls had just gone out of the range of my left, presumably on their way out of the bar. When Mabel began to repeat a long statement by Quincey on the art of narration, and my mind was thus half open to impressions from the trio on the opposite seat, the dialogue of the men was spasmodic, and Penelope with her occasional outbursts of peculiarly liquid laughter seemed to be echoing exclusively the vowelly remarks of Syphilis. I did not at the time consider whether echoing Syphilis in this situation amounted to addressing him, or whether on the other hand she was favouring Smallpox by using the sounds he was used to hearing. By the time Mabel had moved on to the subject of how tedious a long sea-voyage could so easily become, the conversation of the others had grown much more fluent and loud. Penelope, still merry although her two friends had not wholeheartedly accepted her as a talker, had started explosively trying to imitate the sounds they made, and her attempts, possibly because of her preconceived notions about funny noises, were almost wholly consonantal; thus whichever man she had seemed to be more *en rapport* with previously, her attention now appeared to have switched to his counterpart. That Smallpox and Syphilis were arguing is now obvious, and the way in which they clutched in turn at Penelope's fast-emptying glass suggests that the prize at stake in their argument was the privilege of getting her another quantity of dry martini - that or the privilege of staying beside her while the loser went to the bar. One sound which was rhythmically on Syphilis's lips at this time might be written "Ayoul", and it was answered repeatedly by a splutter from Smallpox, "Bvrrh". Penelope, catching the mood even through her own hilarity, began to inject into her imitations a rising placatory note, and the mirth inspired by this seeming success at her game, breaking through her guttural peacemaking in renewed spasms of the fluid laughter, made her appear to be mixing expressions from both forms of the language, and thus making communication a completely three-way affair. It was at about this time, when Irrked and Yaiyer were beginning to respond to Penelope's utterances, allowing her tone to affect the rise and fall of their own dialogue without actually claiming it, that Mabel and I arrived at a mutual decision to go up on deck. What they were talking about when we left I don't of course know, but they were ignoring Penelope's now completely empty glass and were tugging instead at her arms, greatly to her amusement, one on each side: their names for her appeared to be "Eoee" and "Plnp" respectively. What happened during the next few minutes, too, I can only conjecture, as Penelope's memory of the affair is blurred: they may have agreed to go to the bar together, in order to get her more drink of a stronger nature, in a different glass. They themselves do not drink in any of the bars, but they had probably stoked up sufficiently beforehand, in private. In any case, as Penelope continued to drink herself towards a similar state, the illusion of a three-sided colloquy must have crystallised and become something unconsciously assumed, rather than something to be marvelled at. As we seven followed our innocent pursuits on the deck, greater and greater intimacies were achieved and committed below; as I followed the game with half my mind, and the discussion of the relative merits of aeroplanes and ships with the other, the two defective men were happily helping Penelope up from her seat and staggering with her out of the bar. No-one saw fit to interfere with the jovial scene as they half-carried her up the steps; and in short the sight which caused Karl to halt his monologue and grab the telescope was that of Smallpox and Syphilis leading a willing but hysterical Penelope along the deck towards their cabin. Mabel, though sufficiently disturbed to lose her balance, is not so much older than her sister that she feels constantly protective towards her; on the other hand, they were both young enough to be accompanied on the voyage by their parents. Into the magnified circle of ship's scandal Karl saw penetrate a flustered Mr Chew, fluttering a pornographic magazine and glancing from side to side to be sure that his wife was not in sight of the manhandling of their daughter. A moment later, attracted by the distress of this passenger from whatever obscure part of the vessel he had been in, the captain, Lennox Jowler, arrived; and lowering the telescope, Karl, followed by Lionel and Clean-shaven Raoul, also rushed into the circle, hoping to avert the incident. Captain Jowler had succeeded in extricating Penelope and returning her to her father, while Smallpox and Syphilis backed away, gaping at what they had caused. Mr Chew had no idea what to do with his daughter – it seemed he was reluctant to touch her. Captain Jowler was saying, "Who is responsible for these men?", this being the formula closest to a request for an interpreter; Mr Chew responded well to the formula, and Karl to the request, introducing the captain to "Hector Smallpox and Hector Syphilis, both friends and colleagues of long standing." (Lionel was greatly interested in all this). Karl was quite accustomed, he said, to their seeming eccentricity: he had found over the years that their most subversive acts, upon examination into their motives, could be decoded either as their most innocent or as having a moderate constructive element. Mr Chew felt that the response to this should be his delayed outburst of moral rage, and having dealt with the two miscreants, who seemed on the point of flinging their arms round each other for protection, he turned his attention to a point further up the deck, proceeding, "And what do those three think they're doing with Mabel, half-naked as she is? They're some of your lot, aren't they?" The captain stuck his oar in at this point, something to the effect that, although he appreciated Karl's explanation, it was appearances that mattered when appearances were so far-reaching, and he would be obliged if our entire crew comported itself with more dignity in future. This shut Karl and Chew up, but Raoul put in an apology (not exactly complementary to Karl's) saying that, regrettable though such appearances were, they could perhaps be understood, in men that had been deprived of female society for upwards of ten years; at these words Penelope, who was by now nestling in her father's arms, let out a drunken giggle, and Lionel, who had been leaning over in the eagerness of his listening, cried, "I was convinced of it! You've all been on some ship for years on end – you're just the men I want!"

As for what Raoul had seen in the sky with his telescope, inquiry into that was naturally suspended, indeed it had already been forgotten as he made his excuse and bent over fainting Mabel (who I very quickly snatched from under Quincey's nose); but the matter was oddly and with growing frequency recalled to our minds by the incidents of the next few days. I had thought it might have been a cloud: well, it might have been, there's nothing about the subsequent events to say definitely that it wasn't, and clouds can resemble most things, especially when, as you've read, they're behaving strangely and apparently bent on deceiving you anyway. Captain Jowler is a sporting man, and would no doubt have encouraged us to make bets on the question if he had been aware of it. As it is he's spared no pains, Mabel's apprehensions not withstanding, to keep us all amused, and there is enough going on in the way of gaming to distract the sternest scientist from investigation of phenomena outside the ship. In addition to the traditional sweepstake on the distance travelled by the ship each day, there is a larger prize open to anyone who is prepared to speculate in greater detail on the contents of the ship's log, and who is able, in short, to produce by deduction of guesswork an absolutely accurate version of any particular day's entry. The entrant has to pay a fairly large sum each time he wants to make an attempt – hence the size of the prize – and considering that, in order to be successful, his version must be word-for-word identical to the captain's, the task before him would seem to be prohibitively difficult; however, a great deal of enthusiasm is shown by the few consistent competitors, who include Quincey and Jaffa, and the formal reading of their efforts (which are handed to the steward in sealed envelopes immediately before dinner) is always an occasion of excitement and jollity, usually forming the climax of the evening's entertainment. The captain obviously takes great pleasure in the performance, sitting smugly with the log itself open in front of him while the spurious entries are read – it is said that, in the very likely event of the voyage's finishing without anyone having successfully predicted the precise wording of any day's entry, the captain will consider himself the winner and will inevitably keep all the stake money; if this is so, he has good reason for appearing smug. He knows that the layman's conception of a ship's log is a mass of technicalities, and probably he thought to begin with that our entries would be merely random assortments of figures and abbreviations. He did not reckon with our sailing experience, which is solidly behind Quincey, nor obviously with the way in which less knowledgeable players were to benefit by our experience during the readings. His joviality is undiminished, however, and sometimes at the end of the ceremony he will heartily encourage us with some such remark as: "Very close indeed, Mr Horace – make it a little shorter next time and you'll be there." Quincey's attitude is confident throughout – the money is of no interest to him, but the game holds his attention to an extraordinary degree; Jaffa, on the other hand, is always rather tense, and listens to Quincey's attempts with great concentration, sometimes even making notes, which seems hardly fair. We know that he can't be short of money, but on the other hand perhaps he has to account for it to his father, who has after all financed this recruiting-trip of his, and that's what's making him anxious. I personally take no part in this particular game, but I do occasionally find half-an-hour's diversion in following yet another quest with has been organised by our playful captain: it seems that somewhere on the ship there is secreted a blue ball-point pen, with a silver button to extend and retract the point, with "S.S. NABUCCO" stamped on it in gold. Any contestant who, having bought a ticket, finds this pen and hands it to Captain Jowler, wins a prize of fifty pounds. Quincey says he should have nailed the money to the mast, but as the only mast is a little flagpole right at the front end it would have looked rather silly. This competition appeals to me more than the Log Symposium, as the other is called, at bottom because I'd rather be roaming about the vessel, breathing the sea air and generally seeing life, than locked up in the cabin, tussling with mathematical problems and scribbling on pieces of paper. Of the two of us, Quincey is definitely the scribbler: even now I am dictating this letter to you, and Quincey is writing it down. Indeed, he spends so much time writing one document and another that he is beginning to miss out on that general experience and those opportunities for observation which are essential to any writer aiming for success. Aware of the deficiency, he relies to some extent on me to compensate for it, and often when seeking the pen in obscure little corners I am also gathering material for him: for instance, quite soon he will be wanting to write an atmospheric piece concerning the sea and the other elements we are open to on the ship, in order to make our voyage seem more real to you, and as he knows little of their present state apart from what he can see in the little circle of his porthole, I am collecting details of their behaviour, which is admittedly extraordinary, and will later convey them to him. I assure him for my part that the passage several pages back about the clouds and the sunshine is really quite adequate, but he insists that we haven't yet done the thing nearly deeply or comprehensively enough. In the day following the incident I have described, therefore, I spent much time promenading the deck; in the night, too, as I thought this might be what he meant by "comprehensively", and as I didn't in any case want my rival pen-hunters to spot me investigating the rather ingenious hiding-places I had begun to devise. (The nightly noises in our cabin, moreover, had become too loud and impassioned to allow a sleeper any comfort.) During the afternoons I would often find Karl and Bearded Raoul working together, with compass, sextant and plumb-line, either calculating distances or putting together a complete joint contribution to the Log Symposium. I had seen the compass before, of course, and its fellow which had been buried in the desert, but the sextant and the plumb-line were new to me, and I could not imagine where they had found them. Later they added to their equipment a huge chart, done in a dazzling number of different shades of blue and green, over which they would bend, talking in figures, deducing either our position from their observations or the things they couldn't observe from our position; and this too, it seemed to me, was a new acquisition. They were secretive about all their operations, shutting up as soon as they saw me; and Raoul, in another part of the ship with his telescope still pointing up into the sky, did not confer with them. He was to be seen engaged in his studies for increasingly lengthy periods after the morning of Penelope's near-abduction. He became tired of holding the telescope at such an acute angle from the vertical, and on Wednesday afternoon appeared with a tripod, its legs fully extended and spread wide apart so that he could recline in a deckchair, set at its lowest position, underneath it. Like me, he did not confine his activities to the day time: it was when I came upon him one night, recumbent under brass on which the moon and stars glinted, that I realised where the telescope had come from. When we see you in England, as I hope to persuade you that we must, I'll make sure that he returns your property to you. Clouds, then, were not the object of his inquiry, although later an unparalleled thick blanket of cloud, ochre-yellow and opalescent, so oppressive that our lungs seemed full of hot clay and our heads ached noisily, was to cover the stars and moon completely, replacing their white effulgence with its own dull sodium-glare. He may have been trying to remember or even, to work out from scratch – a formidable task – how to plot our course by the stars; on this occasion, however, the telescope seemed to be trained unerringly on the moon, and on another night, when I heard him give a gasp of hope fulfilled, it was following the long, slow curve of what appeared to me to be a shooting-star, obviously unsuited to the purpose of fixing our position.

It was on the Wednesday a week after the first appearance of your tripod that the results of Raoul's researches were made public, if they could be called results. Karl, having convinced the captain of his responsibility during the rape affair, had contrived to join us for dinner at the latter's table; I, of course, had long since endeared myself to the captain by my devotion to his game, and the other regulars were Mabel, Lionel, and Sir James something, an astronomer. Entries in the Log Symposium had been submitted, and the fish soup consumed in the customary atmosphere of expansive tension. The prize for guessing distance only had been presented (to Lionel) before dinner as always; no entrant to the Symposium proper, it is needless to say, was so inexperienced as to have had his hopes dashed by the revelation of this single detail. What kept the impatient guessing was how long after the cheese course they would have to wait, and whether the matter would be resolved while the coffee was still warm. We had in store, we knew (although it was impossible to tell in advance which evening was to be occupied by each of these entertainments) at least one recital by the female singer, Señorita da Roseata, who was sitting at another table; and also a talk on some scientific subject by Sir James, who when pressed says modestly that it will very likely consist of some reflections on the Laws of Probability. This Sir James is very acidic about the log Symposium, maintaining that the prizes being won by anyone but the captain is, of all the ideas he has know, the closest to being a real impossibility. The prize this evening stood at £11,375. We were discussing, at our table, the terms Captain Jowler would have used to describe the odd behaviour of the elements: all concerned were confident of their essential formulae, but some were fearful of the new elaborations he might have introduced to match the peculiarity of the weather; on the subject of which the man himself remained politely impenetrable, to the probings of Lionel in particular. "The sea is especially rough tonight, isn't it?" was one of these, and indeed the unanchored tray of assorted chutney moved at that moments gracefully a few inches to the left, as if intending to tour the table but changing its mind after the first day. Sounds of jollity from the other two tables showed that the wave had been felt there too. Having checked that no-one wanted any more, the captain had the chutney taken away, its freedom of choice removed. Following Lionel's drift, I further excited his fears: "Turbulence of this kind isn't only dependent on the wind, of course." "I thought not." "It wouldn't be enough just to record the wind speed at the usual times." "What is it, then, the moon?" Here Karl was overcome by the heat of the dish, and spluttering into his wine, was sent a reproving look by the captain; Sir James, only half raising his head, said, "I don't know why you chaps are so damn cock-sure about the wind, anyhow; once the captain here knows you've latched onto the six-in-the-morning six-in-the-evening routine, It's obvious he's going to change it, isn't he?"; and to complete the summary of events around the table, Mabel, sitting on my left, was so affected by the violence of a new wave, which wasn't however, so much stronger than the last as to cause much more rollicking among the other diners, that she swayed heavily against me, and as I happened to be reaching for my handkerchief at the time, brought a tight-clad thigh into contact with my hand. The captain, sitting at the end of the table to her left, addressed me: "I hope it isn't on account if the rough weather that your friend Mr Antonius isn't with us?" My relations with Mabel, obviously, weren't such as to make the clasping of her thigh a particularly daring act, as in the lower bunk I had seen a pair of them laid completely open, but it was a new kind of pleasure, perhaps, this sort of private fondling which in our present position could be performed by no-one but me; I lent it weight by turning to look over my left shoulder, obediently seeking Raoul. "The clean-shaven Mr Antonius, of course, I mean," the captain explained as my eye discovered the other in the top right-hand corner. He was unenviably flanked by Smallpox and Syphilis, who had come down for social purposes and were inhaling only boiled rice; as Mrs Chew, on the former's left, however, vacantly smiled at their exotic sallies, Raoul was able to bypass them all in favour of Penelope, who, dressed in exactly the same manner as her sister, faced him from the opposite end of the table. There was a third table, also seating six and also full; and it was true that there were normally seventeen, being minus two Hectors and plus one Raoul. I owed as much to the Captain, but could not explain; I had worked my left hand down the inside of Mabel's thigh and, palm upward, under her posterior, while she, deceitfully raising herself, had then sat hard on my upturned hand, so that I could not free it without powerfully jerking the table. The question was, could the peculiar angle of my arm, tending to its point below the table, mean anything more innocent to the others? I laid down my fork, and immediately regretted it, because I had done so in order to pick up a chapatti with the other hand; and the natural thing being to pick it up with my left, seemed to attach a great weight of guilt to my fixed, disappearing arm. No good to stop now, of course: my right arm must continue its manoeuvre, and put as good a face on it as it might. "What about the colours?" said Lionel, and I leaned over, disproportionately interested: "The colours... the colours..." I said. "As for the chances of the colours in the sea being the same to the captain here as to yourself," Sir James heaved in, still without completely raising his head, "quite apart from the likelihood of his using the same terms to describe them if they were..." he stuffed the sentence with prawns. "It seems to me to be far more probable that he'll be writing about the comets." "The comets... the comets...?" the hot nylon was making my hand sweat, and my forehead too; I pushed an empty plate away as I spoke, and rigidly held onto the wine-glass directly in front of me. The captain looked amused, but it was obvious to me that he had no idea about any comets; and at that moment the steward came in and whispered something in his ear about Mr Antonius, upon which he started (not a long enough start, unfortunately, to cover the extrication of my hand) and said, "Good Lord!" I had just decided I would have to wait for the next wave and pretend to be thrown from my seat, when he said some words to the steward which sent him away, then reflected, said to all of us "The more poetic events, of course, have no place in a ship's log," reflected further, and finally to my tormentor, who had been unusually silent throughout the meal, saying, "Miss Chew, were you and your sister not going to give us a vocal duet? Unless, Sir James...?" It was my salvation: Sir James smacked his lips and said "Not tonight", and Mabel, turning to confabulate over her shoulder with Penelope, who was sitting back-to-back with her, had perforce to raise very slightly her right buttock, in order to pivot on her left. The sisters were directly behind each other because the table at whose head Penelope sat was at right angles to Mabel's: a mere turn of the head would not have been enough – and it was Mabel's right though her left would have been just as useful for my purposes, and Penelope's left buttock which rose, probably because the captain had been the last person to address Mabel, and her mother Penelope – on the same subject, as it happened, although Mrs. Chew had fixed on it more or less at random in trying to escape from Smallpox and Syphilis, whose speech she was finding she could not cope with.

The meal being virtually over, and my right hand free, I was by this time busy writing: no time for social niceties. In order to communicate with Raoul, however, Mrs. Chew must perform with her powers of attraction what might be compared to the move of a knight in chess; she did so, only to find that Raoul was talking in signs with Karl along the diagonal of the room. So poor Mrs. Chew was isolated. Karl, I noticed, was manipulating something under his table: It was not, I felt, likely to be the thighs of either Quincey or Jaffa; as he vigorously indicated it to Raoul, and I almost lay my left cheek on the page in order to see it, I saw it to be a book – and as he swung it round behind his chair, apparently uncertain what to do with it, I began to imagine in the limp leather of its cover a resemblance to the only other book in sight: the log-book upon which the captain was at that time resting his elbow, while he spoke to Quincey. At this point, the steward bringing round coffee and liqueurs, there was a tremendous reshuffle of the seating: Raoul rushed in and began to speak in whispers with his counterpart, as a steward, it seems, had earlier done with the captain; Penelope and Mabel leapt up and went over to the piano, followed from the third table by one of the young men who accompany Señorita da Roseata; Mrs Chew, having spotted this move, and being politely address by Smallpox ("Bvrrh cg, brssdn?") while Syphilis renewed the sounds of suction over his cold rice, virtually flung herself across the room and took the young man's seat adjacent to her husband and the foreign lady, who had been conversing warmly since the start of the meal; and finally the Raoul who had lately appeared finishing his whispered talk with Raoul walked unsteadily round to occupy the chair vacated by Mrs Chew, thus placing himself opposite me. The vocal duet began; it became obvious after a very few seconds that the point of the piece was for the girls to imitate cats. There was accordingly no need for Raoul and me to be silent, unless I needed silence for my writing, as our low speech-tones blended nicely and not at all impolitely with the musical squawling. The others were quite quiet. There was no need for Raoul to be silent, either, because the only people likely to overhear his surprising remarks were Smallpox and Syphilis, who, though they might understand them, could not convey them to anyone but each other since they had abandoned their written notes in favour of spoken language. It seems he had begun to speak to his bearded fellow about the shining object he had just seen falling towards the earth, having earlier blurted it out to the steward and having chosen his twin for a second, more intimate audience; but he had found him in a very excitable state, hissing (or violently whispering) instructions he had really wanted to yell across the room to Karl, upon whom his eyes had been fixed throughout their discussion. He had responded to Raoul's whispered revelations with sidelong jerks of the head which the eyes had not followed, and had mixed up his replies to them with the slightly louder instructions. He had given the impression that the revelations were not sinking in, any more than Karl was receiving or understanding his messages. "Mi-a-u", sang Penelope very prettily. "These things he was hissing," Raoul said to me, "were all to do with something Karl had to foist off on the captain, you know, 'Do it now, he won't notice', 'Pretend you want the sugar', 'He's taken his elbow off it', and so on. I don't know if you've noticed but Karl's got a book in his hand." I said I had. "Do you want to know what I think they've been doing?" "Who?" "Karl and Raoul. That book is an exact duplicate of the captain's log which they've made together. Karl is somehow going to substitute it for the real thing, and once they've got their hands on that they'll copy out today's entry and win the Log Symposium." "But the entries have all gone in – they'll be reading them out in a minute." "Well, I can only suppose that Karl will bring it over to Raoul, they'll copy it out quickly at his place, and seal it in an envelope, and then Karl will go back over there and substitute the new entry for the one they've already got in;" (the small pile of envelopes was now standing at the captain's other elbow) "Or perhaps Raoul will do that – perhaps that's his part of the bargain, as I presume they'll be halving the proceeds – though of course if they change places, the captain is more likely to be on his guard." "I should think that, if this is true, the providing of a place near these two" (Smallpox and Syphilis) "is enough to guarantee Raoul a share of the prize." The girls' voices seemed to be dying away into soft growling purrs, and throughout the room there ran a premonition that they were drawing to a close. I could see the captain's fingers softly drumming on the envelopes which they were itching to open; on the faces of Sir James and Lionel were written distaste and an enduring surprise respectively; Señorita da Roseata, at the other table, had half-closed eyes and a patronising smile, which meant that she would allow no-one to speak however grating she herself found the pretty singers' inaccuracies; while Mr Chew fidgeted to carry on getting to know her, and the presence of his wife made it less likely every moment that he would. Perhaps the only two people positively interested in an encore were Karl and Raoul, whose indecision and impatience were patently increasing; but the young man's contented tinkling, in any case, suddenly erupted again with a volley of howls and screeches from the sisters, and the room relaxed. Lionel began to look green, and seemed on the point of leaving. "On the other hand," Raoul continued, "if it's an exact duplicate, why do they need the real one?" "It's probably identical with the one exception of today's entry, which will be missing. If they had the real one for long enough to duplicate it, it must have been before six o'clock – and if they'd had it after six, they would have copied out today's entry already, and there'd be no need for this substitution." "Unless," Raoul slowly continued, "that's the real one in Karl's hand, and the duplicate in front of the captain." We now became conscious that Karl was standing in the region of the captain's chair. The ship was rolling – had been for some time, more and more heavily; the swaying of Karl's upper half was most conspicuous. Some of the ululations in the singers' voices, too, were not entirely intentional. We did not see the substitution itself: only that he was bending over, perhaps thanking the captain personally for the honour of a place at his table. Then with an increasing stagger he made his way to Raoul's corner. The song was ending and applause bursting out, and in the confusion he and Raoul were busy with some writing, quite of what we couldn't see, mainly on account of the enthusiastic table-thumping of Smallpox and Syphilis. I also was writing. It was of no concern to me whether that particular team won the Log Symposium, or by what method; I felt a faint admiration for their resourcefulness, but certainly no envy or competitive spite. Raoul, losing interest too, was telling me his own story (as told to the steward and Raoul) but I wasn't listening. The girls had taken their bows, smoothing down their dresses, had been kissed by the young man, and were now sweeping and stumbling back to their places. Raoul meanwhile crossed at right angles to their course, leaving the book with Karl but presumably carrying a new sealed envelope with enclosure somewhere about his person. The captain was standing to make his speech introducing the reading, so he'd have to be quick. Something about ending the party at an earlier time than usual, on account of the storm – we must all go and lash ourselves into our bunks. This was not a serious suggestion. I bent to my writing. Penelope flung herself into the chair beside me, breathily hot and excited, obviously ready to talk and already, indeed, making high speech-like noises. I was not prepared to converse but, my right hand being free, I reached over to clasp her knee again. The hand was instantly brushed away with a hysterical movement, and I looked up into the flustered but delightful face of Mabel, who had for some reason during the singing of the song agreed to change places with her sister.

It was shortly after this that we went up on deck to find the atmospheric conditions as I have already described them. The pain and the heat, combined with the swaying, made me think I had drunk too much at dinner: this was not the case, of course, though abstinence might have eased a little this inevitable sickness. Lionel was leaning over the rail again, as if waiting for his indisposition to strike. Above his head little blue flashes played about the edges of the vomit-thick clouds. Penelope had run on ahead to our cabin, and Mabel to theirs, and Quincey and I were lagging painfully, complaining of the weather. We also complained of the fact that, although the girls would not allow us into their cabin, Mabel had to stay there all night; this was in case their mother made enquiries at the door, Mabel being able to imitate the high tones of her sister, but Penelope unable to go any deeper.

"I'm wondering if Penelope is such a good substitute," said Quincey, himself sounding strained. "There's her voice, and the way she cowers against the wash-basin until we go in..." "But you hardly know her. Now, if it were Mabel who came..." "She might be just as bad, and I personally would be justified in speaking, yes: still, she's a fine girl during the day..." "And so is Penelope at night. Leave her to me, I tell you – you know you didn't get on with her at the end of the meal. I assure you it's well worth her staying the night in our cabin."

So we moved on to other subjects, comparing knowledge of Raoul's and Karl's activities from our separate quarters of the dining-room, and examining the lowering sky for any signs of Raoul's flaming object. It was an effort to look up, but we saw it several times, exclaiming, "There it is!" and "Is that it?" as if in anguish.

By the time we reached the cabin, it was with a feeling that the tension must shortly relax, but as we shut the door behind us, things only got worse; the porthole had to remain shut, and the hot little space seemed to oscillate and plunge twice as wildly as the deck. In the darkness – for none of us lit the lantern – Penelope was cowering even more tremulously than usual. After a few seconds she said, very metallically, "It was odd, the captain losing his log-entry like that, wasn't it?", and her tone drew the oppression in closer. She tried once or twice more to get the subject of the Log Symposium going, but Quincey and I had lost even the small degree of sympathy which had been evident during our walk to the cabin, and we merely climbed in unison into our respective bunks, Quincey making some gruff enquiry about the song she had sung, to which she replied, "Rossini".

I like the upper berth because it brings me close to the porthole, through which I have a view of the sea even when my head is on the pillow, and I have always been attracted to windows, as you know. It was only by pure force of personality that I made Quincey take the lower one. Tonight the view was of huge hill-like waves, which still didn't very often burst into foam, but simply rose as if forced upward and subsided again, a deep purple like wine in the hollows, and shot through with the yellow light to make a kind of pale brown at the summits. Sometimes a wave would completely engulf the window, and I would have a momentary vision of its interior, a complex of white bubbles which belied the false colours of the sea's surface. Otherwise the corrugated vista stretched, darkly, further than I could calculate, and unnaturally visible, with a clear luminous space in between the clouds and the sea; as I fixed on that unending emptiness, it was the point where the elements met I sought, not the point where they could be separated.

Turning to the room, I dimly saw the top of Penelope's head as she undressed, and the top of the mirror. The ceiling was very close, and I seemed oddly estranged from events in the lower part of the room; however, the grunts and mewed half-protests almost at once revealed that Penelope had been diverted on her way up to my bunk, and that Quincey was further testing the inexplicable partiality of the sisters. Jealousy did not enter into it, but I was intensely angry, feeling that the situation should be kept as clear-cut as possible, and that Quincey would succeed only in confusing us all; so I began to expound my very obvious theory that the log containing today's entry was now, and had been at the end of dinner, in the possession of Raoul and Karl – that the new entry they had submitted was correct, and that they had failed only in not switching the two logs back after copying it out. Penelope's head appeared, thrusting itself upward, but the expression on her face showed that she was still subject to some interference from below. I helped her up by the arms; from Quincey the only response was, in tones of (surely misplaced) sarcasm, "So unless they give him the book back tonight, he'll be writing out a new entry for today, presumably thinking he's had some kind of black-out." Heat, anger and the aforementioned confusion had unfitted me for sexual activity: I lay propped on one elbow above Penelope's unpleasantly sweating torso, staring at a slightly larger portion of the mirror in which the sea was suggested. After a few seconds Penelope said, in the same voice as before, "I wonder whether he'll use the copy your friends submitted, or..."

The slight turning movement which had gone with this became at that moment a spasm of panic as a violent lurch of the vessel coincided with a volley of deafening gun-shots from outside. She screamed before burying her face, and Quincey leapt out of bed, landing with a thud on the floor. Presumably this was an attack, and he was showing our fitness and courage; pulling on his underpants, he ran out of the cabin. As our tooth-mugs slid off the little glass shelf, however, and the ship continued to swing and toss through what appeared to be a complete hemisphere, although we were doubtless still making some lateral progress, it became obvious that what had hit us was a violent storm; the gunfire, though still like powerful, wide-barrelled cannonry, had become thicker and more extended, reverberating almost continuously. It was thunder blanketing the whole sky, crashing in the foreground and rolling into the distance with the piled-up repercussions of further crashes. The ship stood on its stern for a number of seconds, and I gripped the tubular framework of the bunk above me.

Overhead a lump in the upper mattress showed where Penelope was writhing, whether from terror, sleeplessness or a simple inability to keep her balance. Head raised from the pillow, arms extended and grasping the metal tubes, I was riding the ship as if it were a child's swing; it occurred to me that I might clamber up and stage Quincey's return, but I was enjoying my immediate sensations too well – more like something in a fairground, I decided, with the stomach-turning lurches at the peaks of the vibrations. The joints in the framework were creaking wildly, and in the outer of the two supposedly horizontal tubes which were repeatedly jarred by Penelope's mobile shape, an object, dislodged from some weak former stability, was rattling up and down almost the whole length of the bed, pausing for a moment before following the direction of each new slant. After a minute more of the rocking and imagining Penelope's body, my curiosity drove me to stick a tiny portion of a finger into a hole in the tube, and stop the object in its flight. Impossible to get it out of there, however; at length I crawled out of bed, and winding my limbs round the normally upright corner-post, tackled the end of the tube, undoing a nut which had been jogged loose. The object emerged: a ball-point pen, blue with gold lettering – "S.S. NABUCCO" – only slightly chipped in my struggles with the metal cage. I stared at the pen, and then put it in the breast pocket of my pyjamas. The enchantment of the cabin had gone. I checked that Penelope was hidden by the sheet, and then began to look for the door, holding on to everything that still stood in my way.

The storm was raging: like the thunder, wind and rain were everywhere, and they strove to force everything in nature into ubiquity. Wind thrust observer and pen like shuttles into a vast sequence of new places, and wherever they were they were thrashed as if they hadn't moved. Wind and rain were both pan-pipe shaped, galleries of pulsing cylinders pushing out to any distance and roaring down to any pitch; unseen sources of light shot-wove beams across the two series, flashing into visibility the white pipes of rain in their extending shapes. A search-light pivoted from the ship's funnel; brilliant networks projected instantly into every quarter of the black hemispherical screen; and violently flung lamps exploded everywhere in the air and water, lighting up their own electric curling tracks. The flashes threw the tossed wires and ropes of the ship, too, into momentary agonised shapes. The fury struck the observer as a film, a succession of still moments, each lit from new angles and too short and frenzied for him to see the pattern. Sea in the chaos seemed indistinguishable from rain: the black mass of it was invisible, hidden by a lashing white forest, and the unbroken torrent of the deck went from depth to depth by sudden degrees, giant street-gutter to cataract to a universe of water, in which the ship was lost without angle or depth, without bearings or observer.

Grotesque backsurges of water saw Lionel hanging on his rail, swimming and dragging with his feet, pulled towards the whirling centre of the ship, but pulling with his arms the other way, as if over the rail, arching himself into the sea, and hurling something at it with his body, unheard screamed abuse or answering torrents; others scuttled where they could in little tattered groups, breaking and pulling themselves together again, shouting in each other's faces, and all jabbering about the sky, where through the flickering glimpses of monumental light-patterns two great forces could be seen growing, a source of light and a source of darkness shuddering closer, and beginning to dominate the struggle with their opposed simple answers.

A pit opened in front of the ship, and the black of the sea showed in huge glistening slopes, expanding like shot. The decks tipped down into the field, and the floods see-sawed like the pen in the tube. An infinite number of dark moments passed, then with a clattering of branches overhead we were again at once on the crest and in the gulf, upside-down with a half-imagined crashing in our ears.

In lighted upper parts of the ship Karl and Raoul were leaping like apes, Raoul seeming naked with his trousers cut short at the knees, and Karl in sou'wester and long cape over the evening-dress he had worn at dinner. They were hopping from pinnacle to pinnacle, from the bridge to the tip of a wave, crouching and springing and lying back in the water, trusting the gravity of the ship to bring them down again onto the poop. Like eager looters, they stooped to pick things up and drop them again, or Karl to stuff them inside his jacket, desperately or drunkenly unconcerned about injury and death, probably invulnerable. Of the two forces cutting through the storm, the light was dawn or the sun deprived, like everything else, of its uniqueness and spread uniformly through the cloud. To the observer the shades of greater light were of lessened contrast, and the storm seemed to enter a quieter movement, the thunder clearer and more distant, its reverberations deadened by the thicker blanket. One little group held together on the bridge, and clustered round a telescope; it proved to be Quincey, Raoul and the captain, still with streaming faces, and still clutching things and shouting, but parting to let Sir James Baconbury look through the telescope. They were watching the growth of the darkness, which was to the west of the ship, and near the climax of its geometric expansion.

It was Raoul's flaming object, dulled by the atmosphere and by its closeness. Even before it hit the water the captain had sent the first mate hurrying to start lowering the boats, for it was three times the size of the ship, man-made, with a window. Quincey and Raoul could recognise it, although Sir James showed signs of refusing to believe in its existence. With its shock-wave ended another phase of the storm, and the ship set to rolling in a rhythm violent but familiar. The rain at last made its distinct, powerful voice heard, and the thunder came at intervals, alternating clearly with the lightning. I stayed with the captain as he went down to where the boats were being lowered; the first mate and a number of sailors, dressed like Karl, were working around boat number six in the part of the deck where Lionel was hanging, exhausted, on his rail.

I leapt into the boat as it swung out over the sea, although Lionel was calling, perhaps to me, "You can't go out in that! It'll turn over, leave them to it!" He seemed possessed still by the hysteria of the storm, which we others had forgotten, and as our keel hit the water I heard him screaming to be audible above the shrouds of rain. Through the bottom of the boat the sea was a powerful elastic force; we drove through the waves, the mate standing in the bows to see more clearly. I had taken an oar, and the pen I had thrust into my underpants pressed as I pulled, against my stomach. My whole body was streaming with warm water; I was carefree, like Karl and Raoul, staring at the dripping capes of the sailors.

The mate called out to us how we were to steer; I turned and watched him balancing finely in the prow, and hundreds of yards in front of him the great ship which had already almost disappeared, the thin front end being the last part to show, almost vertically, above the water, with the control-room in the nose, and your room, with its circular window, just vanishing in a turmoil of bubbles and steam. The sky was dark in this quarter; when the sodden survivors began to crawl over the gunwales they were black human shapes, rolling down among the feet of the sailors. Nonetheless I recognised Quincey, drenched not in underpants or pyjamas but in the khaki ex-army stuff I had thrown away when I bought my white outfit. I was resting on my oar and gazing at him as he raised his head; he saw me and whispered, "God!" Then I asked, "Is there another?", and he said, "Yes, out there somewhere." The other two to join us were like Smallpox and Syphilis, and they had contrived to make a buoyant shape with linked arms; one of them began at once to ask for a cigarette in sign-language, which caused a lot of hilarity. Around us the other boats were picking up more of the bobbing shapes; we could only take three, so after all the stopping and turning we pulled back towards the ship, and the mate sat down. The space-ship had gone, still suspended, doubtless, in the dark body of the Atlantic.

Over the ever-deepening thunder a new, sharp percussion was sounding irregularly, touching, like the dawn, lightly on our waking senses. It was not until we were bumping against the side of the ship that I realised it was the firing of a pistol, and the bullets were flopping into the water around us. It was quite dark below the ship on the port side, but I sensed an extra turbulence, or struggling, in the water, and a glutinous quality where it lapped and churned. I wet my hand and held it inches from my eyes, but could not see any dark stain. As we climbed the ladder the shooting stopped, and the first thing I saw on the grey-lit deck was Lionel in the grip of the steward, desperately holding onto his revolver, red-faced and screaming incomprehensibly about 'them' and 'they'; the mate went to help the steward, and they led him off.

That evening (the evening of Thursday, December 6th) there were five of us in the cabin, and poor Penelope was again all but forgotten in the upper bunk, while we four steadily made our way through a bottle of whisky from the duty-free shop, and chatted about our situation; she did, however (the dear girl), get through at least her fifth of the liquor, and between four and five she began to entertain us from the bed with a modified version of her high part in Rossini's duet. The day had been spent in fixing up the newcomers with white clothes, ours being suitably dry as a result of our not having worn them during the storm, and in deciding where they were to sleep, if ever, whether we were to change our names, and such practical questions. Within the other two groups of four no doubt similar arrangements had been made; poor Karl, however, was a special case, having been put in the sick-bay suffering from severe exhaustion and other debilitating illnesses which hadn't as yet been identified. He had caught one of Lionel's bullets in the shoulder, which aggravated his general condition, and in delirium he had not spoken comprehensibly since entering the ship. Karl was sitting with him all the time, perhaps hoping for a word or sign of recognition, and could not be coaxed away. The bullet had been removed, but still the vigil was wasting him, and it had become hard to tell who was the weaker of the two. Lionel himself had not appeared; it was generally assumed that he had been confined to his cabin, not actually in chains, being a distinguished and respected passenger, but perhaps locked in while the hysteria lasted. The captain appeared to feel sympathetically towards him, chuckling when his exploit was mentioned, and refusing to comment when asked whether bodies had been sought or recovered.

Another subject on which he exercised his discretion was that of the land which had been sighted off the port bow. That we were making for it he conceded: we *might well*, he said, have been thrown considerably off course during the storm; we had certainly lost large quantities of fuel, equipment, and provisions, to say nothing of mechanical efficiency, which necessitated our putting in at the nearest port. What he did not reveal was the name of the port. Quincey said that perhaps it was Gibraltar, but this seemed to me on a number of counts to be an absurd suggestion. It was to be supposed that the captain's reticence on all these points was designed to throw us off the scent in the Log Symposium, which figured largely in all his dealings, if not in ours. There was little doubt that he suspected us of somehow effecting his previous day's log-entry's disappearance, whether by hypnosis or some more sinister practice. He was mistaken, of course: we were innocent, and our interest both in Lionel and in our port of call entirely personal; not even bearded Raoul, I think, had taken the trouble to establish our new position. Raoul had in his possession a stack of literature, acquired swiftly over the past two days, all pertaining to the log. Perhaps he was now attempting to interest his three doubles in it, and meeting with various degrees of response.

This competition and the other were, naturally, among the matters to be debated by the four of us over our whisky. Quincey and I introduced the theme by displaying the two pens which we had under our pillows: the one which I had found sellotaped to the underside of a bar table, and had then transferred to the framework of the bed, with the idea of fooling both the captain and Quincey (who had taken the Pen Hunt more seriously than I at that stage, you will remember); and the one which I had discovered upon inserting a rowlock into the gunwale of boat number six, and finding the hole obstructed. The latter had been thoroughly squashed during my attempts to shove the rowlock in, the plastic split and the spring-mechanism destroyed. Both were sorry objects, the legend "S.S. NABUCCO" reduced by several letters, the barrels waterlogged and the whole pens as pens quite impossible to use. The new Quinceys were very conscious of these defects, and although they obviously tried to grasp the significance of the exhibits, knowing that we would not deceive them, they could not see how such battered and worthless trophies had displaced what they saw as their true quest from our minds, or even became a symbol of it; Quincey assured them that each pen was worth fifty pounds, and I, in explaining the Log Symposium, estimated the prize to be offered on the following evening as something in excess of twenty thousand, but these sums understandably meant nothing to them, and all they could talk of, when invited to comment in the light of this on their own concerns, was Lionel.

The one sitting by the wash-basin claimed to have been the invader of the space ship we had seen, rather than the original member of its crew, and that he had killed Lionel. I felt that he was the one I had less in common with, and it was gratifying later to find that Quincey had felt the reverse. He was a little too aggressive, I thought; when we told them that Lionel was actually locked away somewhere on the ship, he drew his knife and was going to demand to be taken to him. You also, my dear Spingo, had been killed again; I'm sure we need make no apology for this, as newspaper reports we have received lead us to believe that you would have taken the same course of action yourself. We have no information until you reply on how you would react to the repeated rape and torture of Miss Keogh. For the time, at least, we succeeded in quieting Quincey, and I hope we have encouraged them to skip a step in the emotional evolution we have all undergone. You cannot, however, expect everyone to have *exactly* the same feelings towards you when we eventually meet. We told them we had written to Lionel, warning him of our approach; we also told them of our later decision that, although it was unnecessary to actually cancel this letter, it would be as well to write a new one, to you, outlining the changes in our intentions, insofar as such vague changes could be outlined. They agreed to subscribe to the new letter.

Again we watched dawn taking over: none of us now had had any sleep for two days and nights, and the light coming through the porthole seemed pulsating feebly, partly the whisky in our heads no doubt making us think we caught fleeting unaccountable shadows round the edges. We roused that extraordinarily pretty girl, Penelope – (she has a sister!) –

who, though after an hour of spasmodic sleep on top of the whisky she must have been feeling awful, sprang up with a wonderful effort to be enthusiastic, and said, "I'd love to see the dawn!"; then the five of us went up on deck. The sea was dead and the air alcoholically clear, so we could plainly see the Mid-Atlantic Ridge where it had pushed itself up at various points around here. There was a cluster of rocks to the left, and twenty or thirty miles behind them an island, purple with the distance. Penelope led a little procession along the rail towards the bow, off which was a second, larger island, about the same distance from us. After a long silence the seafaring Quinceys, in a short dialogue, confessed their ignorance; we told them with a degree of pride that the rocks were the Formigas, and the islands the easternmost of the Azores, Santa Maria and São Miguel respectively. We had known where the space-ship was likely to come down, you see. Quincey, the nominal commander, had hoped until almost the last moment that we would reach Africa, though we seemed to be locked in a slow spiral. Still, it is pleasant to see these islands again, and to be in Ponta Delgada.

I have been reading through the letter, but it is hard to concentrate, and I'm unable to grasp the central theme. It's enjoyable reading in places – I like the passage in the present tense. The other four are slumped in various positions around the table, more or less asleep. Quincey sometimes stirs enough to take a sip of wine, but Penelope's chin is on her breast, her hair in her glass, and she's gently snoring. A dish of crabs and another of oysters, in the centre of the table, remain untouched except by flies. One of the things I appreciate in Quincey's present tense section is the introduction to Mabel, who has been taken, I believe, by her parents on a sight-seeing trip around the city. Have they forgotten Penelope, or even given her up? The others seem wide awake: Raoul has made friends with a whole party of Dutch seamen, and they have noisily blended in, the four of them dotted among the group at the next table seeming a natural part of the rowdy uniformity; and Lionel has emerged, subdued but more friendly, and is sitting in a circle on the harbour-wall with Smallpox, Syphilis, and the newly-christened Cystitis and Streptococci.

I ought to say that these two have accepted without question their names, perhaps inferior as longer, passed to them and to us on pieces of paper. Their language has had to be corrupted, and the communication of the five sitting cross-legged on the harbour-wall appears to an observer like myself an utterly perplexing mixture. There are, I suppose, five spoken languages (or at least three) at three different levels of sophistication and completeness, each spoken by one and understood by two, three, four or five. The words of Smallpox, for example, assuming they are understood by him, are also of course understood by Syphilis; Streptococci, perhaps, understands them if they are at all closely related, despite the discrepancy in development, to those he is used to hearing from Cystitis; but Cystitis himself possibly does not understand them, as they are related only to words he is used to hearing from his own lips; Lionel does not understand. In this hypothesis this language is understood by three; and so on. As spoken language fails, they fall back on the pen and paper, but from the incomprehension with which Lionel scans certain of the sheets I deduce that their speech has begun to affect their writing. The four certainly find more common ground in writing than in speech, and the last resort, sign-language, is virtually universal. Here language begins to merge with Lionel's unformulated gestures – exploratory caresses of their concave sides, and even of their cheeks and lips. I think the subject-matter must be their fitness for duties, special or otherwise, and, again, the crew of the Jaffas' projected space-ship. Still, he is clearly unable to contain occasional exclamations of disgust, which not infrequently elicit an intelligent response from one of the other four.

I have had to tell Quincey that this is not a travelogue but a letter, although I thank him for taking over the duty of documenting these tiresome language developments. Details serve their purpose, but there is certainly a single continuous strand, almost possible to isolate, which is of more interest to you than anything. To continue: a matter of hours out of Ponta Delgada the weather commenced to return to its more saturnine aspect, the breezes strengthening, the clouds thickening again, and so on. I had been sitting in my counterpart's deck-chair, watching this reversion, toying with the pen and sampling my first ever pink gin, when Raoul came out to join me, carrying the April, May and June numbers of Mr. Chew's magazine. This man (Raoul) has a three- or four-day beard in place of his average two-, and others would consider it already fully-fledged, but he claims to be uncertain yet as to how it will go: whether he will shave jaws and throat in order to set the rest in relief, or else restore his average by a period of frequent overall shaving – in which case we might expect one of the others to grow a beard in its place. He even talks, in nonconformist mood, of shaving only lips and chin, thus rejecting high- in favour of bas-relief, and extensive side-whiskers. I was puzzled this morning to see him with "Men Only", and indeed with the furtive behaviour forced on him by his closely-held burden. "Quincey", he said as he sat, the tone and gestures being well-nigh hunted, "I can't find anyone but you to do this with. Karl is in a terribly bad way, I can't get him to understand it." He was riffling through the pages of the magazine. "I don't understand it myself." This was me. "Is Karl sinking then?" He took no notice, but extracted a leaf from April. "Look at this one." It was a page torn from a log-book, headed "S.S.Nabucco, December 5th.-6th., 1973", with columns of figures on the left and "Remarks" on the right. The entries began at six in the evening of the fifth and went through to the same hour on the following day. Here is a sample from a quarter of the way down.

				Wind		Waves				
	Distance travelled in sea-miles	Speed of Engine	Course	Speed in knots	Direction from	Direction from	Period in secs	Height in feet	Pressure in millibars	Temp. °F.
0000	25	Steady ahead	6°	63	6°	?	-	25	999	60
0100	16	"	277°	65	6°	6°	1	30	998	60
0200	9	"	45°	69	6°	?	-	32	996	59

"I can't possibly read this." "Well, look at what happens to our course during the storm." I found the part I have quoted. "Oh, yes, six degrees to two hundred and seventy-seven – a significant change – two hundred and seventy degrees." "Or ninety, if we turned the other way." "Perhaps it was to get to the Azores." "No, they didn't know *where* we were. And what I want to know is, what were we doing in the Azores anyway? We've been doing something like six degrees ever since getting into the Atlantic; we should be off. Two hundred and seventy-odd is what we *should* have been doing all the way from Tangier to get to Ponta Delgada." "Alright, let's have a look." The course continued reverting to two hundred and seventy-seven, and became steadier; at six in the morning, the mid-point, there were spaces for latitude and longitude, here filled with question-marks. The remarks up to this point were mainly concerned with anchoring things and malfunctioning instruments. Every entry, incidentally, was in a different hand, and initialled.

0700 Large meteor, or object in sky not fireball, sighted again 269°.E.N.

0800 Object hit water, 1_ sea-miles 270°. Boats 3,4,5,6 lowered. U.T.

0900 Boats returned and fastened. Overwrought passenger (L Jaffa) sedated. Another (K Waeldermann) in sick-bay. Radio message sent – uncertain success. L.J.

"This is only the watch's log," said Raoul. "Raoul and Karl collected some of these during the storm, and put them back later. Or rather, they collected the same one over and over again, putting it back every time. These things only happened *within* these hours, you see, not *at* them. Would you like to see another?" I was studying the torn edge of the page. There was a dim howling from the sick-bay, and the ship's surgeon hurried past. "Karl," I thought. "They've called the doctor," I said. Overhead the clouds were massing, again, into a thick yellow bank. Raoul plunged into the May number (had Mr Chew bought it in Africa?) and found another page between the folded breasts and knees of the central playmate. "No, this is the captain's log."

Wednesday – Thursday, December 5th – 6th, 1973.

The force of the waves was beyond anything in my experience, penetrating to the control-room, which was wrecked, and to the engine-room. What was thought to be a large thunderbolt proved to be only a continuation of phenomena previously observed in the night-sky. At 0800 a vessel was seen to be foundering at 270° from the ship, but although boats 3,4,5, and 6 were lowered, they were unable to identify her. It was impossible for anyone to survive under the conditions stated. On board, the passengers who frequently make proceedings seem inefficient and cluttered, and for whom we are now not equipped to provide, behaved capriciously but on the whole creatively. Captain Jaffa and Q Horace helped in the impossible task of watching for bodies from the ship, until Captain Jaffa was overtaken by a violent attack of the sickness to which he has already shown himself prone, and retired to his bunk with a sleeping-dose. K Waeldermann's pirate-games in the rigging ended with his seclusion in the sick-bay, injured and chastened. Morale was high, and it is felt that the experience of the storm has been broadening and strengthening. It ended at 0900, when a message was sent forward to Liverpool, though with much electronic interference. At 1000 the meteor-like phenomenon was observed exactly as before, but of course in daylight. Its behaviour is now being watched and chronicled by Sir James Baconbury, who says for example that the distance of the phenomenon from the ship was so much greater at 1000 than 0800 that he is inclined to believe a "shower" is involved. Our position here was 37°18'N 20°W, 312 miles from São Miguel, thus confirming the course-reading of 277°.

"That course is confirmed all the way through this book – yesterday's book, that is. We haven't got the page with yesterday's entry on it because we folded it up and gave it to him in the envelope, as it was, last night. He still didn't accept it, you saw. That was when

Raoul started not understanding it any more – he said he'd take up pen-hunting. The captain had appeared, from somewhere, between Karl and the surgeon, and on account of the surgeon's attempts to escape the trio had drawn closer to us. Karl had turned to the captain and was weeping on his chest, but still they were drawn slowly along by the surgeon's retreats, as if this man had some unshirkable responsibility now that the affair had involved death. "No, it must be today," Karl was wailing, "I can't bear to have him lying about the ship, waiting to be looked at, not rotting – I wouldn't be able to part with him after a day of that – I want nothing of him left but the idea in my head." "Very well," said the captain, who was constantly half-trying to unlace Karl's fingers from his lapels, "if we're sure of the death, and you're sure that's what you want, though we're only three days from Liverpool, or we could even go back to São Miguel. We've got some canvas we could wrap him in, but I don't think we've got the right flag." Karl was obviously sure of the death; Raoul and I looked at each other, but we both felt that he was safe with them. We went on talking about the pens, and meanwhile all around us preparations were begun. Karl was sat down with the surgeon right opposite us, but remained unaware of our presence.

The captain having gone to give orders, two little platforms began to be erected with barrels and planks, one by the rail and one beside our chairs. On the latter bottles of wine with glasses were laid out. I showed Raoul the pen I had been playing with, "But this is it," he said. "This is one of them," I corrected him. "I took this one off Streptococci in Ponta Delgada. He'd found it inside the piano, and it would have been found before if that instrument were used more often. I can't imagine what Streptococci was doing inside it. Before that this one was found by – er – Quincey in the framework of his bunk, and before that by the other Quincey under a bar-table, and before that by the original Quincey built into the handle of a tennis-racket. We've got sixteen of them now, and the idea originally was to put them back in hiding-places not obvious, you know, but likely to be come across by chance. Then they would be found one by one and returned to the captain, and it would be quite a drain on his resources. He can't actually *spend* the Log Symposium money yet. It hasn't worked out like that, though. Streptococci, for instance, was too dim-witted to see what he'd found, and tried to use it for his notes."

"You're sure this *is* the one?" Raoul asked me, having taken it and examined it more closely. "It seems to've been very cheaply made – it doesn't write properly – and those flecks of silver near the top, they might have been anything, mightn't they?"

"It was possibly scraped against the wires by the hammers, if someone used the piano without realising. Though actually, I'm beginning to wonder whether perhaps this is the one that Raoul found in the leg of his tripod – he said he'd been looking for the pen in the intervals between observing his object in the sky, but it hadn't occurred to him that this was the one when he found it – and before that was found by Quincey in the socket of a rowlock he was using in the boat that picked me up, and before that by the other Quincey in the framework of his bunk." Raoul appeared to be asking me a silent question. "I don't know," I continued. People had already begun to gather around the wine-laden table; I suspect that none of them knew precisely what was going on, but they had scented a social gathering, and such things are accepted without question, it seems, on board ship.

"What is this we're drinking?" said Lionel to Mr Chew.

"It is *vinho de cheiro*. We took it on at the Azores," was the reply.

They were standing at the top left-hand corner of the table, gazing vacantly at the rail and at the sea. Srta da Roseata came past them, and Mr Chew's eyes visibly followed her until she reached the wine. Lionel watched as he watched, and as the process reached completion he said to Mr Chew, in a whisper confidential though audible to us, "You know how old she is, don't you?"

"She's possibly sixty," Mr Chew granted, "but then I'm pushing fifty myself, you know, and anyhow she manages to keep those two young lads happy."

"She's eighty if she's a minute," said Lionel, in a voice even quieter though more urgent, "and the things she's done to her body to make it look like that have absolutely no bearing on the way she keeps those two happy."

"Well, if we're going to be absolutely frank I myself am not much over thirty, so the sum's the same. I'm about the same age as those two characters – " (we started out of our listening postures when thus dragged in, and I buried my face in June) " – a bit older than you, and I'll bet you wouldn't turn your nose up at the Señorita. My daughters are in their early teens," he added as an afterthought, but Lionel had begun shuddering at the suggestion about himself.

"She knocks me sick," he had said, with deep trembling feeling.

The volume I had picked up was very cleverly fixed, a whole log (that day's, though of course without that day's entry, which hadn't yet been written) being enclosed immediately within the magazine's cover, and the magazine's original pages, detached, inserted between the leaves of the intact and totally surrounded log. I sifted at random alternately through the entries and the erotica. "The prize tonight…"

"Thirty one thousand, one hundred and seventy-five pounds, if Jaffa does an entry," said Raoul. "We're going to duplicate the book immediately beforehand, and hand it over as it is, as our entry, when the others have been read out. If his copy and ours still turn out to be different, Karl – or anyone I can get to do the job, if he hasn't come round yet – will snatch the captain's and burn it on the spot."

I made one more comment (low-voiced, needless to say) though Raoul was already losing interest: "I see he's beginning to incorporate Baconbury's notes on the flashing objects."

"Yes, Baconbury's drafting a letter to the Astronomical Society, and Jowler's copying it into the log as it comes, alterations and all."

"Yes, here it is…"

"No, please don't read it out. We might be able to see the thing now, I suppose." We looked into the sky, and at once realised how nausea had crept up on us: the vision of the blotted heavens set the ship to reeling beneath us, and with our full awareness of the yellow cloud came shooting pains, the same, I suppose, as previously described.

"There…ooh!" said Raoul once, then we stood up with a common impulse and lowered our gaze to each other. Opposite us the surgeon, Karl and the captain made a gloomy tableau, almost silhouetted against the inadequate glare, as they waited for the arrival of the shrouded Karl. Any odd points of brightness Raoul had seen might have come in electric sparks from the captain's blown hair, as he was standing on the platform, thoughtfully thumbing a large open prayer-book, while the others sat on a box against the rail. These three were silent, though more people gathering round the table were conversing quietly. Gabriela da Roseata had been pressed closer to Lionel and Mr Chew, delighting the latter, though it was to Lionel she… [*the letter breaks off at this point*]

From the journal of Captain Lionel Jaffa, M.A. (Cantab): 1984

September 24th/December 24th

The coroner suspended the inquest for Christmas at 11.45 this morning, and I wandered down to the Black Lion – pretty close to the coroner's court, and conveniently set between the river and the Fullers brewery. I went straight through to the empty snug at the back, and settled myself with a reviving pint.

Though I'd tried in the hearings to look self-possessed, even carefree, I was getting increasingly alarmed by events on several counts. To start with, there were the rigours of the hearing, the murder of my old friend Sir Charles Pink, and the complexity of my relationship with the person who might (or more probably, in my view, might not) be my father. But beyond that, I was becoming more and more anxious that the perturbations that had preceded our arrival on Hampstead Heath had not ceased; yet the demands of the inquest had entirely prevented me from considering this properly. The break in the proceedings was like the removal of a physical burden. I stretched out in a leather armchair, lit my pipe, and took a long, relaxing pull at my beer.

Just after our landing it had seemed to me that the oscillations or shifts in space had ended. Indeed, it was arguable they might have begun to do so earlier, given their regularity during the period of our orbit, and I had had high hopes that the disturbances which had led to them had either become dissipated or passed out of our region of the universe. Nor, so far as I knew, had there been any sign of the supposed duplication of our spaceship being repeated. However, there had recently been a number of minor perturbations of yet another kind, which I suppose one would call time-shifts rather than space-shifts. I now think that the difficulties I had had in climbing the slope towards Isobel's house on our first landing had been due to such an effect. But more recently there had been clearer indications of the same event. I had on several occasions experienced my minor actions rewound by half a minute or so – so that as I put my toothbrush back on the washbasin wet and full of saliva I found myself instead picking it up dry and spread with toothpaste, or that as I put a pint glass down in a pub I found it magically refilled. I could not help thinking that such experiences could be simply the early onset of senile dementia, but I rejected the idea irritably. However, if this was indeed further evidence of the disorderliness of nature in my current circumstances, it could imply wide problems, especially if the tendency increased. I threw my head back against the backrest in a gesture of frustration, but the armchair was quite low, and my occiput collided with something behind it.

I rubbed the bruise, and looked round to see what had caused it. It was a wooden bookshelf fastened to the wall, containing a selection of thrillers by Ian Fleming, Hammond Innes and Neville Shute, a suspiciously sparse-looking box of dominoes, and a small pile of newspapers. My curiosity idly aroused, I pulled out the latter. On top was a copy of *The Times* from 7 December, lying open at an article describing the fall into the sea, near the S. S. Nabucco *en route* from Tangier to Liverpool, of an object such as a space-craft.

I let out a groan, and my mind started racing again. Supposing the ghost-ship to have been real, could this now be yet a *third* copy of our space-ship, and thus further evidence of decay and disintegration in the cosmic order? Were there now four Isobels, four Lionel Jaffas, four – no, three – Charles Pinks? Might a fourth and fifth version of our craft be on their way from orbit even now? I couldn't cope with this without another pint. But there wasn't a counter in the snug, so I stood up and went through to the main bar.

The saloon had by now filled up. People clutching hymn-sheets from a carol service at St Peter's mingled with refugees from the courts like myself. There was a loud hum of conversation and a thick fug of tobacco smoke, all overlain by a Christmas air of bonhomie. With less benevolence I joined the scrum at the bar.

After a moment, however, I found myself listening to a voice which was familiar but which I could not quite recognise, and which seemed to come from a figure with its back to me, expansively waving a glass of champagne. I couldn't see who its owner was speaking to.

"Insisted on cross-examining himself, by God! Never seen that done before. And the man went on and on and on," the voice said, "positively boasting how often he gets drunk and how incompetent it makes him."

Again I couldn't hear the reply.

"Yes, disgusting little tick. Wasting everybody's time too, when they ought to be at home with their wives and mistresses. Top up my glass, old chap: it's Christmas, after all, and I've had to wait until the very last minute before I could relax."

The waved champagne glass went out of sight for a moment, and reappeared filled to the brim. There was another murmured reply.

"No, I'm buggered if I'll do another stroke on the inquest until after Boxing Day. The A3'll be choked all the way to Winchester this afternoon. God knows what time I'll get home."

I still could not hear the response.

"Well, the result's plain as a pikestaff, fortunately. I'll be indicting that creep Lionel Jaffa for murder. That'll make him laugh the other side of his face! Pity the executions aren't public any more: I'd like to watch that one."

I could not believe what I had heard, and played it back to myself a number of times before tuning in again as Sir John Corunna, the coroner (for I now, of course, recognised the voice), began to speak once more.

"No, I won't bother to tip off the police now in case he does a runner: I tell you, I've done quite enough on that sodding inquest till after the holiday. If the police have to run around a bit faster, that's their lookout. Anyway, Jaffa's far too soapy to make a break: he'll be too busy cooped up in his flat looking at pictures of small boys, I expect. You can do what you like, of course, if you fancy telling the police; I expect Barnabas will be around in the Yard at the moment – he can never resist a chance for overtime."

My hands clenched involuntarily, but I controlled my reaction, which was in any event constrained by the tight press of drinkers. However, I had heard enough. I pushed through the crowd, trying to keep out of sight of Corunna and his interlocutor, and emerged into the outdoors.

A light snowfall had begun, and continued as I marched through the streets towards my flat at Stopcombe Close, my mind a whirl like the snowflakes dancing past the Christmas trees in the windows. Surely coroners' courts didn't have power to issue indictments? But then I'd believed all along that this wasn't Earth, after all: maybe they did things differently here. So what about the remark about executions? Had the death penalty not been abolished? Corunna's unpleasant words and voice kept running into my mind, so that whenever I tried to put together the logical pieces needed to answer a question I got distracted before I reached the conclusion. Overall, I was forming the view that I had to get away. It seemed safest to get out of London, but where could I go? The only place I could think of was Charles Pink's house in Westmorland. When I got home (the flat was empty, since I had asked Stanley to stay with my father for the duration of the inquest, an arrangement he had not been at all happy with), I packed a bag, took a taxi to Euston, bought a ticket and just caught the 2.47 pm.

I stowed the bag on the rack above a first class smoking seat, and made my way through crowded corridors to the restaurant car, where a late service of lunch was in train. Only two seats seemed to be free, and I sank gratefully into one, picking up and immersing myself in the menu. Mindful of the risks of British Rail catering when too ambitious, I ordered tomato soup and lamb chops with a bottle of Australian claret, and sat back to collect my thoughts, as the train stopped briefly at Watford. Suppose that Corunna's invisible interlocutor did inform Scotland Yard, or that Sir John himself changed his mind? Could I disguise myself somehow in case a search party got onto the train? Or was there some other expedient? Suddenly there was a noise of apologies and a lady settled into the seat opposite. I looked up, and there was Isobel – a different Isobel, not Isobel as I had last seen her pretending to be called Christabel Cook, but Isobel Keogh as she had looked when I peered at her house that first day of the landing, or when she had first joined our crew.

"Good heavens!" she cried, "it's Lionel! What are you doing on this train?" She smiled happily, and seemed pleased to see me. "I'm just off to Harborough for tomorrow to spend the day with Mummy. I'll be back in town on Thursday at the latest." She peered at me more critically. "You look as if you've aged ten years! How are you?"

I drew a deep breath. Under this pressure of events and circumstance, I saw no alternative to putting myself at her mercy; and some remote part of myself noted that the sexual pangs which I had experienced on seeing her on Hampstead Heath on our arrival seemed now to have disappeared, or at least been suppressed. I briefly explained that the inquest was unjustly going to indict me for murder, that I was a fugitive from the law, that I was on my way to seek refuge from Sir Charles Pink if he was at home at his Lake District house, and that I would be greatly indebted if, should the police board the train at Rugby or later, she would allow us to engage in a prolonged clinch during their inspection of our compartment, so that they would not recognise me.

But she had heard nothing of the inquest, having been, she said, in almost monastic seclusion, drawing up plans for a series of final checks on the engineering systems of my father's space ship. The steward brought drinks. When I started to explain that the inquest had followed Sir Charles's murder, she asked why, if Charles was dead, I was expecting to be entertained by him in Westmorland. And when I began to explain that, she asked what I was doing here in England when I was supposed to be in the Mediterranean recruiting crew members. Before I had time to begin my answer she added that she was anyway only going as far as Rugby.

"Well, it's like this," I began awkwardly, "the fact is that...well, there is more than one Lionel..."

But as I spoke my surname, I found myself back in my flat, alone, closing the zip on my bag. I looked at my watch: it was 2.07 pm. It took me, of course, a few seconds to realise that I had suffered another time-shift. Then I picked up the bag and raced out of the building to catch the train, this time far more conscious that the police might be after me. Once again I anxiously paid the taxi, agitatedly queued at the booking-office, raced pell-mell for the platform, boarded the train with relief. I stowed my bag, went through to the restaurant car, ordered my meal. The train stopped at Watford and pulled away, and then Isobel came and sat at the table. Impatiently, I ran through my part in our previous conversation as closely as I could remember it, and was disturbed to see her from time to time look slightly more askance than I remembered from before. At length we reached the end of our earlier exchange.

"Well, it's like this," I replied awkwardly, "the fact is that...well, there is more than one Lionel Jaffa." I stopped abruptly, since Isobel had vanished. Her lipstick-stained, half-empty glass of wine was still on the table, but she (and, I was to discover, her handbag and overnight case) had gone. The steward brought my tomato soup, and, finding that my companion had left, ushered a waiting traveller into her seat. In considerable confusion I got through the rest of my meal and, on our departure from Stafford, withdrew from the restaurant car. I could only suppose that Isobel, too, had suffered a time-shift, but for some reason had not been able to repair the matter as I had done.

I was already getting anxious whenever we stopped, in case the local police had been alerted, and was disappointed to see that my compartment, being first class, was still empty, and gave no cover. I decided that on arrival at Crewe I would get off the train, muffled in my coat, hat and scarf, and check whether the police were in evidence before re-boarding, rather than run the risk of being cornered by a search party in the confines of a carriage.

It was getting on for six o'clock when we pulled in to Crewe. It was of course quite dark, and the murky electric lighting did little to dispel the gloom as the announcer read out a bored series of stations to Glasgow Central, and then began to give a long list of connections to North Wales, Shrewsbury, Chester, Liverpool and Manchester. Clutching my bag, I moved slowly into the lee of the refreshment room and peered about. A group of men was slumped in seats on the other side of the platform, but nobody seemed to be wearing uniform other than the railwaymen themselves. The train did not look to be about to leave, so I slipped into the refreshment room and bought a Manchester Evening News, opening my coat and scarf to get to my change pocket. Then the departure whistles blew on my train. I turned to go, and as I went out one of the men who had been sitting on the platform passed me at the open door: I looked in his face, and to my astonishment recognised it: it was that of Hector Smallpox.

I sprinted into the train as the porters slammed the last of the doors, nearly running into a uniformed policeman as I did so. He ignored me, however, and in much confusion I made my way back to my compartment and sat down. I tried to take stock. Smallpox had shown no sign of recognising me as I had him, nor did I think there was any chance of the crew having managed to gather up themselves and their kit in time to catch the train. But it had been a narrow escape.

The train pulled out on its way to Wigan North Western, and I sank back into the seat. I felt the rigours of the day overwhelm me, and must have slept, since the next thing I knew was the cold feeling of metal at my throat and a familiar voice murmuring in my ear.

"Don't move," said Quincey Horace. "Just open your eyes slowly, and stay still." I opened my eyes obediently and he removed his knife from my throat, changing places with the burly Raoul Antonius. The compartment was full of people. Next to Antonius was a double of his, who had grown a beard. On the seats opposite were two versions of Horace, Karl Waeldermann and, levelling a revolver, another version of myself, about ten years younger than me.

"So!" said Horace, putting such venom into his voice that even such a stereotyped situation filled me with fear. "We have been waiting for this for a long time. You should have taken the advice in our letters, Captain Jaffa."

"What letters?" I asked. "I've had no letters from you."

Horace seemed disconcerted. "Both of us put a good deal of effort into writing them," he said petulantly, then, returning to his menacing tone, added, "but that does not matter now. Justice is about to catch up with you, Jaffa!"

A wave of irritation passed over me, despite my situation. "Hold on," I said. "who are all these people? And, in particular," I added, looking at my own *doppelgänger*, "where do you fit in?"

The younger Lionel gave a weak smile, which annoyed me rather further, and opened his mouth, but before he could speak Horace's *alter ego* exclaimed, "I like that! First he loses our letters and then he starts orating! It doesn't bloody matter who we are, old cock! We're your Nemesis, that's what!"

"Wait a moment," said the first Horace sharply. "This is not a moment to be hurried. The Captain asked a civil question and he deserves a civil reply.

"May I introduce..." he gestured in turn to each of the company, speaking in measured and self-important tones, "...Raoul Federic Antonius, of your crew; Raoul Federic Antonius, of a replicated version of the ghost ship whose existence in planetary orbit you deduced, which landed in the North Atlantic on 6 December local date; myself you know; my own equivalent on the ghost ship, which we joined and piloted to land in Africa; Karl Waeldermann, of your crew; Lionel Jaffa, who I believe is yourself some ten years and a few months ago before we all took off from Earth, or is alternatively, if this planet is not Earth, an equivalent thereof."

This statement was not received with the respect which I imagine Horace had been hoping for. The second Antonius immediately complained, "I'm not a replica!" while the second Horace said crisply, "That is entirely misleading. You are not handling this as we agreed just now in the other compartment. I think you had better let me deal with it."

The first Horace responded by raising his voice to something approaching a shout. "Now then!" he called. "There was a question asked of Lionel: let him answer it!"

There was a pause while a number of those present drew in breath to speak, and in it my *doppelgänger* said, "Now, look here, I'm told by these chaps that they have a grudge against you for the way you commanded our ship, if I understand correctly what's been going on, which seems dreadfully complicated. Perhaps, before we get onto their grievance, you could just outline your own understanding of how we got to where we are, with so many duplicate people and the present and the future rather mixed up, which seems at variance with my understanding of physics at least."

Had I really been such a pompous twat? My anger redoubled, keeping the feeling of threat at bay. "I think that question might be better put to Isobel," I replied. "It's much more her field. Have you seen her? And what has happened to the rest of the crew?"

"Ah, he's started to worry about the rest of the crew now, that's big of him!" shrieked the second Horace, working himself up into a rage. "Quincey, this won't do, I'm going to take over the questioning!"

"Most of them got left on the platform at Crewe," said Waeldermann helpfully. "We were on our way to London from Liverpool and weren't expecting..."

"Shut up!" said the first Quincey to him loudly.

"I think," said my *doppelgänger* rather crossly, "that I ought to get a proper answer to my question next. I'm still waiting. After all, it is I who have the gun."

"You can't use that in here anyway," said the bearded Antonius. "It would make too much noise, and we couldn't escape from the train."

The first Quincey raised his hand. "Okay," he said. "Lionel gets an answer, but after that I carry on." There were murmurs of grudging acquiescence.

Suddenly the door to the corridor was slammed open. A ticket inspector stood there. My *doppelgänger* hastily stuffed his gun away. "All tickets from Carnforth, please!" The official looked about. "And you gentlemen have moved from another carriage: may I see your tickets, please?" He examined all the tickets carefully, and gave mine back to me. "Yours is fine, of course, sir. The rest of you all have second class to London, but this carriage is first class to Glasgow. You'd all better come with me into a second class compartment and we'll sort the thing out." He slammed the door open again to emphasise his point and stood aside, waiting. The two Antoniuses, the two Horaces and Waeldermann muttered furiously to each other for a while, and then left the compartment. My own *doppelgänger* seemed to be hesitating, but after the two Horaces came back and stared at him for a bit he followed them out. "That's right, gentlemen," said the ticket inspector, and shepherded them off down the train. "See you in Glasgow!" I called after them helpfully.

I wondered what to do next, but the train was already slowing and another ticket inspector going through the corridors calling out "Oxenholme! Oxenholme!". I waited at the door, and as the whistles blew I climbed down onto the platform. I walked briskly to the exit, and commandeered the only cab: it was now just before nine o'clock, and the driver spent the journey explaining how extremely fortunate I was to have found a taxi at that hour on Christmas eve, especially when there had been such snow during the day. The village of Step was twenty miles off, through the centres of Kendal, Windermere and Ambleside, and it was almost a quarter to ten when I paid him off and added the expected large tip. I trudged across the snow to the door of Near Step House.

The building was dark. I rang the bell. There was silence. I rang again, longer. At last there was a light through the fan window above the porch, then a noise of movement. A dog began to bark. "Who's there?" asked a quavering female voice.

"Is Sir Charles at home?" I shouted. "This is Lionel Jaffa."

The voice seemed to give a little squeal. "Oh, Mr Jaffa!" it said, muffled. There was a noise of bolts and chains being drawn, and then the heavy door creaked open, revealing a white-haired old woman in curlers and a dressing-gown. "Oh, Mr Jaffa!" she said again, more distinctly, while a labrador bounded out and gave me the once-over. "How lovely to see you again, Sir! Don't you look grown-up!"

I wasn't quite sure what the last remark meant: "older", perhaps. But it made me remember who she was: Mrs Merriaive, who had "done for" Charles' parents since they married, and whom I had met a number of times during vacation visits in my Cambridge days. Charles's father was now dead, of course, and his mother in a home, but it was nice to be welcomed. "Is Sir Charles in?" I asked again.

"Oh, bless you, no," Mrs Merriaive said, "and I'm awful sorry to come to the door in my night-things, only I didn't know you were coming, Sir." She ushered me in, clucking over my scanty baggage, set me down at the kitchen table and rustled up some cold rabbit pie, potatoes and salad, apologising again for the improvisation. She brought in a decanter of whisky and a jug of water, speaking of the need to ward off the chill. Eventually I prised out of her that Sir Charles was travelling from London by a late train which would go no further than

Preston; he was hiring a car for the rest of the journey and planned to arrive about 3 am. I sent her off to bed, finished my supper, wrote Charles a note, found my room, sat up with the decanter writing this entry, and retired.

Letter from Sir Charles Pink, Bart., to Captain Lionel Jaffa
25 September 1984/25 December 1973, 2.35 am.

Dear Lionel

Thanks for your note. Sensible of you to come here last night: despite our differences you're welcome, for the sake of old times, and I'll do my best to stand by you.

I shall be out when you get up, I expect. As you know, I'm always an early riser, even after a late night; I feel a need to make a showing at the early Communion on Christmas Day and will walk down to Rydal – I got some sleep on the train this evening, so I shouldn't be too rough later on. Don't know what they'll make of my appearing, after the reports of my murder and the inquest, but Mrs Merry seems to believe what she sees in front of her, and I don't see why the local congregation shouldn't do that as well, even if the London lawyers say they still need more convincing. Mrs Merry will look after you at breakfast – but treat her well, for she's a dear old soul, and I know what a bastard you are!

I had a nasty shock last week, some kind of time-shift, reminding me of the space-shifts and oscillations we had when approaching this planet. It seems to have had unfortunate consequences for me. And if there are more of those on the way it will make our lives even more complicated than they are already. Would welcome discussing this with you later on today – Mrs Merry has laid in all the Christmas stuff, and I shall put the capon in the Aga and the claret to unchill before turning in this morning, so we ought to be able to make a decent festive event of it.

Yours ever,

Charles

From the journal of Captain Lionel Jaffa, M.A. (Cantab): 1984

September 25th/December 25th

I slept late this morning, and was woken by Mrs Merriaive with a cup of tea at about ten. I stood at the window to shave: it was a beautiful sunny day and the house stood on top of a hill, looking down on the snow lying bright on the fells, and a fine view of Rydal Water. Downstairs I tucked into Cumberland sausage, with eggs from the ducks who in unfrozen times swam on the large pond behind the house, and glanced through Charles' letter. Then, disdaining the *Westmorland Gazette* which had been left for me, I started to look through the *Manchester Evening News* I had bought on Crewe station. Under the Stop Press was a disturbing item:

Late News

Sources suggest that the London inquest into the death of Sir Charles Pink will conclude shortly with an indictment, and that police are looking for one of the witnesses, whose whereabouts are not known.

Corunna's mysterious interlocutor had, it seemed, not wasted time. Just then I heard, from the hall, a key turning in the front door lock, and I felt a momentary panic, but then Charles came in, pulling off his Crombie, and making much of the labrador. "Ah, Lionel, are you being looked after? Did you sleep well?" He drew up a tall-backed wooden armchair and stroked his moustache thoughtfully. Mrs Merriaive brought in a fresh pot of coffee.

I explained to him what had been happening, in more detail than last night's note, and he listened impassively.

"You're in a fix, aren't you? Still, before we discuss that, let me tell you what's been happening to me." He paused, and poured himself another cup. "As you know, Isobel and I have become very close – for which I make no apology. On board our space ship you spent a lot of time thinking about the oscillations and jumps we made. Now, something which seems related to that happened to me recently, not once but twice; I'll cut the story short, but briefly what happened was that I seemed to jump, not in space as before, but back in time. I'll just describe the incidents first, and then say what I think about them.

"The first occasion was on 3 December – yes, I see that catches your interest, and rightly so. I had breakfast with Isobel and discussed, as we used to, what to do with the day. Then I went to the bank in Hampstead and left by an alleyway alongside it. I got home, and realised that I'd forgotten to pay in some cheques, so decided to go back. This time, Isobel said she would come along as well. We got to the bank without misadventure, but when we left and turned into the alley I was astonished to see someone looking exactly like me straight ahead. I called at him to stop; he turned; well, I don't hold with people impersonating me, and I have a short fuse, and it ended with me hitting him too hard with the butt of my pistol.

"The second occasion was last Saturday. As you know, one of my hobbies is Assyrian cylinder seals; I've been doing some work at the British Museum on a paper about the weapons depicted on them, and I went down there early to get on with it. I was hard at it all day, with a brief break for lunch at the café, and went round to Isobel's afterwards, getting there about six-fifteen. I'd been at her place for about an hour when, when all of a sudden, bang, it was nine in the morning again and I was just going up the steps into the Museum. You can imagine how astonished I was, but as I say it seemed to be rather of a piece with some of the oscillations and jumps we'd had earlier before our landing. I decided to make the most of it, and spent the day working on the next bit of my project, so getting in two days work in one; I started to get tired, so I wasn't quite as industrious as the first time round, taking long coffee and tea breaks and treating myself to a slap-up lunch at the Travellers'. So at the end of the day I put my books on reserve, left the building, and went up to Isobel's; I remember I got delayed a bit compared with the previous time – stopped to buy a paper and missed the Underground train. So I got there, let myself in with my key and went towards the living room where Isobel usually sits in the early evening. Then I heard..." Charles seemed to detach himself from the story for a moment, and collect himself a little. "Well, never mind what I heard, but the long and the short of it is that I saw someone exactly like me again, this time in the bedroom with Isobel. Well, I hadn't meant to kill the previous chap, and I was confused by the time-shift or whatever had happened earlier, so I didn't want to over-react. So I drew attention to my presence quite inconspicuously. I've afraid it caused them quite a surprise, all the same. Well, I won't go into the details, but there was a fair scene. Isobel refused to believe I was myself. She made me return her key, threw me out of the house, and made it clear that she never wanted to see me again, and hanging onto this other chap all the while, too.

"So I decided to come home to Step for Christmas and try and work it out. I'm afraid that in the ship, though I did try to do some work on it, I wasn't really very interested in those oscillations and jumps we had, though you and Isobel clearly were. I was rather puzzled after we landed, though, especially by the date changing, and us going back apparently to the time before we left. I asked Isobel about this once, I remember, but she rushed into a huge explanation about what would happen if it was special relativity theory and the arguments for that and the arguments against, and what would happen if it was general relativity theory and the arguments for that and the arguments against, and wormholes and n-dimensional spaces and quantum uncertainties and multiple continuums and diversity of universes and hierarchies of reality – she obviously found it very exciting, but after about a minute I just switched off.

"Time for a drink, I think." And he rang the bell and told Mrs Merriaive to bring a bottle of champagne.

So, I realised, it was Charles who murdered himself! No wonder that, when I was a suspect, he was so tolerant of my appearance as an uninvited guest for the festive season. I told him that my guess was that the first duplicate Charles that he had met (and killed) had been himself from 10 years ago, and there had been a time-shift giving rise to the second whom Isobel clearly preferred to him. I wasn't able to answer his question why, when he had killed himself in the past, he still existed in the present – or rather, although I had various ideas about that, I didn't think they were sufficiently interesting to try explaining them just now, when what I really wanted to talk about was how he was going to atone for getting me suspected of the murder by helping me to escape from the authorities. I couldn't think of a plan for that, nor even guess how long I had before they thought of sending to enquire at Charles's house. And then there was also the question of the crew who were after my blood, and how long it would take them to find their way here.

Having unburdened himself of his confession of murder, however, Charles showed little immediate interest in my troubles. Muttering that nobody official was going to do anything on Christmas Day, he disappeared into the kitchen, refusing any help from me. Whenever I looked in, he was busy shaking boiled potatoes in a sieve, making Cumberland sauce, putting pork through a mincing-machine, or pursuing other mysteries of the art. There was no television, and only one radio – in the kitchen. I was left to browse in a bookcase of rather heavy-duty classics – I recall that the least intimidating seemed to be *Anne of Geierstein* by Sir Walter Scott – and to continue drinking excellent vintage champagne, of which there seemed to be no shortage.

It was almost dark by the time he roused me from a doze and summoned me to the table, where I was unable to make myself alert enough to manage coherent conversation. I confess that the food was a positive banquet, although after so much champagne I was unable to do real justice to the Chateau Lynch-Bages 1964 which accompanied the capon, nor the Chateau Suduiraut 1966 that came with the pudding, and was altogether defeated by the Taylors 1946 which he brought out with a flourish to accompany the Stilton. I declined a 25-year-old cognac with my coffee, and stumbled off to bed shortly afterwards while Sir Charles was still cutting his cigar. In the night I woke with a raging thirst, and sat up for an hour drinking water and writing up this journal.

September 26th

I was rudely awakened by Charles the next morning. He was full of vigour and enthusiasm, which I thought out of place. He spoke eagerly of the fine sunny day, which was not yet evident at that hour but which I was sure would hurt my eyes, and announced his intention of making an early start and joining the Blencathra Hunt for the day. He implored me to join him, but I firmly refused, whereat he bounced downstairs, and the scents of bacon, kidneys, mushrooms, coffee and toast began to make their way through the door. I turned over and went back to sleep.

I finally woke at nearly mid-day. I went down and found Mrs Merriaive, having remedied the damage of the Christmas meal, seated at the kitchen table with a cup of tea and a Woodbine, waiting to make me breakfast. While I ate it, I considered my options. I was somewhat reassured by the failure of either the police or the crew to make contact the previous day. If I were to disappear entirely, it would surely mean going abroad. That would raise the question of money. I did have a fair amount with me, since it had seemed only prudent to keep it by after our unorthodox and confusing landing. But a life abroad would need all I could muster, and I must at least empty my bank accounts. The banks were not open until the next day, so it seemed to me a reasonable risk to stay put for the moment.

I poured myself another cup of coffee, and lit a cigarette. Then the doorbell rang. At once I sprang up, but I did not know what to do: I went to the door of the dining room and listened as Mrs Merriaive made her arthritis-ridden way to the front door and laboriously opened it. "I'm sorry, Sir," she said, "the master is not here at the moment." Then she cried loudly, "Oh!", and added "Oh, Sir, how did you get outside? I could have sworn you were still in the dining-room."

A voice, my voice and yet not my voice, cried, "Okay, lads, he's here! Come on!" But at the same instant I had raced to the front door, elbowed Mrs Merriaive out of the way, and begun to push.

The reader of this journal has probably not engaged in a trial of strength against himself, and certainly not against himself as he had been ten years earlier. I do not recommend it. I was keenly aware at the time that I had maybe ten seconds before my adversary was reinforced by an unknown number of allies, who would certainly finish the contest; it may be this thought that lent me the effort required to get the door shut. "Quick," I cried to poor Mrs Merriaive as the Yale clicked home, "Where are the bolts? Is there a deadlock?", but even as I said it I spotted and shot home bolts at top and bottom of the door and a chain at the centre.

I put my hands against the door and let my body sag for a moment, as futile drumming began on the other side of the door and Mrs Merriaive uttered a plaintive, "What, Sir? What is happening, Sir?"

"Mrs Merriaive," I replied, "These are bast–" I took a breath. "This is a group of desperate men who are enemies of mine. We must make sure that all the doors and windows are locked, I mean fastened. Do you know of any that aren't?" As I spoke I was starting to run towards the kitchen, where I thought I remembered the back door being; as I finished, Mrs Merriaive gave a little shriek and cried, "Oh, dear, heavens above, and with the master away. It's like the bad old days of the Bassenthwaite maurauders, that old granfer used to speak of!"

She took a few deep breaths, mastering herself. Meanwhile I had checked the back door and the kitchen window. She went on, "Mr Jaffa, I lock up every night faithfully, and never open anything without instruction except the windows when I'm doing the bedrooms...and the front door when the postman comes with a parcel..."

"Are there any other doors to the outside?"

"Apart from the front and the back, no, Sir."

"Wait a moment!" I ran upstairs into my bedroom and fastened the window shut, then into Charles's and did the same. Where did Mrs Merriaive sleep? I called downstairs, "Mrs Merriaive! Please fasten your own window, urgently!"

I went to my own room, whose view was to the front, and looked out. Three versions of Horace were arguing with each other on the drive, with in a circle around them my own *doppelgänger*, Waeldermann and Antonius. I dashed to one of the back rooms. Another version of Horace was there, giving instructions to two versions of Antonius, one of Waeldermann, and what seemed to be four versions of Smallpox. The odds looked bad.

I went onto the landing, where Mrs Merriaive was just emerging from a door concealing a small staircase to the second floor. "Mrs Merriaive!" I cried, "Does Sir Charles have any guns? Where are they?" I had a revolver in my own bag, but limited ammunition; and it would not seem impressive outdoors, while a shotgun would be much better, and given Charles' penchant for country sports there was a good chance of there being one in the house.

Mrs Merriaive appeared now to be entering into the spirit of the thing, and showing enthusiasm. "In the study, Sir, three shotguns and two rifles. The key is in the top left-hand drawer of the desk."

I ran down to the study, got out the key, spotted the gun cabinet. I got out a shotgun and cartridges, and loaded it. Suddenly there was an almighty crash from the hall. I rushed out, but saw nothing. I ran upstairs, while the crash was repeated. I threw open the window of my room and leant out: one version of Horace, Waeldermann and Antonius had found a heavy ladder and were using it as a battering ram against the front door. The door was robust, but I took aim with my shotgun; just before I fired, however, a bullet slapped into the stone mullion of my window. My own shot went astray, and I hastily ducked back indoors. Almost at once I peeped out, and saw that the battering ram party had dropped their ladder and run off to cover; I saw my own *doppelgänger*, who had evidently fired the shot which had missed me, doing the same.

I moved from one side of the house to another looking for movement, and fired off three charges for encouragement, but they were not offering targets. I doubted that another attempt would be made on the front door. Sooner or later, however, they might have a go at the more vulnerable back door or windows.

There were no outbuildings very close to the house, and they had had difficulty finding cover. I thought that five or six were behind a stone shed to one side at the front of the house, which might be where they had found the ladder, while the rest were uncomfortably semi-hidden behind rather narrow trees. I peered cautiously out of the front bedroom window. Mrs Merriaive came into the room with a tray of coffee and Christmas cake, now, apparently, thoroughly involved with the defence.

"Mrs Merriaive," I asked. "What is in that shed over to the right?"

"That's the woodshed, Mr Jaffa, though we keep gardening stuff in there as well."

"Thank you, Mrs Merriaive." I took a bite. "This is excellent cake, I must say." I sensed for a moment that the sky was already darkening, and looked at my watch. There was only an hour, maybe an hour and a half, of daylight left. I could hold them off while the light lasted. "Fetch me a good map, please." Afterwards it would be another matter. They could not batter the doors without making noise which could be shot at. But sooner or later the Horaces would realise that the wood in the woodshed was also a potent weapon, and one against which there would be little defence once it could be laid and lit under cover of dark. Charles would probably be hunting all the hours of daylight, and then entertained to drinks and food before he came home. And even if he got back, our defence would hardly be that much stronger.

Mrs Merriaive returned with an ordnance map, and keeping the corner of my eye on my besiegers I studied it speedily. In two minutes I had a plan. I asked Mrs Merriaive to repack my belongings in a knapsack, and she rapidly returned with it, adding a thermos, a packet of sandwiches and a torch. I thanked her, gave her a huge tip, and sent a couple of revolver shots in the direction of my enemies. Then I ran quietly downstairs. Next I heard a shotgun firing from upstairs: with great surprise I realised that Mrs Merriaive had taken on the burden of the defence herself. I unlocked the back door, threw it open, and ran straight out over the ice of the duckpond on to the fell, followed by incomprehensible shouts from the Smallpoxes.

I cannot tell the detail of the next hour or so. Initially, I gained ground on them fast, since they were afraid of fire from Mrs Merriaive and did not dare venture onto the ice, and also it was only a mile or so to the Langdale youth hostel, where I stole a bicycle. However, my route ran up the slopes of Little Langdale and the Wrynose Pass, which are appalling going for a bicycle, and it was not too long before lights and noise behind me showed me that my assailants had managed to find bikes too and were in hot pursuit. I was heading for Eskdale and the coastal railway, and was now not far away, although the light was already failing. At last I began to freewheel downhill through Hard Knott Pass, only minutes now from my destination. It was at this point that, to my shock and alarm, and ultimate disappointment, I saw two boldly lit police cars driving up the narrow road towards me from the direction of the station at Ravenglass. In desperation, I abandoned the bicycle and struck off on foot up the hill to my right. Before long the slope levelled off onto a broad terrace, and I realised that I was on the spacious parade-ground set in front of the ancient Roman fort. Darkness deepened, and I realised that I was too exhausted to go further. I took out my revolver and prepared to defend myself as best I could. I peered down the south side of the terrace, and saw half a dozen or so of the crew racing up, yelling execrations on me, and led by one of the Horaces with a knife gripped between his teeth. I turned to the west side, and saw half a dozen uniformed policemen running up shouting and waving their truncheons. For a moment, in what must have been the last of the time-shifts, I saw the scene transformed, with crimson-cloaked legionaries alongside me and the attackers painted with woad and waving axes; then almost instantly the current situation returned. I could not decide whether to bring up my weapon.

But suddenly there was a deafening noise, and the whole scene was bathed in blinding light. My assailants stopped in their tracks, shielding their eyes and ears. Behind me there was movement, and as I turned I saw our space ship touching down. The glare and noise continued, but friendly arms encircled me and led me back into the craft. Doors closed. The noise and light diminished. There was a sensation of upward movement.

I looked around. I was in the purser's outer office, near the primary passenger air-lock – though, in the absence of a purser, we had long ago converted it into a secluded library with bar facilities. I was seated on one of the leather sofas. Sitting around me were Sir Charles, Stanley, and the original Isobel whom I had met for the first time on the train.

Sir Charles appeared to have reverted to his customary style of communication. He looked at me displeasedly and wrinkled his nose. "Hm. Merry dance you've led me! After a day's good hunting, too."

Stanley offered me a large gin and tonic, saying tentatively, "Welcome back aboard, Sir."

Isobel pressed her lips together. "After I met you in the train I thought that something ought to be done, and managed this morning to get down to London and pick up this ship – though your father had moved it from the Heath to his house. If it hadn't been for Mrs Merriaive we shouldn't have had a clue what direction you had gone in."

Sir Charles got up. "I'm going to turn in, and I suggest you do too. Isobel's said she will be happy to put the ship into orbit." He left the room, followed by the others. I sat finishing my drink, dog-tired, not even trying to work out what had happened.

I stared blankly at the closed door of the purser's inner cabin, which we had used for private study. Then the door opened. A figure appeared, dressed in an old-fashioned frock coat, its face and hands covered in reddish hair like a marmalade cat, and stopped when it saw me. Its face creased into a smile, and it came forward extending its hand. "Ah, you will be Captain Lionel Jaffa, of whom I have heard so much! I am charmed to make your acquaintance," it said, in a pleasant educated voice. Exhausted and baffled, I mechanically shook his hand. "Permit me to introduce myself. I call myself Doo-endy. I fear that you will find my appearance rather unconventional. Allow me to explain my presence here – but I shall keep it brief, as I am sure that you are fatigued."

Doo-endy helped himself to a whisky and soda, and sat down. He explained that a few months ago he had been going about his business when he had been astonished to be suddenly transported to what he took to be a completely different world, where he met a young lad with curiously smooth and unhairy skin. The young lad had been Stanley, who had taught Doo-endy English, which, having been blessed with a gift for languages, he rapidly mastered. When Doo-endy learned of our travels, he had become extremely interested in our space-ship, thinking that it might be a way of returning to his own world. "Sadly," he went on, "I have now come to the conclusion that what brought me here was a time-shift rather than a space-shift, and that it is most unlikely now that I shall ever return to my people, who, I have reason to believe, are those whom your own scholars have described as the Neanderthals. However, Stanley introduced me to Sir Charles and Isobel, and the latter remarked that I am unusually handy with practical skills, by the standards of your own species, and asked me to stand by as a potential reinforcement to the crew of your ship, should your own (or rather, I understand, your double's) search for crew in the Mediterranean prove insufficient. Let me wish you a pleasant night." He drained his glass and ambled out of the room.

I stared rather vacantly at the door as it closed behind him: this, it came to me, must have been the "hairy man" seen prowling around the ship on Hampstead Heath, who had been so much discussed at the inquest. Then I rose, went to my cabin and cast myself on my bed.

September 27th

The next day, after some coffee, I went to the control room. "Unless anyone disagrees," I said, "I propose that we should now resume the flight plan we were committed to at the time when we first sighted the planet we have just left." No other voice was heard. Isobel reached up and fed a spool of tape into a slot. Sir Charles cleared a space on the chart table and unrolled a sheet, studying it intently. The hum of the engines changed its pitch, and on the display screen I saw the image that represented Earth grow imperceptibly smaller. I looked at Isobel and Sir Charles. "This has been a most distressing planet to visit," I said.

Sir Charles said nothing, but gently stroked his moustache. Isobel gave me a quizzical smile, hardly intimate, but not unfriendly. "What's that poem of T. S. Eliot's?" she asked. "How does it go? '*We shall not cease from exploration/And the end of all our exploring/Will be to arrive where we started/And know the place for the first time....*'"

The Disappearance of Mrs Whiteclock*

My first intimation – of something out of the ordinary, that is, in relations between Geoffrey Whiteclock and his adorable lady – was received at a dinner given by that other good old friend, Mrs Purvis, who had invited, as was increasingly her custom in that period, only the merest sprinkling of people who could be said to fall outside the tightly-knit circle of which we two and the Whiteclocks formed the focus. The remarkable thing was that Geoffrey had turned up in this friendly gathering alone: an omen which has boded well, I should think, for singularly few couples in the history of society, but which struck me as a particularly ill sign in this case.

It was not as if Mrs Whiteclock could be bound up in some private industry, for they were a delightfully indolent pair, and until now had shared their pleasures with the most scrupulous and unfailing fairness. Nor was she likely to be unwell: though undoubtedly of an extreme frailty in appearance, she had a stronger constitution, and less in her of the hypochondriac, than any other person of my acquaintance, with the possible exception of Geoffrey himself; and even if her health had at last failed, yet all else been well, Geoffrey could have been nowhere but at her bedside, reading her passages from Swinburne or some other therapeutic writer about whom they both enthused.

It had frequently been remarked that there was no more overtly affectionate couple in London than the Whiteclocks. Certain old ladies of a cynical turn had been heard to suggest, sufficiently directly, that it would take something more than the traditional felicity of marriage to keep such a demonstrable emotion alive, at least in their own experience; but the rest of us were happy to count their experience inadequate, and to accept the young pair's unselfconscious billing and cooing as a true, indeed perhaps involuntary, manner of expression. One firm piece of evidence was that their behaviour never struck either Mrs Purvis or myself, as the similar demonstrations of less well acquainted lovers so easily could strike us, as embarrassing, or inimical to free conversation. On the contrary, we considered any gathering which did not include them to be insufficiently stocked with innocence and gaiety.

There were reasons enough, then, to justify our being disturbed by Whiteclock's unaccompanied appearance. My own concern, moreover, had been increasing as I watched him move through the developing pleasures of the evening. A far less indulgent hostess than Mrs Purvis would have viewed with positive approval, no doubt, his ambiguous behaviour toward Miss Emma Cavill (one of our most desirable young ladies, to whom he had shown hitherto nothing but the loftiest courtesy, though he was now paying her constant attention); I found, however, as I had expected, upon taking my first opportunity to converse privately with Mrs Purvis on the subject, that she was a great deal more interested in her friend's real

* This story was left unfinished by the author. It has been completed by the editor.

motivation than in his contribution to the success of her party. She was as worried as I over this manifestation of a trait so completely foreign to his character.

"Perhaps after all," she said, "we had only to wait until we could have him on his own, in order to see all this ostentatious charm." It was a falsely playful utterance, delivered with a familiar gesture I could instantly translate: a movement as of settling more comfortably into the sofa, and a lowering of the chin into the lace about her neck.

"But we knew him before they were married," I replied, banishing, in response to her signal, all pretended complacency. "I have never seen a less sophisticated courtship on the man's part, or a woman obliged to work so hard to overcome his deficient confidence."

"Yes, it's true," she conceded. "All the outgoing qualities in the partnership belong to her; it's largely why they're so pleasing together. I have of late begun to think, you know, that my failure to encourage her in the early days showed a sad lack of understanding. I hope I shall not have to revert to my former opinion."

We both had our eyes on Whiteclock, who was standing, halfway across the room, in front of Miss Cavill's chair, slightly inclined towards her – a position to which he had been returning at shorter intervals, and apparently with more and more hilarious matter for discourse, as I observed him; while Emma herself sat straight-backed, attending with the smiling eagerness from which she had rarely been known to lapse.

"He seems demented," Mrs Purvis continued. I agreed. She was not referring, of course, to his manner of addressing Miss Cavill, but to words she had herself exchanged with him earlier in the evening. We had both asked him, individually and in harness, about the absence of his wife, and he had replied in utterly frivolous evasion, as if, quite incredibly, unaware of our questions' serious intent.

"Do you think he's drunk?" Mrs Purvis said.

I thought the idea did not merit a reply. "I'll speak to him again," I said, and set out, therefore, across the polished wooden floor, having to avoid in only my first three steps the glances, delivered from opposite quarters of the room, of both the Ladring sisters. It was always, travelling any distance through an assembly of our friends, reminiscent to me of a moderately rough Channel-crossing: positively invigorating, as I am far too good a sailor to feel the least nausea, but in the end slightly irritating, preventing as it did any moment-to-moment consistency of thought, and lulling with its undulation any sense of purpose into a leisurely acceptance of little things.

I had begun to listen, as I walked, to the music, which still held sway over the conversation – it was played, I think, on a piano and three or possibly four stringed instruments – and perhaps my pace had already perceptibly slowed, when I became aware of the younger Ladring sister at my back, rustling in consequence of her pursuit of me across the room. She overtook me and turned so that we were face to face, but I, more as an immediate reaction to her approach than from a consciousness of my mission, paused only long enough to take her arm, turn her round again, and lead her with me; all of which passed without speech. She sank into position at my side almost gleefully, and her first utterance, "Mr Stopham!", in her perpetually silly voice (which I am ashamed to find charming), although it might have been a prelude to what she had been intending to say, I took as an unguardedly comic expression of excitement.

"There will be dancing soon, I hope," she continued, and concern for my own dispassionate appearance did not prevent me from observing a slight change in tone which confirmed me in my opinion of her mood.

"Indeed. I trust your sister is finding as much pleasure this evening as you are yourself?"

"Where are we going?" she asked, craning forward.

I looked at Geoffrey and Miss Cavill, who were now both standing. "I thought of joining our friends by the piano," I said.

"Oh, Mr Whiteclock! Isn't he wonderful tonight? I think he has changed Lavinia's whole idea of the masculine species, you know, she talked with him so long over dinner."

I was prevented from making any reply to this by our closeness to the man in question, who, our approach being unambiguous, now turned, along with his companion, to meet us. It was apparent at once that, whereas Emma was prepared to glow just as warmly in the company of us all as in that of Geoffrey alone, he, never very happy with an interrupted dialogue, and perhaps particularly unsettled in this instance upon discovering the identity of the newcomers he had to deal with, had no desire to speak to us; indeed, he said absolutely nothing at first, and after a very few moments began to manifest a certain restlessness, gazing about the room and ignoring Emma as completely as he had before been engrossed in her.

All the hard work of the conversation had been undertaken by the two ladies, and a very embarrassing affair it was to any listener, although neither participant, I feel sure, suspected as much; Miss Ladring steered continuously and, it seemed, inexorably, toward regions of innuendo, largely on the subject of Mr Whiteclock, while Emma remained as firmly anchored in areas where, to do justice to Miss Ladring, it was virtually impossible to make any intelligent remark. Emma was concerned solely with plans, both long- and short-term, for future pleasures, whereas Miss Ladring intended to squeeze the last possible drop out of the present situation. I interpolated what I could, slightly piqued, I'm afraid, by Miss Ladring's rather obvious switch from anticipation to enjoyment upon being able to dilute my company with someone else's; I was truly concerned, however, only with Geoffrey, and it was only when he at last spoke that I began to take seriously the business of talking.

"I really believe I ought to go home," was what he inserted, with, for him, an unusually acute sense of timing, into a pause which, in any transcription of the ladies' conversation, would probably have been represented as no more than a semicolon.

It was my opportunity to raise again, without seeming obstinate or tedious, the subject which for Mrs Purvis and me had dominated the evening. "You're going to return to your wife at last, then, Geoffrey?" I said.

His reaction was a complete change of mood: his whole aspect seemed to brighten, and he reversed all the little movements he had made in preparation for his departure – turned to face us fully, and took up his glass again from the musicians' platform, on which he had placed it; he was smiling broadly, as if he had begun to realise that this was a topic which could be expected to yield him some fun. "She is at home, isn't she?" I quickly added, resuming my earnest tone in the hope of resisting his levity; it seemed I was more in danger of becoming a foil for his wit than a bore.

"No, Stopham, she's here – didn't you know?" I glanced around me rather nervously, almost without thinking; certainly without expecting to see Mrs Whiteclock. Then Emma Cavill, whose conversation with Miss Ladring had ceased, as if in deference to this more pertinent treatment of one of its own themes, and who obviously felt that her long private interview with Whiteclock qualified her to make some more or less authoritative statement on the subject, offered me this explanation:

"He means, she's here *in spirit.*" It was not a remark which affected my estimate of the confidence into which Whiteclock had taken her.

It served, however, to remove whatever constraint had existed in my own style of addressing him. "Precisely what *do* you mean, Geoffrey?" I said. "I'm sorry if we appear to be hounding you, but you must understand that the matter is of interest to us." His elation had vanished; the discussion was not to remain as cryptic as he obviously would have liked, and he had never, even in less contrary moods, responded well to obligations and duties which denied him pleasure. He now had the face of a child about to fall into a sulk, and as he did not speak, I continued: "If relations between us had not been unusually close, you would be justified in saying that your wife's absence does not concern me, or anyone but yourself: perhaps you would be justified in any case; but the very fact that we are so familiar with her habits as to see a real cause for anxiety in her staying away – and, indeed, that I am able to speak to you like this in front of these two ladies ..." Under his surly gaze, I lost track of my sentence.

Still no-one else ventured a remark; and the way in which our assembled companions sustained their hubbub around us, and the players on the stage continued unconcernedly to make their instruments heard, began to colour my self-assurance with a fear I had not hitherto experienced. Dancing was indeed in the air; people were standing, and the music might well have been introductory to a waltz; I caught sight of Mrs Purvis, laughing as if in complete unconcern. Nonetheless, I made another attempt:

"Marguerite would not have missed this evening without some compelling reason. She told me herself that she would certainly be here; wherever she is, she cannot be completely happy, without you. And I find it hard to believe that <u>you</u> are enjoying yourself as well as you might, in spite of your exuberant behaviour."

He certainly did not look happy. "Oh, never mind, never mind," he said, taking his eyes off me. The injunction lost some force in being repeated. "She..."; but he hesitated, for at this point the two ladies, who had somehow contrived to put a few extra feet of floor-space between themselves and us (though not so many, I noted, that they were likely to have lost any of our own rather heated conversation) and had begun to exchange an occasional whisper, were approached by those two gallant young gentlemen, Mr Daff and Mr Daker, who evidently intended to relieve us of our admittedly attractive and highly eligible friends, in order to be properly equipped for the more energetic turn which the entertainment was about to take.

"She is here – make of it what you will," Whiteclock continued, in a considerable lower tone. "Now I am going home."

"Will she go too, then?" I asked, following him as he moved off in the general direction of our hostess and away from the quartet of young people.

He smiled at me; I had not, perhaps, been expecting a reply, although my question had not been exactly frivolous. I did not know how to interpret the smile, and partly in order to help myself in this endeavour I asked if I might go home with him. And then, it seemed that he had gone through a complete cycle of moods since I had first taken it into my head to interrogate him, for he clasped me by the shoulders, and was openly affectionate in the rather maternal manner which I associated with moments of qualified intimacy – moments, that is, when he and I were alone but for his wife.

"Don't worry, please don't worry, Richard," he said. "Marguerite and I are perfectly happy. You must, of course you must come home with me, and then you'll see..."

"Oh, Mr Whiteclock, are you going?" The interruption was Miss Ladring's, delivered from a certain distance, to the apparent chagrin of Mr Daker. It emerged that she wanted to know whether Geoffrey had forgotten the picnic – the one arranged by Mrs Whiteclock, in the previous week, for the following Sunday – and whether she and Emma might be authorized to bring to it, provided they limited themselves to members of the present gathering, whichever male companions they chose (Mr Daker, whose face I happened to be watching with momentary intentness, though my mind was occupied with quite other things, was somewhat appeased by this). Geoffrey, of course, answered with perfect courtesy and in the proper spirit of bravado, but I do not remember the precise wording of his reply.

We moved on to take our leave of Mrs Purvis, who naturally showed more interest in Geoffrey's departure than in my own; he, in consequence, spoke first, and his final remark – "We have both enjoyed ourselves immensely" – effectively prevented Mrs Purvis and myself, for the moment, from continuing. "Is he speaking for me?" I thought; and I knew that something of the kind must be going through my hostess's head. Then I gave her my hand, and with my first words – "I, also ..." – conveyed to her (covertly, as I hoped) my own interpretation of Geoffrey's leave taking.

After retrieving our top-coats, and dismissing my carriage (for we had decided to walk to Great Portland Street) we set out along the sodden pavement, keeping our eyes on the ground ahead of us, except when an occasional upward blink, partly intended to dislodge the rain from our lashes, took in a more distant puddle bestrid by the glare of a lamp. There was considerable activity in the street, and the rumble of wheels and the clatter of horses prevented me from making out for certain, much of the time, whether Geoffrey was actually addressing me or merely mumbling to himself. He was speaking, or making some kind of vocal sound, continuously, of that I was sure, although it sometimes became blended with the swish of the rain. Once I caught a repeated "Richard ... Richard" increasing in volume, and turned to find him staring at me, but he immediately, as if with relief, went back to his bowed plodding, saying, "It's alright. It will wait." I did not speak to him. Certainly his wife was either in a carriage or waiting at home; my very curiosity about her was diminishing as disgust at my ungracious treatment of Geoffrey increased. I determined, as we turned into Great Portland Street and began to leave most of the noise behind us, to make him some kind of apology. The wet was hanging onto me like guilt, and the fresh drenching I received every minute had no effect, as if it were the pain of hell, and I had become accustomed to it.

"Geoffrey..." I began; but he immediately broke in: "I hope we shall see you on Sunday" – pause – "They are all interesting people who are going." It at once returned me to my state of wondering doubt, and I continued to stare at the ground. It had been spoken in a tense, breathless tone, as if he were twisted with embarrassment and shyness; I might have been some young lady he was entertaining with inept conversation, as he used to entertain young ladies in the days before his marriage. He went on in the same manner, uttering phrases broken by regular pauses, as if there were a threatening silence to be filled. It meant that I was not to go home with him after all; it withdrew all assurances and conveyed a rising panic, and when I finally looked at him I found that he, too, had raised his head and was glancing from side to side (unconscious of my gaze on him) in search of the catastrophe, whatever it might be. There was nothing but a policeman passing on the other side of the road, his cape glinting, and his complete lack of concern with us reinforcing a picture I had had of our respectable progress down the street. Geoffrey watched him closely, saying, "Mr Daker's translations of Baudelaire..."; then the policeman having passed, he began to increase the pace of his walk, as if uncertainly trying to outstrip me. He had given up his distracted talk, and I was content to walk a few paces behind him, watching his heels, and trying to find something to say.

I knew I could not be rational: I could only grasp two or three facts, and attempt to draw something out of them; but I found something, and lifted my head to say it. I saw the shape of his back, startlingly hazed by only five or six feet of rain; but before I could speak he had started to run, and what little I had formulated swiftly vanished, following his diminishing, jerking figure as it progressively buried itself in the white swathes of rain. I could not run, but I strode after him with a sort of convulsive haste, sometimes uncertain whether what I followed was my friend or a shape made by the millions of falling drops. It danced in front of my eyes whenever it or I was under a street-lamp; otherwise it was merely a mobile part of the darkness, and in my efforts to distinguish it I was led unawares into species of darkness with which I was unfamiliar. Many times, although I did not have the certain knowledge that, among the hundreds of different concussions of raindrops, the sound of running feet was receding in the particular direction I had fixed for it, my steps crossed a swimming kerbstone, and met its fellow on the other side of the mounded street, and sometimes raced along the diagonal to the other side of another street at right angles to the first, without my having registered the name of the place I was in any more than I had established that this was in fact the course Geoffrey had taken.

At last I was faced with an inky blackness, and paused, collecting myself; I was standing at the kerb in front of a pool of water collected in the gutter, and the nearest street lamp had for some reason failed, its pilot light dimly on, but the main burner silent and dark. I looked about: the rain was easing, and I saw that I stood at the corner of Devonshire Street, not far from Geoffrey's house. Confused by his disappearance, but encouraged by his invitation, I made my way to the building and rang the bell; the street was quiet, and I heard it sound somewhere in the interior, but there was no noise of footsteps. I rang again. Then a squally gust of wind blasted down the street, and I saw the door move slightly, as if a ghost were slipping out; I pushed at it, it opened and I moved inside.

I glanced from side to side for Considine, his butler, but there was no sign of servants, and for a moment no sound other than the water dripping from my Inverness cape onto the French tiles of the hall, and the faint swish and clatter of a hansom passing in the street, beyond the front door. Then I heard a chinking of heavy glass from somewhere upstairs, and what seemed like a groan, so that feelings of anxiety for my friend impelled me up the staircase before I had even removed my outer clothing. I stepped rapidly into the drawing room, finding it unlit: the only illumination came from the blazing fire, and silhouetted against the flames was a figure in a winged armchair, facing away from me.

"Geoffrey?" I said hesitantly. "Is that you?"

The figure gave a small start, and did not speak, but pointed to the chair on the other side of the fireplace, whereat I moved slowly round and lowered myself into the seat. The other wore a hat and scarf, but no greatcoat; because of this and the dark shadows, it was difficult to see his face, but from this angle I was sure that it was indeed Geoffrey Whiteclock, although his features appeared to be softened, perhaps by the flickering light. He rose, and, striding to the sideboard without asking my wishes, filled two crystal tumblers with whisky and soda, passed one of them to me with a hand that shook slightly, and resumed his seat.

"I am glad that you reached the house despite the storm, Richard," he said, in a voice that seemed husky and lacking in something of his customary warmth.

"You were walking fast, Geoffrey," I replied, adding, "Should I remove my cape? It will do no good to the carpet," although my concern was in truth more for his own welfare than for that of his property.

"The servants are not about; you may leave it be."

"Are you unwell? Do you not wish to turn on the lamps?" I made to rise, but agitatedly he raised a dissuading hand.

"No, Richard, on no account must the lamps be lit." His manner had quite changed from the gaiety which he had displayed at Mrs Purvis's soirée. His utterances had become more urgent and abbreviated, and a note of anxiety seemed to raise the pitch of his voice. I peered at him, but he settled back into the shadows cast by the wings of his armchair; I took a good sip of my drink, conscious of the aroma of damp tweed about me, which seemed to suggest that my host had changed his blend of whisky. "Tell me, what felicity do you think can be afforded by the closeness of a true friendship?"

I tried to put my concerns aside for a moment and consider his question. "Why, Geoffrey, it is surely the most rewarding of treasures for any man. The philosophers and the poets are agreed on that."

"It is surely difficult to find, though, even between man and woman."

"Some say that it is easier between man and man – but, yes, it is indeed a rarity."

"Yet is it that a friendship of such a kind is in itself rare, or that such friends cannot at the last make it a reality in the deepest and most fundamental sense?"

I could not see what he was driving at. Surely he was not hinting at some dissatisfaction in his relations with his wife? Only an hour earlier he had been asserting boldly that their bonds were stronger than ever before. I hoped that he was not going to seek to betray the secrets of the bedroom. I did not answer, and a pause ensued.

"Marguerite and I have been very fortunate in our marriage, as you know," he at last went on. "But you were surprised not to see her at the dinner this evening. You know that I feel you, as our oldest and dearest friend, deserve an explanation. Yet it is a difficult one to give. Much of importance has happened to us since we saw you last."

I listened to every word as if in a dream, being lulled into a drowsiness by the heat of the fire, the lateness of the hour, the plenitude of the dinner, the inclemency of my walk, the darkness of the room; but I began to wonder what he meant by his last words, since it had been only the previous week when we had all three been together at the opera, and I had had no dramatic news of the Whiteclocks in the interval.

"There are many mysteries in the universe which are not well understood by our polite society," the voice went on. "The two of us are happy to have come to enjoy one which, perhaps, only one couple in ten thousand could benefit from, a privilege darkly hinted at by Plato long ago, and hidden from the world for so very many years."

Silence fell again for a spell, and my eyes were held by the glowing coals. "However, this exaltation comes at a price, and the practical consequences are now something with which we are obliged to engage. We have felt it necessary that you should be brought here tonight to intervene on our behalf, although the consequences for you yourself must, I am afraid, be unfortunate. I should say, in all fairness, that Geoffrey has been very reluctant to take this step, and I have had to press him to it."

I turned, confused by these words, and found myself looking into the eyes of Marguerite Whiteclock. My gaze was held by the shock, but as I peered further into them I became aware that the physiognomy surrounding them seemed hardly to have changed. The face was still surmounted by the black felt hat, and set above the white angora scarf; only, its lineaments were even further softened, so that although the eyes were now quite certainly Marguerite's, one would be hard pressed to declare definitively that the face as a whole was either exclusively hers or really, after all, Geoffrey's.

"Yes," she continued, "I see that now you understand. You observed the harmony of our interests and enthusiasms, our passionate affection for one another, the way in which we found ourselves able to enact all the ideals of marital union. Our true delight in each other only had one final impediment, that of the separation of the flesh. But what a chasm that was, what an impious, unbridgeable, ineluctable chasm! As you see, we have now succeeded in crossing it, and Geoffrey and I shall now be genuinely united for ever."

My torpor seemed to grow. I could see little beyond the eyes bright not only with reflections of the flames but also with some kind of inner eagerness; her words seemed to come from an increasing distance.

"My former corporeal shell, however, remains on the *chaise-longue* in Geoffrey's study. It has become an inconvenience to both of us. When the police arrive, we shall have little difficulty in convincing them of your responsibility for it. You have been a good friend to us both, Richard. I hope you will not begrudge us this last service."

Coast Road

On summer evenings the cliffs fall away
Into nothing, as if the sun had melted sea and sky
Together, and made them insubstantial.
Staring too long into that void, one can feel
Terrified, ecstatic, like the prey of the birds
That float above it, the hereditary overlords.

On the road home from Zennor, we stopped
To watch a buzzard soaring. On the tape
'Love Minus Zero' – an old man, his voice strained,
Singing his old love song. There was no wind
But the bird sailed the currents, as the man's words
Were held aloft by the old, familiar chords.

After each line he strummed the change more loudly
In a careless flourish, as the bird, turning more widely
In the air, fluttered its wing-tips. Two noble,
Fantastic creatures, each in its own way inscrutable
And wise – and yet the bird held fast to the old truth
And the man's song had lost its first simple faith.

Song at Night

Jessica comes through the tunnel up to the pavement. No-one is ever in the tunnel, there is never a sign of any kind in it, not so much as a crack in the wall. Going through it is like closing her eyes, one of those moments in the bed when there is nothing, not herself or anything. In the tunnel there is no way of telling why she is going or where, whether this is an outing to the shop, or one of those that never end. It is on the pavement there is something to see: one man walking away, the same way Jessica has to go; one going past on the other side of the road. They are cold, both wear raincoats though it is dry and grey, both look at the ground and have long trails of pavement behind them. She feels that she knows them and if she can follow this one, not perhaps keep him in sight but at least remember him, there is for the moment still the promise of a destination and an ending. But they don't tell her enough: their walking tells her nothing about the light. Are they hurrying to be home before the dark? Or are they huddled and secret because it is night, and they are ashamed to be seen still sleeping? She cannot tell certainly that the shop will be warm and lit. If only one of them pushed a trolley. But she is never certain, she has always to go right to the door of the shop, even when there is no-one. Nonetheless she wants something from these men more than she has. This one in front of her, she knows his little back and the long pavement behind him, she wants to keep him like that. She sobs once with the effort of walking, and again with a sudden hollowness. Again, not a sob but a quiet angry syllable.

She goes into the shop. She moves along the surface of the yellow light; it supports her and leads her where she is to go. It is an involved current, with a far-off tinkling and closer sounds of sighing like water. She looks down all the time; she needn't look up as the current takes her where she is to go, and the people passing with their trolleys are held by it too, moving in opposing eddies, heads high above the surface. The tins on the shelves are like the stones under it, bright and confused. It doesn't matter that she can't sort them out from one another, there are only three things in the shop that belong to Jessica, and she knows them and that they will reach their hands through the water and connect themselves with her: a dirty bundle of green leaves in plastic, a loaf with red and yellow words, an oblong of lard with paper cold and white like the lard. The only thing to fear is when there is no-one left and they want to lock the doors. She picks up each object and feels it become hers with the touch of it on her palm. The brick of lard, corner of the square in a bright cold gulf, sorts itself into her hand. There is nothing to be afraid of, the people are still thick in the current, only the till at the centre of the long sucked-out spiral, where she sets down her three things and fetches her purse. It is not the girl at the till, Jessica doesn't know her, it is the purse itself and the coins that come out of it. The coins are the things that worry her. At first sight she thinks she knows them, the round one, the one with the corners, the small brown one, all three hard. But then she knows they are not hers, although they seem so closely tied to her, they are following their own course, apart from hers, with which hers merely collides, which she can never understand. Their course is moving further and further from hers. She has lost all understanding of them, and has to set them down flat for the girl to interpret.

Outside the door of the flat again, the needs Jessica has felt and been unable to name, the many failures to understand in her long outing, all are almost forgotten, absorbed in the one remaining problem of the door. The key is like a coin; for that very reason it is foreign, though so obviously hers. The door is such a big question, standing there. What if the key were suddenly not hers, if it simply no longer opened this particular door.

This is the answer: this is what she has been wanting all the time; and yet it leads her into new questions. She had forgotten that there were these. Her sister is in the bed, her sister against the wall looking at her, what is her name? Her eyes are shining but it is getting dark, although the shop was open and she was early going out. She will have to join her sister soon, where it will be warm for a time and the darkness will not matter. This is what she has been wanting all the time, she hasn't been right out of the bed, and yet somehow she doesn't want to go back. She stands by the window and looks at her sister against the opposite wall. The curtains are closed. She has to get away from the dark, of course. These places are bad enough in the light: the door into the next room, blocked by the bed; the mirror on the mantelpiece sandy with dust, holding suggestions of another place. She doesn't look directly at either. And yet her sister's eyes, shining, are like that, they contain places she doesn't know; and she will be lying next to her sister.

Jessica stops by the door. The knocking has sounded: it has ended now but she remembers it. Like a stone thrown into water it has sent rings spreading across the silence, meeting the echoes of the knocking that must follow. She is caught, unable to move because it must begin again, because the man behind the door is still, he too caught between his two knocks. He has asked her for something, he wants only Jessica just now, and he is not her sister; her sister is in the bed behind the wall, perhaps having heard the knock, listening for what she will do. She wants to help the man but she is not free to, although he is innocent. He is there because of all those people who want to push them out of the world, her and her sister Mary: the people who cut off the light, who ask her for the things she doesn't have because they know she doesn't have them, for money because they know it doesn't belong to her. She must pretend to this man that they have already pushed her out of the world. She is held still above the gap between the knocking and its renewal.

Outside the door of the flat the policeman stands, having knocked once, feeling silly, as we do at such moments. There is no-one in the hall, no sound from inside, and yet he feels he must wait between knocking and knocking again. He also makes excuses to himself for waiting: old dears, he thinks, must take them a time to get to the door; although indeed with the lack of sound it would make more sense to think they haven't heard, and need the second knock at once. Is it his errand, the unpaid bills, that makes him so uncomfortable, the coldness or the lowness of it. Social services they need, he thinks, not policemen. He'll make a report if there is no answer. He looks sideways up and down the hall. Jessica isn't watching him, she is looking at the door; but he feels that someone is watching him. Perhaps it is only you and I.

They lie in bed, Mary and Jessica, face to face. Jessica's back is against the wall, and Mary's arms are round her, Mary's knee on top of hers. It is not quite dark in the room, but it is dark between their faces. Both have their eyes open. Neither feels the other's breath. Beside the bed is the fireplace, its film of dust scarred at the edge by fingerprints; the grate is blocked and the electric fire stands in front of it, its filaments coated with fur. On the hearth are the loaf, the greens and the block of lard. Here the dust is broken and there are crumbs scattered, although the bread has not been opened. There is no sound but the almost silent humming of distant traffic. The sound grows and fades but its pitch does not change. The sisters have not moved or spoken. Then a sound comes from Jessica's throat, very quiet, as if she were copying the distant sound of the traffic. Her sound grows and fades and is continuous, just like that. Mary hears it: after a time she makes a sound too, but stops almost at once; then makes the sound again; stops again.

Once Jessica moves: Mary feels her legs move slightly. Now it is lighter in the room. They both lie still, then Mary takes her arms from Jessica's shoulders. Twisting slowly on her elbow, making small sounds as she moves, she reaches down towards the foot of the bed. She holds the hem of Jessica's dress in one hand and begins to pull it up over her legs. After each pull she stops for a moment, and sometimes Jessica shifts a little to help her. When the dress is over her breasts Jessica has to take her arms from under the blankets and move further down in the bed. Mary gets out of the bed, holding the dress in one hand.

Using only one hand, Mary puts the dress in the sink. Then she puts in the plug and turns the tap. A moment, a sound, and then the water comes out of the tap, a clear, cold stream. Mary watches. It takes no time going into the sink, it just appears below the tap, like a beam of light but glittering inside and noisy, and colder than light. It fills her mind while it is flowing, and she feels like a child who has been given a present: there is that delight and sense of coming loss. She turns off the tap and takes another dress from where it is hung on the edge of the sink. The cloth is cold and damp to touch. As she turns away the feeling of loss returns suddenly, immediate and cold, almost like a pain, so sharp that she stops still, gasps and holds her breath. The water having stopped there is silence, and something in the silence has gripped her. It is the emptiness left by the water, that waits behind everything. She has tasted the emptiness behind her thought. She gasps in unbelief that the emptiness has taken her again, that it can take her even while she thinks as she has always thought, that it will invade and is eternal. Her eyes have rested on a cardboard box with the name of some food on the side. It contains some object that was once familiar, some kitchen-thing. She does not read the name but it is there in her mind; the thing in the box is not. Her mind seems to open and close, trying to admit the emptiness. A picture of Jessica lying naked in the bed. A picture of a glass of water. She cannot move.

It is quite dark in the room. Jessica has been asleep but she never dreams. Mary has turned her back on Jessica and is moving; the bed is trembling slightly with her movement. She is leaning on her elbow and reaches down into the fireplace. There is no sound of traffic but there are the tiny sounds of paper and of Mary's jaws as she eats. Jessica cannot see her but believes she can. She lies still against the wall, her eyes open. Mary seems to be a long way from her.

Now Mary's arms are round her, and hers round Mary. It is still quite dark. Jessica makes a quiet sound: it is not like the humming or a sob, it has less voice than those. It is jagged, like a croaking breath. There is a long pause and then she makes the sound again, slightly louder, words half-breathed: I'm thirsty. Her voice drags on the syllables. There is silence again, much longer this time. A third sound, all breath, almost silent. Mary lies awake, her eyes open.

Mary wakes and knows that something has changed. There is some light but Jessica's face is dark. She waits a few moments then tries to move away: Jessica's arm lies across her neck, and as she moves she feels it cold and clinging to her skin. She stops, lifts the arm with her own, moves from under it. Then she touches Jessica's face, runs her fingers over it lightly, then harder. She touches under her breast; feels the arm again; touches the face again. She waits: gets out of the bed.

Mary crouches by the window. The curtains are closed; there is light, fading. She looks at her sister on the bed, against the wall. She has been watching her a long time without moving. Her sister's eyes are open, but dull, her arm still outstretched as if over Mary's neck. Mary is not thinking but her awareness grows and fades, as if in efforts to regain something. She knows it is getting dark, but cannot remember what the darkness means to her. She stares at her sister, knowing that she is linked to her; she is trying to hold onto that connection, trying to remember what the connection is. Slowly the darkness falls. Now there is no light, and neither of them has moved. In the darkness Mary stands and moves across the room. Feeling her way, she climbs back into the cold bed.

Voice from the Dead

No, no silence even here
Now the machine has stopped
The relaxing springs creak
And rust whispers to itself

And I, without a voice
Speak to you, or imagine
As always, that I speak

Nor does time pass as before
Now the springs are all broken
And there are no more words
From which to spin the web of time
And I, without a reason
Still go on, or imagine
As always

Pastoral

Today I took the flock onto the far side of Lover's Hill as usual. I played a melody in the Phrygian mode – an arch-like phrase ascending in steps, then slowly descending likewise in steps, the phrase inverted like a cup. I soon got tired of it. The sheep continue to be stupid. In the morning I played my old trick of running at them, roaring, waving my arms in the air. I first tried this five years ago, and their reaction has never varied. They wander off half-heartedly, as if inclined to believe I am indeed a ferocious monster, and the moment I desist they start to wander slowly back, as if nothing had happened. Of course there are sometimes new sheep in the flock, and there must have been some today who were seeing my performance for the first time. But the fact that they all chose to return, rather than eat the perfectly good grass they could find further off, suggests that the old sheep have taught the young to regard me as their protector. What, therefore, is the lingering doubt they all have in their minds, which prompts them to beware of the least change in my behaviour? How can they not seek to settle this question which is central to their existence?

Tullius once caught me playing this game with the sheep, and at first pretended to be shocked. On the spot we had a heated argument, in the course of which I admitted that it was an irrational act, without intelligible purpose, founded on sheer perversity. In the end he confessed to doing the same thing with his own sheep. It is this sort of pointless hypocrisy which most annoys me about Tullius. He will argue practically any point as if moved by a fierce conviction; but always after a few minutes his interest fades, and he can never be induced to return to the subject. The wonder is that he remembers who he is from day to day. Tomorrow I will make an effort to get myself out of the cynical mood I am in.

My outlook has undergone some subtle change, and the woods and pastures of my youth appear empty and tedious. Idyllic things may once have been enough for me, but I can now see no attraction in them. Unless I discover the cause of this change, life itself will soon have no meaning for me.

Confident that nothing very startling would result, I asked the Sibyl how to revive my flagging enthusiasm. I had been right to expect nothing. After performing some evil-smelling process with items of bodily waste, mostly hers, she decided that the gods had afflicted me in this way for reasons which must remain mysterious. The solution of my problem lay in myself. She had clearly not even listened to my question. It would have been useless to ask how I had deserved this unusual punishment, or which god might have inflicted it.

I'm sure she doesn't know one god from another, or feel the need to identify herself with one in particular. She seemed to think she had given me a reassuring glimpse of the order underlying the universe, thus proving her value as a citizen in spite of doing no work and living on charity. Indeed, one can see why it suits her to think of all the gods as playing the same apparently pointless tricks on men without ever revealing their motives. I do not, however, feel that this view provides an explanation of my vague restlessness. In the afternoon my pipe was silent, and the sheep grazed unmolested, as I sat pondering somewhat sceptically on her words. If there were a divine being, I thought, and therefore a purpose in creation, then, rather than indulge in such petty irritation of his creatures, he would confer with them, the better to accomplish that purpose. Undoubtedly the Sibyl's bloody-minded, ineffectual gods existed only in her enfeebled brain. As I had begun to suspect, the world had no divine creator, and everything in it derived from the inane sequence of cause and effect. Hence the existence of such creatures as sheep and Tullius, who could be part of no cosmic plan.

I was still thinking thus when Tullius himself came up behind me with the two girls, Calliste and Phloxa. It pleased them to approach in silence, and when nearly upon me, to burst into loud wailing. This was the continuation of a joke which has much amused them of late; they have had the idea, seeing my depression caused me to dwell more than usual on religious matters, of making believe my death is imminent – and more recently, since even they tire of a joke which does not develop, that I have already died and they are plunged in grief. When they thought I had grasped the point the girls went looking for some new diversion, Tullius remaining with me to talk of indifferent matters. The vernal equinox being close at hand, the three of them are planning one of their tours of the countryside. I, too, used to take pleasure in these expeditions, whose avowed purpose is to learn the methods of farmers in other districts. Lately, however, I have lost the urge for travel, all places being the same to me. Tullius discourses at length on the opportunities I have missed through my laziness; indeed, since I ceased to participate, he has hoped to gain more from these trips than he ever did to my knowledge. He was still mocking my insularity when the girls reappeared, having found yet another variation of their game. They had made a wreath of ivy, which they proceeded to place on my head with such solemn reverence, perhaps meant to convey that I had been elevated into the pantheon.

Meanwhile Tullius asked the question which always follows talk of travel: would I look after their flocks, as well as my own, during their absence? I did not object, having performed the same function on the last few occasions. A shepherd's duties remain the same, after all, however large his flock. Of course they may yet find some foreigner whose sheep guard themselves, leaving him free to earn a second living from horticulture. When that happens I shall be more inclined to listen to their advice. But from what I remember of their jaunts they spend little time in serious research, being more concerned with picking the berries they find on the way, and simply dallying together in the sunlit glades. Indeed, if any inducement can work with me it is the thought of lying with Phloxa, in whose body, perhaps most of the three, I take intense pleasure. At moments of especial passion with her I have wondered whether, as she says, my view of existence is unnecessarily bleak. Yet even this pleasure, though it allows one briefly to forget the demands of reason, leaves one occupied with the same questions, only a little more earnestly. Still, that is not a reason for denying oneself. The tour having been arranged to their satisfaction, and the girls' wit being for the moment exhausted, we spent the rest of the day pleasantly enough in enjoyment of each other.

If I took a lamb to the shrine this morning it was not an act of piety, but an excuse to take another look at the Sibyl's ménage. There is something in its uncompromising squalor that appeals to my nature. The woman may be blind and stupid, but she has managed to free herself entirely from material need, and has a healthy contempt for worldly matters. There is a girl there, too, who tickled my somewhat jaded appetite. It was the foreign appearance that did it. And only a barbarian could be so happy living with the Sibyl. In fact, there's something unnatural in such self-possession. What has she got to be satisfied about? She does all the messy work, and to look at her you would think it was a privilege. In return the Sibyl probably lets her crawl into a corner of the cave with a bone. I do not know what she gets out of it, but I wish I got the same thrill from tending sheep. She went on with the sacrifice, and I chatted with the old woman. If the Goddess existed, I said, why had she made everything so dull? Every day the sun rose and set, one got up, surrounded by the same old objects, and lay down again. Didn't she ever want to make a complete change, just to break the monotony?

Meanwhile the lamb's blood was all in the bowl, and the Sibyl was waiting for me to leave. Scepticism wasn't getting a response, so I quickly changed tack. What particular favours was the Goddess willing to do for Her devotees? I hoped to draw the assistant into the talk, but she'd gone off meanwhile to skin the carcass or something. The Sibyl began to show signs of life, but still was not exactly communicative. I should not look for any favours save that of making sacrifices in Her honour. Yes, I said, that was all very well, but I was worried in case I was stuck with the melancholy for good. Could the Goddess not be persuaded to say when it would let up? At this she put on her demented look and spoke in a wobbly voice. What I was talking about, she said, was Prophecy. It could be done, but it was a great demand to make of the Goddess. Many offerings would be required. I should keep up the sacrifices for at least a week, and then ask her again.

Now I've skipped a sacrifice, she may decide to be awkward and raise the tariff, but fortunately I have another idea. It came to me while I was watching the sheep, in a blacker mood than ever. While on the subject, this is the last time I'll look after anyone else's sheep. It's never been any trouble before, but then sheep have never had the effect on me they do now. The sight of a single sheep can make me feel quite giddy. And now I find, to my great distress, that the effect increases in proportion to the number of sheep. No Goddess worth the name would have made so many identical versions of such an animal. I was watching them, and thinking about the Sibyl's assistant. I don't know why, but something tells me she could help to alleviate my depression. But so far as I can see she never says a word, and in any case I can't go on sacrificing lambs indefinitely. That was how I got my idea. I could persuade the Sibyl to let her go for a day, to perform some blessing or other on the sheep. It may cost a few more lambs, but if I take one from each flock in turn no-one will notice for a day or two. Once I get the chance to talk to her, she may agree to slip out again whenever the Sibyl's in a trance.

As I thought, the old hag had taken offence at my absence yesterday, and for a long time refused to say a word. I gave the lamb to her assistant, passing a remark about the weather, but she tripped off with her nose in the air as if I were beneath her notice. Hearing my attempt at conversation, the Sibyl butted in with a voice like old parchment, promising me all kinds of doom and destruction.

I lost no time in springing my idea on her. I had sincerely repented my omission, and now, realising that devotion to the Goddess was the only answer, wished to invoke Her protection on my flock. The old woman, smelling more sacrifices, began singing her assistant's praises. She was called Philothea, meaning Lover of the Goddess, and her face was as near divine as made no difference. She had gone straight from her birthplace, via certain pirates, to the market where the Sibyl had bought her at vast expense. Thus she was of guaranteed purity, and so particularly suited to a life of devotion. Anyone violating her would be liable to awful punishments from the Goddess. If only I'd thought at the time, I could have pointed out that the pirates had probably done it already – then perhaps she'd have dropped the price a bit. As it is, I'll have to ask Alcibiades to advance me three months' wages.

I was back among the sheep, wondering if it would be worth it, when someone called my name, and Phloxa came running down the hill. As I'd expected, their important fact-finding soon petered out, and they have now set up temporary camp about a mile and a half away. Phloxa was worried about me, and so decided to come back. She was the last person I wanted to see, as it's her lamb that will have to go tomorrow. I laughed gaily and said I was fine, she should go off and enjoy herself. But she'd made up her mind it wasn't right to leave me alone, with all their sheep, when I'd been acting so oddly. The sheep were a pleasure to look after, I said – they were all perfectly healthy. Then she waxed sentimental – it was her fault I was unhappy, and she'd decided to be nicer to me in future. And she nuzzled up against me, murmuring in baby-talk. I saw that matters would have to come to a head, and managed to do what she wanted, but then was still more anxious to get rid of her. At last she agreed to go, provided I was sure nothing was wrong. She seemed to think they might go to Epizephyrian Locris shortly, having heard that things are happening there. But she promised to come back before they left, to make sure I was all right.

There's evidently something the matter with me. I woke up feeling nervous, and spent an hour trying to think of pious things to say. And that wasn't the strangest thing I did. I don't think it's the fashion to cover yourself with oil, but somehow it seemed a good idea at the time. Gleaming, I turned up at the shrine with the bag of money. The girl had put on cleaner rags and looked almost civilized, but was still somewhat distant. She passed the money to the Sibyl, who instantly showed the other side of her nature. She told us to be as long as we liked – she'd do the sacrifice, and look after things in the cart.

We set off, Philothea looking straight ahead, not saying a word. Sneaking a few looks at her, I found her as fascinating as ever. Not that she isn't pitifully thin, and there are signs that the Sibyl knocks her about a bit. I tried some questions about life at the shrine, but her lips stayed firmly sealed. I was on the point of giving up, when she suddenly launched into a cheerful babble – what she liked was the colour of the blood from the sacrifices. Then for another ten minutes there was nothing intelligible. Still, it was a start.

So I had another try. When she'd warmed up, I was going to suggest we skip the business with the sheep. I asked about home, but soon realised it was the wrong subject. I suppose she forgot her early life doing some rite of the Sibyl's. As that seemed a suitable moment, I asked what rite she was going to perform. It didn't go down well. She frowned, and made a significant pause. Because if it was short, I said, perhaps we could... The frown deepened. What happened, she said, was for me to say. This put me in a bit of a quandary. If she wanted me to specify the details of the rite, it might be awkward to say the least. I went on, a bit more subdued, till we came to the sheep.

There I sat down, to gain time. Somewhat to my surprise, she sat down too. She was frowning, looking at the sheep. I wondered if their case was hopeless. But no, that wasn't it – they looked very small, she said. Small? Yes – she felt that they were actually much larger. What she meant by it remains open to question – but I feel confident in saying, *a propos* this interlude with the sheep, that she didn't know what they were. It was the first time she'd seen a flock, and it hadn't struck her that it was made up of the white woolly things people brought to be sacrificed. For a moment, this discovery produced a slight cooling of my ardour. But then, I reasoned, she couldn't help her upbringing, and at least I didn't need to worry about the rite.

In fact, as the day went on I realised she hadn't a clue what I'd supposedly hired her for. When I explained about the sheep, she looked at me for a minute, then exploded in gales of laughter. I thought she'd spotted the oil, and tried to wipe it off with a bit of grass, but that made her worse than ever. She rolled about, absolutely helpless. I began to think things were going better than I'd expected. There seemed to be no reason why we shouldn't get on famously. We strolled about, and there was no sign that she was planning anything sinister. But every now and then, she'd say something utterly devoid of meaning. For example, some geese flew over, and she waved her arms as if to keep them off her face. I told her they were miles up in the air, but she wouldn't have it. Someone, she said, was blowing them into her face with a fan. And whenever a rapport suggested itself, something like that would come along and nip it in the bud.

So it went on for an hour or two, until we came to Pullo's Pond. I proposed going in for a swim but I might as well have been talking to a lamb. I got undressed and waded in, and she froze in terror. Had I any last request to make of her? she asked. I gave up in disgust, and swam around a bit on my own, and when I got out again she'd disappeared. That worried me a bit, so I went looking for her, and found her scurrying back to the shrine. There was no time for any explanation so I quickly told her my idea about meeting in secret. Again, I might as well have talked to the sheep. It looked pretty certain at this point that she and the Sibyl were in it together, but presently she seemed to change tack: she would perform the same rite again she said, provided I could get the money back from the Sibyl. As it happens I don't mind paying, but I'd still like to know what she meant. Was she offering to help me steal it?

I must admit my heart sank this morning when I reached the shrine and was greeted by the smell. She's a novel enough companion, but her home-background might have been a bit more congenial. She was squatting in the hearth, pretending not to recognise me. The Sibyl, on the other hand, couldn't have been more affable. She grabbed the lamb, and offered me unlimited use of the powers of intercession. Philothea was always available at the same rates, and divination and prophecy came only a little dearer. I left as quickly as possible, determined to find another way. Meanwhile, Alcibiades will give me whatever I like. He was entertaining this afternoon, as usual, and he wanted to show the guests what an enlightened employer he is. What they don't know is the rate of interest he'll charge. There's nothing he'd like more than to have me bound to him for the next ninety-nine years. He thinks I can't possibly run off because of the scrappy bit of land he's promised me when I retire. Things will have to be pretty bad before I'll make do with that. He said he'd heard that Tullius and Phloxa were off on a jaunt, and he hoped I wasn't planning anything of the kind. Ennius was practically under the table, but he came to his senses at this point and tried to look threatening. I wasn't to expect payment from him, he mumbled, for looking after their sheep. It was for Alcibiades to settle up with me one way or another. But if he thought the sheep looked even slightly off-colour, Tullius and Phloxa would get it in the neck.

I don't know whether I've made progress or not. Who was it who said the more you know, the more you realise you don't know? What I do know is, if that's what religion does to people, I'm glad I've steered clear of it. We strolled about as before, everything was fine, and now and then she'd have one of her turns. They exert a kind of fascination and I found myself happily waiting for the next. But there came a point where I realised it couldn't go on, so I sat her down and did some close questioning. It was hopeless. I was forced to conclude that the details of our first expedition had been expunged from her mind. 'Stealing the money', 'pond', 'giant sheep', all left her gaping.

Nothing daunted, I embarked on a more general line of questioning. I haven't worked so hard since the great dropsy outbreak. What I learned, briefly, was this – religion has seriously distorted her view of the world. Since infancy she's had the Sibyl's ravings as her sole guiding influence. As a result the real world is less real to her than the Goddess and her troop of nebulous attendants. When she's asleep they all come and talk to her, and in her case sleeping and waking are much the same. But the worst of it is, this confusion has spread as far as her senses. She doesn't see the real world but another, larger world somehow mixed up with it.

And furthermore, her grasp of people and places isn't any clearer. I don't think she understands, when she goes out with me, that she's moving about in space. For her, the grass isn't entirely distinct from the fur of the Sibyl's cat. We were leaning against a tree, and I'm not sure she didn't think it was the wall of the cave. She has one explanation for all apparent inconsistencies – the will of the Goddess. The Sibyl told her some stuff about learning new rites and moving closer to the Goddess, and for her this is one of the new rites she's learning.

But what caps the lot, though it makes sense if you puzzle it out, is that for her there's no clear dividing line between me and the Sibyl. When I realised that, I must confess I was a bit affronted. But, as I say, she exerts a kind of fascination, and it seems churlish to disagree with her.

In the end we started by knocking about pleasantly much as we had the first time, and the subject of religion didn't get too much in the way. I must have been feeling shaky too, because that absurd warning of the Sibyl's went through my mind. But in the end, she was so obviously normal underneath, I had to do it, in spite of myself. At first she just lay there, stiff as a board. Looking at the clouds, she observed that the Goddess was having fish for dinner. Then she began to get the idea, and by the end she was participating vigorously. But the pirates must have restrained themselves, because it was obviously a new experience. I wondered what idea of it had got through to her mind. She didn't comment, but the thought occurred to me, perhaps inspired by her manner of thrashing about, that it might remind her of the beatings she gets from the Sibyl.

Anyway, I was lying quietly next to her, feeling that everything was really quite all right, when she leapt up and started off back to the shrine. This time I wasn't going to let her go without an argument. Words produced their usual lack of effect, but other measures had more success. I got her to lie down, and to cut a long story short, we did it again. But I could see she was uneasy, until she got into the swing of it again, and when we'd finished she was as keen as ever to go. I was curious to know how, her mind being what it is, the Sibyl had trained her to head for the cave at a certain time. It turned out that she knows about the movement of the sun, though exactly what the Sibyl has told her, or what the sun has to do with the process, I couldn't work out.

In retrospect, it's not easy to explain what I've done today. All I know is, her enigmatic qualities had begun to look like a challenge. I must have been looking for a way of sharing her experience. I was thinking, too, my position with Alcibiades couldn't be any worse, and I might as well make the most of it. The one thing I definitely didn't feel was any kind of fear about the future. Mind you, the day started badly enough. He gave me the extra money without any trouble, then he frowned and did his pillar-of-justice act. It seems the business with the lambs has come out. He didn't want to know anything more about it, he said. In his view, Ennius himself was to blame, for failing to maintain discipline among his shepherds. However, that in no way diminished my own culpability. Compensation for Ennius would be deducted from my wages, and if anything of the kind happened again, I should be dealt with very severely. Fortunately, I already had reason to think it wouldn't happen after today. The consequence is, however, I'm signed up for the next five years of my existence.

But I had other things to worry about, namely the result of my visit to the shrine. When I got there Philothea was bustling about doing the chores, and the Sibyl was just sitting, looking like a frog, as she does. I went straight into Plan A, the prophecy. The Sibyl said I'd made a wise decision, and put out her claws for the money. She felt it, and I think she would have beamed, if she'd been capable of such a thing. Then she told me to wait while she prepared herself. I wandered off, a bit nervous, though I knew there was nothing in it. Trying to simmer down, I gave Philothea a hand.

She was collecting up the sacrificial bowls and knives, to wash them. There were signs that the Sibyl had been at her for being late yesterday. But, believe it or not, she still didn't seem to register who I was. Mind you, that didn't mean she wouldn't let me help her. She proved quite adept at telling me what to do. In the end she just followed me about, watching me do it all. I thought there might be a fuss about my touching the sacred objects, but not a bit of it. Obviously, the Sibyl thinks she's onto a useful convert. I began to feel quite homely, sloshing about by the well with Philothea looking on. It seemed a good omen for the future.

Half an hour or so went by, and then the Sibyl called me in from the next cave. I'll say this much for the old crone – she doesn't stint on the effects. She was wearing some outlandish get-up made of feathers, and the place was thick with foul-smelling smoke. She sat in the middle of it, with her eyeballs rolled up, making the most ghastly noises. I felt a bit *de trop*, and wondered how long it was all going to take. But I didn't say anything, and after a minute or two it sounded as though she was getting somewhere. The noises ended with a kind of choking sound and in the silence came an eerie voice which I suppose was meant to sound like the Goddess.

Whatever I'd expected, it was certainly nothing like that. I'd become Her servant, and one of Her servants would cause my death. I felt swindled, and hung about wanting more, but the Sibyl had keeled over and was faking a swoon. I was pretty sure she'd known exactly what she was doing from the start. The bit about 'one of Her servants' was clearly a reference to Philothea. I suppose she'd rumbled what was afoot, and was doing her best to warn me off. But she certainly knows her business, and the words have a kind of chilly quality that I don't much like to dwell on.

Anyway, I wasn't going to let any hocus pocus like that put me off, so I went through to Philothea and asked if she was ready. She was still washing up, looking about as unlike a murderer as it is possible to do. I don't think she'd heard a word of what had passed next door. Almost before I'd asked, she was out of the cave and heading for the pastures. For most of the day I ambled along behind her, thinking about the life in prospect. But when the time came for her to disappear, I got her to sit down, and launched into my master-plan. It may have been morally open to question, but the way I saw it I was saving her from the Sibyl. Besides, I still wasn't sure she was going to fall for it. In spite of the evidence, it was hard to believe she was as naïve as she pretended.

This was the story: she had reached the final stage of her education. She was engaged in the highest of all ceremonies, after which there were no others. It had brought her into direct and permanent contact with the Goddess – she would therefore forget everything she'd learnt before, and do only what the Goddess now told her to do. Amazingly, she swallowed it all without question. She fell into step behind me, and in the evening I showed her to the hovel. Here there was an unforeseen difficulty – it's not the most inviting of places, and she dug her heels in, perhaps thinking it was a home of evil spirits. But when I'd calmed her down and got her inside, everything was different. It's not exactly a deluxe establishment, but then you have to consider what she's been used to. In short, she must have seen it as some ante-chamber of the Goddess. She lay down in the straw as though expecting divine servants to come and wait on her, which just goes to show what religion does to the reasoning-faculty. Of course, once she's settled in I'll explain the whole thing to her. No doubt in time she'll learn to find it all highly amusing.

As I say, she needs time to settle down, and her old life will intrude a bit at first. It's her dreams that are the most obvious drawback. Once she gets lost in them, nothing on earth will induce her to get up. She just lay there, communing with the spirits, all the time I was preparing the lunch. I pulled her out when I went to get the sheep, but she didn't seem to notice the change. I began her acclimatisation by training her to herd the sheep. At first the results weren't very promising. She still sees them as something other than sheep, and she's more inclined to dance round them in circles than shoo them about. But there came a point where she was getting the idea, and once, or twice she gave one a tentative shove. I tried to make her admit what they were, and she said they were sometimes sheep, but not always: it seems that the Goddess needs sheep to take part in the ritual.

I didn't push the subject any further – I find questioning her only leads to trouble. On the whole, it seemed wise to let her go her own way. Thus by the end of the morning she was covered in mud, and bleeding in several places. She wouldn't eat her lunch until she'd mixed it with bits of earth, and when she wanted to do the same to mine we ended up fighting. But she was mostly content to use her energy without bothering me. She fell down in a fit, or climbed a tree and sat in it singing, and often went on at length about great shining creatures. I was careful about introducing sex again, thinking she might not enjoy it the second time, but that was a mistake on my part. Her enthusiasm is almost frightening. The trouble is, I think she forgets I'm involved. During one particular bout she started frothing at the mouth. Sometimes, looking at her, I wonder again about the Sibyl's prophecy. What worries me is the old toad's unmistakeable air of confidence. After all, I can't be sure she doesn't have secret methods of influencing people. And Philothea's such a scatter-brain, she might be capable of anything.

I don't know why I didn't mention it at the time, but Ennius found a couple of half-starved foreigners to watch his sheep, so that little episode's finished. That was a couple of weeks ago, and since then nothing much has happened, but what with the many delights of married life I'd forgotten all about Tullius and Phloxa. Until, that is, she turned up on the door-step at some unheard of hour in the morning. They're still based in World's End Ravine, but someone's told them Ennius is going to evict them, so they're clearing out to Corcyra. It was all such a surprise I could hardly muster an apology, but then all Phloxa cared about was Philothea.

I made breakfast while they glared at each other, and the air of the place grew progressively chillier. Eventually Philothea gave a shrug, and went out on one of her sprees. Then Phloxa was more forthcoming. Philothea seemed a nice girl, she said. Did she look after me all right? I answered with the appropriate lie knowing there was more to come. I looked worried, she said. Was anything the matter? I knew this refrain of old. No, I said, there was absolutely nothing the matter. There was an underlying memory to all this, but I felt justified in ignoring it. After all, she's never been a great stickler for fidelity. At last she seemed resigned, if somewhat wistful. Why had she never realised, she wondered, that I was religious? I said I hoped she'd enjoy the trip, which may have been a little tactless. It seems there have been reports of pirates in Corcyra. When we ran out of things to say, she left. I felt badly about it all, and in particular about Philothea's rudeness. I questioned her on the subject, knowing the effort was futile. She seemed to have forgotten Phloxa existed. She must have sensed her utter lack of spirituality, and decided she wasn't worthy of notice.

I awoke in blissful ignorance of what would happen today. If I'd known, I'd have gone back to sleep. Not that it would have made any difference. The only clue was that Philothea had gone, and that caused me no particular alarm. I took the sheep out, assuming she'd heard from the Goddess, or else had a fit of absent-mindedness, and wandered back to the shrine. It didn't seem worthwhile to interfere.

But while I was watching the sheep it struck me that this blasé attitude was a bit too much. The sheep themselves prompted the thought. Not long ago, watching them was like a form of torture – yet here I was, gazing at them, and everything seemed fine. I looked round, considering what was different. It's not going to be easy to describe, but since I've started I may as well have a go. There was a change in everything – and it wasn't visible, but only suggested. Everything seemed to have another layer, like an alternative version of itself, that might pop into the light at any moment. And the vagueness of these indefinable alternates had somehow taken the edge off my malaise.

It didn't take me long to spot Philothea's influence on this. She'd talked about her invisible companions until they'd taken to haunting me as well. For a while that was as far as I went. However, there was more to it, as I will now go on to demonstrate. The change was so subtle as to defy description, yet its effect on me was radical. There wasn't any getting round it – I tried, and I couldn't raise a flicker of despondency. The way I argued, fears like that aren't flung into one's lap by chance. Someone must have known that Philothea was the precise tonic I needed. Certainly neither she nor I had foreseen anything of the kind – ergo, some other particularly ingenious person had my interests at heart. I didn't have any trouble working out the rest of it.

Only one person could have wanted to dispel my morose attitude. Not only was it offensive to Her creation – it had led me to deny Her existence, thinking I could get away with it. She had overheard me, and generously pointed out my mistake. You can imagine how small I felt after that. She'd let me go on thinking I'd stolen one of Her servants, when in fact she'd contrived the theft for my benefit. I was lucky she hadn't blasted me off the face of the earth. I went on watching the sheep, wondering what other surprises were in store, and suddenly realised there was a catch. Philothea had gone missing, but her job still wasn't finished. However unconcerned I might be about finding her, she was bound to turn up. I'd been told as much by the prophecy which had now been given the seal of authority.

I decided to take the bull by the horns, and go looking for her. Since fate meant us for one another, we might as well stay together and let it do its worst. However, I felt morally obliged to discuss the thing with her. If she wanted to flee the country, pointlessly in my view, it was for her to decide. I'd do my best to dissuade her – there was the feeble argument that the prophecy hadn't named her – but ultimately I wouldn't stand in her way. Of course, there was a snag in all this. Here was I preparing things to say to her, but judging by past experience, she couldn't stay still long enough to listen.

With a heavy heart I took the sheep in, said goodbye to them just in case, and set out for the shrine. She was there sure enough, squatting in the dirt as though she'd never lived anywhere else. The Sibyl was sitting by the hearth, nodding over her cauldrons, dead to the world. She seems to have gone downhill a good way since I was last there. Judging by her lack of response, I'd say she was deaf as well as blind. But I wasn't taking any chances, so I asked Philothea to come outside. I took her into the wood, just out of sight of the cave. I didn't ask why she'd gone – there'd be plenty of time to argue about that later. I told her the words of the prophecy, and was just getting to the more difficult part when she interrupted me.

She knew all about it. Apparently, the stuff she gets in her dreams includes all manner of prophecies, and she'd got this one along with the rest. But her version went into more detail – she knew she was the person referred to, and she knew the exact programme of events. I was to bring a lamb to the shrine to be sacrificed, and then hang about until she cooked it for the Sibyl's dinner. While helping her draw the water to boil it, I'd look up to say something, lose my footing and tumble down the well. This technical stuff left me gasping a bit, but I pretty soon realised it gave us a foolproof escape-clause. I did a little dance, and told her nothing could possibly induce me to give up one of my precious sheep.

Of course, I'd forgotten that avoiding prophecies isn't really in her line. I explained, and then she was a bit disapproving, but quite capable of grasping the idea. I'd got it all wrong, she said. If I refused to act according to the prophecy, the Goddess would consider herself obliged to fulfil it. In order to escape one's destiny, one must show greater delicacy. Rather than act in opposition to the prophecy, I should approach it obliquely, averting only the event that most directly concerned me. By now I was utterly at sea.

I put the matter entirely in her hands; I said – what did I have to do? Nothing easier, she said. I should bring a sheep along in the morning, and do everything as foretold in the prophecy. She would do the same, only she would tell the Sibyl that the sheep was a lamb, and for the rest I was to leave it to her. I couldn't think of any objection to this. My mind was temporarily numbed. It was only when she was back in the cave, and I was drifting off through the wood, that it struck me what slippery ground I was on. But I still couldn't see any way round it, so I went to the field and picked out a sheep to be sacrificed. I was thinking so erratically, I took the trouble of choosing a doddery old thing that might breathe its last at any minute. That way, I remember arguing, I could tell Alcibiades it had died, and then I wouldn't have to pay for it. I tethered it to a stick outside the fold, and then came indoors. I sat down, and the true hideousness of the prospect finally got through to me. What drove it home was the pathetic bleating of the old sheep outside the fold. I can still hear it now, and my heart throbs in sympathy with the beast. We have about an equal chance of getting through tomorrow alive.

I've decided to give up thinking about the future. I've suddenly been given one again, and I don't know what to do with it. Things may look clearer tomorrow, but at the moment I'm still recovering from shock. All day I've been groping about in a sort of murky grey mist. I dragged the sheep to the shrine, and on the way I kept bumping into trees. I was going to have the whole business out again as soon as I got there. In fact a shadowy Philothea bustled off with the sheep before I realised what was happening. There was an inert brown lump by the hearth which I took to be the Sibyl. She must have been in the same spot since yesterday, slowly disintegrating. I was too far-gone to hear anything about a lamb, but I suppose the message must have got through. The knife went in, and the sheep let out another of its withering bleats. Anything less like a lamb I never heard, but then I don't know what state the Sibyl's ears are in. Philothea dragged off the carcass, and then the worst part began.

I was delirious most of the time. I could see a grassy hillside with a flock of woolly sheep, and I begged the Goddess to let me hear their melodious bleating one last time. When I came to my senses the brown lump was always there, pulsating like a bladder, muttering to itself. If it knew I was there, it didn't let on. A couple of other visitors came to the shrine, and I skulked in the shadows until they'd gone. I kept telling myself I was mad not to make a break for it and go to Corcyra. At the last minute some perverse impulse always held me back. For the life of me, I couldn't see any reason why she should be wrong. After half a million years of this, she gave me a nudge. Dinner-time.

The murky grey mist was now turning black, and I was about to faint. She went over to the hearth, and the Sibyl, after a slight hitch in communication, handed her one of the pots. I still hadn't moved, but she gave me a beady look that said I couldn't get out of it. I clutched the pot and staggered through to the well. I never knew it could be so difficult to find the end of a rope. As for tying it to the pot, I'm convinced it was a physical impossibility. When things have settled down, I'm going to write a thesis about it. At last, commending my soul to the Goddess, I lowered the pot into the well. It hit the water, a thousand feet below, and filled up. I pulled it out again. Nothing. I felt absurdly cheated. In some confusion, I followed Philothea back to the hearth. But little by little, I was beginning to feel safer. She took the pot, and climbing over the Sibyl, poured the water into one of the bigger pots. By now I was convinced my troubles were over. I was on the point of bursting into song, when she pushed me back towards the well.

We had to do another trip. And another, and another. It was like one of those nightmares where you think you'll never wake up. In the end I thought I'd spent my whole life going from hearth to well and back again, with the vague shape of a girl behind me, waiting for the moment when I'd topple from sheer exhaustion into the well. And I was tormented all the time by an idiotic question – why were we using the smaller pot? We could have brought the bigger one from the hearth, and filled it in a single trip. It wasn't so heavy that we couldn't pull it out of the well, or so big that the rope wouldn't go round it. If we'd done that, all this agonising suspense might have been avoided.

On about the fourteenth trip I couldn't bear it any longer. I was on the point of lowering the pot, when I turned to ask the question. As I did so my head struck the pot and sent it flying into the well. Before I knew what was happening, I was dragged across the floor by the rope round my wrist. I came to a stop with my head and chest over the edge, hanging on by my toes. I lay there, watching the evil glint of the water two thousand feet below, and realised what had happened. The mist cleared away, and everything was bathed in a dazzling radiance. I was free!

Philothea stood watching as though she didn't know who I was. I clasped her in my arms, and we rolled round and round the floor and practically into the well. I babbled on about taking her home and living forever in cahoots with the Goddess, and it didn't strike me at first that she wasn't responding. When I got up, she went on calmly with the business of fetching the water. Protests were useless. She'd forgotten that the outside world existed. I stormed off in a rage, went back to argue, and stormed off in another rage.

I went to Alcibiades demanding money. He wanted to know if it was good for my health, then gave me some to get rid of me. I was going to hire Philothea, and find some pretext for keeping her at home. But halfway back to the shrine, I stopped. Did I want to force her to come back? What had happened, I realised, was that the Goddess had achieved

Her purpose, and taken back Her instrument. Her spirit belonged to the Goddess as much as it had at the start. It could never belong to me.

A Dark Figure

He came in a dream. I saw him enter
and stand in the doorway, a deeper shadow.
It was my old room, my old, narrow room,
dark-panelled. Night in the window,
moonlight, clouds flying. He stood
silent in the doorway, his face in shadow.
Something hidden under his coat.
                                        He came
swiftly to the bed. A movement. The knife
came down, severing bone and sinew.
A cold wind passed through my life.
I awoke, the dream flying in pieces,
clinging to the walls, the furniture, the roof-tops
in the moonlit window.
                                The shadow remained.
He was there, in the room, just beyond sight.
Soon I would know him. He had found
What he was seeking, and his work had begun.

The Palimpsest

I shall inevitably run out of pencils. It is this, today, which is my little item of worry, which undermines my creative power, impedes my progress. Like all negative ideas it is futile, for I have pencils equivalent in number to a time greater than any I can conceive. I cannot, it is true, remember the beginning of my own particular time, however long ago that was, but I am convinced that my time so far has not been enough to use a number of pencils equal to that which I have left. I have certainly not yet used half my pencils. As I cannot imagine even that small amount of time I have already passed, and as it has not in fact been enough to use more than the tiniest fraction of my pencils, it follows that to ponder on the unbelievably remote time when I shall use the last pencil is a foolish exercise of my creative power. Perhaps this worry could teach me something, if I let it occupy the whole of my mind, instead of fighting against it. It might, for all I know, become a part of that more important problem, where to go next, instead of distracting me from it, and keeping me here. It does, when given the chance, lead on to little connected problems, some of them almost worth considering. Will it in fact be I, for example, who use the last pencil? I must not now elaborate this thought, or any thought connected with it. The elaboration leads, however, I know, to the idea that my end will come before the pencils have all been used, that some pencils may remain when I am no longer able to use them. It is certainly then impossible to imagine that they will not be used by someone. But there must be no elaboration of this thought. I should be deciding at this moment, it is such an important question, where to go next. And it is not only this problem of the diminishing pencils which distracts me from the question, for every morning when I awake there is one of the old problems, every one of which I know in so many of its elaborations that it almost seems there can be nothing to fear, eating away at my power of movement, subverting my creativity.

A few days ago, for example, I remember it was the problem of the wall, and whether that, like me, might come to an end. I will not pursue this question now. I travel over the surface of the wall, suspended in my cage, to which my four taut ropes are attached, and I lean through the bars to pencil my design on the wall. And here is another of the problems which trouble me in the mornings, for I sometimes awake and then wonder what my design means. I work all day, except when the worries are so bad that I lean and do nothing but rehearse then, for some time, perhaps only a moment or two, the pencil resting against the wall. Sometimes, in starting again, I return, I think, over the work I have just done before stopping, going up where I have come down, or to the right where I have come from the left, and so on. I go over the same lines again, making them darker, or put in finer lines between them, or yet finer lines if I have done that part of the wall more than once. I do not think hard, once I have almost cleared my mind of the other problems, where to go next. I follow the direction of my pencil, and just so long as I know the direction in which it is leading me, that is the direction in which the cage moves. If it is a good day, and I manage almost to clear my mind for longer than usual, I pencil along the edge of the design, if I am close to the edge, and venture an inch or so into the blank. Then the new lines are bold and strong, with large spaces in between. The further I go into the blank the better it is for the boldness and strength of the design. Soon I am glancing through the bars of the cage, down at the blank stretching away, and I think of what I would be doing in that space fathoms below, perhaps this very day, if I could draw a single line from here down to there. But I cannot make the cage move quickly, and while I have been thinking thus it has stopped. Then into my mind comes one of the old problems, and there I wait, everything waits. I may wonder, for example, and this is surely the worst problem of all, whether there is anything behind, whether I should be well-advised to turn, if only for a moment, and see if there is anything behind my back. I might turn, in any case, for so short a time that it was not long enough to see, not enough time for my eyes to work. I am convinced, so far, at least, as I can remember, over all that part of the wall I have known, there has been nothing behind me. It is when I move into the blank, on these good days, which are not, I must confess, after all such good days, that I think there may be something there.

On ordinary days, such as today, having awoken more often than not far from the blank, or far enough to prevent my reaching it that day, I go back over the work I did the day before, or the day before that, or even before that, I do not know. It may be work I have not touched for an inconceivable time, depending on where the pencil leads me, there is no way of telling. Sometimes whole months pass in this way, without my seeing the edge of the design, although I may be close to it without realising. Even so, although on these ordinary days the work I do is not as demanding, or the effect of seeing what I have done, and of imagining what I will do, as overwhelming, as on the good days which I have mentioned, there is a time in every day when I find that I can do no more, and that I must sleep. Perhaps the time comes a little sooner on the good days, but if so I have not noticed, and there is no way of making certain. If I compared the respective periods by measuring my pencil at the beginning and end of each day, there would still be those moments of inactivity, induced by the recurrence of my worries, which could not be taken into account. It is possible, however, that I fall asleep in a certain way on my good days, which might lead to a solution of this problem, for I certainly have at least two different ways of falling asleep.

Sometimes I feel sleep approaching, and then I stop working, look with bleared eyes at what I have done during the day, for on these occasions it is often all in sight, although intermingled with previous days' work, lay my pencil on the stack of those as yet unused, and then almost at once, but prepared, fall asleep. At other times sleep comes upon me unexpectedly, so that, although steadily working in one moment, in the next I am asleep, with no recollection of the work I have been doing. I imagine that I slump forward against the bars, perhaps making a wild line on the wall where none was intended, and the pencil plunges down, past the wall, pencilled or unpencilled, along the lower rope. This is the situation in which I awake, after one of my good days, feeling empty, or rather guilty, for it is not, after all, certain that what I do on these good days is of greater value than my usual slow, methodical work, and in spite of the extremely large number of pencils I have left I do not have so many, surely, that I should be flinging them heedlessly into the gulf, where the chances of my finding them again are, I should think, very slight.

Sometimes, when a pencil has become so short that it is no longer practicable to use it, I drop it intentionally through the bars and watch it fall, but always with a sense of anxiety, as if I were doing something foolish. On my ordinary days, when I think of it, I think that my tendency to lose pencils, some of them almost unused, when falling into sleep of the unexpected kind, should somehow be restricted. It might be possible, for example, to establish a routine whereby I stopped working, before I felt sleep coming on or before it came on unexpectedly, after a certain time, or a certain space covered, replaced my pencil on the stack, and then perhaps did something else, something other than work, until I fell asleep. Sleep might still come upon me unexpectedly, but it would do so less often. As for what I might do in this little period of leisure, I might count pencils. This would take a very long time, very many little periods of leisure, but it would be almost no time compared with the time it will take to use all the pencils, the same number of pencils. I could shift them rapidly, one by one, from the stack on the right-hand side of the cage to a new stack on the left, and keep the number constantly in mind. Perhaps while I was still only a little way into the counting, when it seemed that I was never to finish the counting, the diminishing of the pencils would be less distracting.

The inconceivable time it will take to use them all would be made more conceivable by this ever-present reminder of the tremendous yet almost infinitely shorter time it would take to count them. Then I suppose I might spend less time on the particular worry which is distracting me today, which is that I shall, inevitably, run out of pencils. When, or perhaps if, ever it seemed that I might sometime, within a conceivable time, finish the counting, I would probably stop the counting, be content to know that the number of pencils I had left was greater than the number I had in mind, so that this particular worry, today's worry, would not regain the power it had lost. I might then think of something else to do in my leisure periods. I might calculate the approximate amount of time it would take me to use those pencils I had counted, having first counted how many pencils I used over a certain number of days. Or I might try to restrict all my worrying to the leisure periods, so that when I felt a worry beginning during my working hours I could say to myself, no, I will save that worry until the little period before I fall asleep, there is no need to worry about it now while I have that special period for worrying to look forward to. In this way I could save valuable time, and if I thought about it for long enough no doubt I should find that the supply of things to do in these little periods of leisure was almost inexhaustible. Then after a time I should find that my second, or unexpected manner of falling asleep was beginning to disappear, that I was approaching a state in which I should have only one manner of falling asleep, or half as many as I had before.

The sleep itself, however, would not have changed. The sleep itself, when it comes, is always the same. In it I cannot measure time, any more than I can when I am worrying, nor can I remember the work I have been doing during the day, nor am I conscious of doing any work, or of moving at all, while I am asleep. Depending on the manner in which I have fallen asleep, I awake later either sitting in the usual position, back against the back bars, or slumped against the front bars with my pencilling-arm still extended, hand empty, and feeling either relieved or guilty, as I have explained. In neither case have I any knowledge of the time I have spent in sleep.

Perhaps guilt disturbs my sleep, but I do not know. Nor does either posture help me in the least to remember the work I have been doing. However I awake, the part of the design I see upon awaking is completely unfamiliar to me. Each morning, before I begin work again, I stare with bleared eyes at what is in front of me, and hope it will be something whose composition I remember. If I can recapture the principles whereby this piece was made, perhaps the coming day's work will be somehow more solid, a more valuable elaboration of the design, not that principles are something I know much about.

Never, in any case, upon awaking, can I reconstruct the least detail of what went into the pencilling in front of me, what was going on in my mind, or what were, if I might call them this, the external circumstances, how long the pencil was, which direction I was moving in, and so on, while I did it. Why this should be I do not know, as before sleep I have a more or less clear recollection of what I have been doing, whereas when I awake there is invariably this complete blank, but I have imagined explanations while worrying about this particular question, each of which seemed almost satisfactory at the time. One is that I continue to work while I am asleep, although I am not then conscious of doing any work, and as I have not been conscious while doing it I naturally cannot remember doing it when I regain consciousness. Another, and here is one of the problems which are most likely to trouble first thing in the morning, is that these elaborations of the design have been done by some other person, perhaps by the one who will succeed me, and use the last of the pencils, if my end comes before the pencils have all been used.

The last explanation I will describe is that although I do no work while I am asleep, and although I am not then conscious of moving at all, yet the cage during this time has a mind of its own, and moves without my thinking where to go next, carrying me to some part of the design which was done so long ago, perhaps, that all recollection of doing it and of subsequently elaborating it has disappeared.

And now I find that none of these explanations is entirely incompatible with either of the others. If I take this last one, for example, however far the cage moves during the night, and of course I do not know how quickly it moves when it is released from my control, however long ago that part of the design was made which I face when I awake, if it had been made by me it would be so much like a part of me, so full of my own thoughts and feelings, that I must surely recognise at least certain aspects of it. Some unaccountable change must have occurred if part of my own design, from however long ago, was completely strange to me. Therefore I must assume that the cage moves, while I am asleep, until I am facing the design of someone else, whether done that night or long ago. If there might be one who will succeed me, and use the last pencil, as I have said, it is possible also that there was one who came before me, who used the first of the pencils, had a time equal to mine, and drew a design as great as mine will be when it is finished. It may be, on the other hand, that he comes when I am asleep, takes over from me, goes on from where I left off, but this is a thought which I must not elaborate at the moment. I will assume that he came before me, and that his design was done long ago.

His design is not like mine. Every morning when I awake I contemplate the strangeness of it. He has used so much more elaboration than I, his lines are so many, so intricate and so fine. When I begin in the morning to add to his design I am struck by the simplicity of my additions, by the sweep of my curves, even though mine are often enclosed by his, and must therefore be of lesser extent. I should not like to draw a long curve, intersecting all his lines, crossing and dividing his spaces, if only because the simplicity of the whole design must be preserved, but my curves when I am working at the edge of the design are sometimes quite large, sweeping out it seems almost interminably before they return, and then returning suddenly, not deviating but sweeping back. I am able, moreover, to express myself almost freely even when far from the edge, by enclosing one of his lines with one of mine rather than allowing mine to be the very innermost elaboration. Mine is still enclosed, naturally, by a yet further one of his, but the important thing is that undaunted by the age and elaborateness of his design I have encircled one of his lines, following all the way, on the outside, its every sweep and deviation, keeping always, with great dexterity, the same tiny distance from it, and from that other curve of his which is to encircle mine, never touching either.

Sometimes when my worries have overtaken me, and I have stopped at the end of one of these very difficult and expressive curves, and then restarted, probably in some other direction, it strikes me that there is not, after all, such a great difference between his work and mine. While inserting yet another line between two of these congruent curves, I may become confused and be unable to decide whether the outer is mine and the inner his, or vice versa. It is possible even that I was mistaken in thinking both the original lines his, between which I did my first, so that the relation between our contributions to the design is impossible to unravel, until the next morning, when the cage has moved on and it is all simply strange to me again. The most obvious similarity between our methods is that neither of us will go straight from one point to another. However close the two points may be, on one of our lies, chosen for the purpose of analysis, there will always be some bend or loop in the line between them. When I am going over one of our curves, making it darker, without knowing it for mine or his, I am perhaps most conscious of this tendency we share, and not even thus exactly reproducing the curve helps me to identify it. I should like to see the person who works with me in this way, but I do not think this is possible. Even if he did not come before me, if he instead takes over from me at night, when I fall asleep, the fact that I am asleep when he comes inevitably prevents me from seeing him. It may be that he comes at the very moment when I fall asleep. Perhaps it is as if I simply carried on working, or sat down or slumped for only a moment and then continued to work, but then it is in fact he who is working, while I am asleep, and when I awake perhaps it is as if the same thing happened.

Nonetheless I feel that we know each other, that he is aware of me as I of him. I might perhaps detect his having come, in the morning, by checking the pencil on top of the stack, provided I had not flung the pencil down in my momentary slump, or even flung down two consecutive pencils, when falling asleep and when awaking, checking, that is, that it was shorter than when I had fallen asleep, but it would be very hard to tell. When I try to do this it seems to me that the pencil is no shorter, but it may be that I do not remember, or it may be that he has used exactly one whole pencil, finishing the one I have been using and using as much of another as I have used of the first, I do not know, as I have not counted all the pencils. He may have used two whole pencils, or more, depending on how much time he has. In any case, I do not mind his using my pencils, he is welcome to them. It may be that he is bringing my end twice as close, or closer, if my end is to come before the pencils have all been used, but I do not resent that, I do not see that as an attempt to thwart me. Rather it is that we are together thwarting the third person the one who will come after me, for it is surely better to end than to be left with no pencils, although doubtless even in that situation it would be possible to fill the time.

And it may be that he is not, after all, using my pencils. It may be that he is working now, while I am working, and that he sleeps when I sleep, but in some other place, some other cage. He possibly has his own cage. It is not likely, however, that he has his own ropes attached to the cage, for in that case I should surely see them, or one of them, his upper or lower crossing my right-hand or left-hand rope, or his right-hand or left-hand crossing my upper or lower rope. His rope(s) would become entangled with my cage, moreover. If ever I saw two of his ropes that would mean I might soon be seeing him. But no, if he does have his own cage it is attached to one of my ropes, which is also his rope. It may be that my lower is also his upper rope, for example, but I like to think it is my right-hand which is also his left-hand rope. The rope between us must be very long, for I have never seen him. And our situation ensures, I take it, that I shall never see him, for the rope is taut in between and on either side of us, and when he moves I move, my mind controlling his or his mine, or our minds being simply the same, and when we sleep our cages move together, his to a part of my design and mine to a part of his.

However we elaborate each other's designs they remain identifiable as mine and his. I should like to see him, and perhaps he would like to see me, but we do not speak to each other. We might speak through our designs, but instead we worry about those things we might say to each other. For example, what is this whole design that we are making together, travelling over the wall without apparent purpose, but driven perhaps by the moments' little purposes which go to make up one larger purpose? If there is someone behind, if what is there is another person, he can see the design. It must be a curve of some kind, for we never go straight from one point to another, even, I am sure, from one end to the other of that part of the wall we know. It must be a series of intermediate curves, sweeping out and sweeping back, which go to make up one larger curve, or spiral.

I say this because I remember at that time when I thought I was alone, before the second and third persons had come, although even then I could not remember my beginning, already every morning when I awoke the part of the design which I faced was strange to me. It was not completely strange to me, it was not that someone else was elaborating the design, but I had made curves which swept out almost interminably, and then swept back to within a moment or two of their beginnings, so that at night I could be moved across in a moment from the work I had just been doing to a part of the design which I hardly remembered. I seem to have as many pencils now as I did then, in spite of the fact that they may be diminishing more quickly now, and I seem to have had as many worries then, although I did not yet think of the second person. It was not that he was not there, in his cage or that he did not come when I fell asleep, but he did not appear to be working.

It had occurred to me that there might be one who would come after me, at my end, before I began to see his curves, mingling while I still worked with my own. In other words the third person came before the second. Or perhaps it is this way, that he, whose design I elaborate and who elaborates mine, is also the one who will come after me, that at my end he will simply stay, and I have failed to understand his design, whereas the third person, who has not yet begun to elaborate the design, is also the one who wants to see me, and whom I want to see. Or it may be that they both elaborate the design, and I have not yet learnt to distinguish their work, although they are there, both working while I work, one on my right and one on my left, one whom I wish to see and one who will come after me, or both wishing to see me and yet a fourth, perhaps, above me, who will come after me, or more, above, below and all around me.

But these are thoughts which I must certainly not elaborate at the moment. I will assume that he began to work at this time, when I had already forgotten my own beginning, beginning his design and then some time later, as far from his beginning as I had been from mine when he began, being moved at night from his own design to mine, hardly noticing that, rather than strange to him, as parts of his own design already were, it was completely strange to him. Then he saw that I was working beside him, and together we worked on the curve or spiral, or the two curves or spirals, he being moved to mine and I to his, never seeing each other, making the two curves perhaps only a moment apart. I imagine our curves as lying along each other, reproducing each other, his sweeping out where mine sweeps back, and vice versa, and so on, over all that part of the wall we know.

It would be possible to fill the time. And it may be that he is not, after all, using my pencils. It may be that he is working now, while I am working, and that he sleeps when I sleep, but in some other place, some other cage. He possibly has his own cage. It is not likely, however, that he has his own ropes to which it is attached, for in that case I should surely see them, or one of them, his upper or lower crossing my right-hand or left-hand rope, or his right-hand or left-hand crossing my upper or lower rope. His rope would become
cage, moreover. If ever I saw two of
be seeing him. But no, if he does have
my ropes, which is also his rope. It ma
rope, for example, but I like to think it is
left-hand rope. The rope between us must be
him. And the situation ensures, I take it,
is taut in between and on either side of us,
mind controlling his or his mine, or our minds
we sleep our cages move together, his to a p
his. However, we elaborate each other's desig
and his. I should like to see him, and perhaps h
not speak to each other. We might speak through
worry about those things we might say to each
whole design that we are making together, travel
apparent purpose, but driven perhaps by the moments

In Memory

We met on top of the sea wall
On a cold, grey day.
Through the diminishing-glass of time
I see us there, as in the strange,
Blurred half-light of a dream.

But I do not hear your voice
Or that of the sea below us –
Or rather, your voice is one
I keep in my stock of constant things,
And the voice of the sea is unchanging.

And we must have met before,
Some evening now forgotten – got drunk,
Argued, started building
Our little sandcastle. Why do I
Still see you there, at the sea's edge?